P
MON

THE DEVIL'S CAUSEWAY

*The True Story of America's First Prisoners of War in the
Philippines, and the Heroic Expedition
Sent to Their Rescue*

MATTHEW WESTFALL

LYONS PRESS
Guilford, Connecticut
An imprint of Globe Pequot Press

To Laurie and the girls

All photos are from the author's collection and are in the public domain unless otherwise noted.
Maps by Mary Rostad © Morris Book Publishing, LLC
Project editor: Meredith Dias
Layout: Justin Marciano

Library of Congress Cataloging-in-Publication Data

Westfall, Matthew.
  The devil's causeway : the true story of America's first prisoners of
war in the Philippines, and the heroic expedition sent to their rescue /
Matthew Westfall.
      pages cm
  Includes bibliographical references and index.
  ISBN 978-0-7627-8029-7
  1. Philippines—History—Philippine American War, 1899–1902—Prisoners
and prisons, American. 2. Baler (Philippines)—History—Siege,
1898–1899. 3. Gillmore, James C., 1854–1927. 4.
Philippines—History—Philippine American War, 1899–1902. I. Title.
  DS684.W47 2012
  959.9'031—dc23

                                                        2012011778

Printed in the United States of America

10 9 8 7 6 5 4 3 2 1

CONTENTS

BOOK III

Dramatis Personae

The USS *Yorktown*

Commander	
Charles S. Sperry	
13 Officers	
58 Petty Officers	92 Enlisted Men

The Landing Party

Ensign	Quartermaster
William H. Standley	John Lysaght

The 2nd Cutter

Lieutenant, Commanding	
James C. Gillmore Jr.	
Chief Quartermaster	**Gunner's Mate**
William Walton	Edward J. Nygard
Sailmaker's Mate	**Coxswain**
Paul Vaudoit	Ellsworth E. Pinkham
Ordinary Seamen	**Landsmen**
Silvio Brisolese	Frederick Anderson
Ora B. McDonald	John Dillon
William H. Rynders	Lyman P. Edwards
Orrison W. Woodbury	Charles Morrissey
Apprentices	
Albert Peterson	Denzell G. A. Venville

The Spanish Garrison

Governor
Enrique de las Morenas y Fossi
Lieutenant, Commanding
Juan Alonso Zayas
Lieutenant
Saturnino Martin Cerezo
Contract Surgeon
Rogelio Vigil de Quiñones y Alfaro
47 *Cazadores* (Infantry)

The Spanish Franciscan Priests

Candido Gomez Carreño
Juan Lopez
Felix Minaya

The Filipino Army of Liberation

General
Emilio Aguinaldo
Lieutenant Colonel
Simon Tecson
Captain
Teodorico Novicio
400 Men

The US Army

Commanding General, VIII Corps			
Major General			
Elwell S. Otis			
Commander, 1st Division		**Commander, 2nd Division**	
Major General		**Brigadier General**	
Henry W. Lawton		Arthur MacArthur Jr.	
Commander, Cavalry Brigade, 1st Division		**Commander, 1st Brigade, 2nd Division**	
Brigadier General		**Brigadier General**	
Samuel B. M. Young		Loyd Wheaton	
33rd Infantry		**34th Infantry**	
Colonel		**Lieutenant Colonel**	
Luther R. Hare		Robert L. Howze	
11 Officers	71 Men	5 Officers	61 Men

Prologue
The Boy Venville

This moment was one to be captured for posterity.

Twenty-three gaunt, starving men approached a gray boulder that punctuated the rock-strewn bank of the river. Wracked by disease and riddled with sores, the haggard souls mustered their last reserves of energy to hoist each other up and jostle into position. A small American flag was handed to the dazed senior naval officer of the party, Lieutenant James C. Gillmore Jr., who weakly held it aloft.

That a camera was present there and then, in the war-ravaged Philippines, two weeks shy of the close of the nineteenth century, defied all odds. Brought along by a forward-thinking army lieutenant, the Kodak folding pocket camera had been introduced in the United States just eight months earlier, in April 1899. The hand-sized marvel of photographic innovation had survived a transpacific ocean journey to the Philippines, a grueling months-long march into northern Luzon, pitched battles against insurgents, and a daring mission into the uncharted hinterlands of the Cordilleras to rescue the men now assembled.

But the journey to this site would prove to be just half the miracle: After the single photograph was snapped, consuming the final frame of the last cartridge of film, the Kodak joined the Gillmore party prisoners and 168-soldier rescue column on a harrowing ninety-mile mountain descent along a winding, turbulent river, suffering extremes of mountain frost and stifling tropical heat, and at least two dunkings in the bone-chilling current. Nonetheless, the camera and the cartridge arrived safely in Manila, as did, for the most part, the broken men.

Months later, the improbable portrait of the liberated Gillmore party ran in newspapers across the United States, accompanying a startling tale of siege, survival, and salvation. The account made colorful headlines, albeit briefly: A US Navy mission, sent to rescue a besieged Spanish garrison, had gone horribly awry. A ferocious rebel assault on a hapless cutter crew had left a number of sailors either dead or in captivity. And after more than eight harrowing months as prisoners of war, the survivors had been dramatically freed from insurgent hands by two battalions of US Army volunteer infantry. By many accounts, Lieutenant Gillmore was a hero. His survival and rescue were nothing less than triumphs of civility over savagery, underpinned by America's daunting military might. How could anyone know that these events were just fragments of a larger story, one that had yet to be told?

And then, like all fresh news that quickly grows stale, the account of the US Navy's stunning debacle at Baler, the captivity of the first American prisoners of war in a foreign land, and the US Army units sent to their rescue was lost to time. The photograph of the Gillmore party prisoners on the very morning of their liberation was filed away and forgotten. No further thought was given to the event, nor the great consequences suffered by the men involved and the country in which it occurred.

—◆—

Absent from that photograph was a sailor once under Lieutenant Gillmore's command—just a kid, really, whose name his captors never got right, even after 323 days under their watch. Fair enough; it was a bit of a tongue-twister for a people whose original twenty-character alphabet lacked the letter "v," along with c, f, x, q, and r—all consonants introduced by their Spanish colonizers to cover the loanwords they had brought to the Tagalog language. The lanky, handsome, eighteen-year-old US Naval Apprentice, 2nd Class, Denzell George Arthur Venville, became known throughout Baler, a remote coastal town on the east coast of Luzon, as "Bembio."

When Venville awoke the morning of February 29, 1900, his two fellow captives, the Spanish Franciscan priests Felix Minaya and Juan Lopez, were by his side, as they had been for the past nine months. Their guards, increasingly skittish, were unwilling to let the prisoners wander far from their makeshift bamboo-and-thatch lean-to; they were too valuable to lose. By this time, three of the four gunshot wounds Venville had sustained in the ambush of his US Navy cutter more than ten months ago had healed rather well. One had perforated his ear, another had ripped through his throat, and a third had driven into his armpit and out his shoulder. It was the fourth gunshot, violently shattering his ankle joint, that had healed poorly and left the boy crippled. Just under five-foot-eight and a lean 119 pounds, the naval apprentice could limp about with surprising agility, although he still required a cane for support.

Venville, no doubt, was convinced he had been forgotten by now. After the fateful rebel ambush, he had been too severely wounded to accompany the rest of the American prisoners of war on their forced march to the interior of Luzon, to General Aguinaldo's command, where they would become pawns in a fight for independence. Instead, against his wishes, Venville had been left behind, along with two other wounded sailors. When his companions had sufficiently healed, they too were marched out, leaving Venville abandoned once again. At this point, the boy must have wondered if he would ever get back home.

Home was Sellwood, a small town outside Portland, Oregon. Unlike most other apprentices who had signed up in search of adventure on the world's seas, Venville had joined for health reasons. Behind the gentle boy's bright hazel eyes and warm smile lurked physical infirmity. He had enlisted almost three years earlier, at the age of sixteen, on the advice of his doctor, who thought the fresh sea air would strengthen his sickly constitution and perhaps toughen him up. The medical counsel brought an added benefit: It allowed the youth to exit crushingly difficult family circumstances. Venville was one of eight children living cheek by jowl in a tumbledown shack along a dirt road in Sellwood, supported by their illiterate mother, who struggled to make ends meet as a house servant and washerwoman.

Once aboard the USS *Yorktown*, Venville's weak demeanor and effeminate gestures immediately brought ridicule. "They call me a 'girl sailor,'" he lamented to his mother during one short furlough at home, "but if war ever breaks out, I will show them I'm no girl."

War had indeed broken out between the Filipino Army of Revolution and the United States nearly a year before this February day, but the shot-up Venville, languishing as a prisoner of war, had no role in it. Instead, he had been confined with the two young Spanish priests at ever-changing locations around the town of Baler. They had been joined for a portion of their captivity by other prisoners—a former Spanish Army hospital orderly, a Spanish schoolteacher, and the schoolteacher's son—but not for long. Ominously, without notice, the three additions had been taken away. Venville and the two priests suspected they had been killed.

During the past two weeks, anxiety had swept through the rebel-held town. Reports indicated a large American force—six hundred heavily armed men on huge horses and carting artillery—was marching on Baler. The town's rebel leader, *Kapitan* Novicio, had quickly ordered the three prisoners moved to a series of hiding places that would place them out of reach of their potential rescuers. They were marched to San Jose de Casignan, a small settlement fourteen miles distant, and put into the custody of the local mayor. Days later, when a fresh report confirmed the Americans were about to descend into their coastal valley, the prisoners were again on the move, to a more-secure location deep in the forest. On February 19, just a day before the Americans were to arrive, San Jose fell into chaos as panicked residents packed up and fled.

Venville and the two priests, accompanied by the mayor's extended family and servants, were marched even farther out of reach, this time to an inaccessible clearing in the heart of the jungle. Starved of sunlight by the thick, triple-canopy foliage above, the camp conferred an alarming sense of foreboding on the prisoners. They had been on the move, almost constantly, for the past twelve days.

Kapitan Novicio's decision to move the prisoners from San Jose was timely. On February 20, three companies of the 34th US Volunteer Infantry, one troop of 4th US Cavalry, and a sixty-three-mule pack train under the command of General Frederick Funston did indeed spill through the deserted settlement. At one point, the prisoners and their would-be rescuers were perhaps no more than a few miles apart.

This morning, eight days after the American arrival in Baler Valley, had started out differently for Venville. The mayor's daughter, Agapita, had prepared a hearty breakfast of venison for Bembio. As he savored the unexpected gesture of generosity, four members of the mayor's family approached to inquire if Bembio was interested in joining a fishing expedition on the nearby Diatt River. Proficient with his casting net, a skill he had picked up from local fishermen, Venville was happy to join. It not only meant fresh food—the bountiful rivers in the area offered blue spot and river mullet, sometimes mudskippers, and a good catch of eels, river clams, and snails—but it also meant a chance to take a bath. And it would break the boredom of another seemingly endless day in captivity.

From the forest camp, the group took several trails that opened up into an alluvial valley at the foothills of the verdant Sierra Madres. There, the Diatt River had etched a rocky course from the distant mountains to the shimmering sea. Dressed in his ragged, blue navy-uniform pants, likely barefoot, Venville hobbled to keep up. As the morning sun began to climb, the party of fishermen ventured upstream toward the shadows of the mountains.

Venville may not have noticed it, but there was tension in the air. Maybe, with the several weeks of forced marches and confused rumors, he had become inured to his predicament and no longer worried about his fate. Notably, there is no report of Venville ever having tried to escape; maybe he was actually enjoying his adventure, despite the deprivation and hardship. The group marched on, moving deeper into the canyon. Whether they conversed, and what was said, we do not know. At some point, the four Filipinos dropped from Venville's side, falling back, perhaps suggesting that Bembio go ahead—that they would catch up.

A ferocious band of head-hunting Ilongots, armed with bows and arrows, spears, and razor-sharp steel machetes (known as "head knives"), had been lying in wait since morning. Short and muscular, with long, straight-black hair and clad only in loincloths, the primitive Ilongot warriors were as fierce as they looked, reinforced by a long history of violence against intruders who happened into their mountain domain, and among their own warring people.

It is fair to assume the first arrow—launched from a taut palm-wood bow, and most likely aimed at Venville's back—hit its mark without warning. It was an ingeniously lethal projectile: a jointed, leaf-shaped iron arrow point, barbed and toggled like a harpoon, that was connected to a feathered shaft of bamboo and attached by a lanyard and retrieving cord. This specific arrow was designed for killing the packs of wild boar and deer that roamed the thick jungle. The metal point would drive itself deeply into the heft of the animal; if it ran, it would soon find itself dragging an arrow shaft though the entangling underbrush while the iron point remained wedged deeply in its flesh, causing further damage. But the arrows were also lethal and efficient against other, human prey; this morning, that prey was Naval Apprentice, 2nd Class, Denzell George Arthur Venville. Bembio.

Perhaps the boy turned around to face his attackers; we don't know. Testimony confirms a second arrow was launched, perhaps in near succession, and it dug deeply into the crippled boy. He may have cried out, beseeching the heavens as he had done so often during the past ten months when faced with near death, abandonment, and captivity.

The Ilongots descended on the dying boy, drawing their head knives from their sheaths. Certainly, one Ilongot had been singled out for the honor, for taking a head was a sacred ritual of manhood, a prerequisite for marriage. Whoever the warrior was, he likely seized the boy by his soft blond hair, yanked back his head, and in one violent stroke, sliced off the boy's skull. Holding the grim prize aloft would have elicited shouts of glee, perhaps even a joyful jig. It was a moment of celebration: The boy warrior had just become a man.

The Ilongots were not done. Other knives worked on Venville's appendages; his hands were chopped off at the wrists, and then his feet, one glistening blade efficiently hacking through the deformed joint that had refused to mend. To cover the gruesome deed, a shallow grave was dug along the riverbank. Several of the warriors dragged the boy's dismembered form to the depression and covered it with stones. Clutching their bits of Bembio, the Ilongots then departed, leaving the decaying remains to the gangs of wild boar and feral dogs that scoured the canyon for carrion.

Days after the killing, one of the Ilongots in the head-hunting party passed by the grave with his dogs. Sure enough, scattered about the riverbed were the boy's pelvis and leg bones, lying some thirty feet from the grave.

Not far away, in the neighboring town, the Americans were getting settled, a new garrison falling into place. It was now time to start asking around: Had anyone seen the naval apprentice from the USS *Yorktown*—the boy named Venville who had been left behind at Baler?

BOOK I

The dreams of men, the seed of commonwealths, the germs of empires.
—JOSEPH CONRAD, *HEART OF DARKNESS,* PART I

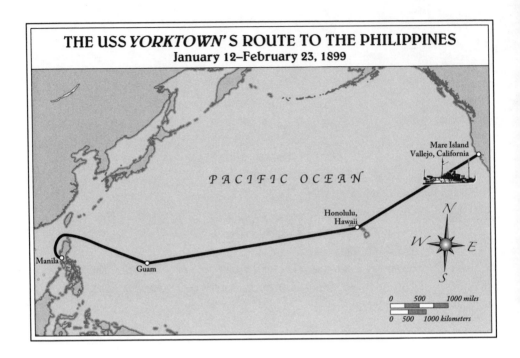

THE USS *YORKTOWN*'S ROUTE TO THE PHILIPPINES
January 12–February 23, 1899

PACIFIC OCEAN

Mare Island
Vallejo, California

Honolulu,
Hawaii

Manila

Guam

0   500   1000 miles
0   500   1000 kilometers

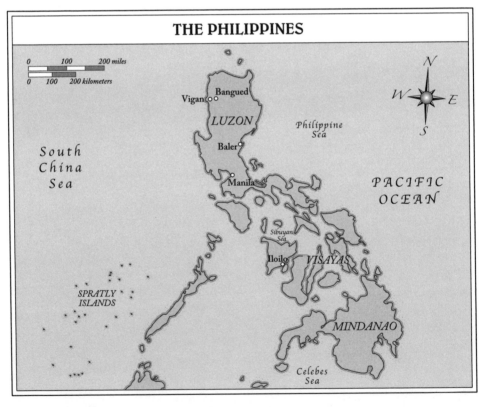

THE PHILIPPINES

0   100   200 miles
0   100   200 kilometers

South
China
Sea

Vigan
Bangued

LUZON

Baler

Philippine
Sea

Manila

PACIFIC
OCEAN

Sibuyan
Sea

Iloilo   VISAYAS

SPRATLY
ISLANDS

MINDANAO

Celebes
Sea

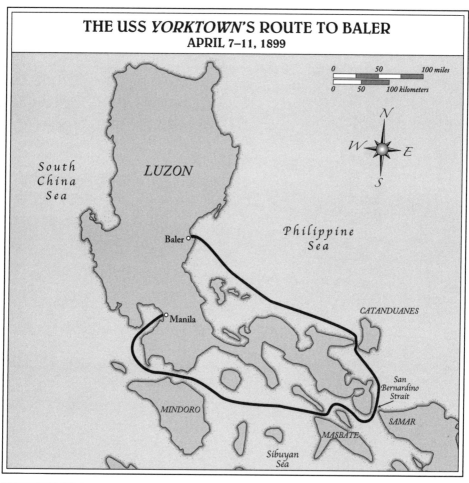

THE USS *YORKTOWN'S* ROUTE TO BALER
APRIL 7–11, 1899

South China Sea

LUZON

Baler

Manila

Philippine Sea

CATANDUANES

San Bernardino Strait

MINDORO

MASBATE

SAMAR

Sibuyan Sea

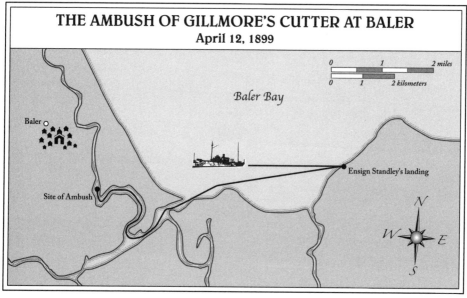

THE AMBUSH OF GILLMORE'S CUTTER AT BALER
April 12, 1899

Baler Bay

Baler

Site of Ambush

Ensign Standley's landing

CHAPTER ONE

Baler, 1897

As the first-quarter moon inched its way into the brilliant canopy of stars above, the young rebel *kapitan* knew he owned the night. From his makeshift mountainside encampment, he surveyed the shadows of the settlement below, firm in the knowledge that his enemy was fast asleep. His spies had told him so. A remote clutch of huts centered around a singular stone church on the Pacific coast of northern Luzon in the Philippines, Baler was home to some seventeen hundred souls. Also in the town was a thin contingent of Spanish infantry, *cazadores*, who were struggling to retain this one tiny fragment of their fraying empire. And tonight they would die.

For the past two weeks, the energetic Teodorico Novicio had single-mindedly prepared for the assault, and he had a lot riding on its success. General Emilio Aguinaldo, a small-town mayor recently elected to lead the Filipino revolution, had promised Novicio the command of Baler, his hometown, if he could rid it of the Spaniards. Electrified by the impassioned rhetoric of revolt during his studies in Manila, the twenty-two-year-old *kapitan* had already made a name for himself in the nascent revolutionary government through a series of violent raids on other Spanish garrisons scattered about central Luzon. Advancement was again in the offing, as soon as Novicio seized control of the sleepy village below.

While his desire to prove his worth to his superiors sharpened Novicio's focus, there was a more-powerful element that fueled the *kapitan's* relentless intensity. Drawn from a less-successful branch of a prominent family in the distant Ilocos region, Novicio had long labored in the shadows of his noted relations—intellectuals well versed in the arts, music, politics, and war. While only distantly related to Antonio Luna, perhaps

General Emilio Aguinaldo, the "center of gravity" to the war against the Spanish and then the Americans.

the most able of Aguinaldo's field commanders, and to his brother Juan Luna, the famed painter, Novicio had laid claim to the lineage.

Novicio, no doubt, was familiar with his relative's most famous painting, *Spoliarium,* which had prevailed over European works in an international art competition in Madrid thirteen years earlier. The twenty-three-by-thirteen-foot masterwork dripped in allegory and symbolism, depicting the battered body of a vanquished Roman gladiator, his contest at the Colosseum over, about to be stripped of his armor. More powerful in this elegy to courage was the implication of Filipino mastery of the arts on par with the Europeans. With the myth of racial or cultural superiority shattered, the Spaniards were more vulnerable than ever. In fin de siècle Philippines, a growing circle of wealthy and educated Filipinos knew that anything was possible.

This emerging sense of national consciousness, however, did little to salve an ill-tempered Novicio, whose second-class status in his illustrious extended family had left him resentful and insecure. It was all revealed in his fits of pique, his brutal tenacity, and his unceasing drive. He carried a tremendous chip on his shoulder, and it dictated his every move.

Teodorico Novicio had been molded for this moment. Raised in Baler, he was the son of farming migrants from the industrious Ilocos in northwest Luzon, who had arrived in waves in search of better opportunities.

COURTESY OF THE NATIONAL MUSEUM OF THE PHILIPPINES. PHOTOGRAPH BY BENIGNO TODA III.

Spoliarium, a massive twenty-three-by-thirteen-foot canvas by Filipino painter Juan Novicio Luna, was awarded a gold medal at the Exposición Nacional de Bellas Artes in Madrid in 1884. The achievement shattered stereotypes.

But coming from a poorer, less-educated offshoot of a clan that had risen to prominence left him keenly perceptive to injustice. Throughout his youth in Baler, Novicio had witnessed the abuses and excesses of the colonial Spaniards, who became a natural target for his anger. He soon came to despise them for their imperious manners and their shameless preying on the town's women. But most of all, he resented them for their one-sided decrees and orders that perpetuated their control over the Filipino people. After schooling in Manila and an immersion in the promise of the revolutionary movement, Novicio was quickly drawn into the fold of the rebel army. He swiftly rose to the rank of *kapitan*, helped by his gilded lineage.

On Aguinaldo's orders, Novicio had set out from the revolution's headquarters in central Luzon and journeyed back home to Baler. Along the way, he persuaded several compatriots to join his cause. Once at the outskirts of his hometown, Novicio sent word to his friends and relatives: *Come join me, as comrades in arms.* With the help of one of the wealthiest town leaders, the former provincial governor Antero Amatorio, Novicio spread his message of revolt, liberation, and the fantastic promise offered by the secret revolutionary society, the *Katipunan*. Odious Spanish taxes would no longer be imposed. Filipinos would not pay tribute to the Spaniards; instead, they would govern themselves. They would be free. In a few short weeks of fiery oratory, Novicio cobbled together a sufficient number of followers—a ragtag band of farmers and laborers—to execute his plan.

Now, Novicio was ratcheting up his game. Baler proper was not much more than a collection of sixty bamboo and *nipa* huts staked out along a few muddy streets, gridded around a dusty, foot-worn plaza and an old stone church. But it did have a strategic location. The Spaniards in the town below did not yet know it, but they were about to reap a whirlwind of violence. Decimation of the Spanish force, the *kapitan* knew, would take the Philippines one step closer to freedom. And it would also lighten the burden on the angry officer's shoulders.

For more than three centuries of colonial domination, the Spaniards had successfully tamped down nationalist dissent through repression, exile, and execution. By 1896, however, the burgeoning Filipino revolutionary movement had spilled over into armed conflict. Provinces fell under martial law. Youthful polymath Jose Rizal, one of the key intellectuals whose powerful and impassioned fictional writings about abusive Spanish rule had inspired the revolt, was arrested, imprisoned, and tried for the crime of rebellion. His sentence—public execution by firing squad in Manila's main plaza, on December 30, 1896—only served to fan the flames of insurrection and unrest.

Spain responded by flooding the islands with fresh troops. Desperate battles were fought and strategic provinces retaken. By mid-1897, the Filipino insurrection that had been under way for the past quarter-century was largely quelled. Aguinaldo's rebel forces were driven into retreat to the relative safety of central Luzon, into the mountains of Bulacan and Nueva Ecija. The Spaniards, in turn, extended an olive branch, cynically hoping to buy off the revolution's leaders with cash in exchange for the rebels' laying down their arms and leaving the country. Called the Pact of Biak-na-Bato, the agreement led to General Aguinaldo's disavowal of the rebellion and his declaration of loyalty to his

On December 30, 1896, Jose Rizal, the intellectual force behind the fight for Philippine independence, was executed in Manila by the Spaniards. His death only fanned the flames of insurrection and unrest.

colonial masters. But soon, both sides violated the terms of the deal. Aguinaldo, using the partial sums paid to him for his loyalty, revived the revolt from his exile in Hong Kong.

In the months running up to the bound-to-fail truce, the Spaniards rightly worried that the unprotected eastern coast of Luzon was being used to smuggle arms to Aguinaldo's forces. In response the Spanish governor general ordered a poorly equipped military detachment of fifty *cazadores*, under the leadership of nineteen-year-old Lieutenant Jose Mota, to Baler, capital of the district of El Principe. Hiking across the Sierra Madres, the north-south spine of mountains that separates the rugged east coast from the rest of Luzon, Lieutenant Mota's detachment arrived in Baler on September 20, 1897. They were greeted by a much-relieved Don Antonio Lopez Irizarri, commandant of the town, and a young parish priest, Candido Gomez Carreño, who explained that until their arrival, the far-flung coastal town had been guarded by no more than a single Spanish corporal of the Guardia Civil and five native guards.

Anticipating the worst, Lieutenant Mota immediately began improving the defenses of the town. He started with the construction of a circular network of trenches, which, if overrun, would provide a path of retreat to the refuge of the church. From behind the church's thick coral and stone walls, he knew, the Spaniards, even if heavily outnumbered, could hold out until reinforcements arrived.

With his plan of last resort in place, and against his better judgment, Lieutenant Mota was forced to scatter his forces about the town, as Baler lacked a structure large enough to accommodate all fifty Spanish *cazadores*. The church was off limits for this purpose, given its importance to the town's religious life. Mota divided his detachment of infantry among the town's three available buildings. He housed ten soldiers in the quarters of the Guardia Civil, another eighteen in the home of the town's schoolteacher, Lucio Quezon, and the balance in the *commandancia*, the office Mota shared with his political counterpart, Don Lopez Irizarri. Mota himself chose to lodge with the priest. For good measure, he assigned a single sentry to stand guard in the town's open and largely indefensible plaza.

After two weeks of toil, the new labyrinth of trenches was complete. Reviewing the reinforced earthen defenses, a cheerful Mota thanked his men for their efforts and took quiet pleasure in his own foresight.

On the eve of the attack, *Kapitan* Teodorico Novicio once more harangued his fighters, all armed with little more than steel bolos, or local machetes:

> *Brothers . . . we will embark on a dangerous operation, which, if we carry out well, will be a remarkable service to our country and one more step on the road to our freedom. . . . Brothers, do you have the strength to follow me?*

Novicio's amateur force of conspirators nervously confirmed their resolve. In his excitement, Novicio appointed a mayor, assigned ranks to a new cadre of officers, and appointed his wealthy benefactor, Amatorio, to head the town's military administration. Novicio then instructed his freshly minted band of freedom fighters to meet at eleven the following evening. Sensing the frailty of his makeshift command and perhaps a tinge of hesitation among his men, a hot-blooded Novicio, rifle in hand, closed with an admonishment: "If any of you fail me, or turn against me, I will shoot you without pity."

The following day, secrecy was compromised and the plot exposed when the talkative Amatorio was anxiously explaining the plan to his wife. An eight-year-old girl overheard the conversation and immediately regurgitated the details to her mother, who, in turn, rushed the news to the Spanish *commandante*. Don Lopez Irizarri dismissed the report with a wave of his hand. Mere child's fantasy.

At eight that evening, the town's uniformed policemen, a force of *cuadrillos*, reported for duty at the municipal hall. All of them were among Novicio's new rebel recruits. After the evening's passwords and signals were exchanged, the guardians of public order became foxes in the henhouse. With unfettered access across the garrison, the policemen-rebels silently tracked the Spaniards' every move.

On Tuesday, October 4, 1897, at precisely eleven in the evening as planned, Novicio's forces stealthily assembled along the forested edge of town. The frenetic *kapitan* ran among them, checking preparations and emphatically imploring each man to kill as many Spaniards as possible in one spectacular spasm of violence. Seize every rifle and every single cartridge of ammunition, Novicio implored. This was their one chance to hit the enemy hard. The glorious revolution depended on their success. And Novicio's own ascension was at hand.

Just before midnight, the compromised *cuadrillos* sauntered across the earthen plaza, following worn trails that cut across thin patches of grass and weeds, toward the lone Spanish sentry posted at the door of the *commandancia*. One *cuadrillo* inquired about the state of peace and order while another played along in the distraction. A third silently approached the Spanish sentry from behind, slowly drew his bolo, and violently smashed the blade through the soldier's skull. The dazed Spaniard swung around, squeezed off a shot from his Mauser, and yelled, "To arms, infantrymen!" A second powerful hack brought the soldier down.

The Filipino insurgents spilled out of the trenches and stormed the *cazadores'* quarters. Jolted awake, the Spaniards stumbled and flailed in the dark toward their rifles. With the element of surprise, the Filipinos mauled their way through the barracks, swinging bladed steel and clubs, collecting rifles and ammunition. As they cut a bloody swath, Novicio, leading one unit, was shot, a bullet piercing his left shoulder. Unable to continue, the *kapitan* escaped the chaos and lurched into the woods. Despite his withdrawal, his men fought on.

At the schoolhouse, brutal fighting degenerated into desperate, frenzied combat. One *cazador* attacked a wave of enemies with his bayoneted rifle, impaling several in a running sprint. In the dark of night, the spirited Spanish defense eventually forced the attackers to fall back. Finally, facing a regrouped and better-armed force, the Filipinos retreated into the forest that fringed the town.

Despite all his public bravado, Lieutenant Mota had quietly heeded the child's warning of an impending attack and had moved to the *commandancia* that night to sleep among the safety of his men. Startled out of bed by the insurgent assault, he raced outside in his nightwear and quickly emptied his revolver at the bolo-wielding shadows darting about. Unable to reload, and thinking his soldiers had been routed, he dashed back to the priest's convent, some twenty-five yards away. Mota was, at this point, nothing more than a half-naked, gun-waving form in a frantic search for refuge. The twenty-seven-year-old priest Carreño was also armed with a revolver. Even a man of God required the means for self-defense in the rebel-infested Philippines.

In the blurred moments that followed, a round from Carreño's revolver found its way into the lieutenant's head, and the priest, in a hysterical panic, bolted into the forest. Whether Mota borrowed the priest's gun, lamented all was lost, and shot himself—later reported as the official story—or was accidentally gunned down by the wild-eyed priest, has been lost to history. Whatever the facts, the outcome remained the same. The lieutenant lay dead by the door of the dormitory, blood oozing from his skull, the priest's revolver by his side.

On the second floor of the *commandancia*, Don Lopez Irizarri stood at the head of the staircase, gripping a Remington rifle. He called out to his men in hiding below, "Come up, my sons, and here, all of us together, we can defend ourselves [until] morning." Several wounded *cazadores* staggered up the stairs, dumbstruck and in shock. As they assessed their dire predicament, a bewildered Spanish infantryman who had broken away from his Filipino captors crashed into the downstairs foyer and started up the steps. The terror-stricken Spaniards unleashed a furious wave of gunfire. The sheet of hot lead lifted their hapless colleague off the stairs and slammed him back against the doorframe. His smoking form slid into a heap on the floor. As the tragic error was realized, the dispirited Spaniards huddled in the darkened *commandancia* and began the interminable wait for the next attack, or first light, whichever came first.

When the sun finally broke over Baler Bay, the morning's hazy light revealed the toll of the devastating assault. Cautiously stepping over their dead comrade in the doorway, the Spanish survivors ventured into the town plaza to find the remains of five fellow *cazadores* scattered about. On the threshold of the convent, Lieutenant Mota lay dead in a pool of congealing blood, a revolver by his side. In total, seven Spaniards were dead and eight missing, presumably captured by the insurgents. More than half of the surviving Spaniards were wounded, their limbs cleaved badly by the violent cyclone of sharpened steel. Only a third of the detachment was on its feet. Worse, of the garrison's fifty powerful Mauser rifles, only twenty remained. Interspersed among the dead were another eight bodies, insurgents killed during the assault, including the town's verbose mayor, whose municipal leadership had lasted but a day.

Disbelief hung in the air as thickly as the morning's humidity, the sun "hidden by dark clouds, as if ashamed by the vile treachery that had been perpetuated in Baler during the night," as remembered by Father Felix Minaya. Later that morning, a passing Spanish warship, the *Manila*, sent its auditor ashore for a routine exchange of views. There was no friendly banter this time; instead, the stunned emissary found the town awash in death and a pale, bleary-eyed Don Lopez Irizarri pleading, "Go back on board your ship and tell your captain to send me some people to help us; we were attacked last night and I am left with only three able-bodied men." A dozen men and a doctor rushed to assist the broken detachment, which had now retreated to the safety of the town's stone church. The ship urgently set sail to Manila to deliver the grim news to the faltering Spanish leadership.

A frustrated Novicio, who would spend the next two months nursing his gunshot wound, no doubt found some satisfaction in his victory. He and his men had not taken the town, but they had inflicted severe damage on the garrison. Novicio surely observed the Spanish ship offloading men and supplies, but it did not matter. The Spaniards could dispatch all the reinforcements they could muster to shore up the town's defenses and dig in even more deeply. Novicio would remain resolute: He would attack them again, and again, until they were gone.

These outsiders would be driven from Baler, once and for all. And Novicio would receive his due.

Freedom was at hand.

CHAPTER TWO

A Defense to Madness

Teodorico Novicio's brutal handiwork at Baler in early October 1897 triggered alarm among the Spanish political hierarchy in Manila. Two steam transports carrying one hundred fresh Spanish soldiers under the command of Captain Jesus Roldan Maizonada were immediately dispatched. The reinforcements would face off with an insurgent force now armed with the garrison's modern, more-deadly Mauser rifles. Landing under fire from Novicio and his men, the Spanish detachment fought its way to the church and relieved the besieged remnants of Lieutenant Mota's men. The battered survivors staggered aboard one of the ships and collapsed on its decks. Within hours, the men were steaming toward Manila, their prayers answered.

For those Spaniards left behind, a new chapter of torment was about to unfold. Sensing weakness, Novicio and his soldiers attacked the reinforcements later that day. Roldan's company, struggling to fight off the insurgents, fell under siege anew. Days dragged into weeks. Hunkered down in the stone church, the detachment faced incessant sniping, with rations running short and relief nowhere in sight. Finally, nearly four months later, on January 23, 1898, more reinforcements arrived—but not to join the fight. Following the peace pact at Biak-na-Bato, the agreement that had bribed Aguinaldo for his loyalty and sent him into exile, the arriving force of four hundred Spanish soldiers under Major Juan Genova Iturbe had marched to Baler simply to assist Roldan and receive the surrender of Novicio, his men, and their weapons. Few insurgents turned up to take advantage of the amnesty, however, and those who did were unarmed. Novicio's fighters, it seemed, were biding their time.

One month later, with the peace settlement in hand and hostilities officially over, Spanish authorities in Manila ordered the withdrawal of Genova's battalion and Roldan's company. In their place, a final detachment of soldiers was dispatched to Baler, essentially to keep peace and order, under the command of a handsome, young lieutenant, Puerto Rican Juan Alonso Zayas.

Alonso was born and raised in the cobblestoned city of San Juan, son of a Spanish officer from Barcelona who was assigned to the Caribbean colony. Drawn from privilege, Alonso had access to excellent schools and had taken up an interest in photography. In November 1888, he decided to follow in his father's footsteps and joined the Spanish Army. At just nineteen years of age, Alonso found himself in Cuba, tasked with quelling the island's simmering unrest. Following further training in Spain, and promotion in rank, Alonso was shipped to Manila, where he arrived in May 1897. Over a depressing nine months, the now twenty-nine-year-old officer had witnessed one loss after another to the Filipinos, followed by a sketchy negotiated peace that had left Spanish authorities with a severely weakened grasp over its upstart colony.

Alonso's subaltern, the thirty-two-year-old Saturnino Martin Cerezo, was from humbler origins. Raised in the fertile valleys of the Caceres region of Spain—known for its fine red wines, rich vegetable stews, and salt-cured ham—Martin had turned to the military to avoid a life of backbreaking labor on farms outside the rural town of Miajadas. In 1897, he volunteered for service in the Philippines, responding to the urgent call to arms from the Spanish authorities there.

Lieutenant Alonso's command consisted of forty-nine enlisted men, who, like Martin, were predominantly laborers and farmers drawn from the hinterlands and outposts of Spain—from provinces such as Castellon, Andalusia, Catalonia, and Valencia, and the far-flung islands of Majorca and the Canaries. The detachment, the bulk of whom were in their early twenties, comprised several bakers, a shoemaker, stonecutter, blacksmith, cook, haberdasher, tailor, locksmith, and boat hand. Few were professional soldiers, but that didn't matter; the revolution's leadership was in exile and hostilities were declared over. The only enemy this new contingent of *cazadores* expected to confront in isolated Baler was the endless boredom of garrison duty.

Alonso and his men set out overland from Manila on February 7, 1898, marching east across Luzon. Joining them were the newly appointed political-military governor for the Principe district, Don Enrique de las

Morenas y Fossi, and a contract surgeon, Medical Lieutenant Rogelio Vigil de Quiñones y Alfaro. Las Morenas, holding the rank of captain, was the most senior officer, an old army veteran from Cadiz. He had fought in the last of the Carlist Wars (1872–1876), a civil war against pretenders to the Spanish throne, and had been retired and placed in the reserves. With the outbreak of a revolt in the Philippines, Las Morenas had been recalled to service. Vigil de Quiñones was a medical doctor, who, at age thirty-six, had joined the army three months earlier for adventure. Prior to his assignment to Baler, he had been working in the main Spanish hospital in Malate, a bucolic, bayside suburb of Manila.

The trek from Manila was an arduous five-day affair, beginning on the Pasig River, a muddy-brown waterway that snaked through the heart of the capital city, connecting Manila Bay with the massive inland Laguna Lake. A clanking steam vessel delivered the Spaniards across the shallow, brackish lake, as they were silently tracked by the sun-wizened fishermen tending their fish pens. The first stop was Santa Cruz, a small settlement on the distant shore. From there, the Spaniards continued on horseback and on foot to the eastern coast, to the town of Mauban. On the final leg, Alonso and his men sailed up the Pacific coast to the remote, mountain-hemmed town of Baler. Upon their arrival at the garrison, Alonso's command took to the urgent task of building up defenses once again. Captain Las Morenas, meanwhile, made plans to repopulate the town. He hoped to lure back inhabitants who had fled, now that the negotiated peace at Biak-na-Bato offered an opportunity for town life to return to normal.

Kapitan Novicio, however, had other plans. The rebel stranglehold on Spanish forces was achieving results in other towns. In Novicio's mind, Baler would fall next. He knew the Spanish were running low on men and lacked the conviction to fight. He also knew that the local populace was once again growing eager for action after Las Morenas had impressed the male population into a labor force. Residents were angry. As the Spaniards alienated the local populace, the rebel *kapitan* knew their days were numbered.

Novicio must have been emboldened by his string of successes: the deadly assault on Mota's detachment the previous October, which had provided his fighters with their first supply of modern Mausers; their surprise attack on the Spanish cruiser as it landed reinforcements; and the corralling and siege of Roldan's force in the embattled church for more than three months. By now, Novicio knew intimately the layout of the garrison, its resources, and its desperate isolation. The next prize that taunted him: fifty newly arrived Mausers and an abundant resupply of precious ammunition. After Novicio captured the garrison in the name of Filipino independence, General Aguinaldo would be pleased, and the *kapitan* was certain that his long-overdue glory and renown would follow.

By late June 1898, an anxious stream of farmers and their families began a quiet exodus from town. Fearing another bloodbath, the Spanish garrison, in turn, prepared in earnest for an attack. They concentrated their forces in the church, drawing together their remaining provisions. Amid the flurry of activity, two local hospital corpsmen, along with Lieutenant Martin Cerezo's servant, deserted their posts and fled into the mountains. As the detachment fretted over their fortifications and supplies, one of the Spanish infantrymen also took the opportunity to run. Things were starting to fall apart.

On June 30, the wait was over. At the bridge on the west side of town, Martin Cerezo's patrol stumbled into an ambush, drawing a heavy barrage of rifle fire from the surrounding thicket. A corporal fell to the ground, severely wounded in the foot. Heavily outnumbered, the Spaniards fell into a full retreat, carrying their wounded comrade. Racing back to the church, they fired on the run, a pack of determined Filipinos in hot pursuit, and burst into the church, slamming the huge wooden doors shut and yanking the heavy iron bolts into place. The wounded *cazador*, his foot mangled, writhed in agony on the floor.

On the last day of June 1898, Teodorico Novicio began what he hoped would be the third and final attack on Baler's garrison. This one, surely, would drive the Spaniards from his town forever.

Holed up in the church, the fifty-two well-armed and defensively entrenched Spaniards—a force of three officers, forty-seven enlisted men, a contract surgeon, and the town's priest—proved a formidable foe. The detachment estimated that their store of food rations and an unlimited supply of fresh drinking water (from a new well dug on the grounds) would allow them to hold out for months. With the Spaniards able to repulse each Filipino attack with ease, a stalemate was quickly reached. Three weeks into what had degenerated into a kind of siege, with each side sniping at the other, the Filipinos received reinforcements under the command of Lieutenant Colonel Simon Tecson. Measured and judicious, the thirty-seven-year-old Tecson, fourteen years older and vastly wiser than the impulsive Novicio, brought a broader strategic mentality to Baler. Drawn from an established family in the central Luzon province of Bulacan, the educated lieutenant colonel was cut from another class of Filipinos, a world above Novicio's rougher, more rakish reality—obvious to all by his striking height and confident bearing.

Tecson's arrival expanded Novicio's force to some 800 men, who were now armed with 137 rifles. After reviewing the standoff, Tecson agreed to order an immediate attack to draw out the Spaniards and finish the siege business once and for all. The church's defenses, however, offered a vastly superior position and would not be easily taken. Tecson's attack left a single Spanish sentry in the church tower wounded, but only by luck. During the Filipinos' four-sided barrage of lead, a single rifle round had ricocheted off the soldier's rifle, slammed into his chest, and settled under his rib cage. The Filipinos backed off, unwilling to lose men to the efficient Spanish snipers. Inside the church, Dr. Vigil de Quiñones treated

US NATIONAL ARCHIVES

The church at Baler (circa February 1900), site of the famed siege.

the wounded soldier, but an infection quickly took hold. Thirteen days later, the *cazador* was dead.

A month into the siege, the Spaniards held their first funeral inside the bolted, beleaguered church, presided over by Father Carreño. The dead boy was buried at the far corner of the sacristy, just before the altar. The funeral would have been far gloomier had the Spaniards been aware of the news outside their walls. In early July 1898, Spain's Caribbean naval forces had been crushed by the Americans in the Battle of Santiago, and the Cuban capital had been surrendered. By the end of the month, Spanish authorities, through the French embassy in Washington, D.C., were proposing an armistice to bring hostilities with the Americans to a close.

As peace between Spain and the United States was being forged, the combatants at Baler continued their tit-for-tat sniping at each other's lines. When rifles proved ineffective, Tecson's forces brought up several cannons and rained shrapnel down on the church walls and roof. The barrage merely splintered the church's doors, but it completely destroyed the roof, exposing the Spaniards to the elements at the height of monsoon season. The miserable, wet conditions led another Filipino servant to desert the Spanish stronghold.

A frustrated Tecson meditated over new approaches to coax the Spaniards into surrendering. He settled on the idea of using two Spanish priests, Fathers Juan Lopez and Felix Minaya, recently captured from

Insurgents patrolling the beach at Baler, circa 1899.

another coastal town fifty miles to the north, in an attempt to persuade their countrymen to lay down their arms.

The two Spanish priests were improbable emissaries between the warring factions. In 1887, Lopez had entered the Franciscan priesthood at age sixteen in his hometown of Pastrana, a once-splendorous medieval village flanked by the Tajo and Tajuño Rivers, in the rolling countryside of Guadalajara. Felix Minaya, one year older and a native of Toledo, had also taken his vows at Pastrana at the same time. For the eight years that followed, the two inseparable men had served together at the quiet hilltop convent, pursuing their godly vocation with youthful passion. In September 1895, Lopez and Minaya sailed together for the Philippines. For the past two and a half years, they had lived and worked together, jointly ministering to their flock in the remote town of Casiguran. Unaware of the siege under way in distant Baler—at the time, only accessible by boat—the priests were largely oblivious to their own deteriorating security. A column of Filipino insurgents arrived at Casiguran on July 20, 1898, and immediately took the two men into custody, stripped them of their possessions and robes, and turned their convent, once a quiet refuge, into a military barracks.

On Tecson's orders, the priests were brought to Baler, given back their robes, and ordered to the front of the church. A parley was called by the sounding of bugles, and flags of truce were raised. Greeted by their ecstatic countrymen, Lopez and Minaya were led inside the barricaded church for a meeting. Sitting with Captain Las Morenas and his officers, the priests were pressed for news. Father Lopez told the Spaniards everything, as incredible as it sounded: Spain had been defeated by the United States of America. Spanish forces were withdrawing across the country. The war was over, they had been told.

As recalled later by Minaya, an incredulous Las Morenas scoffed, "So you have not seen what the insurgents told you about? You have not witnessed any of the major catastrophes you have reported to us?"

"Absolutely none," the priest admitted.

The questioning continued, with Lieutenant Alonso angrily concluding, "So, everything is a pure lie! Those bandits wish to deceive us through all means, but they shall not succeed." Las Morenas then made a decision. "You, dear fathers, will not leave this place; you will remain with us."

Lopez and Minaya objected, fearing they would be killed if they were ever to fall again into insurgent hands. Las Morenas waved off their concerns. The priests would be issued rifles, and from then on, it was agreed, they would rotate on duty at the windows and trenches, like everyone else, sniping at the insurgents when required. Between these tasks, they would attend to their ministry and take confessions. If needed, they would also administer last rites to the dying and pray for their eternal repose.

When the news of the two priests' absorption into the Spanish force filtered back across Filipino lines, Tecson demanded a second parley. Standing in front of the church the following morning, he angrily admonished the Spaniards for their violation of the international laws of war. He closed with a warning: "Felonies such as the ones you are committing shall cost you dearly." And with that, the exasperated lieutenant colonel returned to his office to rethink his strategy.

By September, two months into the stalemate, constant fatigue, limited rations, and an extreme lack of hygiene brought new risks to the embattled Spaniards. Exacerbated by the humid weather, a new intruder stole into the fortified church: beriberi. Little was known of the disease at the time, nor its cause—a diet heavy on polished white rice—but it terrified its Spanish victims. Wracked with intestinal flu, the weakened priest Carreño was the first to fall ill. With his system starved of the critical nutritional building block of thiamine (vitamin B1, readily found in fresh meat, leafy green vegetables, and legumes, among other foods, all absent here), the disease progressed rapidly.

Father Carreño's decline may have started with paresthesia—a feeling of pins and needles—in his feet, a loss of the sense of touch in his hands,

Filipino officers departing to, and returning from, another failed negotiation with the Spanish detachment holed up in the church.

and a feeling of heat in his grotesquely bloated legs. Reflexes in his ankles and then his knees would have failed, followed by severe muscle weakness, crippling him. Over time, Carreño would have suffered from emotional disturbances caused by the onset of psychosis. He would have experienced a profound loss of short-term memory, forgetting where he was or recent events leading up to the siege, while perhaps recalling with startling clarity his childhood. With his brain increasingly confused, Carreño likely began mumbling nonsense. A final wave of damage would have quickly followed: a form of encephalopathy—brain dysfunction. Depleted of essential nutrients, crippled, bloated, in severe pain, and half-insane, Carreño likely fell into a raving delirium before death.

The priest was dead by September 25, 1898, eighty-seven days into the siege.

Five days later, another soldier died of the disease. A corporal and private quickly followed. Fresh graves were dug, hacked out in a small nook alongside the open corral. Eight days later, the garrison's commanding officer, the dashing Puerto Rican officer, Lieutenant Alonso, succumbed.

The command now fell to Lieutenant Martin Cerezo. To stave off further death and despair, he turned his attention to improving sanitation within the church. He ordered ventilation improved and a makeshift latrine constructed on the edge of the corral. Martin Cerezo's men struggled to beat back the swarms of flies that had been attracted to the rotting human filth and refuse strewn about the church. Almost purpose-built vectors for disease, the flies channeled pathogens as they walked, probed, and fed across filth, passing deadly microbes to the Spaniards' food, noses, mouths, and open wounds.

Beriberi continued to take a harsh toll. Another two Spanish *cazadores* died in October, followed by five more men in November. Additional graves were dug and the bodies buried. In late November, Captain Las Morenas reportedly fell ill. Over two days, the captain slipped in and out of consciousness, in great agony. Delirious, he called out to one of his sons, "Little Henry! Little Henry!" He turned to Martin Cerezo and said, "Order them to go back and look for the child. Quickly! The *insurrectos* are going to take him." With his mind gone, Las Morenas died that afternoon.

The captain's death came on November 22, 1898, 145 days into the siege of Baler. The remaining men were now surrounded by fourteen fresh graves.

Meanwhile, further parleys failed. The Spaniards held steadfast to the belief that they were holding out for the honor of Mother Spain. Emissaries were rebuffed and efforts to communicate rejected, in the conviction that these attempts were nothing more than ruses by wily Filipinos bent on luring their colonial masters into surrender. Lieutenant Martin Cerezo was now in command of thirty-one privates, a trumpeter, and three corporals, almost all of them ill. Also holed up in the church were Dr. Vigil de Quiñones, one hospital corpsman, and the two late additions, Fathers Lopez and Minaya. By the end of the year, food rations had fallen to critical levels. Stacked beside the altar were a few sacks of fermented flour, several boxes of maggoty bacon, some old coffee and sugar, and a handful of tins containing sardines. The men were soon veering toward starvation, their bodies falling into a ketogenic state of self-consumption. Hunger, literally, was eating away at their emaciated frames.

On February 13, 1899, the epidemic of beriberi carried off another *cazador*. More than seven months into the siege, the death count now stood at fifteen. Of the original fifty-two men blockaded inside the church, nearly a third were dead, most due to beriberi, but also from the effects of starvation, dysentery, and other diseases.

The surviving Spaniards probably suffered a complete loss of reason, a primary characteristic of advanced beriberi being severe emotional disturbance and psychosis. In short, these men were defending their position while perched on the sharp edge of insanity.

~

Over the months, a cloud of facts and innuendo had inevitably drifted across the mountains and into the hands of Manila's journalists and editors. The press had taken note of the standoff at Baler. Most commentary was directed at the incomprehensible situation of the small garrison that was unwilling to surrender—laudable on one hand, laughable on the other. It was painfully obvious to an incredulous readership: Spain had surrendered the Philippines to the Americans some six months earlier, on August 13, 1898, and the Treaty of Paris had been signed between the United States and Spain on December 10, 1898. The war had officially ended with an agreement to sell the Philippines to the victors for $20 million. And with hostilities breaking out between American and Filipino forces in February 1899, it was no longer the Spaniards' fight. Any further Spanish defense was senseless.

Army of Liberation forces at Baler largely kept their distance and allowed the Spaniards to starve or die of disease. Lieutenant Colonel Simon Tecson stands to the right of the cannon, and to the left, Captain Teodorico Novicio.

Manila's rumor mill was further fed by Spanish officials returning from round after round of failed negotiations at Baler. The refusal of the garrison's officers to obey orders issued by senior officers smacked of disobedience, if not outright mutiny. Anecdotes of death, intrigue, and despair were whispered in the social circles of the Spanish elite. One rumor gaining traction was that Lieutenant Alonso had attempted to climb to the bell tower to take down the tattered Spanish flag and surrender, only to be confronted by a murderously deranged Lieutenant Martin Cerezo, who had cut him down with his sword. Other gossip suggested that a smaller group of soldiers led by Martin Cerezo was holding the others by force and refusing to surrender. But why? Speculation was rife: Was it to avoid being tried for their crimes, be it desertion, mutiny, or murder? Or was it because they had gone stark raving mad?

This much was clear: The truth about the siege at Baler would only be revealed once the crazed detachment of Spaniards threw open the doors of the church and surrendered.

CHAPTER THREE

Arrival

Cavite Navy Yard, Philippines—April 2, 1899

STEPPING OUT OF THE NAVY STEAM LAUNCH, LIEUTENANT JAMES CLARKSON Gillmore Jr. planted his polished white patent leather shoes on the age-worn cobblestones, the first solid ground they had touched in seven weeks. We can imagine Gillmore inhaling deeply, taking in a pungent waft of rot and decay, the humid, tropical vapor feeding his nostrils. And surely, the rich mélange of exotic odors tweaked his pulse, signaling the fulfillment of a long-held wish. Before him was the bustling port city of Manila, now in American hands. The stocky, mustachioed naval officer had been steaming across the world's oceans for nearly two months on a troop transport. Like all cruises, it had surely thickened his short frame a tad more than he liked, but it was a small price to pay to see some action. The forty-four-year-old Gillmore had leveraged every ounce of influence he could muster within the navy hierarchy and finally prevailed. Here he was in the Philippines, coming ashore in his sharp dress whites, on a beautiful bright Sunday morning, April 2, 1899, just weeks into the fighting.

⌁

By the time of Gillmore's arrival, the city of Manila had been under American control for eight months. Yet, in the resulting vacuum of power left in the Spaniards' wake, the balance of the Philippines was ripe for the taking. The Americans understood they would need to act quickly. Other powers—the Germans above all—were just as keen to expand their footprint into Asia and were probing the region with their formidable warships.

For most of America's leadership, the foray into Asia was a natural step in a process long under way, and intrinsically tied to the very founding of America. The United States was forged, in the words of Thomas Jefferson, as an "empire for liberty." Over the course of the century that followed, an insatiable hunger for expansion pushed America over the Appalachian chain, across the Midwestern heartland, into the fringes of Canada and Mexico, and on, to the Pacific coast. Through treaties, purchase, and outright conquest, America spilled over into new lands with an unshakable belief in its own exceptionalism—moral, legal, and otherwise—which justified an unstoppable expansion of the boundaries of frontier for the greater good.

Coupled with this geographical expansion was a revolution of science and technology. In the twilight of the nineteenth century, America began its ascent as a world power, dominating the fields of science and invention, infused with a vision of a new global order. Front and center to the growing nation was an entirely new conception of sea power and its role in commanding the world's oceans. An ambitious steel-armored shipbuilding program, begun in the 1880s, led to the deployment of powerful new fleets of ships, many that straddled the divide between old and new, one age and another, both wind and steam. With its growing military might, America was effectively positioned to extend its reach across the Pacific.

Emboldened with its newfound military prowess, America went to war with a weak and eviscerated Spain, its rebellious colonies and unkempt empire in collapse. The United States achieved an astonishingly swift victory. At Manila Bay on May 1, 1898, Admiral George Dewey and his Asiatic Squadron of seven warships crushed the forty-vessel Spanish Armada, killing three hundred Spaniards and destroying its Pacific fleet. Dewey's squadron incurred the total loss of one fatality: an overweight chief engineer who dropped from heat prostration as his ship, a revenue cutter pressed into service as a coal carrier, slipped past Corregidor the night before the battle. As a result of his success at Manila Bay, Admiral Dewey became a beloved hero and household name across America.

The culminating Battle of Santiago de Cuba followed. Attempting to break out of Santiago harbor, Admiral Pascual Cervera's Spanish squadron was intercepted by the American fleet under the commands of Rear Admiral William T. Sampson and Commodore Winfield S. Schley. In a

Admiral George Dewey, hero of the Battle of Manila Bay on May 1, 1898, aboard the *USS Olympia,* flagship of the Asiatic Squadron.

running fight, brutal American firepower reduced Cervera's four armored cruisers and two torpedo-boat destroyers to burning wrecks. Again, the casualties were grossly one-sided: 323 Spaniards killed versus a single American, twenty-five-year-old Chief Yeoman George H. Ellis, who was decapitated when a large Spanish shell rocketed across the USS *Brooklyn*'s main deck.

These back-to-back naval victories, stunning in their brevity and destruction, led most Americans to believe the United States Navy and its armor-clad fleet were nothing short of invincible. The Spanish-American War lasted only four months, marking the end of the Spanish Empire and leaving the victor with the new island possessions of Guam, Puerto Rico, and the Philippines.

But there was one problem with that last acquisition. The Filipinos were not simply going to relinquish their sovereign claim to new colonial masters. The Americans had inherited the same predicament faced by the now-vanquished Spanish colonizers: a tenuous foothold in a porous and unmanageable capital city, their forces surrounded by entrenched insurgent troops; a revolutionary government that rejected their presence and demanded recognition; and across the disparate, fractious islands, a heterogeneity of competing interests and ethnic groups united only in their restiveness and resistance. After diplomacy had failed, fighting erupted on February 4, 1899. A full-scale onslaught against Filipino insurgent positions by the American military was well under way by the time of Lieutenant Gillmore's arrival on April 2, 1899.

The naval officer's transport was one of many arriving each week from the United States, adding thousands of fresh American troops to the campaign. Regular army units serving in the Cuban theater were quickly redirected to the Philippines. Since the outbreak of hostilities in early February, five regiments had arrived in Manila, allowing major gains to be made. American forces had routed insurgents across Manila's suburbs, and the southern islands of Cebu and Negros were now occupied. By March 31, 1899, the headquarters of the Filipino Army of Liberation at Malolos, Bulacan, located twenty miles to the northwest of Manila, had been overrun. General Emilio Aguinaldo—back from exile in Hong Kong, and the figurehead of the nationalist movement—was in retreat. The prospect of a quick, decisive win over the now scattered and disorganized *insurrectos* seemed inevitable.

—◦—

Coming ashore on liberty, an invigorated Lieutenant Gillmore had just completed his first responsibility—paying a courtesy call to Admiral Dewey aboard his squadron's flagship, the impressively armed USS *Olympia,* to receive orders. It was now official: In a few days, Gillmore would report to the USS *Yorktown,* one of the many warships standing at anchor in the bay, to serve as its new navigator.

This was welcome news. Gillmore had now been in the navy for twenty-two years, seven months, and twenty-two days. As was his custom, he had left his wife Mary and son Stuart—along with two African-American servants, Lizzie and Helena—in Washington, D.C., comfortably ensconced in their four-story brownstone, nestled amid the mansions and statuary of fashionable Dupont Circle. After almost seventeen years of marriage—spending nearly half of those at sea—the lieutenant had found himself mired in a distant and increasingly unhappy union. With his travels, he barely spent any time with his eight-year-old son, and when he was at home, his marriage constituted little more than an ugly silence punctuated by alcohol-laced conflict. Gillmore had been stalled at his rank of lieutenant for nine years, at the top of his pay grade, earning $216 per month. The situation was surely oppressive to a man of his pedigree and talent; he knew that he deserved better. Something had to change. Something, finally, had to go his way.

Lieutenant Gillmore had served as an officer on twelve different ships. His next ship—his thirteenth—would hopefully be a lucky one. It was time to make up lost ground. But first, the streets of Manila beckoned.

Crammed with some 225,000 residents, including 3,000 Spaniards and 18,000 Chinese, the "Pearl of the Orient" had been overrun by merchants, traders, and entrepreneurs, all seeking to capitalize on the massive influx of Americans and relieve them of their gold. In just a few short months, the incursion had reshaped the previously sedate, verdant city. Beyond the old walled city of Intramuros, built by the Spaniards two centuries earlier, just across the Bridge of Spain, was the premier commercial district of Escolta. Lieutenant Gillmore would have found Escolta, presumably his first stop, home to upscale American- and European-run retail shops, the best restaurants, bakeries, and cafes. Just a third of a mile long, the narrow Escolta was a constant jostle of elbows, carts, and cries, incessantly fed by a deluge of shoppers delivered by horse-drawn, sixteen-person omnibuses, called *tranvias*, that ran along a five-line, ten-mile rail network connecting the city's neighborhoods. Escolta's vibrant, electrified, two-story commercial strip offered everything from clothing to candy, printers to perfume, saddleries to saloons. Topping the shops were second-floor offices that billeted the city's leading lawyers, brokers, dentists, and doctors.

Elsewhere in Manila, Gillmore would have found America's presence looming large. Advertisements on once-barren stone walls colorfully pitched Schlitz, Budweiser, and Cyrus Noble whiskey, which were arriving by the shipload to slake the thirsty throats of the thousands of soldiers and sailors spilling into the colonial city. In less than a year, more than

Lieutenant James C. Gillmore Jr., at age forty-four, was looking for an opportunity to reinvigorate his sagging career.

four hundred saloons—operated by a roguish mix of Spaniards, Americans, Filipinos, Chinese, and Japanese entrepreneurs—had opened their doors. Knowing Gillmore's record, and the habits of nearly all of his naval counterparts, he quickly found a way to slake his thirst.

And then, more diversions beckoned: Long a port city with a dark underside, Manila's sex trade was experiencing a veritable stampede of women and their handlers from seedy ports across Asia—Yokohama, Hong Kong, Singapore, and even Calcutta and Vladivostok. With the invasion, a neat crossroads of formerly tranquil streets in Santa Mesa had degenerated into a raucous zone of debauchery, described as "two whole streets filled with drunken soldiers, rioting, yelling Americans and half-naked women."

To be sure, Manila was a port that could keep a sailor busy. And Lieutenant James C. Gillmore Jr. had two days to squander before reporting to his gleaming gunboat, at anchor in the bay.

———

The freshly revamped USS *Yorktown* was a marvel. She was named after the Siege of Yorktown at Virginia, the history-changing assault by American and French forces on the British in 1781. Under the command of General George Cornwallis, seven thousand trapped and hungry redcoats, low on ammunition, had no choice but to surrender. The decisive victory triggered a negotiation that ended the Revolutionary War.

Witness to another revolution, the *Yorktown* was the first of her kind—a new class of ship specifically designed for the kinds of naval warfare imagined by Washington's military planners. Her keel laid down in 1887 at the William Cramp & Sons Shipbuilding Company in Philadelphia, the *Yorktown* was a $445,000 hybrid of technology that spanned two ages: three tall masts and a set of sails to harness the wind, with steam-powered propellers below, fueled by massive bunkers of dark, filthy coal. She was a steel-hulled, twin-screw gunboat with a heavy armored deck, 244 feet long, 36 feet wide, and capable of accommodating a 191-member crew. Lashed about her decks were eight additional boats: a steam launch, three cutters, two whaleboats, a dinghy, and a punt. Recently overhauled, she was now armed with six rapid-fire six-inch guns, each capable of hurling armor-piercing, highly explosive shrapnel and canister shells at targets over six miles distant; in addition, she boasted two three-pounder guns, two one-pounder guns, and two spanking new Colt Automatic machine guns. The USS *Yorktown*'s designation as "Gunboat No. 1" was a misnomer; she was, in fact, an armored cruiser capable of delivering tremendous destruction.

Gillmore would be reporting to Commander Charles Stillman Sperry, who had taken the helm of the *Yorktown* the previous November. The Brooklyn-born son of a clockmaker had a rougher start in life than most. At age nine, Sperry lost both his parents, which left him and his five sisters orphaned and impoverished. Raised by an older uncle, Sperry gained an appointment to the United States Naval Academy in 1862 at the age of fifteen. Dismissed twice for medical deficiencies, and then reinstated through his uncle's intervention, Sperry graduated eleventh in a class of seventy-eight in 1866.

Sperry's naval career began less than auspiciously. His first cruise, as a midshipman aboard the USS *Sacramento*, ended in disaster. Shipwrecked in the Bay of Bengal in June 1867, the entire crew was left adrift on a

US NATIONAL ARCHIVES

The *USS Yorktown*, designated Gunboat Number 1, was Lieutenant Gillmore's thirteenth ship.

raft for days, without water or provisions, until a passing steamer came to the rescue. Things improved from there: stints in the South Pacific, on ships based at the West India, Asiatic, and Mediterranean stations, and as a professor at the US Naval Academy. Sperry had been promoted to commander in July 1894, and now, at age fifty-two, was a respected officer known for his temperate behavior and professionalism.

Being orphaned as a child likely explained Sperry's deep devotion to family. He married well, taking the hand of Edith Marcy, the daughter of a former secretary of state, and together they raised two sons. While away at sea, Sperry wrote his beloved wife almost daily—lengthy, handwritten accounts of his activities, ruminations, and concerns for his family that arrived in batches at their home in Waterbury, Connecticut, from distant ports around the world.

Despite a generous and loving spirit toward his family, Commander Sperry ran a very tight ship, strictly by the book. A tight ship, he knew from his years at sea, was a happy ship. With his solid reputation, Sperry was tasked to helm the *Yorktown* for a year or two of what he called "bushwhacking" in the Philippines. Assuming he excelled, he mused to his wife, a promotion to captain awaited.

On January 7, 1899, the US Navy's Bureau of Navigation ordered the *Yorktown* to set sail to the western reaches of the Pacific Ocean and to the port of Manila. For the next five days, the *Yorktown* rushed to secure herself for the voyage. On January 12, the last of the deliveries and stores arrived: one hundred tons of Australian coal; hundreds of pounds of beef, vegetables, and bread; and one hundred bags of mail. At 4:45 p.m., the *Yorktown* called all hands, and under cloudy, cool skies, with a slight southwesterly breeze, got under way. She stood out at the harbor, sailed through the Golden Gate Strait, breezed past Alcatraz Island, and cut into the open sea.

On board was a crew of 164 men comprising officers, petty officers, enlisted men, and apprentices. In addition to Commander Sperry, the *Yorktown*'s thirteen officers included an executive officer, two lieutenants, a chief engineer, a surgeon, and a mix of seven ensigns and midshipmen. The officers, by and large, were graduates from the Naval Academy, indoctrinated in its traditional values of duty, honor, and integrity.

The complexion and lineage of the rough-and-tumble men said as much about them as it did the country they had volunteered to serve.

Commander Charles S. Sperry helmed the *USS Yorktown* at Baler and later rose to the rank of admiral.

Fully one-third were foreign-born, drawn from Canada, Denmark, England, France, Hungary, Ireland, Norway, Russia, Scotland, and Sweden. Most were skilled seamen who had deserted foreign-flag merchant ships over the years, attracted to the US Navy's better pay and work conditions. The younger sailors were by and large native-born Americans, caught up in anti-Spanish "Remember the *Maine*" war fever—a call to arms shouted after the suspicious sinking of the USS *Maine* in Havana Harbor on February 15, 1898. Fifteen others—Chinese cooks and mess attendants—hailed from either Hong Kong, Shanghai, or Canton.

Dictating the itinerary of the *Yorktown*'s ocean jaunt across the Pacific were critical stops at Hawaii and Guam to take on board a precious resupply of fuel. Black anthracite coal—combustible sedimentary rock formed over millions of years from the swampy forests that once covered the Earth—was in fact the Achilles heel of the modern navy. The *Yorktown* could only travel as far as her coal reserves could take her, and like all the ships in the new steel-hulled fleet, her appetite was voracious. At full

The *USS Yorktown* under full steam.

power, with her boilers cranked to maximum steam pressure, she chewed through 222 pounds of coal per nautical mile, leaving a thick acrid arc of black smoke in her wake. She consumed 2,730 pounds per hour to achieve a full cruising speed of thirteen knots, and this, on smooth seas. The *Yorktown's* coal bunkers, however, held only 400 tons under normal conditions, which allowed her to sail, in theory, at this breakneck pace, unimpeded, for only twelve continuous days, covering just 3,500 nautical miles. Of course, the ship also had her three masts outfitted with powerful square sails, which provided supplementary wind power and, as a result, much greater reach.

The *Yorktown* arrived at the Port of Cavite late on Thursday, February 23, 1899, just as a spectacular orange sun dipped below the horizon. The previous day, Filipino rebels had torched major parts of Manila, causing massive conflagrations in the districts of Santa Cruz, Tondo, and Binondo. The fires had razed block after block of bamboo and *nipa* palm structures, reducing entire neighborhoods to smoldering black ash. Firefighters and soldiers battling the blazes had also been targeted by insurgent snipers, which compounded the chaos. For the *Yorktown's* crew, though, Manila's sky was lit to a beautiful, pulsating red glow, the arsonists' handiwork just coming under control as their ship dropped anchor in the bay.

The following morning, the *Yorktown* received signals from Admiral Dewey's flagship, the USS *Olympia*. The messages granted permission for Commander Sperry to lower her steam launch and declare a general field day for the crew. The *Yorktown* gave a resounding thirteen-gun salute to the Asiatic Squadron's flagship and received a seven-gun salute in return. The ship's officers, for the most part, began their rounds of official visits and courtesy calls. The balance of the crew stumbled ashore and, by and large, tramped to the city's more riotous quarters, where most of them quickly slid into a blurred state of liberty in one of the many ramshackle saloons, brothels, and bars.

Over the course of the next six weeks, the *Yorktown* was tasked to hunt for German gunrunners rumored to be sailing routes from Hong Kong to bands of insurgents operating along the unguarded Luzon coast. With Commander Sperry at the helm, the *Yorktown* chased down and boarded suspicious merchant ships, checked documentation and cargo, and, in one case, fired blank charges to stop a suspected gunrunner. There were a few run-ins, a chase or two, but it appeared the *Yorktown* had missed much of the action in the Philippines during its long cruise at sea. Manila, by now, was firmly under American control. The larger confrontation with the Filipino insurgent forces seemed to be winding down, as well. From every indication, hostilities would all be over soon.

On Tuesday, April 4, 1899, the *Yorktown*'s log noted clear and pleasant skies, with light air to breezes from the southeast. The logbook also methodically recounted the day's activities in sequential order. The crew offloaded tons of coal, delivered by barge, into bunkers belowdecks. A working party was sent into Cavite port with condemned six- and eight-inch manila hawsers—long thick ropes used for tying up the ship—to be turned into the Navy Yard storehouse. And reporting for duty that day was the ship's new navigator, Lieutenant James C. Gillmore Jr.

CHAPTER FOUR

A Generous Mission

HAD THE MEN UNDER SIEGE IN THE CHURCH AT BALER SURRENDERED to Lieutenant Colonel Tecson's insurgent forces, they would have soon learned they were not the exception. By April 1899, General Aguinaldo's revolutionary forces were holding some nine thousand Spanish soldiers, several hundred friars, and an eclectic group of hapless civilians, as prisoners of war. Moreover, Aguinaldo had no intention of releasing them anytime soon. The captives offered valuable leverage in future negotiations with both Spain and the United States, once Philippine sovereignty was acknowledged.

Since mid-1898, rumors had seeped across military lines to Manila, alleging that these prisoners were suffering from abuse, torture, and starvation. The Spanish government, with its military forces in collapse, was helpless to respond. A number of negotiations through an array of emissaries had failed. When credible reports trickled back that certain Spanish priests in captivity faced imminent execution by Filipino forces, however, the issue was brought before the Vatican in Rome. The eighty-nine-year-old pontiff, Leo XIII, a chess-playing devotee of the poetry of Virgil and Dante, was incensed and demanded action. On July 31, 1898, the Vatican's secretary of state urgently cabled the apostolic delegate in Washington, D.C., sharing the Pope's dire concerns: "The Holy Father wishes that you take steps at once to have the Government of the United States prevent this evil."

The Vatican's request trickled down through diplomatic channels to the War Department and on to General Elwell Otis in the field. Any action, the American commander knew, was next to impossible at the time. The Spanish priests were not in areas under American control, and his own forces had their hands full battling the insurgency in Manila, a city on which they had only a tenuous grasp. Further, the Americans were suffering their own losses. A few hundred Spanish priests and the thousands of Spanish soldiers being held in the insurgent-ruled north was of minimal concern to Otis.

In this stalemate of inaction, the rotund, bespectacled Bernardino Nozaleda, the Archbishop of Manila, saw opportunity. It was a startling turnaround for the ruthless and unforgiving religious leader, who had weathered the Filipino revolt that first broke out in 1896. At that time, Nozaleda demanded that Spanish authorities exterminate the insurgents by "fire, sword and wholesale executions." When the then-Spanish administrator, Governor Blanco, did not sign on for such draconian measures, Nozaleda forced him out. Soon, with Nozaleda's blessings and encouragement, public rifle-fire executions of rebel leaders—including the charismatic and influential Jose Rizal—became a regular spectator sport on the Paseo de Luneta, the city's bayside promenade and park. It was this iron-fisted approach, in part, that created the violent backlash that had at first undermined—and then led to the wholesale collapse of—Spanish colonial rule in the Philippines.

In April 1898, with Dewey steaming toward Manila to confront the Spanish Armada off the coast of Cavite, Archbishop Nozaleda turned his ire on the Americans. He urged his Spanish brethren to drive the Americans out, arguing that they would be enslaved, their liberties denied, and their true Christianity uprooted if America's ungodly Protestantism prevailed. A week after Dewey's startling victory at Manila Bay, the unchastened archbishop penned a scathing diatribe against the admiral and his forces, to be circulated in parishes throughout the country:

> *A sad day has dawned upon this country. A North American Squadron has taken possession of our beautiful bay, and notwithstanding the heroic defenses of our sailors, has succeeded in destroying our vessels and in establishing his flag there. You are not ignorant of this enemy nor his pretensions who thus trample upon our rights. He is a foreigner who wishes to subject us to a hard yoke. He is a heretic who wishes to take our religion from us and tear us from the Maternal bosom of the Catholic church. He is an insatiable shopkeeper who wishes to increase his fortune with the ruin of Spain and her possessions. Alas, poor Spain! If the invader succeeds in his intention! Woe, Filipinos!*

And then the archbishop issued a call to action: "This, this alone is your only hope of salvation: to arms and to prayer in unison."

Nozaleda's passionate appeal failed. The average Spaniard was in no mood, or position, to take up arms against the Americans. Nozaleda cynically turned elsewhere. He sent church emissaries to General Aguinaldo to make the case that his embattled Spaniards and the Filipino rebels—whose revolutionary movement he had so deeply despised—should stand as one against the invaders. This appeal was also rejected. Instead, the increasingly brazen Filipino Army of Liberation seized the initiative, taking advantage of the power vacuum in their country. They took over more towns across the Philippines, imprisoned Spanish friars, and seized church property. Aguinaldo also ordered Filipino clergy to fill the void in parishes vacated by the Spanish priests, in blatant defiance of the Vatican. Filipinos, he argued, had had enough of Spanish dominion and their corrupt church in Rome.

Archbishop Nozaleda—smart enough to know when the jig was up, yet not above crass self-preservation—fled to Shanghai after Manila fell to the Americans in August 1898. But that was not the end of him. He skulked back after the December 1898 signing of the Treaty of Paris, which brought the Spanish-American War to an end. In a shamelessly opportunistic fit of obsequiousness, Nozaleda suddenly announced his hearty support for the benevolent Americans, his newfound friends. Above all, the archbishop was a realist, and a practical man.

On March 23, 1899, a letter, eloquently crafted in English on stationery from the archbishop's palace, arrived in Dewey's wardroom.

Admiral:

The magnanimous and noble spirit that adorns you fills me with confidence that you will lend your favorable attention to a subject which I beg you will allow me briefly to lay before you:

At Baler, Capital of the district of Principe, a small detachment of about forty Spanish soldiers still hold out against the Insurgents, being the only post in Luzon which refuses to surrender to them.

We are informed that these intrepid men have constantly repulsed the terms of capitulation, however honorable, that have on several occasions been offered to them, including those presented by a Commander of the Spanish Army, commissioned to that effect by General Rios.

Such a courageous resistance can only be explained by supposing that all those who compose the detachment have taken the irrevocable decision to perish to a man rather than to surrender to the Insurgents; for they know well that however honorable may seem the terms for their capitulation, they will be certain, if they accept them, to share the miserable fate of their companions in arms and fall victims to the perfidy and want of honor of which on many occasions the Rebels have given proof.

For these reasons it is evident that the only hope of saving these brave fellows is to send to their rescue by sea. Baler is situated about a mile from the shore. The road to the town is not offering any great difficulty, and although the beach is rather low and moving, the pilots assure me that at this season of the year it is pretty easy to land.

And then, the pitch:

To carry out this enterprise, to rescue this little band of devoted men, I count, Admiral, on your generous assistance and efficacious cooperation. Better than anyone can you appreciate the merit of such heroic constancy, which, while it will excite your sympathy, will also, I trust, move you to adopt measures as shall be necessary to obtain their release from the dire alternative of death, or of what would seem far worse, especially after such a long and courageous resistance—an odious captivity.

Offering you my sincere thanks for the interest I feel sure you will take in this affair as if it concerned a detachment of your own troops.

> *I beg you to accept,*
> *Admiral,*
> *The assurance of my high esteem and of respectful consideration.*
> *P. Nozaleda*
> *Archbishop of Manila*

Why the archbishop felt compelled to intervene in the affairs at Baler is not known. Perhaps he had been prodded by the Vatican, or, aware of the news reports, felt it his responsibility to seek the release of the two priests held in the church. Notably, Archbishop Nozaleda's missive failed even to mention the captivity of the priests at Baler, most certainly his and the Vatican's primary concern. Instead—and most likely by design—the crafty Nozaleda appealed to the admiral's sentiments with a tale of last-stand courage and honor by his Spanish brothers, who, by every report, seemed hell-bent on defending one last piece of empire at all cost.

Known for energetic and bold actions, Dewey mulled his options. Already a national hero at home, the admiral was planning his triumphant return to America, where "Dewey fever" had swept the country. Dewey had nothing to lose; in fact, he had the freedom to demonstrate magnanimity at this closing chapter of his brilliant naval career. And, if successful, a bit more publicity couldn't hurt.

Whatever his motivations, Dewey summoned Commander Sperry to his flagship to discuss a new mission, one to be carried out in secrecy, and, if successful, to have the potential to pay significant military and political dividends. In the quiet confines of his wardroom, the admiral huddled with the commander, shared the archbishop's letter, and laid out his plan. When back aboard the *Yorktown*, Sperry wrote to his beloved Edith, unable to contain his excitement.

> *[Admiral Dewey] has laid out an "interesting cruise" for us as soon as we can get our coal in. We are to go down south among the islands, looking for filibusters, and then go out through the straits of San Bernardino to a place on the east coast called Baler in latitude 150 50' near Cape San Ildefonso. The Archbishop has written the Admiral that at Baler there is a garrison of fifty Spanish soldiers who have never surrendered to the insurgents and never will, and we are to go around there and rescue them if possible.*

Sperry spelled out the rare opportunity for recognition:

> *The Admiral remarked that they might decline to be rescued, but he would make the attempt, and I told him we would get those Spaniards if they could be had. He said it would be an excellent stroke of policy, and if we succeeded he should telegraph the report, so you see he is giving me a good chance, and as he says, a most interesting cruise.*

The commander sprang into action. Standing in port at Cavite, Sperry made preparations to sail, ordering the *Yorktown's* hungry bunkers filled with coal and her stores stocked with provisions. Official orders followed from the USS *Olympia* on April 4, offering a backup plan in the event the rescue failed. "If the soldiers do not wish to return to Manila, or if, for any reason, you are unable to rescue them," Admiral Dewey advised, "proceed with the vessel under your command to Iloilo, and report to the Commanding Officer, USS *Charleston*, delivering to him the enclosed orders."

Commander Sperry gathered his officers, including Lieutenant James Gillmore, who had reported aboard ship that same morning. A navigation chart of the island of Luzon—a land mass about the size of Kentucky—was rolled out before them and the secret rescue mission explained. The officers intently measured distances, assessed tides, and checked depth curves and soundings on the chart. Together, they planned the approach to their objective: a distant and isolated town held by insurgents on the remote east coast of the island.

On April 5, as Commander Sperry paced anxiously about the ship, activity about the decks quickened. Coaling continued into the following day. As the bunkers filled with the dusty black fuel, a score of additional men joined the *Yorktown*, replacing others who had been detached. The ship's paymaster received $5,000 in Mexican silver and another $2,360 in American gold. Another 506 pounds of fresh beef and 399 pounds of assorted vegetables were hauled down to the ship's refrigerated storage, replenishing its stores. The ship took on 30 tons of fresh water for steaming purposes. Monthly salaries were paid.

Everything was going so well that the commander allowed the ship's enlisted men an unusual luxury: a swim in the sparkling, blue waters of Manila Bay, an activity officially tagged as exercise for the crew. Within minutes of the announcement, scores of the ship's sailors were crashing into the bay, tattooed cannonballs of laughter under the relentless tropical sun.

As the *Yorktown's* crew relaxed, their commander was lost in thought. This new mission was a lot more than bushwhacking. Admiral Dewey had placed his trust in Sperry, and was giving the commander a real chance to shine. Could a promotion to captain be very far behind?

An excited Sperry again wrote his wife, his imagination ignited. "We have been filling up with coal at the Cavite arsenal, and tomorrow we sail direct to Baler on the east coast in an attempt to rescue the garrison of forty Spaniards who never surrendered." The commander worked over scenarios and planned his actions. "Of course, they will not come to me as prisoners as I am simply to rescue them, and if their tale of gallant resistance is true, I shall certainly salute their Spanish flag with twenty-one guns when they haul it down."

On Saturday, April 8, as the *Yorktown* cruised by the island of Mindoro, the new navigator, perhaps still exhausted from his nocturnal excursions about Manila, struggled to plot the ship's course and fix its position. Sperry checked Gillmore's calculations, and to his shock, found a serious navigational error. Sperry exploded, severely castigating the lieutenant for his incompetence. The news of the dressing-down quickly spread throughout the ship. There were no secrets aboard a small man-of-war, and as the crew all knew, Commander Sperry was "quite an expert at a 'balling-out' party." This time, the reprimand went down as a warning. Lieutenant Gillmore, however, had been on the ship for less than four days, and already his fellow officers had sized him up as careless and unreliable.

On Tuesday, April 11, at exactly 11:40 a.m., the *Yorktown* came to anchor in Baler Bay, at nine fathoms port to forty-five fathoms starboard chain, seventeen hundred yards from shore.

CHAPTER FIVE

Reconnoiter

THE SIGHT MUST HAVE BEEN IMPRESSIVE AND ALTOGETHER OMINOUS TO the band of poorly armed rebels. Hidden in the dense underbrush along the shore, they watched the heavily armed cruiser round the southern chain of forested mountains that edged their perspective and slip into the bay. The warship's smokestack spewed thick, acrid smoke that tainted the crisp blue morning sky. The Filipino revolutionaries could only have wondered: What would today bring?

Kapitan Novicio ordered his men to assemble.

❧

Commander Charles Sperry's first actions were to have soundings taken about Baler Bay and attempt to establish communications with the insurgent forces ashore. While approaching their anchorage, an officer on the deck of the *Yorktown* spied several Filipinos waving a flag of truce on a sand spit at the mouth of the river. The rebels appeared keen to parley with the Americans; this was indeed a good sign.

Sperry ordered his navigator, Lieutenant Gillmore, into one of the ship's whaleboats, armed and equipped, to sound inshore. For the more-challenging task of making contact with the insurgents, Sperry turned to his trusted protégé, Ensign William H. Standley. Twenty-six years of age, the Ukiah, California, native was tall, handsome, and well-liked by the crew. The young ensign had been taken under Sperry's wing, enjoying favored access, and by all reports, was destined for advancement. Sperry ordered him to take charge of a crew on the 3rd cutter, and open communications with the insurgents. Standley was also tasked with checking whether the Filipinos, if friendly, were willing to deliver a letter written by

Archbishop Nozaleda to the besieged Spanish garrison, which explained that the Americans had come to bring them home. Standley brought with him the *Yorktown's* pilot, Ansolme Lachion, fluent in Spanish, to serve as his interpreter.

As the cutter's oars splashed in the water, Ensign Standley noted that the white flag spotted earlier by the river was no longer visible. The Filipinos had also disappeared. Standley hoisted a white flag of his own and pulled toward the beach. A group of five Filipinos emerged from the brush and came down to the water's edge, which the ensign took as a friendly gesture. Landing on some rocks in the middle of the mouth of the river, the ensign and the interpreter disembarked, and together made their way toward shore while the cutter and its crew waited. Lachion was unarmed; Standley carried only his sidearm.

Approaching the beach, Standley scanned the Filipinos before them. One was armed with a rifle, three with bolos, and the fifth, who seemed to be in charge, carried a cane. One of the bolo men waded out to the rocks to meet them while the others kept their distance. The sole Filipino rifleman kept his weapon trained on the two *Yorktown* men as they treaded through the surf.

Stopping to communicate with their escort, Standley and the interpreter asked about the Spaniards at the church. The bolo man, however, could not speak Spanish. He abruptly turned, waded back to shore, and, following his four compatriots, jogged into the brush.

Left behind in the shallow river, an increasingly worried Standley and Lachion pushed on to the beach, stepping ashore just as another Filipino, dressed in a Spanish uniform and armed with a Mauser rifle, emerged from the dense thicket and came toward them. Four more men armed with rifles stepped out of the foliage. Suddenly, they set a skirmish line.

Standley remained poised as his pulse quickened. The situation could turn ugly at any moment.

The Filipino officer accosted them sharply in Spanish, both hands gripping his rifle. The man's anger was obvious: a taut stance, aggressive eye contact, accentuated breathing. His eyes darted back and forth from Standley to Lachion, making it clear they were not welcome. Standley could not have known, nor would it have mattered: This was *Kapitan* Teodorico Novicio, Baler's insurgent leader, who had led the series of bloody assaults against the Spanish garrison and had initiated the siege.

The diminutive officer standing before them was, in fact, the catalyst to the events that had brought the *Yorktown* to Baler.

Hoping to defuse the tense situation, Standley calmly asked why the Filipino insurgents had hoisted a white flag in the first place, which suggested a request for a ceasefire and parley. Novicio either couldn't or wouldn't answer. Standley pressed the rebel officer to put one up now, but Novicio responded that they did not have one. Standley was baffled.

Unknown to the ensign at the time, the entire basis for the parley had been, in fact, a comedy of errors. The Filipinos had not raised a white flag of truce earlier; they had no desire whatsoever to communicate with the Americans. What the officers on the deck of the *Yorktown* had seen was simply the laundry of an insurgent soldier, hanging on the brush to dry. Standley and Lachion had just walked into a rebel stronghold with none of the protection offered by a flag of truce.

The conversation continued. Novicio confirmed that the Spanish detachment and several priests had taken refuge in the town's church. The Filipinos had not yet bothered to make a serious all-out attack on the church, but they had stationed sentries around the building to keep the Spaniards—whom they deemed their prisoners—from escaping. The Spaniards, in return, refused to communicate, and fired on anyone who came within range. To Standley it may have seemed less a siege than a standoff—and a rather pointless one—between two hardheaded and essentially impotent parties.

Standley explained that he had a solution—that the Americans had come to Baler to accept the Spaniards' surrender and to take them to Manila. No doubt the ensign gestured to the awesome warship standing out in the bay under the dazzling sun, and the 3rd cutter sounding offshore, to give visual proof of his words.

This was not possible, Novicio countered. If the Spanish government formally requested Aguinaldo's revolutionary government to turn the prisoners over to the Americans, he explained, they would be happy to do so. Otherwise, the Americans could not take the Spaniards away. Standley nodded diplomatically, accepting Novicio's point; this was not going to be easy.

Standley next attempted to clarify the protocol for future contact, as the present situation was far too confused. He carefully explained that if the Americans again landed under a flag of truce, the Filipinos would need to hoist a white flag of truce as well. Or, if the Filipinos wanted to communicate with the Americans, they should also hoist a white flag and the Americans would come to them. This was how it worked, Standley said.

A skeptical Novicio, perhaps misunderstanding the point, responded that he would need to consult his commander, and he suddenly disappeared into the brush.

The searing noontime sun blazed overhead. Standley and Lachion stood impatiently on the sandy beach, sweat streaking their faces. In the distance, the *Yorktown* cut an impressive silhouette against the shimmering blue-green sea. And in front of them, the armed picket kept their rifle sights beaded on their heads. Offshore, Gillmore and his crew continued to sound the bay, keeping an anxious eye on their colleagues.

After fifteen increasingly uncomfortable minutes, Novicio returned out of the brush with a man of European complexion in tow. Dressed in what appeared to be a Spanish uniform and armed with a bolo and revolver, the man claimed to be on a mission from Manila, sent on orders of the Spanish General Rios. He had permission to take the Spanish prisoners to Manila, he explained, but so far, the besieged detachment refused to even speak with him. Standley, in a subsequent official report, mistakenly guessed this man was a Spanish deserter turned insurgent. He was, in fact, exactly who he had claimed to be.

Novicio now angrily interjected, cutting off the conversation. His commanding officer did not wish to communicate with the Americans any further. Unless a white flag was hoisted on shore first, there was no point in the Americans trying to approach. Novicio had four hundred soldiers under his command, and would fire on any boat attempting to land. As the confused discussions continued, at least fifty more insurgent soldiers emerged along the scrub brush to back up the threat.

Standley then made a judgment call: He would not pass on the letter from the Archbishop of Manila, doubting that it would be delivered to the Spaniards in the church. The parley came to a close, and Standley and Lachion cautiously withdrew. The two boat crews—Standley and his men in the 3rd cutter and Gillmore and his crew in the whaleboat—returned to the *Yorktown* slightly after 12:30 p.m. The two boats were hoisted and stowed.

Sperry, after debriefing Standley and Gillmore, summed up the difficult situation to his fellow officers. They had no map or plan of the town of Baler, which was unfortunately set back from shore and hidden from view. The beach was absolutely deserted. They had not seen any civilian boats or fishing vessels, which suggested little chance of locating any friendlies who might share their knowledge of the place. And the insurgents had openly threatened violence if they returned. Until the town could be located and distances and locations ascertained, the *Yorktown*'s big guns could not target the insurgents or any of their defenses without the risk of shelling the church and killing the very men they had been sent to rescue.

The officers discussed approaching the town by the river, where Standley and his interpreter had landed. It was twenty yards wide, no more than a creek, really, with a rocky bar at its shallow mouth. From Gillmore's initial soundings, they judged the *Yorktown*'s cutters would only be able to pass over the bar at high tide. From their anchorage in the bay, the officers could see no more than three hundred yards upriver, after which the channel turned abruptly to the north and disappeared. Steep mountains edged the river to the south. To the north, dense underbrush obscured the low alluvial plain on which the town presumably lay. Where it all led, no one could say.

The men discussed the various ways to secure more accurate information. Commander Sperry, Lieutenant Commander Chauncey Thomas Jr., his executive officer, and Lieutenant Gillmore were of the same view: Sending a boat expedition up the narrow creek would simply invite destruction.

Ensign Standley, studiously watching the back-and-forth, offered a new way forward. He volunteered to climb the mountain to the south, which presumably overlooked the insurgent camp, the church, and any defenses in place. From the summit, he would be able to map the town, which would then allow for the ship's guns to direct a barrage of shells that would clear the way for a landing force. The ever-cautious Sperry immediately objected to Standley's proposed mission. It would be extremely hazardous, prone to numerous and unknown risks, including insurgent attack. The Filipino officer had earlier claimed a force of more than four hundred armed insurgents, the commander reminded the assembled officers, and no one knew where they were entrenched. Further, his men had spied a ferry raft at the mouth of the river, which meant the location served as a crossing point for locals. A landing party would be far too vulnerable and exposed.

The men debated the idea further. Several of the officers argued that Standley's proposal was not so farfetched after all. Sperry reviewed his options and finally relented, but with conditions. Ensign Standley could proceed with his risky survey from the mountain, but not alone as he wished. Anything could go wrong; something as simple as a fall might disable him. Sperry was emphatic: There would be no tragedies, no loss of men; not on his ship, and not on his watch. Standley would need to bring another man, also armed, to serve as a lookout during the reconnoitering. Sperry assigned Quartermaster 3rd Class John Lysaght to the task.

Later that afternoon, to put the insurgents on notice and to alert the Spaniards in the church, Sperry ordered his men to fire several blank charges from the ship's six-inch guns. The commander's intended message? *Make no mistake; the Americans have arrived.* The booming reports shattered the calm of Baler's quiet blue skies, sending bands of frightened birds flitting skyward from the shoreline's foliage.

That evening, a still-uncomfortable Sperry called Thomas and Gillmore back to a second conference on the poop deck. The commander needed a senior officer to backstop Standley's mission, someone with years of experience and sound judgment who would "check any disposition to rashness." He turned to Gillmore, a logical choice given the navigator's earlier role in sounding the bay.

The orders were explicit: Gillmore was to lead a crew of fourteen men in the ship's twenty-eight-foot 2nd cutter, armed with one of the *Yorktown*'s Colt Automatics, and land Standley and Lysaght before daybreak. Gillmore should continue to take soundings along the beach; this would occupy the time usefully, and serve as a ruse to conceal the true objective of the cutter's presence. The lieutenant should then be ready to take the ensign and quartermaster off the very instant they returned to the beach, which, under daylight conditions, would be risky. In addition to the Colt, the cutter crew's Lee rifles and Gillmore's sidearm would provide sufficient firepower against any threat. If and when any insurgents turned up, Gillmore's boat should provide covering fire at the river crossing. Commander Sperry reiterated his concern for his favored ensign: Under no circumstances was Standley to attempt to land unless accompanied by Lysaght, and they would need to be collected quickly to avoid any confrontation with insurgents.

The conversation between Sperry, Thomas, and Gillmore lasted nearly an hour, covering the orders and a "full and exhaustive discussion of their purposes and intent." As Sperry later recounted, "I can think of no point which had not been covered to the entire understanding of Lieutenant Gillmore, the Executive Officer, and myself, when we separated."

That evening, not knowing if his ship's guns had achieved their desired effect, Sperry ordered the cruiser's new, powerful electric searchlight flashed toward the town. This act would again inform the Spanish garrison of the presence of an American warship standing in the bay. The shoreline offered up nothing more than utter darkness in response. Sperry surely wondered if the Spaniards had gotten the message.

━ ⌣ ━

Earlier that afternoon, back at the church, Lieutenant Cerezo, his half-starved *cazadores,* and the two hapless priests were jolted to their feet by the bone-rattling boom of cannon fire, from what they thought was the direction of the bay. They stared at one another, speechless, and then, as the significance of the barrage dawned on them, leapt for joy. Surely this meant a Spanish rescue mission had been sent to save the embattled garrison! The soldiers scrambled into the bullet-pocked church tower, taking turns to look out to the sea, squinting against the sun to make out any sign of their rescuers. Was it a ship? Had the Spaniards finally sent a man-of-war to their rescue?

After the sun set, a bright electric searchlight swept the bullet-ridden church tower, illuminating its tattered red-and-gold flag. The dancing light and shadows whipped the Spaniards into a second frenzy. Some of the ragged men broke down into tears while others simply sighed in relief; with the help of the priests, surely all thanked God. Their long-awaited rescue was at hand.

━ ⌣ ━

For the following morning's mission, a crew of enlisted men was picked from the *Yorktown* to accompany Gillmore, Standley, and Lysaght in the ship's 2nd cutter. Fourteen men—an eclectic assortment of sailors who fell into two subsets. The first five were thoroughly experienced sailors, mostly former merchant mariners, averaging thirty-four years of age, whose sun-etched faces and tattooed hides revealed a lifetime of riding the world's seas and stumbling through its ports. The second nine, a gangly collection of bright-eyed kids nearly all in their teens, were all slightly built, weighing a mere 128 pounds on average, on their first adventure, very far from home.

Chief Quartermaster William Walton, one of the most senior petty officers aboard ship, was a natural for the assignment. The heavily tattooed, German-born sailor had just turned thirty-five. Another, Sailmaker's Mate Paul Vaudoit, an iron-haired, forty-one-year-old from France—described by one commanding officer as "one of those excitable Frenchmen who seems to antagonize everyone"—was on Sperry's hit list. The ornery old salt's latest transgressions included turning up "tight from leave" while on liberty in Hawaii and, weeks later, talking back to an officer. Sperry had him charged with insubordination, resulting in five days' solitary confinement on bread-and-water rations.

If Vaudoit was trouble for the commander, Coxswain Ellsworth Everett Pinkham, a sun-wizened seadog with a foul mouth and tattoos to match, was even worse. His operation of the ship's steam cutter at the coaling stop in Hawaii, "so much under the influence of intoxicating liquor on board ship as to incapacitate him for the proper performance of duty," earned the thirty-three-year-old sailor from Kittery, Maine, ten days in solitary in chains on bread-and-water rations, and forfeiture of pay.

The two other petty officers included Coxswain William Henry Rynders, a short, thirty-year-old Dutchman from Amsterdam, who had been recently disrated and demoted to the rank of seaman by Commander Sperry for some unknown infraction, and the twenty-nine-year-old Gunner's Mate 3rd Class, Edward John Nygard, a naturalized Polish-American mariner and musician. A well-grounded family man, Nygard had recently settled in Brooklyn, New York, with his wife, Sophie, and their son, Edward Jr., who had just celebrated his first birthday. A second child, sister-to-be Ellen, was scheduled to enter the world in five months. As the gunner's mate for this mission, Nygard would be responsible for the powerful Colt Automatic mounted on the cutter's bow.

The balance of the cutter crew, the nine young men, were essentially the muscle for pulling the 2nd cutter's oars: three ordinary seamen, four landsmen, and two apprentices.

Among the three seamen were two nineteen-year-olds: Orrison Welch Woodbury, a ruddy-faced, crooked-toothed merchant marine from Lynn, Massachusetts, and Silvio Brisolese, a dark-haired Italian American from

San Francisco. The third, two years older, was the stick-thin, soft-spoken Ora Butler McDonald from Monterey, California. At almost five-foot-ten, McDonald towered above his crewmates. Three landsmen included Fred Anderson, a blue-eyed, nineteen-year-old from Buffalo, New York, Lyman Paul Edwards, a cheerful, twenty-year-old former bookkeeper from Peru, Indiana, and the lanky Charles Albert Morrissey, also twenty, hailing from landlocked Lincoln, Nebraska.

The cutter's crew was rounded out by two more boys: the tall, slightly built Apprentice 2nd Class Denzell George Arthur Venville, age seventeen, and freckle-faced Apprentice 3rd Class Albert Peterson, also seventeen, who weighed in at a wind-blown 111 pounds.

A fourteenth man, quick with his mouth and whose name has been lost to history, was the last and final sailor assigned to the landing party.

Just after 4:00 a.m., the cutter crew assembled on the *Yorktown*'s main deck. Commander Sperry arrived from his wardroom to oversee the boat being quietly lowered into the inky bay. Conditions could not have been better: a moonless, pitch-black night, which would cover the cutter's movements. The distant shore was nothing more than a black impenetrable mass, barely illuminated by the shimmering stars overhead. As he surveyed the men, Sperry overheard the fourteenth sailor bitterly complain, mumbling something about this "damned landing party business." The commander did not tolerate such insubordination and angrily ordered the sailor out of the boat. A replacement was quickly scared up—Landsman John Dillon, a red-haired, blue-eyed Irishman from Galway who had enlisted at the port of Honolulu where he had been working as a barber.

Stepping belatedly into the cutter, a confused Dillon wondered aloud, "Where are we going?" Coxswain Pinkham, perhaps sober for more days than he cared to count, couldn't resist and gruffly shot back with a fearful grin, "You are going to meet your Jesus."

The fourteen men quietly jostled into position: ten assigned on oars, five to a side. The oars were placed in the rowlocks and angled. Any anxiousness among the crew was surely calmed by the straight-pull, bolt-action, 6mm Lee Navy rifles stowed snugly below the gunwale, in canvas pockets that had been snapped in place with protective leather flaps and heavy wooden toggles. And beyond those, there was the squared-off silhouette of the all-powerful Colt Automatic on the cutter's bow. Ensign Standley and Quartermaster Lysaght then climbed into the boat, followed by Lieutenant Gillmore, who took command. At 4:45 a.m., with hushed voices and a growing sense of excitement, the cutter shoved off. Under muffled oars, the boat and crew began their journey toward shore.

In a huddle of whispers, Gillmore reconfirmed the plan with Standley and Lysaght. After the drop, he would pull down to the mouth of the river. By daylight, he would be sounding near the bar. As soon as Standley signaled, he would return to pick them up. Gillmore would only open fire if insurgents tried to cross the river. Any firing, then, meant the enemy was coming their way. The ensign and the quartermaster nodded.

The cutter landed off a beach, some five hundred–plus yards to the south of the mouth of the Baler River. Standley and Lysaght gathered their gear: brass binoculars, a length of rope, a sketchpad and pens for impromptu mapmaking. Lysaght shouldered his Lee rifle, Standley checked his pistol. They climbed out of the cutter, dropped into waist-deep water, and waded toward shore. On the deck of the *Yorktown*, the officers peered intently into the night with their telescopes. They were unable to see a thing.

Now out of the water, Standley and Lysaght double-timed down the sandy beach, heading toward the mouth of the river. They waded across a deep, narrow slough up to their chests and began an arduous, wet climb up the small mountain. They scrambled over boulders and threaded their way through dense, thorny underbrush, following a course nearly parallel with the river. Suddenly, the tropical sky began to lighten to a cool, star-studded blue.

Meanwhile, Gillmore's cutter moved slowly toward the mouth of the river to begin the Americans' ruse. In the forward bow, Apprentice Venville ran the lead line, marked in feet, and quietly called out soundings to Quartermaster Walton, who repeated the depth readings and recorded them in a notebook. Aboard the *Yorktown*, as first light broke, Sperry could see the boat and the busy movement of the crew taking soundings. The boat remained on the middle of the bar a short time and then drifted out of view. Finally, to the commander's puzzlement, the cutter disappeared from sight. It was 5:50 a.m.

After an hour of difficult climbing, a winded Standley and Lysaght emerged through the brush onto the summit. The perspective was better than imagined, offering a commanding view of the bay. But owing to the thick brush and high trees that surrounded them, little could be seen in the direction of the town. As the men searched about for a better vantage point, three shots rang out below, close together, followed by desultory firing. Standley figured that meant insurgents were crossing the river, which meant time was of the essence.

At a spot farther west, just off the summit, the two sailors found a tree that, once climbed, would afford a proper view. Together, they tossed up the rope. Standley tied in and climbed to a branch that he prayed would hold his weight. As Standley settled down to sketch the panorama spread out before him, Lysaght stood anxiously at the foot of the tree, rifle in hand, his finger on the trigger, fully expecting a band of insurgents to burst through the trees at any second.

From his perch, the ensign rapidly sketched the layout of the small town, the serpentine river network, and the contour of the beaches below. The tortuous route of the Baler River, he noted, almost doubled back on itself. Flying from a pole on the church tower, he believed, was a Spanish flag fluttering in the wind. The town, to the west and north of the church, was well situated for strong defense, surrounded by rivers on two sides, exposed terrain on another, and dense brush along the beach. It was increasingly clear that they would need to shell the entire peninsula with canisters of shot and shrapnel from the *Yorktown*'s big guns before making any rescue attempt.

Even as Standley was carefully mapping the geography below, the gunfire had him deeply concerned. Lysaght counted hundreds of shots. Then, they both heard a man call out in Spanish, *Mira ese hombre!* ("Look at that man!"), followed by more excited but ill-defined shouting. Standley saw six or seven men—were they insurgents?—splashing about in the water at the second bend of the river, around what looked like a boat. From this distance, however, Standley couldn't make it out clearly. Maybe these men are bathing, he said aloud.

Around 7:00 a.m. Standley's sketch was complete. He quickly admired his cartographic handiwork, packed it away, and climbed down the tree. Together with Lysaght, he made his way back down to the beach. As agreed, the two sailors threw up the signal flag, hanging it on a bush, to call back the 2nd cutter. It was now twenty minutes after seven.

Aboard the *Yorktown*, Executive Officer Thomas broke a signal flag to repeat the message, to visually advise the 2nd cutter to collect the men.

The cutter was nowhere in sight.

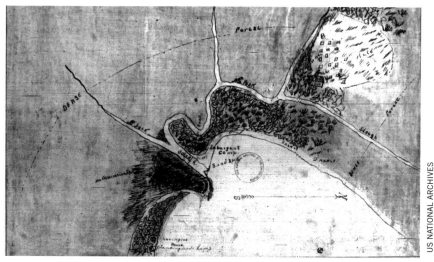

Ensign William H. Standley's sketch of Baler, completed from the perch of a tree branch on a hill overlooking the town, April 12, 1899.

There was no time to waste. The landing party, exposed and at risk, needed to be taken off immediately. Thomas quickly dispatched a whaleboat from the *Yorktown* to collect the two men.

As the whaleboat got under way, Sperry and Thomas scanned the horizon with their binoculars. Their eyes met, and they shared a look of alarm.

Where the hell was Gillmore?

CHAPTER SIX

Trouble

In the thickest of shadows, Lieutenant Gillmore and his fourteen sailors had watched Ensign Standley and Quartermaster Lysaght straddle the cutter's gunwale and slide into the water. With muffled oars, they then pulled toward the mouth of the river. "Not a sound was made," recalled Gillmore, "and we were flattering ourselves that the stupid Filipinos had been completely outwitted; but at that critical moment, as we were pulling out of the cover, the day came upon us."

The tropical dawn rapidly pushed across the sea, lifting the *Yorktown* and the cutter out of darkness. Gillmore scanned the shore with his glass and spied a single insurgent patrolling the beach, his gun held at a lazy angle. The Filipino suddenly looked up, locked his eyes on the boat, squeezed off a shot in alarm, and dashed into the brush. The cutter's crew nervously glanced about, bracing for whatever might come next. Gillmore, while concerned that the sentry had witnessed the landing, still adhered to his plan of deception. He ordered the cutter closer to the mouth of the river and began to take soundings. At the bar, he had the men on oars stop rowing and continued his ruse. When the panicked insurgent failed to return, the sailors' anxiety waned.

And then it happened.

We will never know what was going through Gillmore's mind at this pivotal moment. Perhaps the middle-aged lieutenant was still bitter from Sperry's stinging rebuke just days earlier for his egregious navigational error. Gillmore may also have felt slighted by Sperry's obvious favoring of the much-younger Standley, who had been chosen to parley with the rebels and undertake a daring reconnoiter of insurgent defenses.

Gillmore likely did some math, as well: What hope did a ragtag band of insurgents have against the powerful Colt Automatic appended to the cutter's bow? Just under 41 inches long and 40 pounds in weight, the machine gun could deliver 400 rounds per minute, each 6mm bullet capable of traveling 3,000 yards at an eye-blinking 2,469 feet per second. Anyone on the receiving end of the gun's staccato burst of lead had scant chance of survival. And if that wasn't enough, the cutter was also equipped with powerful Lee rifles buttoned up along the gunwale. Gillmore's arrogant calculus perhaps discounted, if not completely dismissed, any risks.

Or maybe, no matter the peril, he felt this was his ticket to glory.

Whatever the spark, whatever the motivation—perhaps planned, or possibly spontaneous—Lieutenant James C. Gillmore Jr., while on a high-risk mission, did what no senior naval officer is ever supposed to do: He broke from his orders and commanded the cutter up the narrow river.

As a seasoned officer, Gillmore knew beyond all doubt the gravity of his decision. It ran against the consensus of his fellow officers and violated

The Baler River as it looked to Gillmore and his crew on the morning of April 12, 1899.

his own words and oath. It not only put the lives of Standley and Lysaght in danger, but also brought his cutter crew potentially into the line of fire. At its most basic level of impropriety, it was a rejection of Sperry and his authority, a denial of a commander's control over a subordinate.

The crew, not privy to Sperry's explicit orders to Gillmore, was oblivious. But that didn't matter; few sailors would question an officer's order in any event. The men obediently heaved on the oars and shifted direction. The cutter pushed over the shallow bar.

Pulling slowly up the river, Gillmore ordered the cutter to turn north to a channel that seemed to lead toward town. The narrowing river threaded a steep, thickly wooded riverbank on their port side and a low, marshy shore, covered with high swamp grass, on their starboard side. As they cut through the silted current, the starboard riverbank lifted into high wooded ground some fifty yards ahead. The men saw a lone sentry standing there, tracking their progress. The Filipino angrily shouted in Spanish for the cutter to halt. Gillmore ignored him and urged his men on. A few seconds later, the sentry raised his rifle and fired a single shot of alarm. Then he disappeared from view.

The cutter crew looked to Gillmore for a response. The lieutenant urgently ordered the cutter's course reversed, but his men were bucking a down current and the cutter barely moved.

Stalled in the water and hoping to reason with the insurgent, Gillmore called into the foliage in English. A Filipino responded in Spanish, reiterating the order to halt. Unknown to Gillmore at the time, it was the same rebel officer who had been engaged by Standley, *Kapitan* Teodorico Novicio, a man now furious that the Americans had ignored his earlier warning. At Gillmore's command, Sailmaker's Mate Vaudoit and Seaman Brisolese yelled back in a mix of French and Italian, a potpourri of linguistic confusion that did little to help matters. Efforts to communicate were getting nowhere.

At this juncture, Gillmore would boast later, he was still not worried. He could pull farther off to a safe distance, and of course, there was always the powerful Colt Automatic mounted on the bow. "Trouble was coming—that was clear enough—but on the whole we were rather glad, and we had not the slightest doubt the other fellows were going to at least get their fair share of it."

Trouble then came quickly. A blast of muzzle flashes exploded from the woods. An insurgent force let fly a barrage of lead, a first volley from an estimated twenty-five rifles, about forty yards out. Charles Morrissey, the lanky landsman from Lincoln, Nebraska, pulling the bow at starboard, his lightning-rod form peering out above the others, was the first. He took a round in the forehead, a bullet that blew out the back of his skull and splattered his brains across his horrified comrades. He fell back into several sailors and slid to the bottom of the boat, dead.

The portly, redheaded Dillon, seated in front of Morrissey at starboard, frantically pulled his oar to turn the cutter. Moments later, a second volley cracked from the insurgent firing line, slamming a .45 caliber Remington slug into the landsman's head, just above his right eye, killing him instantly and fulfilling Pinkham's grim prophecy. The former barber's body flew back into the boat, knocking over the boy Edwards and spraying others with a warm slap of blood. Several sailors pushed Dillon off his stunned comrade, sending his broken form tumbling to the cutter's deck.

The Filipinos fired more volleys, which came as fast as they could reload. On starboard stroke oar, the Holland-born Rynders was next. A round smashed against the coxswain's left hand that gripped the oar, shredding three fingers. The remaining sailors struggled to back-oar, to push the boat farther out, away from the withering rifle fire. Others desperately grappled for the Lee rifles stored down in canvas pouches along the gunwale, fighting the stiff wooden toggles that locked them into place.

Bullets whizzed and zinged about the cutter, one grazing Arthur Venville's ear, another tearing through his neck, and a third bullet drilling into the side of his chest and exiting out his armpit. A fourth shot slammed into the apprentice's ankle joint, shattering the bone.

A dumbstruck Gillmore crouched at the stern of the boat, watching in stupefied horror as his men fell in a bloody slaughter. Whatever his thoughts, the words did not come; under fire, the cutter crew heard nothing but stunned silence from their commander. Gunner's Mate Nygard, having been caught fully off guard, was still fumbling with the ammunition belt for the Colt Automatic. Coxswain Pinkham scrambled to the front of the cutter, yelling at Nygard, "Damn you, I hope you get shot!" As if on cue, a .45 caliber slug burst through Nygard's chest, its forward spatter misting Ellsworth in blood. Before the gunner's mate could cry out, a second round sliced into his thigh, severing his femoral artery and flipping him to the deck.

The Filipino insurgents aimed their next barrage at the Colt. Round after round shattered the ammunition box and cut the loading tape to pieces. One lucky shot slammed into the right side of the Colt's breech, effectively destroying the gun. The directed volley shot the visor off Walton's cap and riddled Vaudoit's jacket with bullets. Other rounds smashed into the Colt in rapid succession, spinning it around, knocking Walton into the gunwale. The wind knocked out of him, a breathless Walton began to slide over the side. Apprentice Albert Peterson reached over and yanked the wheezing quartermaster back into the cutter.

Seaman McDonald took the next hit. The force of the bullet's impact on his thigh kicked out his shattered leg from under him and threw him into the mass of mangled bodies below. The surviving men knew that if something didn't happen very soon, everyone was going to die. With the Colt out of commission, the desperate sailors' remaining hope lay with their Lee rifles hanging along the gunwale. When the *Yorktown* had been rebuilt at Mare Island, all of its equipment had been replaced, including the cutter's hardware, and it had yet to be broken in. The sailors frantically clawed at the stiffened toggles and rope beckets, struggling to free their rifles. For Pinkham and several others who succeeded, their momentary hope was quickly dashed: The ammunition had been stowed separately, and as a result, the unloaded rifles were completely useless.

An artist's depiction of the ambush on Gillmore's cutter. In reality, the sailors never returned fire.

The cutter's hull, punched through with insurgent lead, was taking on water and threatening to sink in the shallow river. The few sailors left manning the remaining oars were unable to control the craft, which began to drift with the current toward the shore, neatly into the insurgents' sights. Pinkham and Landsman Edwards jumped overboard on the port side to lighten the boat and fought to push her stern out of the rebels' line of fire. Seaman Woodbury joined them, but not by choice; an insurgent bullet hit his cartridge belt and blew one of his own rounds into his rib cage, the force of which threw him overboard. When the effort to float the cutter failed—it was too heavy with water, bodies, and blood—Pinkham tried to swim the boat out, holding the boat with one hand and frantically sidestroking. If he could get her to the distant bank, her shattered hull could be used as a breastwork from which to fire. This effort started to succeed when the insurgents moved from their cover to a new promontory on the sailors' flank. The Filipino riflemen raked the cutter from fore to aft. The sailors could not fight the current. The boat drifted slowly to a bank of sand and then struck.

The rebels, rifles up, inched toward the grounded boat. Lieutenant Gillmore saw the hopelessness of the situation and finally found his voice. He called his men to surrender. "It is useless for us to try and overpower a greater force, and I think I'm doing right to surrender," the unnerved lieutenant explained to his men. Pinkham, disgusted, threw his yet-to-be-loaded rifle in the water. Woodbury later recalled that as the deadly ambush unfolded, "Gillmore behaved like an old woman when the Filipinos fired on us . . . we waited for an order, but he never gave us one."

Rynders, his one hand severely damaged and missing digits, raised a white flag, but this just incensed the Filipinos further, and a new volley of rifle fire was unleashed. The flurry of bullets shredded the flag and wounded Rynders again in the wrist. No one dared move in or alongside the cutter. By now, the vessel was stuck fast in the mud, its gunwale down to the water.

Kapitan Novicio called out in Spanish from the starboard shore, ordering the Americans to put down their rifles or else they would all be shot to pieces. The men did not need any translation and quickly complied; there was no other option. Before dumping their rifles, several sailors had the foresight to remove and throw away the extractors, hoping to render the guns useless to the enemy. For the same reason, the reversing gear from the damaged Colt was tossed into the river.

On the opposite shore, a crowd of a hundred or so inflamed insurgents had assembled. They lunged forward, swinging bolos and spears in a ferocious, if not ridiculous, display of bravado. Novicio angrily waved them off and the theatrics quickly ceased. On the starboard shore, with bolos drawn and rifles at the ready, a force of some sixty insurgents approached. The sailors were ordered out of the boat and lined up along the riverbank, where they were stripped of their coats, hats, shoes, and anything else of value. Seaman Brisolese, not undressing fast enough, had his pants sliced off with a knife. Woodbury had his prized silver watch confiscated. Gillmore's gold Annapolis graduation ring and wedding band were pried from his stubby fingers, along with his watch, chain, cuff links, and hat.

At Novicio's order, the Filipinos tied the Americans' hands with hemp cord and forced them to kneel. A firing line, assembled at twenty paces, loaded and aimed their rifles.

Execution was imminent.

Perhaps regretting his earlier display of cowardice, Gillmore demanded that his hands be untied if he was to be shot. He was an officer and a gentleman, a prisoner of war, he argued, not a criminal. Walton, struggling in poor, broken Spanish and hand gestures, attempted to repeat this request, which was seemingly understood. The confused Filipinos quickly huddled, rifles still trained on the sailors. Gillmore's curious demand initiated a debate. Novicio presumably shrugged, as if to say *Why not?* Several Filipinos walked over to Gillmore and untied his hands. The bonds on the rest of the sailors' wrists were similarly removed.

The men on the firing line again took their positions, rifles raised. It is not known how the stunned *Yorktown* men responded at this moment. Some likely bowed their heads in final prayer. Others less spiritually inclined may have stared defiantly at their captors, or even spat a torrent of colorful seafaring epithets. Perhaps the youngest of the boys wept in despair.

Death had arrived.

Breaking the dark moment, another Filipino officer appeared, galloping along the riverbank on a small pony, angrily waving a sword, shouting, *Alto! Alto!* It was Lieutenant Colonel Simon Tecson, the Filipino Army of Liberation's senior officer at Baler. He dismounted and began to berate Novicio and his soldiers. Whatever he said to them postponed the execution, and the admonished rifle squad stood down. The Americans were ordered on their feet and told to push the cutter to the opposite bank, to the head of the trail that led to town. Gillmore and the surviving members of the crew climbed back into the bloody boat and attempted to row. The cutter, however, refused to budge; it needed to be baled and its holes plugged. The few able sailors got to work.

Shot to pieces and its starboard oars splintered, the cutter's deck resembled a slaughterhouse. Two men—Dillon and Morrissey—lay dead in the bow. Two others—Nygard and McDonald—lay at the stern, losing blood from severe leg wounds. Three others were wounded: Rynders, with severed fingers on his left hand and a shattered right wrist; Venville, with four gunshot wounds and a severely shattered right ankle; and Woodbury, with a gaping wound on the right side of his lower back. Gillmore, having avoided the blistering line of insurgent fire while crouched in the hull, had a superficial wound to his knee from a spent bullet, but it was not disabling.

At the opposite bank, another Filipino officer and his men assembled to receive the cutter. Baled and plugged, she was heaved across and beached on the opposite shore. Tecson followed on horseback and the others waded across the chest-high waters. With the Filipinos' permission, several of the sailors moved the badly wounded McDonald and Nygard from the boat to the foot of a shady tree. The older petty officers, Pinkham and Walton, fashioned makeshift tourniquets from nearby vines and tied off both men's legs above their severed arteries to staunch the flow of blood. Venville, badly crippled and in agonizing pain, was carried by the sailors to join the two wounded men on the riverbank. Tecson ordered the rest of the cutter's crew to march up the trail toward town, but the men protested. Their wounded comrades were dying; they needed immediate medical attention. And they needed to bury their dead.

Through sketchy communication, Tecson assured the Americans and told them not to worry; their friends would be cared for. One of Gillmore's men scavenged a bucket from the cutter, filled it with river water, and placed it between Nygard and McDonald. As the men attended to their wounded shipmates, the Filipinos insisted with their guns: It was time to go.

Still fuming over the fiasco, Tecson ordered his adjutant, Quicoy, and Novicio to deal with the wounded men, while he took the prisoners up to the town proper. Venville, lying helpless on the ground, begged not to be left behind. A compromise was struck with Tecson: The wounded boy could be carried by the other sailors, but they had to go now. Venville was hoisted up on the shoulders of one sailor, and the column started toward

Baler, Tecson and his pony at the lead. Along the way, Brisolese tore off the tail of his shirt and helped Rynders wrap the three smashed fingertips left hanging by the skin on his bloodied hand.

Staggering along a narrow trail, the stunned American captives, prodded along by their armed guards, were brought to Tecson's office, a bamboo and *nipa* structure. Sensing their fear, the lieutenant colonel quickly informed Gillmore that he and his men would not be executed. What had happened at the riverbank, he explained, had been a terrible mistake made by inferiors. Filipinos were civilized, and conducted themselves in strict accordance with what he called "the international rules of war." The partial apology calmed the sailors and lightened the dark mood. Perhaps they would survive after all.

Tecson's conversation shifted to the subject of the besieged Spaniards at the church. He was eager to see the embattled Spaniards leave. While they were viewed as prisoners, they were wreaking havoc on the town, Tecson explained. But the obstinate Spaniards refused to believe the war was over or that their empire had been lost. From the bell tower, Spanish snipers controlled most of the town's productive, arable land. The deranged detachment had been there for eight long months, and continued to shoot at anyone who came near. It was exasperating; the Spaniards had to go.

Tecson then made a stunning offer: If the Americans could get the Spaniards to surrender, they too would be given their liberty. They, and the Spaniards, could all return to the *Yorktown* and simply leave. All the Filipinos wanted from the Spaniards were their arms and any remaining stores of ammunition.

Gillmore quickly agreed, though he doubted Tecson's sincerity. Yes, he would try his best; in fact, that was the very intention of their mission to Baler. One of his sailors, Vaudoit, could converse in Spanish, Gillmore added, stretching the truth. If a parley could be called at the church, Vaudoit could negotiate with the besieged Spaniards in their own language and surely persuade them to surrender. The *Yorktown* would then take the Spanish detachment to Manila.

Tecson must have smiled in agreement. Finally, he had a solution to his intractable problem at the church.

While waiting under guard for the parley to be arranged, Gillmore quietly conferred with his crew. A consensus view emerged: They didn't trust the Filipinos to hold to their promises. What guarantees did they have? Several American sailors had already been killed. It was unlikely that they, or the Spaniards, would ever be allowed to leave Baler peacefully. More likely, they would all be slaughtered. Tecson was just using their presence to coax the Spaniards into surrender. The only thing the Filipinos would understand, it was roundly agreed, would be the force of the *Yorktown*'s big guns.

In a hushed voice, Gillmore outlined his ruse. Vaudoit should get as close as possible to the church under the flag of truce, without arousing Filipino suspicions. Then, instead of speaking in Spanish as Gillmore had suggested to Tecson, Vaudoit should speak in his native French, a language which only the Spaniards—surely not the Filipinos—would understand. The insurgents would be in the dark about the content of the ensuing conversation. Vaudoit should first explain to the Spaniards that he was from an American warship anchored in the bay, but had been taken prisoner. Then, he should advise the Spaniards quickly to open the church's huge doors, and he would run to join them. Once inside, Vaudoit would climb up to the cupola and signal his ship. With this basic information in hand, the *Yorktown* could then shell the insurgents, destroy their defenses, and launch a rescue.

Gillmore's men silently nodded in agreement. The plan was brilliant. And it was probably their only hope.

Later that afternoon, Tecson sent for the sailmaker's mate and went over the plan with him. Vaudoit was instructed to go before the trenches of the church under a flag of truce. He should announce that if the besieged Spaniards were to lay down their arms, they would be marched down to the beach and turned over to the American man-of-war. Vaudoit nodded in agreement.

Vaudoit was walked out to the church, several hundred yards from the *komandante*'s office. He carried the cutter's Stars and Stripes in one hand and a white handkerchief, serving as the flag of truce, in the other. A Filipino bugler sounded the call for a parley. Then, to Vaudoit's consternation, the bugler vanished. The sailmaker's mate was on his own, in front of the church, unarmed and exposed. With a flag raised in each hand, Vaudoit cautiously stepped forward.

A Spaniard, rifle in hand, popped up in the trenches at a distance and called out. What was his business, the soldier angrily inquired in

Spanish. Vaudoit broke into French. He explained who he was and the plan they had hatched. Inside the church, the rest of the mentally diminished Spaniards looked on, unable to make sense of the flags or the man's words. They first mistook Vaudoit for Captain Olmeda, a Spanish officer with whom they had parleyed in the past, one of the occasional envoys sent from Manila to coax the detachment into surrender. They then surmised that the emissary, despite being dressed in a sailor's uniform, was an imposter somehow trying to impersonate Olmeda, as part of a new Filipino ruse.

Making little progress with the first *cazador*, Vaudoit yelled out, asking if anyone in the church spoke French. Minutes later, Lieutenant Cerezo appeared. Vaudoit again explained the plan in his native French. Cerezo, his usual skeptical, paranoid self, responded in French that he did not know that American and Spanish hostilities had ceased. Vaudoit explained that not only was this true, but also that the American warship anchored off the coast of Baler had brought a letter from the Archbishop of Manila for the Spaniards, certifying that the war was over. Cerezo was incredulous. Surely this was more lies, more deceit—and in half-gibberish French, no less! Cerezo called back in Spanish, telling Vaudoit that he would need to confer with his officers. In the meantime, Vaudoit should step away from the church and await their response. When Vaudoit quickly complied, it added to Cerezo's suspicions: So this imposter understood Spanish, too!

Vaudoit stood silently, both flags growing heavy in his raised arms. After several uncomfortable minutes, the response came from the Spaniards in the church: two simultaneous Mauser rifle shots, one just grazing Vaudoit's cheeks. The sailor dropped the flags and dove for cover. Parley over.

A downcast Vaudoit returned to the *komandante*'s office under insurgent guard to share the bad news. The Spaniards weren't willing to listen to him and had no interest in departing with the Americans. They had even tried to kill him. Tecson slowly digested the unfortunate outcome, the ramifications becoming clear. First, the Spaniards and the siege at the church would continue. Without resolution, their constant sniping and harassment would further wear on the town. And now, Tecson's hands were full with this foolhardy band of American adventurers who had stumbled into his midst. With every passing minute, their presence posed an ever-greater risk of a naval bombardment on the town, or worse, a heavily armed American landing party, itching for a fight.

Tecson needed guidance. Runners were sent to the distant town of Pantabangan, where a message could be sent to Aguinaldo's command.

The general would know what to do.

CHAPTER SEVEN

Off Beach and Bar

As instructed by Lieutenant Colonel Simon Tecson, Adjutant Quicoy and *Kapitan* Novicio had returned to the scene of the ambush, where several of their subordinates stood watch over the dead and wounded American sailors. Seaman Ora McDonald and Gunner's Mate Edward Nygard—alive and in agony—were both sprawled out on the muddy riverbank. The contorted bodies of the two landsmen—John Dillon and Charles Morrissey—still lay at the bottom of the bullet-ridden, blood-soaked cutter, their broken forms already in a state of rapid decay in the stifling humidity, a swarm of electrified blowflies bouncing about the mess.

Nygard, the Polish musician from Brooklyn, looked in very bad shape. With a sucking chest wound, he wheezed each fragile breath, and his left leg was shattered. Slipping in and out of consciousness, he weakly begged for water to slake his parched throat. Nygard's time was near.

McDonald, the twenty-one-year-old landsman from Monterey, California, had been shot in the middle of his right thigh. His femoral artery had been severed. The makeshift vine tourniquet had temporarily halted the loss of blood, but still, shock had set in. Perspiring profusely in the rising morning heat, his breathing labored, McDonald was unable to move. His eyes darted helplessly in every direction, struggling with a limited line of sight: Verdant green foliage edged his peripheral vision, and a shimmering blue sky hovered above. Around him, all he could hear were the insurgents chattering in a language he could not understand.

Adjutant Quicoy and *Kapitan* Novicio needed to get the mess cleaned up. Novicio ordered several of his soldiers to run back to town and pull together a grave-digging crew. Four men should do it. The *kapitan* rattled off some civilian names.

As detailed court testimony would later attest, the first of a four-man grave-digging crew, Balbino Sindac, arrived around 9:00 a.m., armed with a piece of bamboo with which to dig. The other three soon followed—Pablo Paulo and two brothers, Tomas and Luiz Gonzales—local residents who were not in a position to say no to Novicio's demand. They picked a site nine yards back from the river, off the trail heading up to town, set apart from the heavy undergrowth in a small clearing. By 11:00 a.m., they began digging in earnest with simple bamboo shovels. At the rate they were going, hollowing out a grave would be a three-hour job.

As the men dug, Novicio ordered the bodies of Dillon and Morrissey moved from the damaged cutter. A pack of obedient soldiers clumsily hauled out the bloodied men, their skulls blown open and brain matter dripping, and laid them beside a horrified Nygard and McDonald.

No doubt, Nygard knew his time was short. He likely pondered the impact of his impending death on the family he had left behind in their new apartment on Atlantic Avenue in Brooklyn—his wife, Sophie, their baby son Edward, and daughter-to-be, Ellen. If this was it, he would never meet her. With these sad and tragic thoughts swirling in his head, Edward John Nygard's pulse weakened, his eyes narrowed, and he slipped into unconsciousness. Death closed in.

By 2:00 p.m., working through the sweltering midday heat, the four grave diggers completed a large hole, five feet deep, six feet long, and five feet wide. It was large enough for two bodies to be placed in a row, side by side. One of the grave diggers turned to Novicio and asked in Tagalog, "Captain, are we going to bury them now?"

Novicio curtly responded, "Bury them."

Obediently, the civilians carried the stiffening bodies of Dillon and Morrissey to the grave and laid them at the bottom, side by side, against the moist earth. They then stepped back into the shade, fell into a squat, and waited for the two other Americans to die.

McDonald, in shock and unable to move, again begged for water—*"Agua, amigo"*—fighting for his life. One grave digger somberly walked to the nearby river, scooped up some cool water in the bucket, and fed McDonald a few sips, bringing relief to his cracked lips and parched throat.

McDonald looked to his fellow sailor, who had gone silent. The soldiers motioned to the grave diggers to check. One placed his fingers against Nygard's skin—the warmth of life was dissipating; he was gone.

McDonald watched as the grave diggers circled Nygard, picked up his expended form, and shimmied toward the grave. With a swinging heave, the gunner's mate's broken body was dumped on top of the two dead sailors, momentarily scattering the clusters of blowflies.

It was now 2:30 p.m. and the two Filipino officers were growing impatient with the one stubborn American who refused to die. Fed up, Novicio motioned to the men to put McDonald in the hole. The four men picked the sailor up, his eyes now wild, his severely weakened body writhing, and placed him in the grave alongside Nygard's still body. Delirious, his life draining away, the barely conscious sailor sensed the horror about to befall him. He squirmed among the bodies below and beside him. The nervous grave diggers stepped back, their eyes averted, and paused.

Kapitan Novicio yelled over to the men to hurry up—to get it done so they could all leave.

Gingerly, one of the grave diggers began to shovel the freshly dug dirt on top of McDonald, starting at his feet. Shovel after hesitant shovel brought the dark, loamy soil up to McDonald's neck. The sailor moaned in despair. One of the Filipino soldiers walked over and looked in. He quietly urged in Tagalog, "Have pity on the man."

Grave digger Tomas Gonzales, in the hole spreading the dirt, called out to Novicio, standing six yards away, "What about this man? He is still alive."

An irritated Novicio did not hesitate. "Go on burying him."

With their bamboo shovels, the troubled grave diggers heaved the moist soil over the dying sailor's face. McDonald, terrified, was incapable of emitting anything more than an anguished groan. If he tried to shake off the first shovelful or squirm in helpless desperation, it was of little use. The damp dirt kept coming, closing off the radiant heavens above. Then came darkness, and the sailor's tortured last gasp stolen by the earth.

The grave diggers tamped down their handiwork, completing the communal grave. A small wooden cross was added to mark the site. Their job done, the two officers, the contingent of Tecson's soldiers, and the four exhausted civilians somberly climbed back up the trail toward town.

❦

By now, collected by another cutter sent after them, Ensign Standley and Quartermaster Lysaght were back aboard the *Yorktown*. Standley's report to Commander Sperry had "excited the gravest apprehension" among the ship's officers. An uncharacteristically anxious Sperry ordered an armed picket boat—the ship's 3rd cutter—to patrol the beach throughout the day, hoping that Lieutenant Gillmore and his sailors would stumble out of the brush.

Toward sundown, without any news, Sperry reassessed his options. Shelling the town might injure any of the *Yorktown* men in hiding or captured, but it would at least deliver some pain to the insurgents. As a blood-orange sun dipped behind the Sierra Madres, the cruiser lobbed an introductory five-round salvo of six-inch shells toward land. The concussion of the huge guns sent shells whistling through the sky. Molten shrapnel sliced through the dense tropical brush and blasted tree trunks. Red-hot beads skipped across the bow of Gillmore's sunken cutter and dug harmlessly into the freshly turned soil of a new grave. Sperry could not have known that the Filipino fighters had long since retreated back to the town, to their homes and families, to their tables for dinner. Their fighting day was done.

The bamboo-and-thatch shelter that was housing Gillmore and the sailors was rocked by the *Yorktown*'s booming guns. The sailors exchanged knowing looks; this first barrage surely signaled that a landing party had been sent. The inevitable rescue was finally under way—probably marines with the second Colt Automatic, which this time would do its job with deadly efficiency. The grinning men fought to contain their glee.

That evening, Sperry ordered three armed boats—two cutters, as well as a smaller whaleboat—to patrol off the beach where Standley and Lysaght had landed and later been retrieved. Throughout the night, signals were made every half-hour with the ship's brilliant electric searchlight, indicating, "Boats waiting off beach and bar." The crews scanned the dark shoreline throughout the night, hoping for Gillmore and his sailors to break through the brush and make for open water. As they waited, small bands of Filipino soldiers darted about the beach, occasionally taking poorly aimed potshots at the boats. They missed every time.

The American patrols had rattled the insurgents. Novicio had bluffed Standley with the threat of four hundred armed insurgents—the number was about right, but most were armed with nothing more than bolos. A well-armed landing party, backed up by the devastating big guns of a steel-hulled battleship, would have easily overwhelmed their meager, ill-equipped forces. Strangely, that did not happen. The Americans continued probing the shoreline, waiting. Tecson and his men could only wonder—waiting for what?

Throughout the night, the Spaniards heard the intermittent rifle fire echoing through the air. They assumed a Spanish landing force, supported by a vessel of war, was on its way to their rescue. But no one arrived.

The following morning, a frustrated Lieutenant Cerezo ordered his men to fire three consecutive volleys into the air. The shots would confirm that they were indeed still alive and defending themselves. Aboard the *Yorktown*, the ship's log noted thirteen individual reports, followed by two loud volleys. But it wasn't clear where these shots were emanating from, or why they had been fired. If the Spaniards meant to send a message, they had failed.

The day sped by for the Spaniards, without a rescue. Night fell, without an answer.

Then, the *Yorktown*'s electric searchlight once again swept over the church tower. The Spaniards climbed into the tower, this time armed with a long bamboo pole wrapped with a kerosene-soaked rag. Once lit, the blazing bamboo pole was waved crazily with calls to their would-be saviors. *Yes, we are here! Help us!* To their alarm and growing dismay, they received nothing but silence in return.

Lieutenant Gillmore and his men, now captives of Lieutenant Colonel Simon Tecson, were faring no better. That same morning, Gillmore and seven other sailors without injuries were lined up and advised that they would be marched to a new location. The wounded men, too weak to make the trek over the mountains, would need to stay behind with Tecson and his command until they were well enough to follow. Gillmore and the seven sailors bade farewell to their three wounded comrades—Rynders, Woodbury, and Venville—not knowing if they would ever see each other again. The men set out on a dirt trail heading into the forested mountains, escorted by twenty-two Filipino guards, most armed with bolos. After several hours of marching, the column arrived at a small settlement, San Jose de Casignan. Exhausted and unfed, the prisoners were locked in the community's one solid structure, a squalid stone church. The tropical sun again quickly dipped behind the tree line, announcing the prisoners' second night in captivity.

Commander Sperry ordered the armed 3rd cutter, with eleven sailors and four marines, to once again patrol along the shore throughout the night of April 13. The crew anxiously scanned the beach, illuminated by only a sliver of moonlight, hoping for just one of Gillmore's crew to stumble through the brush and wave them down. But again, nothing.

At daybreak on April 14, Sperry ordered the cutter recalled. As the morning sun rose, the exasperated *Yorktown* commander again sent two boats, flying flags of truce, toward shore. And again, the insurgents refused to communicate. The cutters were rowed back, hoisted, and stowed.

Sperry's heart began to sink. It was now evident that this had become a grand naval disaster, an unnecessary loss of an officer and men sent on a mission of mercy. A seasoned officer well familiar with navy bureaucracy, Sperry began to assemble a paper trail to document his command decisions. From Thomas, Sperry requested an account of the exact orders given to Gillmore. From Standley, he asked for a summary of the reconnoitering mission and his assessment of Gillmore's intentions. Both reports, delivered within the day, solidly established that Gillmore had gone up the river on his own, against repeated and direct orders not to do so.

For the moment, Sperry was covered, but it did little to relieve his brewing anger. As he would write in a private letter to his wife Edith a week later:

> *The plain truth is poor Gillmore yielded to a desire for adventure, violated his instructions, did what he had expressly said would be sure defeat—that is, he went up the narrow creek only sixty feet wide with a jungle on each side—and probably none of them were left after the insurgents fired three volleys. Not only did he sacrifice himself and fourteen men, but he [also] exposed Standley to serious danger and made it impossible for me to shell out the town for fear that some of our people might be there alive.*

Unspoken and even more infuriating, Gillmore had also embarrassed his commander before the great Admiral Dewey. He had stolen away Sperry's one grand moment of glory. It was an outrage.

After a third day of waiting, Sperry's hope for survivors waned. Any determined person could get off the beach, he reasoned, there being no heavy surf. Even if a boat could not be used, "the most trifling assistance in the way of a wooden float would enable a man in the warm, smooth water, to reach the ship." It did not seem possible that with life at stake, any surviving American sailor could not reach the *Yorktown*. Or, for that matter, a besieged Spaniard who likely knew every foot of the jungle. Any further waiting offshore was simply a waste of time.

The only other option, Sperry knew, was to go in after the sailors and the Spaniards. Such a high-risk gamble, however, was not compatible with the commander's cautious, considered character. Any large landing would be difficult given the considerable swells to the east. They had only the knowledge of the local geography that Standley had quickly acquired. Standley's report suggested a rebel force of four hundred armed men, though this had not been verified. Lastly, it was unknown whether a landing force would even be welcomed by the beleaguered Spaniards. The *Yorktown*'s marines might fight their way through insurgent defenses only to confront even more armed resistance at the church.

Sperry concluded in his written assessment to Dewey, "To land eighty or ninety men from this vessel, absolutely untrained in operations on shore, without guides, under such conditions would have been simply inviting destruction, even if it had been possible to thoroughly shell out the enemy's position, a course which could not be taken if the safety of the Spaniards was to be considered."

The commander of the *Yorktown* was at a dead end.

During the late-afternoon shift on Friday, April 14, the *Yorktown*'s guns were unshotted and the boats secured. Auxiliaries were started. At 5:45 p.m., the fire under boiler D was set.

Sperry likely stepped out onto the main deck of the cruiser, brass navy binoculars in hand, to scan the beach and hills one final time. As the last rays of the sun fell from view, his crew preparing for sea, Sperry must have contemplated his unenviable position. *How had it come to this?*

Engines and steering gear were turned at 9:45 p.m., with fires now in boilers A, B, C, and D. Fifteen minutes later, the anchor was brought up, and twenty minutes after that the *Yorktown* got under way, swinging out to the north-northeast. Once in open water, she changed course to the southeast.

Under cloudy skies with intermittent rain squalls, light east-northeasterly airs, and the barometer holding steady, the *Yorktown* sailed from Baler— minus one officer and fourteen of her men.

The mission had failed on a scale beyond Sperry's imagination. The old admiral had been right. It had become one interesting cruise indeed.

BOOK II

The reaches opened before us and closed behind, as if the forest had stepped leisurely across the water to bar the way for our return. We penetrated deeper and deeper into the heart of darkness.
—JOSEPH CONRAD, *HEART OF DARKNESS*, PART II

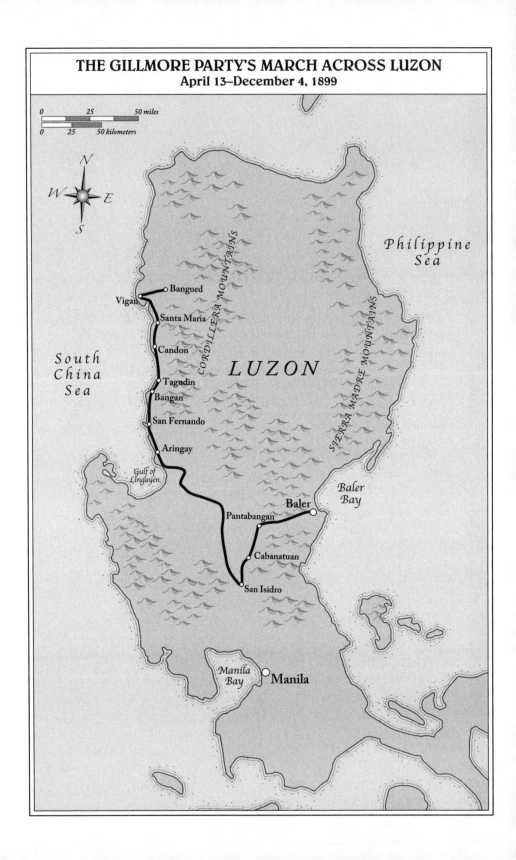

THE GILLMORE PARTY'S MARCH ACROSS LUZON
April 13–December 4, 1899

0   25   50 miles
0   25   50 kilometers

N
W — *E*
S

Philippine Sea

Bangued
Vigan
Santa Maria
Candon
Tagudin
Bangan
San Fernando
Aringay

CORDILLERA MOUNTAINS

LUZON

SIERRA MADRE MOUNTAINS

South China Sea

Gulf of Lingayen

Baler Bay

Baler
Pantabangan
Cabanatuan
San Isidro

Manila Bay   Manila

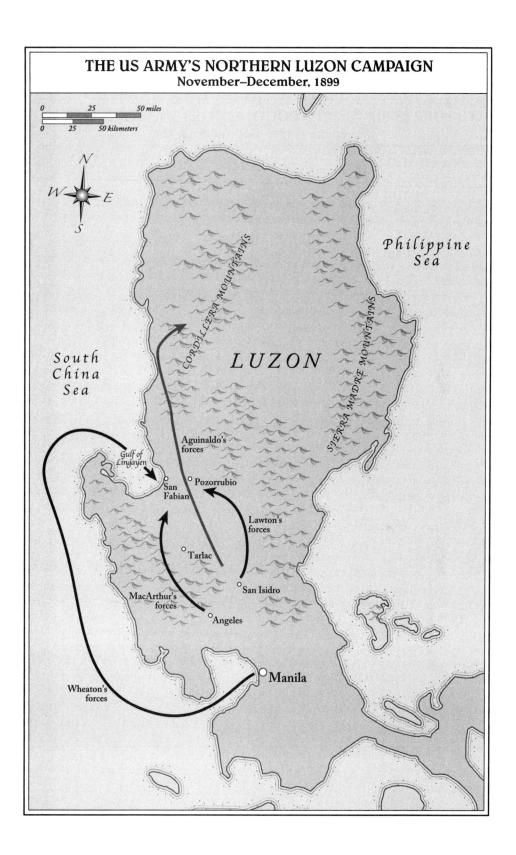

THE US ARMY'S NORTHERN LUZON CAMPAIGN
November–December, 1899

0   25   50 miles

0   25   50 kilometers

N
W   *E*
S

*Philippine
Sea*

*South
China
Sea*

CORDILLERA MOUNTAINS

L U Z O N

SIERRA MADRE MOUNTAINS

Aguinaldo's
forces

*Gulf of
Lingayen*

San
Fabian

Pozorrubio

Lawton's
forces

Tarlac

San Isidro

MacArthur's
forces

Angeles

Manila

Wheaton's
forces

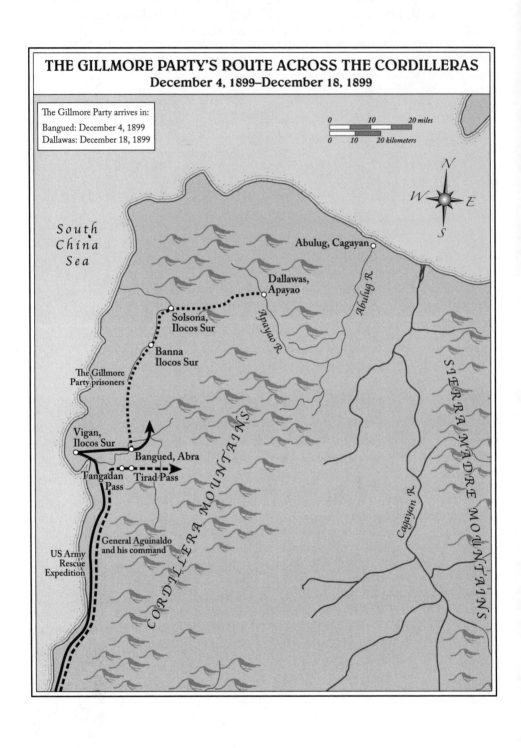

THE GILLMORE PARTY'S ROUTE ACROSS THE CORDILLERAS
December 4, 1899–December 18, 1899

The Gillmore Party arrives in:

Bangued: December 4, 1899
Dallawas: December 18, 1899

0   10   20 miles

0   10   20 kilometers

South China Sea

Abulug, Cagayan

Dallawas, Apayao

Solsona, Ilocos Sur

Banna Ilocos Sur

The Gillmore Party prisoners

Vigan, Ilocos Sur

Bangued, Abra

Tangadan Pass

Tirad Pass

US Army Rescue Expedition

General Aguinaldo and his command

Abulug R.

Apayao R.

Cagayan R.

CORDILLERA MOUNTAINS

SIERRA MADRE MOUNTAINS

CHAPTER EIGHT

Sierra Madres

AT SAN JOSE DE CASIGNAN, THE ROOSTERS WERE CROWING WELL BEFORE the sun steamed through the early-morning haze. Lieutenant Gillmore and the seven sailors with him stirred from an uncomfortable slumber on the hard floor of the stone church, a dark one-room affair that now served as their makeshift jail. Offered bowls of boiled porridge—rice, plantains, and scrawny bits of chicken—the famished sailors greedily slurped their first hot meal since supper on the *Yorktown,* three days earlier.

The cutter crew naturally gravitated into two groups, split by age and experience. The first, made up of the three older petty officers, Chief Quartermaster Walton, Coxswain Pinkham, and Sailmaker's Mate Vaudoit, formed a tough, weathered set of mariners. A second brought together the four younger boys, seaman Brisolese, landsmen Anderson and Edwards, and apprentice Peterson, naive and wide-eyed, and about half the age of the petty officers. Gillmore, the sole officer among the captives, sat off by himself, reluctant to mingle with the enlisted men.

While there is no record of what the men discussed as they entered their third day in captivity, the cost of their reckless adventure on the river was now clear. Shock likely gave in to frustration and anger as they relived the blurred moments of the ambush, the mind-boggling failure of the Colt, the stunning, bloody deaths of their comrades, and the alarming ease with which they had been taken prisoner. More galling, probably, was being captive to a ragtag band of insurgents who lacked any conception of the hell that would most assuredly be paid for their ill-considered assault. And all this, no less, while on a mission to rescue a detachment of Spaniards, who until recently were their sworn enemy. So much for "Remember the *Maine.*"

The rigid schedule of shipboard life was replaced with anxious waiting and a host of unknowns. Tethered together by rope, the sailors did know this: The odds of a rescue, now that they had been moved away from the coast, had diminished. And escape, if possible, would only place them at greater peril, facing an unfamiliar enemy on his own terrain.

The following morning, April 15, a runner arrived with orders: The prisoners were to be marched across the mountains to central Luzon, to General Aguinaldo's command at San Isidro. The captives were too valuable to be left near Baler, where patrolling American warships might attempt a rescue. Within an hour, the men were hurriedly started on a dirt trail that led to a wide, rock-strewn river. Climbing into the thick forest ahead, the column crossed the river more than twenty times by one count, chest-deep in places, with a current "swift as a mill race." At one crossing, Walton slipped, sprained an ankle, and broke a big toe, hobbling him for the rest of the march.

Prodded along, the column made slow progress, each step an ascent into the majestic Caraballo Mountains, the arcing volcanic spine of the

PHOTOGRAPH BY TOMAS ERIC SALES

Marched under armed guard on treacherous trails across the Sierra Madres to General Aguinaldo's headquarters, the *USS Yorktown* sailors would soon become valuable pawns in the Filipino Army of Liberation's fight for freedom.

southern Sierra Madres, which shared a name with other ranges throughout the Spanish-influenced world. By afternoon, squeezed dry of sweat, the older, visibly less-fit sailors began to flag. Moving into a steeper canyon, Vaudoit melted, falling senseless to the ground from heat stroke, and the column stopped for the night. After a thoroughly unsatisfying dinner of boiled plantains, a torrential tropical downpour fell from the sky, unleashing a wall of rain so dense, one sailor recalled, that it seemed to seize his breath. The drenched Americans lay uncovered among the rocks, harassed by mosquitoes, plumbing new depths of misery. The amused guards, having fashioned broad palm-leaf hats for themselves, squatted comfortably among the boulders, and while one kept a lazy watch over the prisoners, fell into a deep, perfect sleep.

If the sailors thought they and their guards were alone in the isolated fastness of the Caraballos, they were mistaken. They had hiked from the windswept eastern coast, an alluvial valley inhabited by Tagalog-speaking farmers and fishermen, across an invisible boundary, and into the mountain domain of the bark cloth–clad Ilongots, a fierce tribal people of the forest. It was a territorial demarcation the lowland Tagalogs respected and violated with the greatest care, as the Ilongots were fierce, prone to violence, and as innumerable assaults over the years had confirmed, inveterate hunters of heads. With all likelihood, the Ilongots were silently tracking the column's movements, ensuring that the strange intruders observed territorial boundaries and continued on their way. If there were doubts, the Ilongots would not hesitate to attack.

It was not just encroachment or invasion that could drive the Ilongots to violence. Their head-taking was an established rite of passage. Bands of long-haired warriors, their blackened teeth chiseled to sharp points, ambushed and killed their victims for the body parts they believed contained the essence of the person's strength—the head, toes, and fingers. After a raid, these appendages were carved off and brought back to the village for an elaborate celebration. The heads were scalped, the tops of the skulls chipped away, and the brains removed, creating morbid vessels for a potent brew of fermented rice wine. Under the stars, amid a cacophony of gongs and bamboo zithers, the warriors danced as if in a trance, teasing their cranial prizes until sunrise. One or more of the boys were then anointed as men, crowned with an ornate headdress crafted from the brilliant red beak of a Rufous hornbill. So attired, an Ilongot warrior was transformed from boy to man, and now could rightly take a girl's hand in marriage.

Thankfully for the oblivious Americans and their wary contingent of armed guards, on this night, on this mountain, the Ilongots were not in a warring mood, nor in search of manhood.

The forced march continued the following day. Despite the torment of their captivity, the sailors were awestruck by the natural beauty surrounding them. They were hiking through old-growth tropical rain forest, part of the geologic backbone of Luzon, where the thick, verdant cover supported a stunningly vast biodiversity. "Under other circumstances, this would have been a wonderful trip," recounted Landsman Edwards. Within a day, the thirty-man column had moved from beach and strand forest—vegetated with *pandan, agoho, talisay, dapdap, malibago,* and *kalumpang* trees—into lowland evergreen forest. Towering above were dipterocarps, a family of hardwood tropical trees, of every variety—red *lauan, apitong, yakal, tangile, narra, dao,* and *molave*—rattan, bamboo, and massive strangling fig trees with trunks many yards in circumference. Along the trail, legumes, aroids, palms, lichens, mosses, hepatics, and ferns jostled for their moments in the fleeting shafts of sunlight.

And there was much more, most of it unseen: A host of exotic mammals flitted about the thick forest floor—golden-crowned flying foxes, crab-eating macaques, warty pigs, and bushy-tailed cloud rats, among them. Screeching, cawing, and chattering about the majestic triple canopy were hundreds of bird species of every description—among them, noisy fluorescent green parrots; boisterous red-beaked hornbills; crop-raiding, bright white cockatoos; and a symphony of woodpeckers, spider hunters, babblers, shrikes, and kingfishers. In the shadows of the towering trees, eagle owls stood sentinel, eyeing the forest floor for any movement of edible prey. And soaring above, awesome monkey-eating Philippine eagles ruled the skies.

In total, the Sierra Madre Mountains were alive with an estimated 3,500 different plants, 84 species of birds, 38 kinds of mammals, 17 amphibians, 40 types of reptiles, several hundred kinds of butterflies, and a legion of insects too numerous to count. Gillmore and his sailors were moving through one of the world's most lush and diverse biospheres, virginal primary forest yet untouched by commercial loggers who would devastate this pristine heritage in the decades to come. Yet to the

Lyman P. Edwards, circa 1900.

Americans' untrained eyes, it was likely no more than an unforgiving and seemingly impenetrable jungle.

As the captives climbed higher, the temperature dipped. Without shelter, and battered by heavy rains, new risks arose. Vaudoit, having collapsed earlier, was dehydrated, underfed, and, like most of the sailors, out of shape for such exertion on steep, mountainous terrain. As he fell in and out of a delirium on the second night, his comrades, sprawled out on the rocky riverbank around him, debated whether the old French sailor would survive. A darkening gloom of despair set in.

Set apart, with a sliver of moonlight illuminating the shadows, Gillmore spent the entire night staring into the noisy darkness that enclosed him, trying to make sense of his predicament. "I sat on a boulder in a pool of water till daybreak," he recalled, likely ruminating over the unexpected turn of events, yet another twist in a life thick with setbacks and forged by trial. It was all the more bewildering, he may have thought, given his origins. By every measure, he had been provided with all of the ingredients for a life of wealth and privilege. How had it come to this?

❧

Life had begun for James C. Gillmore Jr. in Philadelphia, Pennsylvania, on July 10, 1854. His father, James Clarkson Gillmore Sr., a wealthy merchant engaged in the silk trade, was rebuilding his family after the loss of his first wife, Elizabeth Ann Dunlap. Her passing, from tuberculosis a day after Christmas 1849, had left the senior Gillmore, a busy man of twenty-seven, with two daughters in his care. Unable to raise them on his own, he gave guardianship to his in-laws, with whom he had been living. Within a year, Gillmore was remarried to Augustina J. Hagner, a woman of means nine years his junior, and descended from old Washingtonian stock. Their first child, a daughter named in memory of Gillmore Sr.'s first wife, Elizabeth, was born in 1853. Then came their son, James Clarkson Gillmore Jr., a year later.

Two months after his arrival, the infant James was dealt his first family tragedy: the loss of his older sister, at eighteen months of age, to pneumonia. Sister Annie was then born in 1855, followed by Ida in 1856. With a steady stream of profits, the wealthy patriarch settled his family at two homes: one in Philadelphia proper, at 1713 Arch Street, located a few blocks from his ornate dry goods shop, and a second on a seven-acre estate in posh suburban Germantown. Supported by three Irish servants, a coachman, and a gardener who maintained the residence's sprawling grounds, life for the wealthy Gillmore family was, at this point, nothing short of idyllic.

Little baby Florence arrived in May 1862. That same year, Gillmore Sr., now settled, opted to reclaim his two eldest daughters, Ella, now fifteen, and Clara, thirteen, after their maternal grandmother, who had been caring for them, passed away. James Jr., turning eight, soon had a full house with five female siblings, all under one well-appointed roof. Wealth and privilege may have spared the elder Gillmore from military service in the Civil War, but it could not stave off life's unexpected tragedies. Less than a year later, on February 2, 1863, James Gillmore Sr., at the prime age of forty-two, was cut down by a brain aneurysm. Three days later, the Gillmores' elegant Arch Street home was filled with family, friends, and business partners for a late-morning funeral. A glum, uncomprehending huddle of six children watched the sad event unfold.

And then, another shocking loss followed on the heels of this tragedy. With her husband's business affairs in shambles, the grieving thirty-three-year-old Augustina, still weak from childbirth ten months earlier, was stricken with rheumatic fever. The disease was rapid and violent in its devastation, damaging the valves of her broken heart. On March 3, 1863, one month after James Sr.'s death, Augustina died. A second funeral was held, attended by the same grieving group of family, friends, and business associates. Augustina was interred at Laurel Hill Cemetery, next to the freshly turned plot of her husband, James.

The children, now orphans, were scattered to whoever could be found to care for them. But before those arrangements could be finalized, the looming hand of death again visited the Gillmore household to take baby Florence, who, since the loss of her mother five months earlier, had become tormented by convulsions. The family plot at Laurel Hill was again visited, and a third addition made, accompanied by a small headstone noting Florence's brief, difficult life.

In less than a year, the family had experienced three heartbreaking losses. Amid a world of plenty, the five surviving Gillmore children could not have felt more alone. Luckily, their father's estate provided each child with a sum of $10,000—equivalent to $240,000 in today's dollars. The children, scattered to guardians, watched helplessly as the safety, security, and cohesion evaporated from their once-privileged lives.

The two older Gillmore daughters married as soon as they were eligible. Clara married at age eighteen to an army officer in 1866, Lieutenant Butler D. Price, 4th Infantry, giving her younger brother an important family connection in the military. Bounced between guardians, in September 1868, James Gillmore Jr., then fourteen, and his two younger siblings, were shunted to a third legal guardian, their deceased father's business partner, Lucius P. Thompson. The wealthy Princeton graduate welcomed the Gillmore additions into his own palatial family home in prestigious Germantown. While it may have approximated the lifestyle the Gillmore children were familiar with, it likely did little to heal the fissures in their heavy hearts.

Common among those of privilege at the time, James was packed off to boarding school, the Pennsylvania Military Academy for boys in Chester. Life at PMA under the leadership of Colonel Theodore Hyatt was strictly disciplined, with each rigidly ordered day starting with reveille before dawn, followed by inspections, mess-hall meals, and marching to and from classes in uniform. Hyatt, an exacting taskmaster, inculcated a sense of superiority and distinction in his boys. Each cadet was groomed to view himself as set apart from others, and to embrace a destiny of manhood defined by education, chivalry, and honor. It was a mind-set that would stay with Gillmore all of his life. Born into privilege, raised amid great wealth, Gillmore was part of the elite—both by birth and training—and he knew it. He was, much like his country, an exception, which the colonel's academy only reaffirmed.

The day before final exams in June 1869, Colonel Hyatt chartered a boat and sailed his cadets up the Delaware River. Arriving at the League Island Navy Yard, Philadelphia's sprawling shipyard located at the confluence of the Schuylkill River, the yard's commanding officer, sixty-year-old Commodore Oliver S. Glisson, toured the wide-eyed boys through the stable of ironclad warships at anchor in the harbor. Glisson was an impressive old salt with tales of adventure and daring on the high seas during the Mexican War in the 1840s, while accompanying the Perry expedition to Japan in the 1850s, and battling Confederate forces in the 1860s.

It was on this day, it would seem, that the juvenile Gillmore set his heart on a new aspiration: to become an officer in the United States Navy. It was a career that offered not only the prospects of honor and glory, but also, for Gillmore—whose childhood had been steeped in turmoil and loss—a chance to escape, to take to the world's high seas and start anew.

—◆—

At daybreak on April 17, 1899, following a few mouthfuls of rice for breakfast, Gillmore, his men, and their guards once again set out, marching among more boulders, along rock-strewn riverbeds, and wading the rushing river with exhausting frequency. As if to add insult to injury, they struck a section of the trail off the river, Gillmore would remember, where a platoon of monkeys in the trees overhead, "jabbered angrily and threw nuts and twigs" as they passed. Covering forty miles since Baler, the narrow mountain trail finally broke onto the western slope of the range, leveling out at the town of Pantabangan. Bursting with curiosity, residents mobbed the captives, eager, it seemed, "to see the terrible Americans arrive."

That same afternoon, after three days under full steam, the *Yorktown* arrived at the port of Iloilo. Sperry had pushed her for all she was worth, working the ship's four boilers, but at a cost: The searing heat had prostrated one of the sailors in the fire room. The ship dropped anchor at 14.5 fathoms, in sight of its sister ships, the USS *Charleston* and the USS *Concord*, the latter of which was just getting under way.

A junior officer was sent ashore with a secret 308-word cipher message carefully constructed by Sperry. By 6:40 p.m., the telegraph operator had finished converting the text into Larrabee Code, the navy's cipher for telegraphic transmissions. The operator began tapping out the message, sending faint electronic pulses—encrypted dots and dashes—along an undersea copper cable that connected the distant port of Iloilo to Manila.

> *Couchera repecchino initiarem*
> *Apura aggricarem subfibrous*
> *Achucharon domans picaroon . . .*

The tapping went on for twelve pages.

At Manila, a receiving telegraph operator worked the cipher backward against the navy's Larrabee tables. The translated message was raced to Admiral Dewey, who surely winced at its contents. The debacle at Baler represented a major setback in the Philippines. There would be no hiding it—news of the fiasco would need to be urgently conveyed to Washington. After a day of meditation, Dewey drafted a new message, presenting the calamity in the best possible light. Gillmore's perplexing behavior, if not outright defiance of an order, was not raised. Dewey's staccato report was cabled late the following evening, also in cipher. It arrived just before lunch, April 18, in Washington, D.C., to an alarmed navy brass:

> *The Yorktown visited Baler, Luzon, east coast of Luzon, Philippine Islands, April 12th, for the purposes of rescuing and bringing away the Spanish forces consisting of fifty soldiers, three officers, and two priests, which were surrounded by four hundred insurgents. Some of the insurgents armed with Mauser rifles, as reported by natives. Lieutenant J. C. Gillmore, while making an examination of the*

apr 17, 1899

THE EASTERN EXTENSION AUSTRALASIA & CHINA
TELEGRAPH COMPANY, LIMITED.

IN CONNECTION WITH

THE EASTERN TELEGRAPH COMPANY, LIMITED.

Manila Station.

(No. 42.)—Receiving Form.

PREAMBLE.

Del. From.

Foreign No.

309/308

REMARKS.

U S govt

Clerk's Initials

No. 16

At 6 40p m. on 17 of 4 189 9

Received the following TELEGRAM:

From Iloilo dated 17 Time 6 Pm.

To

Address Dewey

☞ No inquiry respecting this Telegram can be attended to without the production of this Paper.

The Public are expressly requested to take Notice that Messages are only forwarded by THE EASTERN EXTENSION AUSTRALASIA AND CHINA TELEGRAPH COMPANY, LIMITED, on the condition that no responsibility is incurred for delay in transmission or delivery, or for non-transmission or non-delivery, or for mistakes from whatever cause they may arise.

Manila

Conchera	ripecchino	initiarem
apura	aggricarem	subfibrous
achucharon	edomans	picaroon
ailodarons	argutes	tontedad
acendron	concedante	asseroabis
substylar	rundheit	spathose
appilante	binario	affichioris
centinando	edecimeris	babyish
accuorare	argudarse	alluciare
dehortar	saledizo	bethinking
sinaitic	conchoidal	truncemus

William Brown & Co., Ltd., Export Stationers, &c., London, E.C.

The first page of Commander Sperry's encrypted message to Admiral Dewey, sent from Iloilo to Manila on April 17, 1899. The telegram carefully explained the ambush and Sperry's loss of men at Baler.

mouth of the river in an armed boat, was ambushed, fired upon, and captured. Fate unknown, as the insurgents refused to communicate afterwards.

The telegram concluded with a list of the fifteen missing men and their hometowns of record.

Back at Iloilo, news of the deadly ambush at Baler quickly spread to the other ships, and to the garrison of US Army soldiers stationed ashore, triggering calls for revenge. Amid rumors that Aguinaldo was suing for peace, Sperry wrote to his wife:

The Tennessee regiment here is wild to go up and clean out Baler, and if peace does not come I hope the admiral will see that they have the chance. He can certainly be trusted to do the right thing, and the matter is in his hands.

In fact, Dewey was weeks from departing Manila for his triumphant return to the United States. The mess at Baler was the last thing he needed. The great admiral, beloved hero to a thankful nation, could do little now but stoically await the fallout that would inevitably follow from his devastating message to Washington.

The Navy Department, keen to demonstrate the selfless sacrifice being made by American forces in the Philippines, immediately shared the dispatch with the news media. The following morning, America awoke to breathless headlines. The *Washington Post* ran the story on its front page, top of the fold, a cascade of grim headlines:

DEWEY'S BAD NEWS
Lieut. Gilmore and Fourteen
of the Yorktown *Crew Ambushed*

FIRST DISASTER TO THE NAVY
Unknown Fate of a Naval Party Sent Ashore at Baler, Where They
Were Surrounded and Surprised by Four Hundred Natives
List of Names of the Missing

Dewey's dispatch caused tremendous excitement in naval circles, it was reported, as the navy had prided itself thus far on its immunity from any reverses. Sensitive to complaints that America was not doing enough in response to appeals from Spain to help liberate its own prisoners, the *Washington Post* story emphasized the noble cause that underpinned the failed mission at Baler:

> *That the capture should have been effected while the American forces were on a mission of mercy toward the Spaniards, rather than the prosecution of the campaign, led to the belief that Spain would have no further ground for questioning the good faith with which the Americans were seeking to relieve the condition of the Spanish prisoners.*

And so it continued, in hundreds of papers, in every city, in every rural town. Overnight, the tragic tale of the good Lieutenant Gillmore and his cutter of unfortunate sailors, their noble mission of mercy to save a besieged band of Spaniards, was the topic of conversation in office hallways and street corners, in shops and at dinner tables, across the nation.

In Washington, along the corridors of power, military planners and decision-makers wrung their hands in fresh frustration. The campaign of pacification in their new and distant possession had just grown colossally more complicated.

CHAPTER NINE

San Isidro

AFTER A SHORT RESPITE IN THE TOWN OF PANTABANGAN, GILLMORE and his band of sailors were marched another three days, dropping into the prosperous and well-populated central Luzon valley. At the town of San Isidro, the prisoners ran an ugly gauntlet of several thousand Filipino soldiers and residents, hooting, jeering, and throwing stones, calling them "all manner of names in Tagal and Spanish," Gillmore recalled.

But the Americans were not to be outdone: "Our sailormen, after the manner of their kind, hurled back at them as good as they sent, or perhaps I should say worse."

Amid a cacophony of vulgarities, the prisoners staggered across the threshold of the town's derelict stone jail, collapsing in exhaustion as the wrought-iron doors clanged shut behind them.

Inside, the American sailors found they were not alone. Eager to make their acquaintance were six ragged, hungry prisoners, a mix of American soldiers and foreign civilians who stepped forward to make introductions and share their tales of woe and misfortune.

Albert Sonnichsen, a vagabond from Springfield, Massachusetts, had dropped out of school at age sixteen. Working alternately as a trapper, ranch hand, art student, and typesetter, he most recently had been employed as the quartermaster on the *Zealandia,* a tramp steamer chartered by the US Army to haul troops and supplies about the Philippines. The twenty-one-year-old merchant marine had struck out from Manila with former classmate and now fellow prisoner, nineteen-year-old Hospital Corpsman Harry Huber, to the insurgent capital at Malolos, to take pictures and hunt for souvenirs. Armed with cameras and a revolver, their excursion behind rebel lines was an exotic adventure, and it had been a successful one. So, on January 27, 1899, they shucked their American identities again, dressed up as Englishmen, shifted their accents, and caught the train north to Malolos. This time, their thin charade fell apart, leading to their arrest as armed, camera-wielding spies.

Three of the prisoners were US Army privates who had managed to stumble into captivity one way or another. William Bruce and Elmer Honnyman, enlisting together in the 1st Nevada Cavalry at Reno, were taken by insurgents on January 30, 1899, while sightseeing in San Roque, a small town outside Manila. On April 12, 1899, Private Albert O. Bishop, Battery K, 3rd Artillery, a tall, bearded, twenty-six-year-old bookkeeper from St. Charles, Iowa, had been on the receiving end of a surprise night-time assault by Filipino revolutionaries at Malolos. Rousted from sleep in the town's church, separated from his men, Bishop ended up hiding on the wrong side of the lines in a muddy ditch, only to be discovered the following morning, as soon as daylight arrived.

And then, there was a civilian: John O'Brien, a thirty-year-old British Army veteran, had been studying Shakespeare and English literature at Salt Lake City, Utah, when he was swept up in the gold rush to the West. Hearing rumors of the vast untapped mineral wealth of the Philippines, he had sailed to Manila and traveled north to Malolos to secure permission from the revolutionary government to prospect for gold. Somehow, he thought his mix of disinterested citizenship and entrepreneurial zeal would exempt him from the ongoing hostilities. He was wrong. Arriving in Malolos on February 3, 1899, the Englishman was arrested, divested of the $240 he was carrying, and locked up.

Altogether, there were now fourteen prisoners of war in the hands of the Filipino forces at San Isidro.

There was a fifteenth man, a prisoner of sorts, a dodgy, slick-tongued, Canadian ex-preacher named Williams, who was operating under the alias David Brown. He was, in fact, a criminal on the run. Newspaper stories later tagged Brown as a Methodist minister who had fled North St. Paul, Minnesota, after being accused of sexually assaulting a young woman in his congregation. To avoid arrest, Brown had hightailed it to Seattle and caught the first steamer to the Orient. On board, unable to control himself once again, Brown was caught stealing money from his fellow passengers and put ashore at Honolulu. But it was to be a temporary detour. The wily hustler managed to find his way to Manila, where he picked up work managing a local restaurant. His latest transgression was a foolish one: Following a night out in Manila with a bottle of scotch, a severely inebriated Brown had staggered beyond the safety of American lines, collapsed in a delirium, and awoken among a band of insurgents. The bleary-eyed, cotton-mouthed Canadian was immediately taken captive, another valuable prize.

Once imprisoned, Brown worked every angle at San Isidro. Keen to win favor with his jailers, he revealed an escape plan to the warden, instantly earning the contempt and loathing of his fellow prisoners. Just prior to the Gillmore party's arrival, the conniving Brown had managed to slip out of confinement; using his well-honed powers of persuasion, he cleverly convinced the provincial governor of the merits of learning English. After making his case, Brown transferred to the politician's residence to serve as his personal, full-time language instructor. "We all felt pleased to have him go," Huber explained, "because there was this feeling of hatred against him that none of us could resist."

Lieutenant Gillmore and his sailors were now officially prisoners of war of the Aguinaldo revolutionary government, and, like the other prisoners held at San Isidro, were now extended a small daily per diem by the jail's warden. Prison life, the men soon found, was not equal for all. Each prisoner was given a daily stipend of ten *centimos*, in cash, allowing them to purchase food from local vendors who passed by the jail. The men quickly learned that this amount didn't buy much, nor did their diet vary. Staples included rice, bananas, sugar, and *kamote*, a local sweet potato. Gillmore, due to his rank, was treated far better. He was given a double allowance—twenty *centimos*, or one-fifth of a silver *peso*—and quartered separately with the warden, the *alcalde*. The double per diem allowed the lieutenant to splurge on the occasional chicken or fish, and to enjoy the local cigars. Such were the privileges of a commissioned officer, a successful graduate of the rigorous program of study at the United States Naval Academy. Had they known the truth, his fellow prisoners and jailers would have been astounded at how close the Annapolis graduate had come to failure.

~~~

After two years at the Pennsylvania Military Academy, the teenage Gillmore ambitiously looked to admission at the prestigious Naval Academy in Annapolis, Maryland. To secure an appointment, he turned to his guardian and benefactor, Lucius Thompson, who sought the intervention of his influential friends. Unfortunately, while awaiting a response from Annapolis, Gillmore was again visited by tragedy. His oldest sister, Ella Gillmore Pearce, having married a few years earlier, died during childbirth. The fresh loss reduced the Gillmore family once again, to James and his sisters Clara, Annie, and Ida.

As the surviving Gillmores grieved, a four-month barrage of letters ultimately worked their magic with the Naval Academy. An appointment letter for James C. Gillmore Jr., Cadet Midshipman, was issued on September 5, 1871, to fill a vacancy in a congressional district where no nomination had been made, and in which the seventeen-year-old Gillmore had never set foot—Arizona Territory.

All the influence in the world could not diminish Gillmore's new set of tribulations. Gaining admission to the Academy was one thing; prospering once there was another. As a fourth-class "plebe," Cadet Gillmore began to falter. Errant behavior led to permanent demerits—eighty-two in his first year alone—which marred his class standing and placed him at risk of dismissal.

In the fall of 1872, during Gillmore's second year, a new plebe from South Carolina captured the nation's attention: James Henry Conyers, the first black cadet to be appointed. The first weeks for the sixteen-year-old Conyers passed peacefully, without much more than ugly yet harmless epithets thrown in his wake. On October 11, it turned violent: Twenty white cadets converged on Conyers after a heated exchange and beat him without mercy. It took a midshipman, intervening with his sword drawn, to break up the assault.

The following day, Gillmore and the other cadets involved in the attack were slapped with ten demerits each for "hazing, or encouraging the hazing, of a 4th classman." The story of the brutal assault found its way into the newspapers and caused outrage across the country. The navy was forced to take action. An investigative panel interviewed twenty-five plebes, fifteen midshipmen (including Cadet Gillmore), and three officers. In its final report, the panel implied that most of the boys were lying in their responses to questioning. Two cadets were recommended for dismissal. Another four had their ten demerits' penalty confirmed, were confined to the Academy grounds for the remainder of the school year, and were publicly reprimanded. Gillmore, however, managed to avoid punishment completely. The ten demerits he had earned were retracted, without any explanation in the written record for the highly unusual reversal.

Gillmore, who had slid by as an unpunished coconspirator, watched his performance slide in the months that followed. He was not turned in at taps, he failed to keep his room swept, and he was "inattentive at dress parade and indifferent at signals." On other occasions, his table was in disorder, he talked at formation, spoke disrespectfully to a professor, and answered back improperly when spoken to at sea drills. He was caught "skylarking" on the staircase and in the lower hall. By the end of his second year, Gillmore had buried himself under a fresh avalanche of 170 additional demerits.

During his third year, Gillmore's performance slipped to new lows, with misbehavior earning a raft of punishing demerits on his record. Over the year-end holidays, Gillmore decided to stay behind at the Academy, perhaps to wallow in his loneliness. It was a bad decision, and led to a fresh incident. On Christmas Day, he was caught on campus in a state of intoxication, and slapped with another ten demerits. By the spring of 1874, the errant cadet had collected 173 demerits for the year, breaking his previous year's record of disinterest, defiance, and sloth.

In his senior year, the cocksure Gillmore racked up 39 demerits in one month alone. At an inspection in November, footprints were found on his windowsill, evidence of a previous night's escape: two demerits. Eleven days later, failure to post regulations in his room: another demerit. And then on November 18, Gillmore was again slapped with 10 demerits for a second bout of drunkenness, part of an unrecorded yet gravely serious incident in which he crossed the point of no return. On November 29, 1874, the United States Naval Academy had had enough—James C. Gillmore Jr. was dropped from its rolls.

Unlike the many others who had been forced to make an early exit due to poor academic performance or behavioral issues, Gillmore refused to go quietly. Within days, Secretary of the Navy George Robeson began to receive a stream of urgent appeals on behalf of the dismissed cadet, pleading for a second chance. The entreaties assured the secretary that Gillmore possessed all of the attributes required of a fine naval officer. His guardian, Mr. Lucius Thompson, the letters noted, was a highly respected member of the Philadelphia business community and an important

James C. Gillmore Jr. was appointed in 1871 to the United States Naval Academy, where he fared poorly and was disciplined for a raft of infractions. In November 1874, after one egregious incident, Gillmore was expelled.

political fund-raiser for the Republican Party. Other letters arrived from publisher George Childs; Alexander Gilmore Cattell, a wealthy, well-connected grain merchant and former US senator; and James W. Paul, a relative who later married into the famed Drexel banking family. Congressman Alfred C. Harmer personally endorsed Paul's letter, pleading for the secretary's intervention while Paul made the boy's case:

Mr. Gillmore lost both his mother and father when only seven years old and had no near relatives to take care of him and supply a parent's love except an aged grandmother, who is also dead. From his assurances, I am confident that if the letter of dismissal was withdrawn, and Mr. Gillmore reinstated, that the Department would have no further cause of complaint. His mother was Mrs. Paul's first cousin and a very lovely woman. If the present application was granted I would esteem it a personal favor, as I am desirous of saving my young friend from the disgrace attached to a dismissal for an act which he is heartily ashamed of and which he promises shall not be repeated in the future.

Against all odds, and in a striking departure from precedent and procedure, Gillmore was allowed to return to the Academy. Demerits locked into his official academic record were physically altered, by persons unknown, leaving a visible scar of erasure. With the resulting revisions in the math, Gillmore's future in the United States Navy was reestablished.

Incredibly, Gillmore returned to Annapolis not chastened by his experience, but even more self-assured, somehow skirting disaster while accumulating a host of new infractions: loitering in the washrooms, straggling to formation, being out of uniform, arriving in class unprepared to recite, appearing tardy and inattentive, and in one failed deception, leaving "two lights burning while absent from room."

In 1876, Gillmore graduated, ranking an astonishing twenty-fourth out of a class of forty-one, miraculously surviving the cuts and dismissals that had pared the entering class five years earlier from its original one hundred cadets. At his graduation ceremony, likely without any family members in attendance, Gillmore proudly wore a gold class ring on his left hand, inscribed with Neptune's trident and the Academy's motto of the day: *Ex scientia tridens*, "From knowledge, seapower."

Cadet-Midshipman

DATE. 1874	DELINQUENCY.	
Oct. 1	Unprepared to recite at 11.45 A.M. recitation	
" 6	Books not neatly arranged at A.M. Inspection	
" "	Room not properly swept, dust in corners	
" "	Out of uniform wearing double-breasted white coat at "recit."	
" 13	Disobedience, reading a newspaper while kept q. 2 floor or somthg	
" "	Careless and inattentive as kept q. 2 floor whereof ? thing	
" "	smoked in their room about 12.30 P.M.	
" 14	Washing suit not marked in accordance with order	
" 15	At evening talking marching from 10.45 recitation	
" 16	Non regulation shirt at breakfast formation (held over)	
" 19	Untidy, dirt under bed A.M. Inspection	
" 25	Cadaverous slippers under bed 9.30 A.M. Inspection	
" 26	Skylarking on Veranda	
" 27	Books not neatly arranged on table ? ? ? 10 A.M. Inspection (2nd offence)	
" "	Unmilitary, allowing disorder in section	
Nov. 6	Foot marks on window sill 11 A.M. Inspection	
" 17	Regulations not posted in room	
Dec. 22	Out of uniform supper formation	
" "	Intoxication Nov. 18	
" 27	No name on bed or wardrobe 10 A.M.	
" 31	Loitering in wash room 12.30 P.M.	
Jany 2	Straggling from position marching marching from recit.	
" 7	Room not ready for Insp. dust on washstand	
" 9	Name not posted in room 10. A.m. Insp.	
" 31	Careless — in dress as waistcoat with full dress	
Feby 8	Loitering in wash room A.M. station	
" "	Careless trousers torn about the feet	
" 11	Receiving visits	
" 17	Towell not neatly arranged on rack 10 A.M. insp.	
" 23	Careless and indifferent at boxing skylarking	
" 24	Books not in order on top of wardrobe	
" 26	Rain Coat not of place A.M. insp.	
" "	Staring mess hall at breakfast	
Mch. 3	Unprepared to recite 10.45 recitation	
" "	Inattentive at drill	
" 19	Dirty wash stand at 10 A.M. insp.	
" 25	Tardy donner formation	
Apr. 1	Bringing manuscript to drill and reading them	
" 16	Noisy on stairs about 16.30 P.M.	
" 24	No ? on ? at ?	

The Naval Academy's record of demerits for Cadet James C. Gillmore Jr., from October 1874 through April 1875. In an unusual move, the November 18th incident and its demerits were removed from Gillmore's disciplinary record.

Gillmore 2nd Class.

REPORTING OFFICER.	DEMERITS.			REMARKS.
	DAY.	MONTH.	YEAR.	
Lt. Crosb. Terry	2			no excuse
" " McCalla	1			" "
" "	1			" "
" " Schuler	1			" "
" " Caldwell	2			" "
" "	2			" "
" " White	2			" "
Lieut. Simms	6			" "
" "	6			" "
	0			excuse accepted
Lt. Simons	1			no excuse
Lt. Com. Caldwell	1			" "
" " McCalla	6			" "
Lt. Simons	2			" "
Prof. Smith	6			" "
		39		
Lt. for Caldwell	2			" "
Lt. Cornwell	1			" "
		3	42	Amd. 3 Ag 39
Lt. for McCalla	1			no ex
" Caldwell	10			"
Mr. Simons	2			"
Lt. McWalling	2			"
		15	54	
Lt. Com. Dimble	6			excd
" McCalle	1			
Lt. Cornwell	1			
Lt. Com. McCalla	1			
		9	63	
Lt. Com. McCalla	1			
	1			
C. M. Winch	21			
Lt. Simons	1			
Lt. Com. White	1			not sat.
" McCalla	1			ney
Lt. Cornwell	1			
C. Lt. Com. Winslow	6			
		14	77	
Lt. Rodgers	2			ney
Lt. Rodgers	1			
Lt. Cornwell	1			
C. M. Coffin	1			
		5	82	Rem. 5 Rg 77
Lt. Com. Caldwell	1			ney
"	1			
Lt. Simons	1			
		3	80	Rem. 3 Rg 77

The erasure had followed the intercession of wealthy family friends. Gillmore was taken back by the Academy and given a last chance.

Twenty-three years later, Gillmore was a captive of Filipino revolutionaries, and the evidence of his narrow survival at the Academy had been stripped from his hand at Baler. It did not matter; even without the token of his own exceptionalism, he assumed it would not be any different now. Already, he may have mused, his web of powerful connections and patronage was working, behind the scenes, on a plan for his rescue. And, surprisingly, he would have been right.

On the day the Gillmore party arrived at the town of San Isidro, the *San Francisco Examiner* headlined its Sunday-morning edition with a story about President McKinley, who, under increasing pressure, was directing Navy Secretary Long to cable Admiral Dewey for information "concerning the fate of Gillmore of the *Yorktown* and the party under his charge captured or killed by the insurgents at Baler." McKinley instructed "both the army and navy to send relief expeditions to Baler both by land and by sea, and to spare no effort to either rescue the members of the naval party, or to punish the insurgents if they are dead." Indeed, the reach of Gillmore's influential family and friends extended directly into the White House.

The prisoners passed their time playing checkers, shooting pool on a makeshift table, and debating the slush of rumors swirling about the prison yard. Ramon Rey, an old Spanish officer who had befriended the American prisoners, finally delivered one tale with substance. A thirty-year resident of the Philippines who had married locally, Rey gushed forth with dramatic news: American forces were heading north in a major campaign to rout Aguinaldo and his diminishing band of officers. Liberation was but days away.

Meanwhile, the prison-guard force was doubled, as rebel soldiers and their trains of hastily loaded *carabao* carts scrambled toward the mountains. In the wake of their retreat, swarms of Spanish prisoners stumbled into San Isidro, pushed up from towns and villages as the fighting neared. It was now obvious: Filipino rebel forces were on the run.

The US Army, following its seizure of the insurgent capital at Malolos and a successful campaign eastward to Laguna Lake, was pushing north on two fronts. Two divisions, each wrapping around the eastern and western flanks of the Candaba Swamp in central Luzon, were now heading into the provinces of Pampanga and Bulacan. In the muddy slog north—rainy season was upon them—one division, under the command of General MacArthur, had captured the towns of Calumpit and San Fernando. In parallel, a second division, led by General Lawton, had captured the towns of Norzagaray, San Rafael, and Baliuag. Filipino units, demoralized and in retreat, were disintegrating as a conventional fighting force.

The two battle-hardened American generals—both Congressional Medal of Honor recipients for actions in the Civil War, and veterans of the bloody Indian Wars that had pacified the West—brought a wealth of military experience to the fight.

General Arthur MacArthur Jr. had entered the US Army in 1862 as a lieutenant in the 24th Wisconsin Infantry. Brevetted twice for bravery during the Civil War, MacArthur rose to the rank of colonel by 1865, only to endure decades of mundane, peacetime service as a captain in the Regular Army. Despite a rather smug bearing, long-windedness, and reputation for ambitious politicking and self-promotion, MacArthur, in fact, had proven his capacity to lead.

Major General Henry Ware Lawton—towering over his men at six-foot-three—was a hard-drinking, hot-tempered commander who devoted "every ounce of his 210 pounds . . . bone and sinew" to his military career. Battling chronic depression and alcoholism during much of his nearly forty years of military service, Lawton was one of America's most celebrated soldiers, and rightly so. Enlisting in the Civil War at age eighteen as a sergeant in the 9th Indiana Infantry, he saw action in twenty-eight major engagements. Later, Lawton studied law at Harvard, and then returned to the army for the Indian Wars, burnishing his reputation as a tenacious fighter. In 1886, Lawton won national fame for his capture of Geronimo, the fearless Apache leader who led one of the last organized Native American forces against the United States. Lawton went on to fight in the Spanish-American War, leading six thousand men in a confused and poorly managed fight at the Battle of El Caney, Cuba, finally linking up with forces at San Juan Hill to take the city of Santiago.

When not in a fight on the battlefield, Lawton was often at war with his own demons. Following the ineptly handled operation at El Caney, Lawton was appointed the island's military governor in August 1898, and immediately found himself adrift. During a weeklong, liquor-fueled binge, he broke up a local saloon and assaulted the local police chief, leaving his career in ruins. Begging for President McKinley's forgiveness, the aging Lawton was shipped off to the Philippines, with his beloved wife, Mame, and their four children. It was his last chance for redemption.

Now, on the soggy expanse of Luzon, the two US Army divisions under the generals' leadership were coping with an oppressive climate, poor supply logistics, and horrendous muddy tracks that comprised the country's primitive rural road network. They were slowly inching north, one arduous step at a time.

San Isidro soon fell into chaos. Gillmore and his sailors could see Filipinos—soldiers and civilians alike—running to and fro, streets filled with *carretons*, or native carts, "laden with all manner of household effects, and surrounded by panic-stricken, jabbering men, women and children, breaking for the mountains." On May 4, eleven short days after the Gillmore party's arrival, the prisoners were again ordered to move.

The Spaniard Ramon Rey, too old for drama and unwilling to leave his Filipino wife and family, had been feigning illness by dragging himself around with a cane in the hope that he'd be left behind. For the moment, it seemed his ruse was working. As his imprisoned American friends prepared to march, Rey offered to quietly pass on any messages once US Army forces arrived.

Albert Sonnichsen seized the opportunity to write to General Otis, commander of the US Armed Forces in the Philippines, to plead for a rescue mission. Gillmore also took time to craft a letter, but his was not addressed to his military superiors. Perhaps he did not expect their support, given his startling lapse in judgment at Baler. Or, perhaps he believed he knew a better way to instigate a rescue. In any event, Gillmore decided to write to his brother-in-law, Major Butler Price, commander of the 4th Infantry, who was in residence with his wife Clara, Gillmore's sister, at Manila's stately Hotel de Oriente. Since his marriage to Clara thirty-three years earlier, Major Price had served at army posts across the American West, fought the Utes in Colorado, and had seen action in Cuba at the Santiago campaign; in short, he was known as a man who could get things done. Gillmore again opted to play on his connections, this time pleading for his brother-in-law's personal intervention.

The fourteen prisoners were paid their per diem for rations and marched out of San Isidro's crumbling prison gates, accompanied by their Filipino guards and fifty Spanish prisoners. The retreating column totaled some eighty men, led by a rebel officer and Gillmore on ponies, and most others on foot. Those too ill to walk were pulled along in *carretons* by lumbering *carabao*. The procession tramped along rain-soaked roads, fording lagoons and swamps that seemed to never end. On May 29, having covered 136 miles over twenty-five days spent marching and camping through the settlements they passed, they dropped into a beautiful valley in the province of La Union. Edged by the foothills of the Cordilleras, the sun-splashed valley consisted of organized little villages that interspersed lush paddies of rice and vast fields of corn, sugarcane, tobacco, and bananas. By now, hundreds of additional Spanish prisoners had joined the column, swelling it to more than five hundred men.

A day later, all arrived at the shimmering blue South China Sea. The Gillmore party had just marched across the width of Luzon, east to west, from one coast to the other. Sixteen days behind the prisoners, American forces captured San Isidro after engaging a large insurgent force on its outskirts. But with supply lines exhausted, the Americans' northern campaign was about to stall. While the military offensive had been a success by many measures, it had only pushed Aguinaldo's army farther north and scattered the fight across even more demanding terrain. The insurgent capital had moved from Malolos to San Isidro to Tarlac, a frustratingly mobile government that eluded capture. Aguinaldo was on the run, but the unforgiving monsoon season had arrived. Further gains by the Americans would need to wait for better weather and additional reinforcements. For the time being, a waterlogged stalemate, provoked largely by nature, was at hand.

━ ⌒

On the distant eastern coast of Luzon, the three *Yorktown* sailors left behind at Baler were now being held under guard in a structure located across from the bamboo and *nipa* hut residence of the rebel *kapitan*, Novicio. Little record has survived of what transpired during the initial months of their captivity, but it appears the American prisoners were fed well enough, and at some point, their wounds were attended to by the Spanish surgeon, Dr. Vigil, who was otherwise holed up with his comrades in the church. The Filipinos had wisely allowed the doctor unfettered access from the besieged church to the town, where he attended to the medical needs of the wounded rebels and residents. Under Vigil's care, the three terminal phalanges of Coxswain Rynders's left hand, which had been cut off cleanly with a surgically sharp bolo, healed without further problems. Ordinary Seaman Woodbury was also lucky: The gaping wound to his torso, from a round on his own cartridge belt that had been driven deep into his flesh by a ricochet, avoided infection, and soon the boy was back on his feet.

Venville faced the most difficult recuperation. The rifle round that had clipped his ear had left a disfiguring loss of cartilage, but it was not life-threatening. And the penetrating ballistic trauma he had incurred from a bullet slicing cleanly through his neck—which miraculously missed his carotid arteries, jugular veins, windpipe, and gullet—was healing well. Two other injuries were more worrying. First, there was the deep gunshot wound that had entered his armpit and exited his shoulder, creating an unpredictable puncture wound that had caused severe tissue damage. Then there was the devastating gunshot that had ripped through his ankle, piercing tendons, muscles, ligaments, nerves, and bone, leaving the mechanically complex joint shattered beyond repair. The injury had completely disabled the boy, leaving him with an excruciatingly painful wound in a highly exudative state—meaning, it was a leaking, open mess. Without medicines to help fight infection and pain, we can be assured that Venville, already saddled with a weak constitution, was reduced to tormented agony day and night.

Across the Pacific Ocean, in the small Oregon town of Sellwood, just outside Portland, Venville's thirty-nine-year-old mother, Emily Mash, was mired in her own distress. The news of her son's capture at Baler, playing prominently in the *Portland Oregonian*, triggered great alarm at the Venville home, a simple, two-room shack that housed Emily, six children, two in-laws, and ailing husband Henry, who was in a long, miserable decline toward early death due to chronic lead poisoning from his job as a painter at the Puget Sound Naval Yard.

Emily, however, was a survivor: A poorly educated English immigrant from the tightly packed, disease-ridden tenements of Wolverhampton, an industrial West Midlands town known for its endless foundries, mills, and mines, she and her first husband, Densell Venville, a painter, had bravely forged a new life in America. When she faced Densell's sudden death in St. Paul, Minnesota, to unrecorded causes, Emily simply married her second husband, Harry Mash, another Englishman, just four months later, and pushed on to Oregon in search of better opportunities. Trained in England's woolen mills, Emily labored as a spinstress and weaver, and when those jobs dried up, toiled as a house servant in the wealthier local homes on the other side of town.

But now, the news of her oldest child's trial in the Philippines overwhelmed her. Her boy, she knew too well, was vulnerable and frail; indeed, he had taken to the sea in an effort to strengthen his precarious health. Perhaps they shared a special bond. He, the oldest boy, had dutifully dropped out of school to work at a local shop to help her make ends meet. She was the doting mother who would fret over his health. While at sea, Venville would write home regularly, and while it wasn't much, he would send along some of his meager nine-dollar-a-month salary. With Henry, the family's primary breadwinner, now unemployed and dying, toxic lead stripping his gut and causing bouts of confusion and irritability, those small financial contributions were surely missed all the more. For Emily, her son Denzell George Arthur Venville—Arthur, she called him—had served as her best hope for the future.

Unable to craft a written plea herself, Emily called to her daughter Regina, then thirteen years old, to compose the first of her letters. On April 19, 1899, Emily elected to shoot straight for the top, writing the Secretary of the Navy, seeking answers to her distress. It would be the first salvo in a relentless campaign in search of the truth.

<hr />

As the US Army bogged down in central Luzon, the Gillmore party was marched along the northwestern coast of Luzon, passing through a string of small towns, each anchored around an ancient stone church. After a total of thirty-three days on the move since leaving San Isidro, the column arrived at Vigan, the country's second-largest city. Threading a labyrinth of narrow, cobblestoned streets, the column again attracted a dense throng of curious onlookers. The prisoners pushed through the growing swarm, spilling into a large plaza ringed by handsome buildings and elegant shops, a number with large, plate-glass windows. With a boisterous mob at their heels, the prisoners were led through the iron gates of their new home: the pestilential city jail. It was Monday, June 5, 1899.

At this stage of their captivity, since departing the jail at San Isidro, the fourteen prisoners had covered over 226 miles on foot, most without shoes, subsisting, one remembered, on "the same daily ration of rice and rumors." Gillmore and his sailors had covered an additional ninety miles from Baler, bringing the total they had covered on foot to well over three hundred miles. At this juncture, they knew very little except this: Each step was taking them farther away from the US Army advance, making the odds of a rescue more remote than ever.

Perhaps they wondered whether Ramon Rey's ruse had indeed succeeded—if the Spanish prisoner, feigning infirmity, had been allowed to stay behind at San Isidro following the Filipinos' retreat. In fact, after the Americans arrived, Rey approached General Lawton and shared the letter of introduction he had been given by the American prisoners. With his identity confirmed, Rey then turned over the additional correspondence to the general, who assured him that the letters—from Sonnichsen, to the army, and from Gillmore, to his brother-in-law—would be delivered without delay.

Contact was about to be made.

CHAPTER TEN

A Ray of Light

SINCE THE BLOODY AMBUSH OF THE *YORKTOWN*'S 2ND CUTTER ON APRIL 12, 1899, life for the Spaniards holed up in the church at Baler had grown increasingly desperate. By May, after more than eleven months under siege, the last remnants of their coffee and beans gave out. Sustenance was now reduced to a kind of paste made from swamp cabbage, *kangkong,* mixed with rice and the remaining cans of sardines. Other sources of protein were now fair game: an errant dog, a passing cat, hapless lizards, and an ensnared crow or two. Tropical land snails, found in abundance, became a staple. The vegetation around the church was methodically stripped bare of its leaves, regardless of taste or toxicity. As the Spaniards edged toward starvation, angry sniping with the Filipino insurgents wore on.

On May 7, 1899, a *cazador* was gravely wounded in an exchange of gunfire and died days later. On May 19, disease carried off another man, this private succumbing to dysentery and becoming the seventeenth man to be buried on the church grounds.

In late May, an exasperated Lieutenant Colonel Tecson attempted another parley with the Spaniards. This time, he sent a newly arrived emissary, Cristobal Castañeda Aguilar, who had been tasked by Spanish general Diego de los Rios to bring in the unyielding detachment. A confused daylong negotiation ensued. Lieutenant Cerezo was obstinate; he refused to believe his fellow countryman was who he claimed to be, and he waved aside the news Aguilar shared. It was inconceivable that the Philippine colony had fallen, or that the war with the Americans was over. Cerezo was convinced that this parley was another ruse. Making no headway, a thoroughly frustrated Aguilar threw up his hands and prepared to withdraw. As a final act, he left a bundle of recent Spanish newspapers on the ground, a last-ditch effort to provide the crazed holdouts a glimpse of the world beyond their blinding realm of madness.

Inside, as extreme hunger loomed, Cerezo and his emaciated men initiated a new plan to escape to the surrounding forest, make their way to the coast, and flag down a passing Spanish warship. It was their only chance, they believed. Otherwise, with rations exhausted, they would surely starve to death in the church. The plan was set in motion on the morning of Thursday, June 1, 1899. All extra arms were collected and destroyed, to ensure that they did not fall into Filipino hands, and the remaining Mauser ammunition for the rifles was distributed among the men.

To ensure stealth and speed, Cerezo decided to exclude from the plan Corporal Gonzales and Private Menache, the two prisoners being held for attempted desertion. They could easily undermine the plot. Without much hesitation, Cerezo ordered the two men executed. The soldiers were solemnly marched out to the corral, blindfolded, and backed up against the low stone wall. A firing line was assembled, and without legal formality, the Spaniards were shot and buried on the grounds of the church.

The sun began to set over the mountains, revealing on that crisp, clear night a yellowing half-crescent moon. Along the *insurrecto* trenches, however, Cerezo and his men sensed renewed vigilance. Had the Filipinos learned of their impending flight? Or had the volley of gunfire from the executioners' rifles suggested an escape plan unfolding? A choice had to be made: They either had to charge through enemy lines and race to the forest, or, delay their escape until the Filipinos lowered their guard. After deliberating, the Spaniards decided to wait.

The besieged men passed the night fitfully. Cerezo slept less than the others, more paranoid than usual, troubled by Aguilar's Spanish newspapers. Something was wrong. The sophistication of the latest ruse was remarkable, as the newspapers looked almost genuine. Under the cool blue morning light, a bleary-eyed Cerezo again revisited the papers, marveling at the deception. As he turned the pages of *El Imparcial,* he glanced from one headline to another. *Astonishing, really, how well the Filipinos can imitate,* he thought. His eyes fell on a small notice, several lines only, referring to a lieutenant of the Infantry Reserve, Francisco Diaz Navarro, who had been ordered to take a post at the Andalusian city of Malaga. Coincidentally, the officer had been Cerezo's close acquaintance at a previous post. Only Cerezo knew that his fellow lieutenant was planning to ask for an assignment at that Mediterranean coastal city, where his family and sweetheart lived.

Suddenly, Cerezo knew that the news about Navarro could not have been invented. Logically, he reasoned, if that fact was true, the other facts were also true, and the newspapers were real. The colonies indeed had been lost. More striking, the little bit of earth that he and his men had "defended even to madness" was not theirs. The entire siege, and the steep human cost incurred, had been pointless. He later wrote that as these realizations swept over him, it was as if "a ray of light suddenly illumined the pit in which we were about to fall headlong." The race to the forest was a high-stakes gamble in the first place, hinging on the ability to flag down a Spanish warship. Now, given the impossibility of encountering such a ship, a trek into the unforgiving forest meant almost-certain death.

A sickened Cerezo called his men together and shared his epiphany. He struggled to articulate the reality he now knew to be true. The stunned men alternately wept and objected. Finally, it was agreed, only one option remained: surrender.

On Friday, June 2, 1899, three days before Gillmore and his fellow prisoners stumbled into Vigan, the targets of their failed rescue had negotiated the terms of their surrender at Baler with the Filipino forces that had encircled them for eleven deadly months. The earth-filled crates that had barricaded the entrances to the church were removed and its doors cast open. Apprehensively, the hollow survivors, dressed in rags and shod with worn leather scraps and twine, stepped into the sharp sunlight. Greeting them was an angry town in devastation. Some nine-tenths of Baler proper had been burned to the ground during the Spaniards' hit-and-run arson attacks, and now, some fifty homes were little more than charred timber and ash. The dazed Spaniards relinquished their Mausers, the very weapons with which they had so relentlessly punished their besiegers.

The broken Spanish detachment entered a new world of freedom with great fear, and, for the first time, unarmed. Tecson ordered Filipino sentries posted at the doors of the church, fearful that local citizens, furious at the havoc the Spaniards had wrought, might seek revenge. The men were obviously starved, and in a gesture of magnanimity, the *komandante* ordered fresh meat and other foodstuffs delivered to the church.

After 337 days, the siege of Baler had come to an end. Of the fifty-two Spaniards originally locked in the church on June 30, 1898, fifteen had succumbed to disease, two had died from their wounds, two had deserted, and two had been executed, leaving thirty-one alive. With the later addition of the two priests, a total of thirty-three men had survived the ordeal.

Franciscan priests Lopez and Minaya had refused to sign the surrender agreement, claiming they lacked the authority to do so. It was a decision they would soon regret. As the Spaniards packed for their march to Aguinaldo's headquarters in Tarlac, and then on to Manila, Tecson advised that the priests would not be allowed to leave. They had been prisoners of the Filipinos before they had fled in cowardly fashion into the church. They were not part of the surrender agreement. An infuriated Cerezo argued with the *komandante*, but the point was not negotiable. The priests stayed.

Just as the Spaniards (pictured here) capitulated to Filipino forces at Baler and were returning home to Spain, their failed American rescuers, Lieutenant Gillmore and the sailors from the *USS Yorktown,* were being marched deeper into Luzon as valuable prisoners of war.

Tecson decided to use the cover of the Spaniards' departure to move the three remaining *Yorktown* prisoners farther north, into the mountains of Nueva Vizcaya province. There, they would be out of reach of any American forces that might attempt a rescue. Since the ambush of Gillmore's cutter two months earlier, Rynders and Woodbury had sufficiently healed, but Venville was still crippled and in poor health. Since Venville would not be able to undertake the strenuous march, Tecson ultimately decided to keep him at Baler, along with the two Spanish priests.

On the afternoon of Tuesday, June 6, Tecson ordered his men to bring Rynders and Woodbury to the church in preparation for their march across the mountains. Presumably, with a distressed Venville looking on, the two sailors packed the meager belongings they had accumulated during their seven-week stay at Baler. It is not known whether the American men discussed how they might bring Venville along. Tecson, however, had forbidden it, thinking perhaps that the crippled boy would only slow the column down and place it at risk. No doubt with heavy hearts, Rynders and Woodbury bade their comrade Venville farewell.

At the church, Rynders and Woodbury, finally meeting the objectives of their failed rescue mission, were "made most welcome by the Spaniards," though "this reception was a bit cock-eyed, of course, on account of nobody understanding each other's lingo." Woodbury, recounting events in the church for the 34th Infantry regimental historian, Charles Manahan, recalled how the men whiled away the evening after a rich dinner of rice and beans. "Here's a little unimportant thing that occurred that night in the church, which I have not forgotten and never will—it's not a very polite thing to put in words in a letter, but I think you'll understand. We used to do it occasionally in the Navy, and you birds in the Army being no more or less human must have also, and that was a contest of real 'Bronx cheers.'" Unable to converse, the two *Yorktown* sailors and the surrendered Spanish detachment communicated with one of the universal languages at their disposal—bodily sounds from the passing of gas. The vanquished Spaniards and wounded Americans spent the evening in laughter, competing in a contest of farts.

The next morning, Rynders and Woodbury, along with the Spaniards and their guards, began the grueling journey over the Sierra Madres. Unbeknownst to them, their path would trace the route taken by Gillmore and their crewmates less than two months earlier. The two young priests, held behind and surely knocking themselves for their own stupidity, were transferred to the house holding Venville, taking the place of the two Americans who had departed.

For the Spaniards now being marched, unconditional surrender did not eliminate their woes. Over the many months of the siege, the tale of their lengthy sniping campaign on Baler had been widely shared. As a result, during their march to Aguinaldo's headquarters, they were harassed, stoned, spit upon, and beaten by an angry local populace bent on seeking vengeance. At Pantabangan, Cerezo escaped an attempt on his life by jumping from a window, severely dislocating his ankle in the process. A day later, Cerezo's personal effects, along with those of Surgeon Vigil, loaded on a *carabao*, were stolen. The angry Spaniards attempted to file a complaint with the Filipino officer in command, but their efforts were ignored.

At the town of Bongabon, the two American sailors, Rynders and Woodbury, were separated from the Spaniards and marched another sixty miles in a northern direction, to Bayombong, the capital of Nueva Vizcaya province. Here, under the watchful eye of General Fernando Canon and his forces, the two sailors could be held safely, far from the reach of American forces.

Cerezo and his fellow Spaniards continued their march west across central Luzon. An astute Aguinaldo was keenly aware that the newspapers in Manila, and perhaps in Spain and America, were characterizing the Spaniards at Baler as a plucky band of heroes who had survived the Filipino siege against all odds. In this, the rebel general saw an opportunity to demonstrate the civility of his leadership, which in turn would strengthen his claim to self-government. Upon the Spaniards' arrival, Aguinaldo showered the surrendered men with gifts and praise. He issued a decree that declared the survivors "worthy of the admiration of the world for the valor, determination, and heroism with which that handful of men, cut off and without any hope of aid, defended their flag over the course of a year, realizing an epic so glorious and worthy of the legendary valor of El Cid and Pelayo."

Aguinaldo was clever, appealing to deep-seated Spanish sentiments by referencing the nation's foremost heroes—Pelagius of Asturias, the eighth-century Visigoth nobleman who had led the Christian reconquest of the Iberian peninsula from North African Moors, and El Cid Campeador, Rodrigo Diaz de Vivar, the eleventh-century Castilian nobleman who carried on the struggle against the Muslims, conquering Valencia and emerging as a symbol of Spain's national awakening. Aguinaldo boldly announced that the liberated Spaniards were to be treated not as prisoners but as friends.

A parley was held between Filipino and American forces to secure safe transport of the Spanish detachment through the lines of battle. Once in Manila, the stupefied survivors were feted with financial aid, congratulations, and entertainment. Yet, despite the accolades, abundant skepticism swirled in circles of gossip and the media. What impelled the defenders of Baler to prolong the siege beyond the realm of reason? Did they fear punishment? And was it true that Las Morenas and Alonso had tried to surrender, only to be struck down by their own men? Those seeking answers were met with a conspiracy of silence. No one, it seemed, was talking.

On July 20, 1899, the survivors sailed for Spain, where they were greeted with great fanfare. In the weeks that followed, the nation's heroes dispersed and went their separate ways, returning to their hometowns to receive more rewards, medals, and honorary pensions.

Months later, the Spanish newspaper *Heraldo de Madrid*, still smarting over the collapse of empire and military defeat to the Americans, published a brash, albeit wildly inaccurate, story. It claimed that American forces then in Baler had been forced to surrender to rebel forces. It concluded with a summation of the Spanish detachment's experience:

Baler was consecrated by the blood of martyrs and heroes, and such achievements as theirs are not to be paralleled, cannot be boasted by any other nation. Haughty North Americans have immense riches, extensive possessions, but she has no Siege of Baler, and she never will.

CHAPTER ELEVEN

Prison

IN THE SQUALID VIGAN JAIL, THE HEALTH OF THE PRISONERS WITH Lieutenant Gillmore began to fail. Insufficient food, poor sanitation, and exposure to disease drained the color from their faces and carved away their weight. A few fell violently ill. Gillmore wrote a series of urgent letters to the town's mayor, the *presidente,* and the Filipino military command, demanding medical attention for his increasingly listless prisoners. The entreaties fell on deaf ears.

Sonnichsen, the civilian quartermaster, suffered from festering tropical ulcers on his right foot that completely disabled him. Landsman Edwards, battling violent diarrhea, visibly wasted away. "This, together with the ragged state of our wardrobe, gave us the appearance of an advance guard of famine, or we might have been the crew of that ship in which the 'Ancient Mariner' made his eventful voyage," Sonnichsen recalled.

Vigan's residents, and surprisingly, the *alcalde* (prison warden), took pity on the prisoners. It could have been the novelty of American captives, or the cultural importance to hardworking Ilocanos to be seen as gracious hosts. Or maybe, given that American forces were rumored to be on the advance, they thought a demonstration of compassion might pay dividends in the future. Whatever the motivation, the *alcalde* visited the men, accompanied by wealthy local merchant Pedro Rivera. Trailing behind was Rivera's servant, his arms overflowing with a stack of clothes. Rivera cheerfully explained that he had collected the items from his many friends about town, all of whom were eager to give what they could. "Help yourself," he urged. The grateful prisoners rummaged through the pile, sorting coats, shorts, pants, and pajamas in all sizes and colors.

News of the unusual delivery trickled back to the Filipino officer in command of the region, General Manuel Tinio, and it enraged him. That same evening, he summoned Rivera to his office and threatened the merchant with imprisonment if he ever again attempted to help the enemy. For good measure, Tinio declared the prisoners *incommunicados,* and posted additional guards. The threat of death hung over anyone who engaged the prisoners. From then on, even casual passersby avoided going anywhere near the jail.

General Tinio, almost twenty-two, was now in control of the Gillmore party's survival. Appointed governor of the Ilocos province and commanding general of northern Luzon nine months earlier, the handsome ladies' man had rapidly ascended among the ranks to become one of four senior commanders of Aguinaldo's Army of Liberation. Tinio's military force stood at just under eighteen hundred men, including officers, bolo men, armorers, medics, telegraphers, artillerymen, and, to help with the design and construction of defensive trench works at strategic points across the region, two Spanish engineers. Now, Tinio had a band of American prisoners who might one day have value. For the time being, the youthful general was happy to leave his enemies to rot in prison.

General Manuel Tinio (center) with fellow officers and aides de camp.

The greatest risk now to the Gillmore party was not the violence of war, but the impoverished landscape of the Philippines itself. Pathogens swirled in their midst, encouraged by a trying climate that bred infection. Dysentery, typhoid, and malaria stood as ever-present killers. As Walton recalled, "In the daytime we had to put up with great swarms of flies, and at night the mosquitoes gave us no peace. We also had a full allowance of bedbugs, lizards, rats, and mice." Sonnichsen was the first to fall violently ill, with bloody diarrhea, abdominal cramps, and fever, leaving him curled up in agony on the bamboo-slat bed in his dank, fetid cell.

And if the threats of bacteria, parasites, and malnutrition were not enough, the high heat and humidity presented a final, almost insulting blow to their health. All the men suffered from severe skin irritations and Dhobie itch—a persistent skin ailment of the crotch. Some battled tropical, or phagedenic, ulcers, often originating from small, even innocuous wounds around the ankle or lower leg, caused by something as simple as a brush against a sharp rock, swiping a barbed plant, or the bite of an insect. The small abrasion quickly became infected from exposure to an anaerobic bacterium, *Fusobacterium ulcerans*, found in the island's muddy, stagnant water. The wound then swelled into a blister that would eventually burst, leaving a raw, festering ulcer that refused to heal. A necrotic black coating formed, emitting the stench of rotten flesh. On some of the prisoners, the depth of the putrid ulcers revealed tendon and bone. In these desperate conditions, the prisoners were starting down the slow spiral path toward early death.

Gillmore's increasingly strident letters to his captors appealed for relief. Finally, around July 2, Tinio's adjutant, Lieutenant Colonel Blas Villamor, visited the prison. He took note of the wasting prisoners and promised to send along a doctor. Having dead Americans on their hands, rather than pawns for some future exchange, obviously served no purpose.

Holding true to his promise, Villamor dispatched two Spanish hospital stewards, *practicantes*, to the jail the following day. Sonnichsen, gravely ill, was transferred to the local hospital for treatment. Located along the town plaza, the facility catered to dying Spaniards. Not much more than living skeletons, many of the patients were suffering from a lethal mix of malnutrition, beriberi, and dysentery. The Filipino doctor on duty at the facility, Gabino Castro, assessed Sonnichsen's condition and doped him on opium, the drug of choice for dysentery, sending the quartermaster into a senseless, deep sleep for a period of several groggy, forgotten days.

On July 8, it was Apprentice Peterson's turn to fall seriously ill, and he was moved to the hospital that evening. On arrival, the sailor looked so bad that Sonnichsen barely recognized him. A week later, a third prisoner succumbed to dysentery and joined the growing patient list. Around the Americans, the Spaniards continued to die of disease. Over the course of his two-month stay at the hospital, Sonnichsen kept a grim body count of the dying Spaniards—fourteen—whose remains were carted away for burial.

A resilient Peterson was soon back on his feet and returned to the jail, swapping places with Army Private Bruce and Landsman Edwards, the next set of patients. Bruce was suffering from the first stages of tuberculosis, while Edwards battled a severe stomach ailment. Prisoners came and went, but Sonnichsen remained hospitalized; his dysentery was cured, but deep tropical ulcers now attacked his legs. On July 19, Vaudoit fell ill and was transferred to the hospital. It had become a medical merry-go-round.

The monsoon rains continued through August. Under a leaking jail-cell roof, the increasingly irritable prisoners slept poorly, moving about constantly to avoid falling and the ever-increasing pools of water. At the end of their tethers, civilian prospector O'Brien and Army Private Bishop exchanged words, tempers flared, and soon the men were throwing punches. Too weak to do much damage, they exhausted themselves just as their Filipino guards charged into the cell with fixed bayonets. Staring down at the battered, wheezing men, the guards demanded to know why they were fighting, but neither spoke. After news of the fight was delivered to Tinio, he ordered the Englishman O'Brien separated from the Americans, assuming it was a clash of cultures.

On August 18, five bruised and beaten Spaniards were thrown into O'Brien's cell, where they shared an extraordinary tale. They had attempted to escape in a fifteen-foot boat they had found along the shore, but ended up fighting a heavy wind and uncooperative sea for two exhausting days. Driven back into the coast, they washed up less than ten miles from where they had started, only to be met by an angry pack of bolo-wielding insurgents. Assuming the escapees were Americans, the Filipinos had prepared to kill them. The Spaniards had frantically proved their nationality and were taken into custody. Marched back to Vigan, they were brought before their former captors and tried for the crime of escape. Each man was sentenced to receive twenty-five lashes, which took place in Vigan's plaza, in front of an excited crowd.

Over a group supper, one of the men, a Spanish quartermaster, explained that he had somehow insulted Tinio during the trial. Well known for his short temper, the general had exploded. He unholstered his revolver and held it to the man's head, threatening to shoot him dead if he uttered another word. The quartermaster kept silent, and while his life was spared, he earned an additional twenty-five lashes for his supposed insolence. The Spaniard pulled up his shirt to show the result of the fifty lashes he had received. Deep lacerations had torn the skin and left raw, bloody, exposed flesh, from shoulder to rump. "If that man got any sleep he must have got it standing up," surmised Hospital Corpsman Huber, "for I am positive, a person in such condition he was in, could neither sit nor lie down and sleep."

Three days later, Tinio made a surprise visit to the jail. He had received a desperate letter from Gillmore a few days earlier and wanted to see for himself how the men were faring. The Americans played it up, sending the four most pathetic-looking among them to stand dejectedly against the prison bars. Tinio came as far as the arched gateway that led into the yard. The gazes of the general and the half-starved men locked for an uncomfortable moment before the general withdrew. The men were sure they had made an impression, and they were right. Five days later, orders arrived that granted the men permission to walk for an hour each afternoon along the road fronting the jail, fifty feet in each direction. The opportunity for sunshine, fresh air, and exercise was a huge relief, helping the men to cope with their filthy, claustrophobic confinement.

In early September 1899, with American warships on patrol along the coast, the prisoners heard fresh rumors that suggested American infantry were making gains to the south and were on their way to Vigan. The prisoners assumed they would be relocated once again to a more-distant location, and they were right. Early on September 6, the fourteen prisoners, under a guard of twenty-four rebel soldiers, were marched out of jail and loaded on rafts along the banks of the Abra River. For two days, they pushed up the river, past the settlement of San Quintin, and into the Cordillera Mountains. At Bangued, the capital of the province of Abra, the prisoners were led to a new jail and again confined.

Although the new prison was cramped, the captives' new *alcalde* was a man of some warmth and generosity. Gillmore was given a room at the front of the building, with ample sunlight and a pleasant view overlooking the plaza. The other prisoners, due to space limitations, were confined to the only other option, a large, gloomy cell in the rear. Sonnichsen, still suffering from his ulcers, was transferred to the town's small infirmary. Brown, the Canadian, was still working his angles, and managed to take up quarters with the local priest. And because he wasn't a prisoner, he was given liberty of the town. Occasionally, Brown stopped by the jail to deliver tobacco to his expatriate comrades, and one day made the effort to deliver a small, reddish-brown, long-tailed macaque to Harry Huber. The monkey brought a bit of rare laughter and amusement to the men, the con man Brown proving to have some use after all.

Bruce and Edwards fell upon a plan to eat better by roping Gillmore into their mess hall arrangements. They brashly proposed to Gillmore that they would do all the cooking for their group mess if the lieutenant would contribute his generous twenty *centimos* per diem to the kitty. With a combined total of forty *centimos,* all three men could eat better, and Gillmore would avoid having to cook for himself. Gillmore quickly agreed to the lopsided arrangement, Edwards recalled, "as he was very vain, and being an officer, above the common herd." Gillmore felt that cooking his own food was beneath him; for Bruce and Edwards, this aspect of the lieutenant's arrogance turned out to be an unexpected boon.

By now, the *Yorktown* sailors held Gillmore directly responsible for their predicament. As Edwards assessed:

> *He was a more or less harmless guy, one who I would assume would appear to be at his best in a cocktail lounge surrounded by young Geisha girls who would swoon at the presence of anyone wearing an officer's uniform covered with gold braid. He was a little out of his element on this part of the trip, but since most of us thought he got us the tickets, we saw to it that he could not make the pretense to the natives of us being his servants. Several of the fellows made it pretty clear that he was just another prisoner.*

The enlisted men had sized Gillmore up just about right. Born of fleeting privilege and wealth that had since evaporated, the lieutenant still possessed an unshakable sense of entitlement. It was all the more remarkable given his middling achievements in the navy. Gillmore's worst enemy, proven time and again, was his own deep-seated arrogance and abiding belief that he was exceptional.

———

Gillmore's career, despite his initial foundering at the Naval Academy, had started out well enough in August 1876, as midshipman aboard the USS *Hartford*, a twenty-year-old Civil War–era sloop-of-war that served as the flagship for the North Atlantic squadron. Gillmore then started the long, slow climb up the navy hierarchy, deploying on a mix of ships in the Atlantic and Pacific squadrons, and making the rank of ensign three years later. By 1879, he was aboard the 1,150-ton USS *Jamestown*, a thirty-five-year-old sail- and steam-powered sloop that had been tasked to the Alaskan port of Sitka, helping to sort troubles that had been brewing between white settlers and native Tlingit Indians. Between keeping the peace and negotiating often-fractious issues between residents, the *Jamestown* undertook a survey of the new possession, charting the Alexander Archipelago and Glacier Bay, where the crew named much of the geography after themselves. Today, five small spits of land in Sitka Sound are known as the Gillmore Islands, and other islands, glaciers, coves, straits, and islets remain a part of the *Jamestown*'s legacy in Alaska.

At this frozen outpost, Ensign Gillmore fell in love. Mary S. Ball, the belle of the post and daughter of Alaska's chief customs collector, Mottram Dulany Ball, had caught his eye. On May 12, 1882, James Gillmore, twenty-seven, and Mary, twenty-one, were married.

After a brief honeymoon, and with Mary ensconced in a new home in Washington, D.C., Gillmore was back at sea, aboard the USS *Iroquois* for a three-year cruise that brought him to South America, Hawaii, Australia, and the Pacific Islands. It was largely uneventful, except for a brief brush with action in April 1885, when the ship was rushed to Panama to put down a brewing rebellion. At the port of Colon, the terminus to a critical railroad link that traversed the Isthmus of Panama and connected the Caribbean Sea to the Pacific Ocean, Gillmore was responsible for landing a battery of Gatling guns that allowed marines to fend off rebels and protect the expatriate community. By all reports, it was a commendable performance.

In time, Gillmore was keen to come home to his bride. He pursued a series of desk assignments in Washington—at the Naval Library, Navy War College, and as a torpedo service instructor. Promotion to lieutenant junior grade followed. But just several years on the home front were apparently enough, and by 1887, the open seas, higher pay, and prospects for further career advancement all beckoned. At his insistence, Gillmore was assigned to the USS *Marion,* an aging sloop-of-war in the Asiatic Squadron, for another three-year cruise.

Gillmore returned home in June 1890 and focused on starting a family. On January 17, 1891, his son Stuart was born, just as Gillmore reached the rank of lieutenant. Between assignments at the Bureau of Equipment, Gillmore was ordered out on several short cruises: on the 839-ton USS *Bancroft,* one of the navy's new steel gunboats; on the 1,170-ton USS *Machias,* a new schooner-rigged gunboat, for a seven-month shakedown cruise; and on the one-of-a-kind USS *Vesuvius,* a 930-ton experimental unarmored dynamite gunboat, for another seven months. By 1894, after twelve years of marriage, boredom once again set in, and Gillmore chased another long-term assignment at sea. Assigned to the *Machias* for a second time, tasked to patrol the Far East, the forty-year-old Gillmore was exposed to a wide swath of Asia and its raucous ports.

It was around this time that Gillmore began to falter. While on liberty in bustling Shanghai in October 1895, the naval officer spent an evening at the plush Shanghai Club, considered the port's most exclusive club. It rapidly spiraled into a night of excess, with the lieutenant imbibing an unhealthy portion of what the *New York Times* hailed as the club's famed stock of "rare wines, excellent brandies, better whiskies and unsurpassed cigars." As the evening unfolded, likely starting with an elaborate meal in one of its dining rooms, and then moving to perhaps the library or billiards rooms, if not straight to the bar itself, a heavily intoxicated Gillmore lost control. A discussion with fellow patrons grew into an argument and then spilled over into physical confrontation. In a fit of cursing and invective, Gillmore slapped another officer, an English captain from the P&O, the Peninsular and Oriental Steam Navigation Company, whose ships ran the mail for the British Admiralty. For those present, it was behavior that crossed the line.

Within days, the Shanghai Club issued a letter that permanently banned Gillmore from its premises, but that was just the start of it. Gillmore's commanding officer, Edwin S. Houston, having warned the lieutenant to take control of his drinking just a week prior, suspended him from duty. In a spirited defense, a dissembling Gillmore refuted the charges:

I must call attention to the fact that the offense for which I was punished was reported by civilians, that I was given no opportunity to make any defense nor to rectify the serious error which has been entered on my record. . . . The absence of reliable witnesses of my own nationality renders it particularly difficult to substantiate this denial. . . . I consider the whole affair an exaggeration of a trivial difference between the person whom I slapped and myself. . . . and while I regret having lost my temper, under what I consider sufficient justification, there is no question of influence of liquor in the action.

Drink would again get the best of Gillmore eight months later. At the port of Yokohama, while attending a high-society event at the elegant Grand Hotel, a deeply inebriated Gillmore staggered onto the dance floor. The details of what followed are sketchy, but we can imagine the scene. More than likely, he approached several society ladies and slurred some unknowable inanities while pawing at them as a sailor might grope the cheap hookers found elsewhere around the port. Maybe he forced them to dance, roughly swinging them about, himself barely able to stand. Perhaps he collapsed on the floor, a total drunken mess. Whatever occurred, he deeply embarrassed several ladies in his company and completely disgraced himself in front of his fellow officers.

Confronted again by Commander Houston, Gillmore flatly rejected the accusations, writing, "I must plead ignorance of any behavior that could be so construed, and I assert, most positively, that I have always endeavored, and I believe with a fair measure of success, to do a gentleman's duty toward a lady as long as I have been in the service. I regret that such a stigma should be attached to my record after 25 years of service."

The defense didn't wash. Gillmore was suspended from duty, placed under arrest, and ordered to face court-martial proceedings aboard the USS *Detroit* at Yokohama. Unable to muster a defense, Gillmore pleaded guilty to "the disgrace brought by this officer, upon himself and the naval service, by his appearance in uniform, in the presence of ladies and gentlemen, in a confessedly drunken condition."

To keep Gillmore from further trouble, the court ordered him confined to the limits of the ship for three months. However, the lieutenant quickly became a nuisance and perhaps kept on with his drinking.

An exasperated Houston finally ordered his incorrigible subordinate to the Naval Hospital at Yokohama to dry out. After six weeks, chastened and apparently sober, Gillmore slunk back to the ship, but with his career in tatters. He was yanked from his cruise and assigned to a desk job at the Coast Survey. Aboard ship, the navy had decided, the lieutenant was a liability.

Gillmore's exile to land was short-lived. By early 1898, as war with Spain began to brew, the navy needed all of its officers on deck. The desk-bound Gillmore soon found himself back at sea, assigned as a navigator aboard the USS *Saint Paul,* a massive 14,910-ton, 554-foot-long former passenger vessel that had been hastily outfitted with guns and pressed into service. On June 28, 1898, in waters off Puerto Rico, Gillmore was on the bridge of the *Saint Paul* as she fiercely engaged the *Terror,* a 370-ton Spanish destroyer. The encounter between the unwieldy former ocean liner and a nimble warship brought a surprise outcome: The *Terror* took a direct hit, leaving her badly damaged and the captain with no choice but to beach her on the shores at San Juan. Gillmore, finally, had seen some real action.

In September 1898, as the war came to a close, Gillmore took command of his first ship, the USS *Porter,* a 165-ton torpedo boat, but only shepherded it to decommissioning at New York. His next assignment, less than three months in duration, was equally uninteresting: command of a 775-ton civilian steam yacht, a two-masted rigged schooner used for running dispatches from Guantanamo. His orders were to bring her out of Cuban waters for a retrofit into an armed gunboat. Gillmore, at this stage of his career, was little more than a ship jockey, running vessels to and from ports for either maintenance or salvage.

Languishing at the rank of lieutenant at age forty-four, Gillmore knew that if his naval career was to prosper, he needed to see combat service. At the moment, the growing insurrection in the Philippines offered the only opportunity for such adventure and advancement. Gillmore pressed hard for an assignment. By late 1898, despite his checkered reputation, the politicking prevailed. On January 14, 1899, Gillmore was ordered to Manila, and within days of arrival, found himself in charge of the *Yorktown*'s cutter, on a quiet, misty morning, at the mouth of the Baler River. Gillmore must have known that this was likely his last chance for a display of heroics that might advance his sagging career.

The high altitude and relatively cool climate of Bangued proved a boon for the Gillmore party prisoners. Moreover, the jail was clean, the *alcalde* relaxed in disposition, and the residents downright friendly. Community leaders visited in their cells and gifted the prisoners with tobacco and food as tokens of goodwill. Three days after arriving in Bangued, the prisoners were given even more stunning news: The *alcalde* announced that the captives would be allowed to go about the town, freed from their cells at sunrise with the expectation that they return by dusk.

Through this unusual arrangement, civilian prisoner Sonnichsen was introduced by Brown to the wealthy Don Isidro Paredes, a former lawyer in Manila who had served as a representative at the Malolos Congress. In his early thirties, the stout man with sharply cut features was well versed in the arts, literature, and law. He spoke passionately about the importance of education for the country's next generation. Sonnichsen seized on this idea and suggested setting up an English class for the town's children. Within days, fourteen children from well-to-do families were assembled at the Paredes residence for classes taught by Sonnichsen.

Such was the success of the program that Don Isidro requested lessons for himself, along with his younger brother Quintin, a boy of fifteen. Sonnichsen was soon earning ten *pesos* per month between his teaching two English classes and his prisoner's per diem. Hospital Corpsman Huber joined, teaching another two of the Paredes boys. Not one to miss out on an opportunity, Landsman Edwards took up teaching a group of five Chinese traders, which earned him a small amount of cash, along with salted eggs and candied fruit. Soon, the British civilian O'Brien and army privates Bruce and Honnyman jumped on the bandwagon. Even old Vaudoit, the *Yorktown*'s sailmaker's mate, found one resident keen to learn his native French. Suddenly, Bangued was the country's epicenter of foreign language instruction.

On September 16, 1899, the *Boston Globe* provided new information about the fate of Gillmore, while passing harsh judgment on the US Navy for its lack of progress in securing the rescue of the lieutenant and his party. "It has been more than six months since the Navy Department heard anything definite in regard to the fate of Lieut. Gillmore and the party of 14 enlisted men from the *Yorktown*, who disappeared at Baler," the paper reported, adding, "[N]othing appears to have been done toward finding Gillmore and the bluejackets." A Spanish planter identified as Señor Garza had escaped, the story claimed, and made it to Manila, reporting he had seen Gillmore and his men at Vigan, "where they were subsisting off of a meager quantity of rice, in quantity not more than can be purchased for one *peseta* per man per day." All were showing "the effect of their confinement and the poor and insufficient food." Garza explained that the captives "could not stand such hardship and such fare much longer."

The Spaniard provided further intelligence on the Army of Liberation. Its forces contained eight thousand men under arms, who were increasingly being equipped with Mausers and better weapons "at an alarming rate." Some of the Filipino soldiers donned the uniforms of American soldiers, including new cork helmets, which were looted from the steamer *Centennial* after it had run into a reef in northern Luzon. "The ginger ale," the story concluded, "which was part of the plunder, was shipped to Aguinaldo's camp."

On September 18, the captives were presented with a new surprise: the remainder of three *carreton*-loads of provisions sent by the US government across enemy lines to the prisoners the previous June, when they were marching to Vigan. The prisoners had learned there were three large carts of provisions hauled by *carabao*, as the Canadian Brown had earlier managed to finagle a portion of the supplies for himself. Of the original thirty cases, less than a half of one remained. The rest had been waylaid, picked through by the Filipinos, and spoiled by exposure; what was left was now only arriving, nearly three months later.

The delivery included twenty-one tins of condensed milk, ten tins of peaches, a tin of Boston baked beans, two pounds of spoiled ground coffee, seven half-empty bottles of ginger ale, six packages of tobacco, and two empty jars of jam. Dividing the provisions among fourteen men left each with just a few tins and a deep sense of disappointment.

Despite these setbacks, by now Gillmore owned several changes of clothes, and had managed to buy himself a pair of fine boots with his accumulated per diem. Others in the Gillmore party also made out well. A Chinese merchant had given Sonnichsen a pair of canvas shoes and two pairs of socks in exchange for teaching him a few phrases of English.

Villamor had gifted him with a new straw hat, and the local hospital doctor's wife had her servants handle Sonnichsen's laundry. On balance, not bad for a prisoner of war. "But for whatever little comforts we enjoyed," Sonnichsen would recall, "we did not owe any thanks to the Government, but to the good people of Bangued."

In October, the eldest daughter of Don Isidro was to be married, and Sonnichsen and Brown were invited. It was a lavish affair, beginning with a 6:00 a.m. wedding at the church, the wedding entourage arriving in festive *piña* cloth, flowers in all the bridesmaids' hair, conveyed in a carriage drawn by two white horses. The groom and his groomsmen, dressed in smart black suits, followed in another carriage. Following the ceremony, with a brass band leading, the crowd of one hundred strong started off to Don Isidro's house for a sumptuous breakfast feast. Lucas, the eldest brother of Don Isidro, played the piano, accompanied by a violinist, while groups of guests danced and played card games, chess, and dominoes. Between dances there were recitations, followed by a luncheon and more speeches.

Lucas made the most memorable speech of the day:

But let us all be merry this day at least, and let the good feelings of brothers and friends exist among us. We are assembled here, Spaniards, Americans and Filipinos, representatives of the three factors in the present trouble. We may all be good patriots to our different causes and countries, and fight for our different flags if necessary, but why should the troubles and quarrels of our respective governments be imitated by individuals? Although we may be at war with Spain or America, may we not clasp the hand of a Spaniard or an American and call him friend? I think we may. I am Filipino, and always will be, but when I clasp the hand of a friend I do not ask: Is he also a Filipino? Or is he a Spaniard or a German? That he is my friend suffices, that he is a man and has good qualities of a true man—therein lies the distinction. Let us then today forget politics and national prejudices, and meet on the common footing of friendship. Today we are neither Filipinos, Spaniards, nor Americans, but men, just common, ordinary men—friends.

The crowd burst into applause.

By afternoon, the partygoers had broken up for their siesta and were later awoken with chocolates and cakes, followed by singing. With wine flowing all day, and dinner served at 8:00 p.m., the merriment only grew. At midnight, as the party drew to a close, Brown and Sonnichsen staggered to their respective homes—the con man to his accommodations with the town priest, and the captive back to prison.

On the succeeding day, all the American prisoners were invited for a grand post-wedding dinner just for them. Gillmore bowed out, explaining that he was too sick to attend. It was a lavish affair, with turkey and cakes and several kinds of good wine. After toasting the bride and groom, wishing them a lifetime of happiness, the prisoners adjourned to a music room where they were entertained for a few hours with songs and dancing. Some of the girls tried to persuade the Americans to dance, but their damaged feet forced them to decline. They did, however, sing a few American songs, which brought forth great applause. In the early evening, they bid the hosts farewell and returned to their jail cell to remember one of the most enjoyable days of their captivity.

On October 31, the *Washington Post* again headlined the latest news.

CLINGS TO PRISONERS;

AGUINALDO REFUSES TO RELEASE CAPTURED SPANIARDS;

LIEUT. GILLMORE HELD AT BINGAT [*SIC*]

The story updated readers on efforts (to date unsuccessful) for a Spanish commission—which had entered insurgent lines a month earlier—to negotiate for the prisoners' release. The commission arrived with money to support the huge population of Spanish prisoners, but also noted that around Tarlac alone, some two hundred sick Spanish soldiers were in the town's hospital, where "the Filipinos ill-treat and ill-feed them, refusing to surrender them, as well as the other Spanish prisoners."

The story indicated that Gillmore and his men were being held at "Bingat," alluding perhaps to Vigan. The commissioners further noted that "Aguinaldo, who is still at Tarlac, wishes to continue the war, although he has a high opinion of the American officers and soldiers. Gen. Lawton he calls *El General de la Noche* (the night general), because the commander has attacked him so often at night in the darkness that he never knows when to look for him."

❧

The American military campaign into northern Luzon would soon rattle the prisoners' lives. On November 10, a rumor conveyed that American warships, having shelled coastal towns to the south, were moving on Vigan. Soon, a flood of ailing Spaniards held at Vigan's hospital stumbled into Bangued, followed by an unending stream of other Spaniards. Within days, some 2,500 Spanish prisoners were milling about the town's cobblestoned streets and plaza. Prices for goods in the local market soared as shelves were stripped bare. Without an official per diem on which to subsist, the hungry Spaniards were reduced to looting outlying villages, stealing chickens, goats, and anything else they could grab.

The deteriorating situation, the prisoners could see, was not sustainable. Sonnichsen, acting as the go-between with Gillmore and a group of Spanish officers, helped forge a new plan. They agreed to send an emissary to communicate with the American warships, explain their predicament, and request that marines be landed. If the captives knew with certainty when American forces would be arriving, they could time their escape accordingly, overpower their guards at Bangued, and meet their rescuers halfway. Gillmore provided a letter scratched out in navy cipher, addressed to his superiors. In it, he outlined the plan and introduced the messengers—Sonnichsen, who had reluctantly volunteered to take the dispatch to the coast, accompanied by three Spaniards. The coded communication was rolled up and concealed in the hollow of a bamboo cane.

At dusk, in a light rain, Sonnichsen and his companions slid out of Bangued and made their way to Vigan, where the plan quickly fell apart. They found the beaches under heavy guard and ran into a bolo-armed gang of irate farmers who chased them into the woods. Frustrated and frightened, the Spaniards deserted the American. Alone, Sonnichsen stumbled around aimlessly for two days, and then badly tore up his leg on sharp-edged fish pens while swimming across a river.

After two miserable days on the run, Sonnichsen had had enough. Hungry, abandoned by his comrades, his gut inflamed, and his leg bleeding, he staggered into Vigan's plaza, ditched his cane in the nearby bushes, and surrendered to a clutch of Filipino guards on duty. Taken before

General Benito Natividad, the drenched, wounded escapee was given a fresh set of clothes and a per diem for food. Natividad advised that he would return Sonnichsen to Bangued himself, but first he would allow the prisoner to get the medical attention he obviously needed. The civilian quartermaster was soon back at Vigan's hospital, where he had languished for months, to heal once again.

Within days, three American warships—the USS *Samar*, USS *Oregon*, and USS *Callao*—quietly arrived off Vigan's shores, just as the rumors had suggested. The townspeople solemnly awaited the inevitable bombardment. Sonnichsen, aware an attack was imminent, realized he needed Gillmore's message. Without it, the arriving Americans would not believe anything he said, or that he was who he claimed to be. Slipping out of the hospital, he limped back to the plaza to retrieve his cane and its secret contents from the shrubs where it had been stashed.

On November 26, 1899, it began. A deadly hailstorm of naval artillery from the *Oregon*'s thirteen- and six-inch guns rained down on the largely defenseless town. The *Callao* and *Samar*, in support, fired their three-inch cannons and Gatling guns. The *Oregon*'s commander ordered the shelling directed toward uninhabited areas, hoping to instill fear in the enemy and achieve a quick surrender. Despite the effort to avoid casualties, one shell burst on the riverbank, mortally wounding a mother and her child. Two miles away, another shell exploded in a muddy rice field, killing a farmer. Strangely, the two adult victims were brother and sister, killed by two separate shells, miles apart. Then, as suddenly as it had begun, the American shelling stopped.

Sonnichsen, pressed into service to assist with the capitulation of the town, joined a group of provincial representatives in a horse-drawn carriage. They bounced toward the coast with a large white flag of surrender flapping in the wind. In his hands, Sonnichsen gripped the bamboo cane. The carriage passengers stopped on a hill outside Vigan to watch the Americans arrive—two hundred marines of the *Oregon* under the command of Lieutenant Commander Alexander McCracken. A gleeful Sonnichsen, jumping from the vehicle, raced ahead to embrace his countrymen. As the Americans circled around, Sonnichsen turned to a marine, asked to borrow his knife, and carefully sliced open the cane. After extracting the message, he passed it to McCracken. It was a message from Lieutenant Gillmore, Sonnichsen explained, watching as the commander's eyes lit up.

A triumphant Sonnichsen led the Americans into Vigan's plaza, a boisterous local brass band at the head of the column, where he introduced McCracken and his officers to the provincial governor and his staff. Within minutes, the Stars and Stripes were flying above the town plaza, on a flagstaff above the balcony of the governor's *palacio*. That night, during a hearty dinner, Sonnichsen shared all he knew with McCracken— about the remaining prisoners at Bangued, the size of their guard, and the urgency of a rescue. McCracken advised Sonnichsen not to worry; he would pass the message up the chain of command. He was sure steps would be taken without delay to liberate the Gillmore party.

Two days later, Sonnichsen was aboard the *Oregon*, heading to Manila. Outfitted with a new set of clothes, he regaled the officers in their wardroom with tales of his captivity, a mug of beer in one hand and a loaf of bread in the other. That night, he would recall, "[I] slept as if I had been drugged by poison." A day later in Manila, Sonnichsen met with Admiral Watson, Dewey's replacement in charge of the US Navy's Asiatic Squadron, and reported to General Otis. As a courtesy, Sonnichsen also called on Gillmore's sister Clara, at the Hotel de Oriente, to provide an update on her brother's captivity.

Afterward, Sonnichsen made the rounds with his journalist friends, leaking bits of the diary he had kept to the newspapers, keen to drum up publicity for a book about his captivity that he hoped to publish. Finally, he joined a Thanksgiving celebration hosted by the US Army where he made the first speech of his life. He concluded with "a toast to the hope of having Gillmore down by Christmas, which was loudly applauded, especially by the officers present." Lieutenant Gillmore was indeed the talk of the town.

❧

On November 29, 1899, twelve new prisoners—four US Navy sailors, seven US Army soldiers, and an American civilian—stumbled into the prison yard at Bangued. The fresh batch of captives, this time from Tarlac, were being moved just as the Gillmore party had been, to ensure they were well beyond the reach of the advancing Americans. As the arrivals told their stories, the rest of the prisoners prepared a modest Thanksgiving dinner. The highlight was a fine fatted goat, a gift from the generous Paredes family.

The men's tales of woe were compelling. Three men were sailors from the forty-two-ton USS *Urdaneta*, which had been ambushed while on patrol on September 17, 1899, after it ran aground in the soft muddy banks of the Orani River along the Bataan peninsula, about twenty miles northwest of Manila. A fourth sailor was taken with much less violence, at San Fabian, Pangasinan; during General Wheaton's landing, he was jumped by a band of insurgents after going off to find breakfast in a nearby village. The other prisoners had been captured in similar ways, most waylaid or clubbed unconscious inside American lines, and dragged across into insurgent lines.

Quite amazingly, two US Army prisoners had walked voluntarily into their captivity, though this was not divulged at the time. Descended from a long line of American patriots, Private George T. Sackett, Company H, 3rd Regiment, apparently fed up with army life and disgusted by a war he felt was unjust, stole into enemy territory to offer his services to the rebels. As records later showed, the revolutionaries were unimpressed and instead tossed the idealistic deserter into detention.

A second prisoner, Corporal Frank McDonald, Company L, 21st Regiment, had far less altruistic intentions. Descended from Revolutionary War stock, McDonald's real name was William Duff Green. Adopting an alias, following a conviction years earlier for desertion, had allowed him to reenlist. Once shipped to Manila, "McDonald" promptly ran afoul of the law. After an incident during which he stole $107 in Mexican silver (one of the currencies used in the Philippines at the time, a holdover from the Spanish colonial period) from a local ferryboat captain, McDonald was arrested, tried by court-martial, and found guilty. The sentence was harsh: a dishonorable discharge, forfeiture of all pay, and three years of hard labor in Manila's Bilibid Prison.

But the wily McDonald had other plans. While being transferred to his place of confinement, McDonald gave his military guards the slip and headed straight for the rebel lines. Almost immediately, he was detained and imprisoned by the Filipinos. In the eyes of the US Army, Frank McDonald was an escaped military convict on the run.

And finally, there was a civilian among the prisoners, a man who had nothing to do with the hostilities at hand: George William Langford, an upbeat American entrepreneur from Minnesota who had been working in Manila as a commercial agent for Pabst Blue Ribbon beer. The cheerful

Langford had been captured four months earlier, on July 27, 1899, while traveling by sailboat from Malolos to Manila.

A thirteenth prisoner had not made it all the way to Bangued: Charles Baker, Battery L, 3rd Artillery. Months earlier, he had left his quarters without permission, failed to return, and had been declared a deserter. In fact, Baker had gone to visit a Filipino girl whom he had been courting. Along the way, he was ambushed by insurgents, hit over the head, and taken captive. On a forced march to the north under General Tinio's command, Baker fell violently ill. Unable to continue, he was put on a stretcher and carried by his guards. Around November 19, 1899, on a trail south of Santa Maria, Ilocos Sur, American forces began to close in. Anxious to push on, but burdened by his column's slow progress, an infuriated Tinio rode back to the laggards hauling Baker's litter, dismounted his horse, and ordered the guards to put Baker down. Unwilling to allow the prisoner to fall back into American hands, a livid Tinio unsheathed his bayonet and plunged it into Baker's heart. There, now they could move faster. The column's load lightened, they moved out at pace.

With the twelve new prisoners, the Gillmore party at Bangued had grown to twenty-six. The gaunt, hungry arrivals settled into the prison courtyard just in time for the sparse Thanksgiving meal that was being prepared. When served, their meager shares of the rich goat stew, ladled over cups of hot, white rice, were incrementally larger, in part due to the generous contributions from the other prisoners, and the tragic fact that one of their own—Private Charles Baker—had not survived the march to join them. It was a somber meal, for which the men gave thanks.

CHAPTER TWELVE

The Center of Gravity

IN PURSUIT OF GENERAL AGUINALDO AND HIS REBEL COMMAND, THE US Army had pushed into northern Luzon in fits and starts. The previous April, mired down by monsoon rains, General Lawton's division had only advanced as far as San Isidro, the old insurgent capital. On arrival, they had searched the town but found little of interest until they stumbled into the decrepit jailhouse. There, etched on the grimy stone wall with a flint of charcoal, was a list of names of the Gillmore party. The disturbing find made headlines across America. On May 24, 1899, the *Los Angeles Times* ran a front-page story with the following headline:

REBEL BRUTES
Filipinos Use the Lash on an American;
Yorktown *Prisoners Receive Outrageous Treatment*

More details spilled into the newspapers once the prisoners' letters, turned over by Ramon Rey to General Lawton, made their way home. On August 16, 1899, the *New York Times* broke with a story that explained how the names of the *Yorktown* sailors had been "scratched into the walls of the jail" at San Isidro, adding that letters from the prisoners had been found secreted under stones and turned over by a friendly Spaniard. In one, a prisoner wrote that he and the others were being "starved, beaten, and bound, and moreover, were in rags." The prisoners "begged that aid be sent to them." Another letter, from Albert Sonnichsen, added a depressing aside: The Spanish prisoners were being treated even worse, "and hundreds were dying of dysentery and disease."

As grim as the news accounts were, they sent a sigh of relief through military circles in Washington. At least some of the *Yorktown*'s sailors had survived the ambush at Baler, and were likely still alive.

With his forces extended well beyond their lines of supply, Lawton could do very little at this point. He had neither the means nor the mandate to move farther. Then, to his dismay, orders arrived from a temporizing General Otis. Anxious to keep his forces within reach, Otis ordered Lawton's men to withdraw thirty miles to the south, to Baliuag. Not surprisingly, Filipino forces quickly filled the vacuum, reclaiming the abandoned territory in the Americans' wake. Across the Candaba Swamp to the west, General MacArthur and his division had pushed as far north as Angeles, where he, too, was placed on hold by Otis. Altogether, for the past eight months, from February to October 1899, American forces had ventured no more than sixty miles from Manila. Aguinaldo's forces took advantage, strengthening their grip on the towns they held and entrenching their defenses.

During this rain-swept lull, a continual stream of troop transports had dropped anchor at Manila Bay, disgorging thirty-five thousand federal volunteers who had been sent to replace the state militia soldiers. Washington's decision-makers hoped the troop surge, comprising twenty-five newly formed regiments, would allow Otis to bring the bloody insurrection—a war by nearly every definition—to a close. With a decisive victory over Aguinaldo and his forces, the Americans could focus their attention on the original task of executing McKinley's policy of "benevolent assimilation," which sought to establish United States sovereignty over the islands with a gentler hand.

Without a crushing, final defeat of the rebels, Otis feared Aguinaldo might scatter his forces into the mountains of northern Luzon and continue a low-intensity guerrilla campaign for years to come. Otis also worried about extending his troops too far into insurgent territory; he knew that the more distance the Americans covered, the greater the risk that supply lines from Manila would fail.

Otis mulled over his options. Studying the geography, it appeared likely that Aguinaldo, if pressed, would withdraw from his current headquarters at Tarlac along the railroad line to Dagupan, on the northwest coast, and make his way to the mountains. Otis conceived a new plan: a three-pronged pincher movement that would trap Aguinaldo's forces. If

MacArthur's division could pin down the rebels' main body in central Luzon, Lawton's division—highly mobile and predominantly composed of cavalry—could sweep around their eastern flank and block access to the Caraballo and Sierra Madre Mountains. A third force, under the command of General Wheaton, and taken by ship to the Lingayen Gulf for an amphibious landing at San Fabian, could cut off all access to the northern Ilocos region and the Cordilleras. MacArthur's men would then advance north, forcing Aguinaldo and his army into the waiting hands of Lawton or Wheaton, where they would be forced to surrender or face annihilation, once and for all.

A historically successful military strategy used time and again over the centuries, the three-pronged pincher movement was aimed at destroying the remnants of the revolutionary army while they still constituted a formal force. This would avoid a costly and frustrating hit-and-run guerrilla conflict and depose the rebel ringleader, Aguinaldo, who served as the rebellion's inspiration, the Army of Liberation's center of gravity. As political and military figurehead, he provided much of the cohesion, strength, and will to fight among his insurgents. Capture Aguinaldo, the argument went, and the insurrection would collapse.

The seemingly elegant plan was put into effect in early October 1899, with Lawton's column pushing back up to the territory it once held in San Isidro. Almost immediately, the Americans ran into problems with weather, equipment, and logistics. The column's three thousand men trudged through waterlogged rice fields and muddy roads, driving off entrenched enemy fighters as they advanced. Their lifeline to Manila was an untenable supply train of 22 wagons hauled by four-mule teams and 110 bull carts powered by straining, obstinate *carabao*. Under stifling heat and with their cavalry horses helplessly mired in earthen muck, the advance staggered into Cabanatuan at the end of the month, completing a nearly four-week slog, largely on half rations. There, they stalled. They had covered all of fifteen miles.

On November 7, another prong of the pincher movement—Wheaton's force of two thousand men—arrived by sea at San Fabian, Pangasinan. Much like Lawton and MacArthur, the foul-mouthed, sixty-two-year-old Brigadier General Loyd Wheaton had risen through the ranks during the Civil War. Enlisting as a sergeant in the 8th Illinois Infantry, the heavily built, dark-bearded Wheaton had been brevetted three times for gallantry and awarded the Congressional Medal of Honor for his efforts during the assault on Fort Blakely, Alabama, in April 1865. Despite these early heroics, Wheaton had done little in the thirty years that followed, save for supervising a company of soldiers. At the outbreak of war with Spain, Wheaton raced to Cuba only to miss all the action. But now here he was, once again in the thick of it—a key element of a three-pronged drive set to crush the heart of the Philippine revolution.

Commanding a battalion of Wheaton's 33rd Infantry was a far more battle-hardened colonel: the forty-eight-year-old Luther Rector Hare. The oldest of six children of a politically connected Republican judge, Silas Hare of Sherman, Texas, the foul-mouthed Hare possessed an impressive résumé. As a young lieutenant with the 7th Cavalry in 1874, Hare was posted at the garrison at Colfax, Louisiana, where he helped lock down the county after the nation's worst and most deadly race riot a year earlier.

In 1876, Hare survived the Battle of the Little Bighorn, where General Custer and his battalion of 210 men were annihilated by the Lakota, Dakota, and Northern Cheyenne in a last-stand action. In that engagement, with Reno's battalion in panicked retreat, Hare reportedly shouted, "If we've got to die, let's die like men!" He let loose a rebel yell and then hollered in self-proclamation, "I'm a fightin' son of a bitch from Texas!" His caustic admonition for his men to not "run off like a pack of whipped curs" is said to have jolted the company into standing its ground.

A year later, Hare joined the Nez Perce Expedition, fighting at the Battle of Canyon Creek, Montana, and on the Dakota frontier, taking part in the Sioux Ghost Dance War. During a subsequent assignment in Arizona Territory, Hare helped chase down the last of the renegade Apaches. After twenty-four years of loyal service with the 7th Calvary, Hare, a devoted family man and father to three girls, had only risen to the rank of captain; however, this was soon to change with the outbreak of war in Cuba in 1898, and appointment to the Texas Volunteer Calvary as liutenant colonel and, in quick succession, colonel. Over the years, Hare had earned a reputation as a serious, war-scarred military officer who got the job done.

At San Fabian, Wheaton's troop transports anchored at a safe distance while the accompanying six warships—three cruisers and three gunboats—patrolled the coast to locate Filipino defenses. After a few hours of observation, the bombardment began. The American naval guns poured a rain of hot fire on the town, while mosquito craft—smaller,

US NATIONAL ARCHIVES

Colonel Hare and staff officers, 33rd Infantry. Front row, left to right: Captain Edgar A. Sirmyer, Lieutenant Colonel John J. Brereton, Colonel Luther R. Hare, Major John A. Logan Jr., and Captain James M. Burroughs. Standing, left to right: Captain James S. Butler, Lieutenant George L. Febiger, Captain Thomas Q. Ashburn, and Captain Charles W. Van Way.

faster, shallow draft steam launches stripped from the larger ships—crept up to the beach, pulverizing the Filipino trenches with blasts from their Colt Automatics. By the time the first landing party struck the beach, the Filipino soldiers had fled.

A few days earlier, to the south, a skirmish between Lawton's men and a band of insurgents led to the capture of important Filipino documents. Found within them was information that suggested Aguinaldo was once again planning to move his headquarters, this time from Tarlac to the capital of Nueva Vizcaya, Bayombong, located another seventy-five miles north. Time was of the essence. Aguinaldo could not be allowed to reach the mountain passes that Lawton's men had intended to block, or else the three-pronged strategy to encircle and destroy his rebel forces would fail.

To move at speed and close off Aguinaldo's routes of escape, a new approach was required. One of Lawton's officers, Brigadier General

Young, presented a proposal to lead an advance cavalry brigade that could charge ahead and cut off Aguinaldo's retreat to the mountains. Young was fairly sure he could catch Aguinaldo, but he and his men would have to be highly mobile and stripped of nearly all wheeled transportation. If the ration carts could not keep up, they would need to be ditched, and in that case, his men would need to live off the land, surviving on their own ingenuity and wits. With luck, Young's advance could close the strategic mountain passes before Aguinaldo's command disappeared into the vast Cordilleras. Young's proposal was unconventional, but if it succeeded, the Americans would be able to bring the conflict to a close.

If Brigadier General Samuel Baldwin Marks Young knew anything, he knew how to hunt down an enemy. At fifty-nine, the white-haired bear of a man from Pittsburgh, Pennsylvania—who towered over his men at six-foot-four, weighing a hefty 250 pounds—had nearly three decades of military experience under his belt. Known for his competence and daring, Young had raced through the ranks during the Civil War, first enlisting as a private in the 12th Pennsylvania Regiment in 1861. He was brevetted four times for gallantry at battles with Confederate rebels in Virginia, and promoted to the rank of brigadier general of the volunteers by 1865. At the end of the Civil War, Young entered the Regular Army and spent the next thirteen years leading campaigns to subjugate the Apache and Navajo.

Lawton liked Young's idea—a high-risk strategy, yet one with the potential for high reward. Currently out of communication with the cautious and calculating Otis in Manila, Lawton allowed Young to charge ahead as proposed. Lawton, meanwhile, planned to stay behind in Cabanatuan to focus on nagging supply-train issues that seemed to defy resolution.

On November 7, Young led eleven hundred men—squadrons of the 3rd and 4th Cavalry, a battalion of the 22nd Infantry, and some attached artillery units—on a frenetic race north. Immediately they ran into the same hardships and obstacles earlier encountered: dangerous river crossings, incessant rains, and impassable roads. Ration carts were pulled apart in the muck by straining mules and *carabao*. Artillery pieces sank in the mud. Infantry on foot, lugging heavy rifles and ammunition, passed a cavalry troop that, incredibly, had covered only two miles over a thirty-six-hour period. By the time they reached Lupao, Nueva Ecija, three days later, anything with wheels had been abandoned.

Brigadier General Samuel Baldwin Marks Young

Young's fraying column pushed on the best it could, engaging pockets of shadowy insurgents while slogging through central Luzon's seemingly endless waterlogged rice fields. Over the course of five days and fifty miles, the column was dispersed, without rations or shelter, and living on rice and fresh *carabao* meat. The soldiers' shoes had come apart and most were now barefoot. Exposed to the elements, the soldiers were exhibiting a raft of medical problems: fever from malaria and dengue, diarrhea from dysentery and poor sanitation, raw tropical ulcers on their ankles and shins, and a persistent Dhobie itch in their rotting crotches. Above all, they were hungry.

Meanwhile, at San Fabian, Wheaton's 33rd Infantry was looking to the southwest, assuming that the main body of Aguinaldo's force would approach from the coastal province of Zambales. Battalions were sent to scout the country, destroy telegraph lines, and engage insurgents. In the process, they learned that one brigade of insurgents, under the able leadership of one of Aguinaldo's key officers, General Tinio, was already in their midst. Consisting of perhaps twelve hundred men, Tinio's Brigade was reportedly entrenched at the town of San Jacinto, six miles to the east and preparing for battle. On November 11, eleven companies of the 33rd Infantry under the command of Colonel Hare went looking for a fight.

En route, Hare's troops encountered five miles of some of the worst road seen in Luzon, encompassing a succession of creeks and miry ditches in which the men sank to their waists. Every bridge was unserviceable and had to be repaired along the way. The horses towing the heavy Gatling guns needed to be unhitched and walked around the worst patches. In these instances, the soldiers themselves dragged the wheeled carriages by hand through the quagmire. Three miles from San Jacinto, just as the men reached another boggy depression in the road that left them knee-deep in mud, a sharpshooter on point spied the enemy some fifty yards ahead. Rebels were entrenched on a stretch of road surrounded by a coconut tree grove. Hare ordered his three battalions to spread out for an assault. One battalion, led by Major Marcus D. Cronin, took the right flank; another, led by Major Peyton C. March, took the left flank. A third, under the command of Major John A. Logan Jr., advanced from the center.

~ ~

Nearly all of Hare's officers were West Point graduates like himself, steeped in the traditions of service and sacrifice. Nearly all had worked their way up through the ranks on hardscrabble posts across the American West, and were toughened by combat in the Indian Wars. All but one: Manning Alexander Logan. He came with a pedigree, though. He was the son of famed Civil War general John "Black Jack" Logan, who had led the Union Army to its first major victory at Fort Donelson, despite being shot three times and losing half of his 606 men. Awarded the Congressional Medal of Honor for his gallantry at Vicksburg, Logan Sr. served as a three-term senator, working tirelessly on behalf of enlisted soldiers. Credited with establishing Decoration Day, later to become Memorial Day, Logan Sr. was, in every facet, an archetype of the American citizen-soldier.

The greatness of Logan Sr.—if it is possible to transmit such a thing across generations—was never unlocked in his son's genes. Adopting his father's first name as an adult, and prodded on by his demanding mother, Logan Jr. dabbled in a state military academy and the National Guard as a youth. He made it to West Point, but crashed out in spectacular fashion following two separate court-martial trials—first, for unloading on a member of the Guard with a mouthful of profanity, and second, for smuggling liquor into his room. On November 10, 1884, faced with dismissal from the Academy, Logan beat them to it and resigned from his appointment. In later years, Logan's epic failure as a cadet would be disingenuously attributed to poor eyesight.

Three years later, Logan married well, taking the hand of Edith Andrews, the daughter of an iron and coal magnate worth an estimated $3 million (equivalent to $60 million in early-twenty-first-century currency). Logan had himself appointed president of one of his father-in-law's businesses, and spent his time breeding racehorses on a sprawling country estate. At the age of twenty-three, Logan was living a gilded life as a corporate executive, country gentleman, and social dilettante, but it was not enough. The shadow of his father's legacy seemed to always loom over him. Over time, he realized that only a war would give him the same opportunity for prominence and honors that had been afforded his father.

In April 1898, that opportunity arrived when war broke out with Spain. A brief enlistment as a major with the 2nd Ohio Volunteers, which saw minor action in Cuba, only fueled his military ambitions to new heights. With his persistent mother stirring the pot, the White House and War Department received a deluge of letters from prominent politicians and business leaders in support of an officer's appointment, which eventually bore fruit. On August 17, 1899, the War Department, worn down by the increasingly uncomfortable barrage of correspondence, finally offered Logan a commission as a major with Wheaton's 33rd Infantry.

Five weeks later, in late September 1899, Logan, accompanied by his personal valet Morley, set sail to Manila aboard the US Army transport *Sheridan*. During the voyage, Logan managed to enrage the entire ship of enlisted men. Perhaps the ship's beloved mascot kept him up one night with its barking, or maybe it mischievously befouled his quarters or urinated on his leg—the cause was not documented. Whatever the spark, a short-fused Logan threw the helpless dog overboard and into the churning sea. From that point on, "a certain class of men used his action as a subject for strong talk."

The 33rd Infantry arrived in Manila on October 24, 1899, minus its canine mascot. Now, less than three weeks after arriving in the Philippines, Logan was charging headlong on his mount into battle at San Jacinto as battalion commander. The thirty-three-year-old son of a hero was leading on point, keen to seize his long-delayed glory.

Before the Filipino entrenchments, Logan dismounted and floundered across the bog. On reaching the other side, he discovered a head peeping out of a trench. Pointing his riding quirt toward the trenches, he yelled out, "Go for them, men; they're insurgents!" The next instant the battle began.

For several minutes, bullets rained about the Americans, coming from the front, flanks, and rear. One soldier was shot, then another. Logan could see that the main insurgent column was still deploying and had not yet opened fire. He called to twenty-two-year-old Sergeant Major Albert E. Gebert, a bookkeeper from Illinois, to order their men to cease firing, as they were recklessly shooting in Logan's direction. The order was given, but rifle fire continued to zing past Logan from several directions. A wounded man lying on the ground cried out, "Look in the trees; they're full of goo-goos!" Logan and his men looked up; sure enough, nestled in the tops of a number of coconut trees, were Filipino riflemen, not twenty yards away.

In the meantime, Logan's soldiers were dropping. A twenty-one-year-old corporal was hit in the first volley, superficially, followed by the officer leading point, and then another private, a twenty-one-year-old laborer from Kansas City. Seconds later, a cook from Indian Territory was shot through the neck with a Mauser round, "instantly killed by a missile of unknown origin." Logan, passing the first wounded private, stooped over to help the boy. In the same instant, a bullet slammed through Logan's skull, entering just above the right temple and blowing out the left side of his head—a straight-line trajectory that would seem to suggest fire from the ground, not the trees above. As Logan slumped lifelessly to the ground, the regimental surgeon and a sergeant major struggled to move the hefty battalion commander to safety. The surgeon called to a hospital steward, who dutifully ran over to assist in pulling the dying Logan onto a sledge.

As the hospital corpsman struggled to lift the mortally wounded Logan onto the sledge, blood from the major's head wound flowing over his hands, another rifle slug found its mark in the medic's chest. The bullet tore through his heart, killing him instantly. The soldier collapsed on top of the lifeless Logan.

The 33rd Infantry immediately gave the snipers their attention and began "knocking them out of the trees like squirrels." The battalions advanced along a two-mile skirmish line to the trenches, across "water-soaked rice fields, ditches, creeks and thickets," overwhelming rebel forces through sheer numbers and superior firepower. The Filipinos held their own in places, sometimes waiting for the Americans to advance within twenty yards before opening up with their own rifles. A thirty-year-old sergeant from Columbus, Indiana, deaf in one ear and missing teeth, raced headlong toward one trench, only to be knocked back with a Mauser shot to the chest, killing him on the spot. Another private was luckier: A similar Mauser slug slammed into his chest, between the left nipple and sternum, and failed to exit, leaving the twenty-five-year-old wounded but alive. On the left flank, Major March's men pushed to one trench more quickly than expected, and poured heavy fire onto the packed line of exposed insurgents, slaughtering scores.

After three and a half hours of incessant fighting, the three American battalions reached the outskirts of the town. Five insurgents, firing from the broken bridge they hoped to hold, were quickly dispatched with a smoking burst of automatic gunfire from a Gatling gun. Upon entering San Jacinto and finding only two residents remaining—a blind boy and one old woman—the spent Americans stopped to catch their breath and collapsed in exhaustion.

On the battlefield that day, Hare's forces killed 134 insurgents and wounded 160 others, while taking about 25 casualties themselves. Losses included Major Logan and 6 enlisted men killed in action, and 15 wounded—2 of whom succumbed later to their wounds.

Deciding not to hold San Jacinto or to move farther west, Hare's men returned to the coastal town of San Fabian. Pushing on logically would have allowed them to connect with Young's advancing command coming from the east, and join forces. By not doing so, a critical gap was left open, as the two commands had yet to come together to close the slowly constricting circle around Aguinaldo's main body of soldiers. But so far, the three-pronged pincher plan seemed to be working. Aguinaldo's rebels were being pushed up through central Luzon by MacArthur's division, a sprawling force of 4,800 men.

～

Two days later, on November 13, Aguinaldo and his senior officers met with troops under the command of Generals Gregorio del Pilar and Manuel Tinio, along with their commands, at the town of Bayambang, Pangasinan. Huddled in a council of war twenty-three miles south of Wheaton's 33rd Infantry forces at San Fabian, the Filipinos reassessed their increasingly dire situation. The rout at San Jacinto demonstrated that traditional resistance against the unstoppable and well-armed American military machine was futile. It was decided to disband their main fighting force, break up into small bodies, and pursue a more-asymmetrical guerrilla campaign. Orders were issued for their soldiers to discard their uniforms and disperse. It was a tactic they had used often, but never on such a scale. Obediently, the revolutionary fighters transformed into civilians and prepared to melt into the surrounding towns, villages, and thick forests beyond. Against the Americans' forceful advance, there was no time to lose. Throughout the night, Aguinaldo, several officers, and a lean body of his guard marched north, on foot, toward the town of Pozorrubio.

A new phase of the war against the unwelcome American occupiers was about to begin. While a lackadaisical Wheaton remained on pause, Young was moving quickly to close the gap. He ordered a squadron of cavalry under Major Samuel M. Swigert to race to Pozorrubio to close off any opening that might allow Aguinaldo and his men to make it north. Swigert's guide, however, led their squad to the wrong town—likely by design—to Manaoag, where they ran headlong into Aguinaldo's eight-hundred-man rear guard.

The fifty-three-year-old major at first balked at engaging the enemy, but at the insistence of Lieutenant Colonel James Parker, detailed from Young's staff to accompany the squadron, the force was charged and dispersed. Swigert bristled at the interference of his command by an officer, who, despite his seniority, was eight years his junior. Words were exchanged. Critical time was lost, adding to Aguinaldo's advantage. A disgusted Young arrived on the scene later, adding, "The only reason that the guide who led us to Manaoag instead of Pozorrubio was not shot was because he could not be found."

The following morning, November 14, a cavalry squadron departed for Pozorrubio, led by an angry, lethargic, and thoroughly demoralized Swigert. Parker, though still detailed to accompany them, decided not to join, as the previous day's confrontation was still raw and emotions were running high. On arriving at the outskirts of Pozorrubio, Swigert learned he had missed Aguinaldo by just a few hours. Rather than pursue the almost-unguarded rebel command, and in a startling display of bureaucratic parsing and passive-aggressive dysfunction, Swigert ordered his men back to the 33rd Infantry's command, which was now near the town of Binalonan.

On arrival, the major was quizzed about the rebel leader.

"Oh yes, he was there. He left Pozorrubio as I entered."

"Why did you not pursue him?"

"I had no orders to pursue him."

And with that, an unbelievably lucky Aguinaldo slipped through the Americans' grasp, making a total mockery of Otis's three-pronged pincher movement and dashing all hope for a quick end to the insurrection.

While the northern campaign had failed to contain Aguinaldo or crush his forces, it resulted in one unintended surprise. As the Americans pushed up through Luzon, Lawton recognized that he would need to cut off all options for Aguinaldo's flight. This also meant taking towns where Aguinaldo's rebel command might again relocate. Rumors had repeatedly pointed to the mountain town of Bayombong, Nueva Vizcaya, to the east of the drama unfolding at San Fabian and Pozorrubio, Pangasinan. Strategically, the military importance of Bayombong had diminished with Aguinaldo's move to the west, but Lawton wanted to garrison the town anyway, if only for good measure.

A company of soldiers, led by 2nd Lieutenant James N. Munro, 4th Cavalry, set out from MacArthur's command, climbing through Balete Pass at an elevation of three thousand feet. On the evening of November 26, they arrived at Dupax, eighteen miles south of their objective. Intelligence suggested that Bayombong was being held by a large rebel force that would not surrender without a fight. The following morning, as Munro and his men formulated a plan of attack, they encountered an exceptional stroke of luck. Staggering into their camp, broken with fever, was a twenty-six-year-old American prisoner, Private Aram K. D. Minassian of the Hospital Corps, who had escaped from Bayombong the previous night.

Minassian's arrival was almost too good to be true. The Bulgarian-born Armenian, an Egyptian Army veteran and now American citizen from St. Louis, Missouri, had been pressed into the US Army's Secret Service by General MacArthur. On August 30, 1899, armed with a French passport and letters of introduction from an influential Filipino in Manila, the five-foot-four, 121-pound soldier had set out on a bold mission to infiltrate Aguinaldo's headquarters at Tarlac. At some point, the mission failed, and by November 1899, Minassian was a prisoner at Bayombong.

Now, Minassian was able to provide invaluable intelligence on the three-hundred-man insurgent battalion holding Bayombong. He described the Filipinos' morale, and sketched out the location of their trenches. Even more important, he explained that the rebel commander, General Fernando Canon, was laboring under the impression that Munro's forces tallied several thousand men, and was contemplating surrender.

With Minassian's guidance, Munro hatched a ruse to deceive Canon. It would have to be good: Canon, the son of a watchmaker from Binan, Laguna, and a classmate of Jose Rizal at Ateneo, was no fool; in fact, he was a gifted guitarist, poet, and inventor who had been trained as an engineer in Spain. Minassian proposed that the Americans craft a message to the general—in Spanish, and under the forged signature of an insurgent source—which explained that American forces were descending on Bayombong with thousands of troops. The false confirmation of troop numbers, coming from what looked like a legitimate rebel source, would play into Canon's erroneous assumptions. The message was crafted and translated into Spanish by Minassian, who volunteered to run it to an insurgent-held telegraph office located in a nearby town, five miles away.

When the alarming message arrived at Bayombong, an overwhelmed Canon knew he had run out of options. On November 28, Munro and his fifty-three men accepted the surrender of Canon's forces, six times larger than their own. The successful ruse also resulted in the release of 139 Spanish prisoners, including the province's former Spanish governor, and, to their surprise, fourteen American prisoners being held in the town. Among the ragged group of captives were two *Yorktown* sailors: Ordinary Seamen William Rynders and Orrison Woodbury.

The sailors' captivity at Bayombong would have been a source of envy for their compatriots being held at Bangued. Since their arrival from Baler five months earlier, Rynders and Woodbury had been given leeway about the town, as "the natives of this province seemed to be lukewarm toward Aguinaldo and his independence business." Rynders, in particular, made the best of it. As Woodbury remembered, "That old pirate Rynders gets himself a Philipino *senhora* and lives with her day and night in their own little hut—she cooked his rice, rolled his cigars and done his washing, and he even kicked because once a day he had to roll off his mat and go to the *presidente* to sign for his daily allowance of one *paseta*."

On December 2, 1899, the ecstatic former captives began their walk south to Manila, accompanied by a column of several hundred Spanish soldiers, priests, families of soldiers, other officials, and an American detachment of 4th Cavalry. After a grueling march across mountain trails, and Woodbury's brief stay at a US Army field hospital along the way to treat a bout of malaria, the two sailors staggered into Manila. A rail-thin Woodbury tipped the scale at ninety-seven pounds, having lost 25 percent of his body weight from his already-slight frame.

But compromised health would not hold the sailors back. Once in bustling Manila, Rynders and Woodbury spent a raucous two weeks celebrating their freedom in the city's saloons with their newfound friends from the cavalry, "feeding up & drinking bottled beer from the US . . . between the fever & chill spells." With some reluctance, they eventually reported to Admiral Watson aboard the flagship USS *Brooklyn* to share an account of their ordeal. Wracked with dysentery, malaria, and tropical ulcers, both men were sent to the naval hospital at Cavite, where they would spend some two months struggling to regain their health.

Two of the *Yorktown* prisoners were now free. Meanwhile, for Gillmore, the seven other sailors, and the odd and growing assortment of other captives who had joined their party, a new adventure was about to begin.

CHAPTER THIRTEEN

Pursuit

BRIGADIER GENERAL SAMUEL B. M. YOUNG WAS IN A QUANDARY. His plan to move at speed and corner General Aguinaldo had broken his men. Of the original eleven hundred men under his command, he now had less than one-third still on their feet—eighty troopers from the 3rd Cavalry and three hundred native scouts—the rest having succumbed to exhaustion or illness. His nemesis, Aguinaldo, was making good time with Generals del Pilar and Tinio, backed by a strong rear guard to protect their retreat. Having advanced almost 150 miles north of Manila, out of telegraphic range of his superiors, without rations or supplies, and with most of his men barefoot, Young needed to decide whether to renew the chase or call it a day.

On November 17, Young's command received information that the fleet-footed Aguinaldo was heading north across Pangasinan. A day later, Young and his men were on the move, sixty hours behind the revolutionary leader, pushing into the province of La Union, "to prevent the uniting of their scattered commands and follow up those having prisoners in their charge and to release them all." But Young lacked men, and his force "was too small to allow any concentration of the enemy." He needed more men if they were to corral the enemy at one location for a full-scale confrontation. Runners were sent with an urgent message for General Lawton, who had remained behind with his command in Cabanatuan, in central Luzon: "I need forces but cannot wait. A battalion of light Infantry which can march without impediment should follow on my trail, with an officer in command who will push for all he is worth." No more Swigerts or slackers. It was crunch time.

With his thin, weary force, Young reached the outskirts of Aringay only to encounter another huddle of entrenched insurgents. One of Young's officers was wounded, and a native scout killed, while a lieutenant, who took a round to the chest, miraculously survived thanks to a fat plug of chewing tobacco in his shirt pocket that absorbed the impact of the slug.

Two days later, Young and his men reached the coast at Bauang, but more had fallen ill. Now desperate, the general signaled a navy gunboat patrolling offshore, the USS *Samar*, requesting help to secure their next objective to the north, the coastal town of San Fernando. The gunboat commander was only too happy to oblige. In a joint assault the following day, Young's band of fighters, supported by the *Samar*'s three-inch guns and deck-mounted Gatlings, dispersed three hundred insurgents. The Americans pushed on, hammering Tinio's forces at every turn. Young's men marched another five arduous days, battling insurgents in skirmishes along the way. The column arrived at the town of Namacpacan, where it essentially collapsed as a fighting force.

As his exhausted men slept, Young reassessed his situation. He had been pushing north with everything he had, aware that Aguinaldo was within his grasp. Fresh intelligence suggested the rebel general intended to continue up the coast into the province of Abra, where, it was rumored, the Gillmore party prisoners were being held, along with some four thousand Spaniards. Young wrote to General Wheaton, who was still languidly camped at San Fabian:

> *My forces are much depleted and worn out. Aguinaldo has been playing hide and seek. One day in the mountains, the next day he and some of his generals are on the coast road. . . . The Infantry force promised has not arrived. . . . Aguinaldo is an outlaw and fugitive in the Mountains and can be caught with fresh troops. If you can assist me in this matter, I don't see how he can escape.*

To drive home the urgency of his request for reinforcements, Young ordered his hard-charging adjutant, Lieutenant Colonel James Parker, back to San Fabian on the USS *Samar*, to make the case. Young hoped that Wheaton would agree to land forces north of Vigan, to cut off another possible route of escape for Aguinaldo. It was, in a sense, a new pincher movement, adapted to the evolving circumstances. But for it to work, Young needed men, and he needed them now.

The choice of Parker—a product of Phillips Academy at Andover, Rutgers University, and West Point, and a veteran of the Indian Wars who had helped Lawton to capture the famed Apache leader Geronimo in 1886—could not have been better. At San Fabian, Parker made an impassioned plea to Wheaton. With fresh troops landed at Vigan, he argued, one of the last remaining routes open to Aguinaldo could be closed and the noose tightened.

But Wheaton was unmoved. Without General Otis's approval from Manila, he pedantically refused to support the unauthorized expedition.

Exasperated yet undeterred, Parker gave up on Wheaton and turned to the navy instead. It had worked once already during the assault on San Fernando—why not again? Parker approached the commanders of the USS *Callao* and USS *Oregon,* two warships anchored off the coast, and persuaded them to join an assault on Vigan. On the morning of November 26, the attack began. The *Oregon* initiated shelling from its devastating thirteen- and six-inch guns. The *Callao,* joined by the *Samar,* followed with heavy fire from their three-inch and deck-mounted Gatling guns. Once the smoke cleared, sailors and marines were landed, only to be greeted by an ecstatic Albert Sonnichsen, the town's enthusiastic leadership, and a noisy brass band.

Farther south, on the same day, Young's desperate pleas for reinforcements finally bore fruit. A battalion of the 33rd Infantry under the command of Major Peyton C. March arrived to augment the general's expended men. The thirty-five-year-old Pennsylvanian had a well-deserved reputation as an effective, inspired officer. March had attended West Point, served in the 3rd and 5th Artilleries, and had led the famed 102-man Astor Battery, a light artillery unit, during the Spanish-American War. The Astor Battery was a unique conception, independently underwritten by the multimillionaire and later victim of the *Titanic* disaster, John Jacob Astor IV, at a personal cost of $100,000—equivalent to $2.7 million today. The unit attracted a core of well-heeled college graduates from some of the nation's top schools, performed admirably in Cuba and Manila, and earned March accolades for his organizational skills and leadership.

More good news was about to arrive. Several days behind March, another battalion from the 34th Infantry, under Lieutenant Colonel

Howze, was on its way north from MacArthur's command. Howze had started with 180 men at San Fernando, Pampanga, on October 25, reaching San Fabian to join Wheaton's command one month later. Although forty of his men had dropped out due to exhaustion and illness, an undeterred Howze was forging ahead to catch the hard-charging Young.

Lieutenant Colonel Robert "Bob" Lee Howze was, like Lawton, Young, and Hare, steeped in the Indian Wars of the American Southwest. Son of a former Confederate cavalry captain, the Texan was a graduate of Hubbard College, where he attained a degree in business, and West Point. Assigned to frontier duty in New Mexico with the 6th Cavalry, the stern, square-jawed lieutenant had seen action in the Pine Ridge Campaign in 1890, and, notably, in a bloody fight on New Year's Day 1891 at Little Grass Creek. That battle had occurred just days after the debacle at Wounded Knee, South Dakota, a tragic massacre of three hundred Lakota Sioux men, women, and children who were trying to surrender to the 7th Cavalry. Howze was leading a fifty-three-man cavalry escort to protect a supply train as it lumbered across the partially frozen White River near the mouth of Little Grass Creek, when hundreds of Lakota warriors attacked to exact revenge for the senseless slaughter at Wounded Knee. The lieutenant and his men desperately fought off the attack and miraculously survived. For this effort, Howze and five of his comrades were awarded the Congressional Medal of Honor.

Howze's military career then took him to Chicago, to quell the Pullman railroad strikes in 1894, followed by a stint at West Point as an instructor of military tactics. In February 1897, then-Captain Howze married Ann Hawkins, daughter of General Hamilton H. Hawkins. In 1898, he sailed to Cuba with General Shafter and fought in the Santiago Campaign. On July 6, 1899, he received a telegram from fellow Rough Rider Theodore Roosevelt, advising that the "President wires me he will appoint you Lieutenant Colonel if you are to accept." Without hesitation, Howze signed on and arrived in the Philippines three months later. Howze was a can-do guy who performed well under pressure, a welcome addition to the hunt for Aguinaldo.

On November 28, 1899, Young's men captured a letter that indicated Aguinaldo's small column had moved once again. This time, the intelligence suggested that he was moving into the Cordilleras, through Tirad Pass, and on to Angaki, Ilocos Sur. Separately, it was reported, Tinio's

Left to right, front row: Major Julius A. Penn, Lieutenant Colonel Robert L. Howze, Assistant Surgeon Frank M. Foxworthy, and Captain Frank L. French, joined by fellow staff officers of the 34th Infantry.

Brigade—with some twenty American prisoners and more than four thousand Spanish captives—had taken another route into the Cordilleras, through a second pass called Tangadan, into the province of Abra.

Aguinaldo's plan was obvious to Young: divide the American forces pursuing him and draw both elements into the thickly forested and near-impenetrable Cordilleras. Along narrow, uncharted trails, across steep terrain, and through hostile tribal settlements, the Americans would lose every advantage they currently possessed—speed, superior firepower, and a greater number of men.

On November 30, 1899, reinforced by Howze's battalion of 34th Infantry, Young faced a critical decision. His quarry had now split in two separate columns, each requiring pursuit. Aguinaldo, the center of gravity who served as the political, martial, and inspirational cohesion to the Philippine insurrection, had taken one route. Tinio, along with the Gillmore party prisoners, had taken another. Gillmore was, in his own right, a cause célèbre, and could not be ignored. His imprisonment, reportedly under the harshest of conditions, represented a wholly unacceptable state of affairs that offended the sensibilities of every officer in army and navy service.

Young grappled with the question: With Aguinaldo and Tinio having split their forces into two, how should he direct his very limited resources? Devoting all of his forces to the hunt for Aguinaldo beyond Tirad Pass might bring an early termination to the war, but there were no guarantees the leader could be caught. Chasing Tinio, and securing the liberation of the famed Gillmore and his party, might result in an accomplishment of even greater importance and bring a horrible chapter of American debacle and defeat to a close.

Young then made a fateful decision. Instead of focusing on an either/or proposition, Young opted to split his already-meager and under-resourced force into two and pursue both objectives. March and his battalion would head into the mountains toward Angaki, hot on the trail of the retreating Aguinaldo. Young, with Howze's battalion, would continue north to Tangadan Pass, to destroy Tinio's remaining forces and chase after Gillmore and the other American prisoners.

Was Young taking Aguinaldo's bait? Or was he judiciously allocating his resources for the greatest chances of success? The brigadier general could not have known it at the time, but his strategy would have startling consequences, and would alter the course of the war.

March and his battalion—a force of four companies totaling some three hundred men—were sent by Young in urgent pursuit of Aguinaldo on November 30, 1899. Two days later, they ran headlong into the rebel general's rear guard on narrow, zigzagging trails at Tirad Pass, at a mist-shrouded elevation of 4,400 feet. A sixty-man defensive force, led by the twenty-two-year-old General del Pilar, had taken positions behind a stone barricade, where they enjoyed excellent lines of fire from which to rain down rifle fire on the advancing Americans.

Seeing that a frontal attack was impossible, March ordered a company of his men to climb the steep mountain face on the flank. He ordered another group of sharpshooters to a nearby hill to pick off any insurgent foolish enough to raise his head above the stone works. For three hours, the flanking force scrambled up near-vertical terrain, groping at branches, hauling each other up with belts and blankets, and dodging boulders rolled down the mountainside by the enemy above. Led by

Lieutenant Frank Dean Tompkins, a former grocer and father of three from New York City, the company finally made the summit. From this vantage point, Tompkins and his men initiated a barrage of suppressing fire, covering March and the balance of their men as they assaulted the Filipino positions.

Despite a five-to-one advantage over del Pilar's force, two American privates were immediately killed. Two others fell with serious gunshot wounds. Yet, March's men spilled over the defenses in a blaze of rifle fire. When the smoke cleared, they counted fifty-one insurgent dead sprawled across the trenches, including del Pilar. Their sacrifice, however, had bought the fleeing Aguinaldo a twenty-hour lead. As thick clouds rolled in and night fell, the Americans set up camp and prepared to bivouac. For the moment, the chase for the day was over. Savoring their victory, March's men dined on a cache of rice left behind by the slaughtered rebel force.

The hike after the Gillmore Party prisoners in December 1899. Lieutenant John Lipop, 33rd Infantry, carried a Kodak folding pocket camera. That images of the rescue expedition exist at all is remarkable.

At sunrise, encouraged by reports from straggling Spanish prisoners that Aguinaldo was at the settlement of Cayan, only seventeen miles ahead, March's battalion pressed forward. Along the route, at the town of Cervantes, March ran into a distraction. Swamped by some 575 Spanish prisoners, 150 friars, and a ream of conflicting intelligence, the major fatefully opted to spend the entire day of December 4, "resting the men and sifting evidence" regarding Aguinaldo's whereabouts. Back on the trail at daybreak on December 5 with a contingent of one hundred selected men, March tackled the steep climb to the settlement of Cayan, only to find that Aguinaldo and his core of officers were long gone. The precious day's delay at Cervantes had extended the rebel command's lead to two and a half days.

With his men starting to drop, Major March dallied again at Cayan to accept the surrender of a Filipino general, Venancio Concepcion, through an exchange of letters and a proposed interview that afternoon. As the remnants of daylight fell, March ordered camp set for the night. The next morning, realizing he would need to travel even faster to catch Aguinaldo, March weeded his men to his best eighty-six. This leaner, faster force continued at pace across the jagged mountain terrain. Reaching Bontoc, they learned that Aguinaldo had been replenished with fresh ponies and bearers. With what had now become a three-day advantage, Aguinaldo and his command had fled deeper into the Cordilleras. With his forces out of steam, March knew further pursuit was futile. The chase for Aguinaldo was over. The usually effective March had failed.

The pursuit had been the major's best effort given the limited resources at his disposal. Perhaps with the balance of men who had been sent to confront Tinio's Brigade and chase down the Gillmore party, March could have leapfrogged ahead and denied Aguinaldo his escape. But that was not to be. Aguinaldo would now disappear from American sights for the next fifteen months, retreating to the relative safety of Luzon's mountains, where he would continue to orchestrate a bloody and protracted guerrilla war from afar.

Farther north, the American hunt for Tinio's Brigade was under way. Young's beleaguered column, reinforced with two battalions in response to his urgent pleas for help—one from the 33rd Infantry, led by Major Peyton March, whose men had faltered while pursuing Aguinaldo at Tirad Pass, and one from the 34th Infantry, led by Howze, which had marched up from MacArthur's command at Cabanatuan—was to receive a welcome surprise. Unknown to Young at the time, a third battalion was now also making its way to him, having left San Fabian on November 23: Hare's battalion from the 33rd Infantry, comprising 270 men. Wheaton, it seemed, had finally come to his senses.

Hare and his men were making good progress up the coast, covering an average of twenty miles per day. At that pace, they aimed to make Vigan, 130 miles north, within the week. Once Hare's battalion arrived, Young would have double the men at his disposal.

The one officer missing from Hare's staff command was John Logan, the major who had been shot and killed in a muddy swamp outside San Jacinto. Logan's death caused a stir across the United States in the weeks that followed. Fueled by soldiers' letters home and a robust grapevine of gossip, newspaper stories suggested that he had been killed by his own men. When the rumors refused to dissipate, the War Department launched an investigation. The finding: The story had originated from a lowly freight clerk named Koppitz. Hunted down by investigators, the poor man denied ever uttering such a tale, much less to the media. Nevertheless, Koppitz was dismissed from service; someone had to take the fall. The *New York Times* ran a story with the headline WAS LOGAN KILLED BY HIS MEN? NO ONE WILL ASSUME RESPONSIBILITY FOR THE REPORT. If Logan indeed had been shot by his own comrades—perhaps in revenge for tossing their beloved regimental mascot overboard—no one was talking.

The blistering pace of Hare's column, racing to bolster Young's forces, began to take its toll. Men dropped off from exhaustion and a raft of medical ailments. The number of men on the sick list spiked. The stress of the march hit the men hard, particularly Hare's most senior officer, Lieutenant Colonel John J. Brereton.

That the slight-statured Brereton was a man of few words was not surprising, given the heavy burdens that had dogged his domestic life. Widowed twice and left to raise his only daughter, Alice, on his own, Brereton was also afflicted with an ailment he could not shake: deep-seated pain from chronic inflammation of his optic nerve, apparently caused by a severe viral-bacterial infection he had contracted at West Point. During bouts of inflammation of the orbital branches of the fifth nerve of his right eye, Brereton was only able to read or write for a few minutes at a time. He wore sunglasses whenever venturing outside in daylight, and was unable to sleep unless heavily dosed with narcotics. The pain, headaches, and severe discomfort—relentless and enduring—followed him from West Point to Indian Territory to his tour of duty in the Spanish-American War, where he distinguished himself at the Battle of Santiago.

Now, with his optic nerve inflamed under the intense physical torment of the grueling march up the coast of northern Luzon, the headaches worsened. Brereton began to exhibit increasingly erratic behavior. On the afternoon of November 29, near San Fernando, La Union, he disappeared on his mount, leaving his fellow officers mystified. While Hare could barely spare the men, he ordered Major Lieberman, his battalion surgeon, accompanied by Sergeant Major Robert E. Wilson, Hospital Corpsmen Manuel Campa, and a Filipino servant, to head south after Brereton to coax him back to the command.

Reaching San Fernando that evening, Lieberman was handed several notes by a courier who had been sent by Brereton from the town of Bauang. The letters were studies in madness. Brereton alleged that several officers in the regiment were trying to kill him. Bizarrely, in response to the provocation, he explained that he had killed Major Sirmyer. The problem with all this, of course, was that Sirmyer—whom the men had just left at camp—was alive and well. From a medical perspective, Surgeon Lieberman was convinced "beyond a doubt" that Brereton had gone insane.

At daybreak, Lieberman and his men charged south to catch up with the deranged officer. They found Brereton "riding aimlessly" on his horse and complaining of a mind-numbing headache. Lieberman fibbed: He was on his way to get supplies at San Fabian; if the lieutenant colonel would be so kind as to accompany them, they'd also be able to get him some relief for his headache. Brereton bought the story and rode with his compatriots throughout the day. Upon reaching the town of Santo Tomas late that evening, they agreed to camp at the *presidencia* building, joining a detachment of 3rd Cavalry already bivouacked there for the night. They would make for San Fabian at first light.

In the decrepit stone building, Brereton collapsed into an exhausted sleep, gripping a loaded and cocked revolver against his chest. Studying their patient from a distance, Lieberman and Wilson agreed they needed to disarm the lieutenant colonel for his own good. They approached quietly and slipped the revolver from his hand. Lieberman carefully released the hammer to a safe position and withdrew, leaving the mentally confused officer to his dreams.

Before dawn, Brereton jumped from his sleep and, finding his revolver gone, "raised Cain." Lieberman and Wilson tried to calm him down, but the lieutenant colonel was unstoppable. He stormed out of the room, closely trailed by Wilson, and into another part of the building where the men of the 3rd Cavalry were quartered. Brereton suddenly grabbed a Krag-Jorgensen .30-40 cavalry carbine lying about and turned the gun on Wilson. He demanded that the sergeant major lay his gun on the floor or else he would be shot. Wilson slowly placed his revolver on the wooden floor, stepped back, and exited the room. Then, in a blur of unfathomable insanity, Brereton flipped the rifle around toward his own forehead, aimed its barrel between his eyes—the focus of his blinding headache—and squeezed the trigger. The gunshot blew off the top of his head and splattered his brains across the old stone wall behind him. At 5:50 a.m., as the tropical sun began its searing ascent into the sky, Lieutenant Colonel John James Brereton was no longer in pain, and his beloved twelve-year-old daughter Alice Eleanor—safely ensconced with relatives in New Jersey—was now an orphan.

Lieberman wired San Fabian to send an ambulance for the body. Hare's regimental command, en route to assist the beleaguered Young in the capture of Aguinaldo, the attack on Tinio's forces, and the rescue of the Gillmore party prisoners, was now short one more officer.

This time, though, the men of the "Fighting 33rd" mourned. They had lost one of their own.

CHAPTER FOURTEEN

Buying Time

ON DECEMBER 3, 1899, BRIGADIER GENERAL SAMUEL B. M. YOUNG, Lieutenant Colonel Robert Lee Howze, and their bedraggled column stopped at the foot of a steep canyon pass carved by the mighty Abra River. They were a day's hike from their next objective, the city of Vigan. At camp, however, new information trickled in about a more-immediate objective. Ten miles to the east, heavily fortified trench works had been built at Tangadan Pass by the Tinio Brigade as a defensive effort to close off a strategic route leading into the Cordilleras. Known as *La Bocana*, the "mouth," Tangadan Pass was reportedly the route taken by General Tinio to elude the Americans and divert attention from Aguinaldo's retreat at Tirad Pass to the south. More beguiling to Young, the report suggested that beyond the canyon, in Tinio's grip, the Gillmore party languished.

The trench works at Tangadan Pass, constructed with the assistance of Spanish engineers, were a marvel. Tinio had assigned some one hundred laborers to the effort over the course of a year, part of his plan to hold out in the mountains beyond. The defenses terraced the mountainside, providing a line of fire across the entire valley below. The interconnected labyrinth of "bombproof" trenches were permanent in nature, "with slopes and sodded revetments supported by timbers," providing "perfect approaches" for defense and retreat. Tinio did not expect the Americans to even consider attacking the defenses, which were seemingly impregnable. With limited men already nearing exhaustion, the logical course of action for the Americans would be to move on to the more-comfortable confines of Vigan, which was already under their control. In any event, if the approaching Americans were that bold, Tinio fully expected the trenches to hold.

Defending Tangadan Pass was a force of 1,060 men under the command of Lieutenant Colonel Blas Villamor, an educated man from Bangued, Abra. In his late twenties, Villamor was Tinio's chief of staff and second in command of the brigade. His men had about a thousand rifles, though most were old Spanish Remingtons in barely serviceable condition. Tinio was emphatic: Villamor and his men were to hold Tangadan Pass, sacrificing their lives in its defense if necessary. It could not be allowed to fall.

Itching for a fight, Tinio was not content with an entirely defensive posture. He knew the Americans had taken Vigan with a limited force and had stockpiled vast stores of ammunition throughout the town. An offensive assault would put the Americans on notice: Their foray into the Ilocos would be costly. From Bangued sixteen miles distant, Tinio ordered four hundred men to float down the Abra River on a flotilla of *bancas* and bamboo rafts and infiltrate Vigan under the cover of darkness. They were to attack the Americans with impunity and deal a deadly blow.

Vigan at this point was lightly defended. Lieutenant Colonel Parker, Young's executive officer, had arrived on the USS *Oregon* and was by now supported by 84 men of Company B, from Hare's battalion of 33rd Infantry, who had been sent to relieve the marine contingent that first took the city. Another 153 men from the 33rd Infantry had arrived under the command of Major Cronin, all suffering from disease or other medical ailments. In sum, the American force at Vigan totaled approximately 250 men, the majority of them on the sick list, who had been scattered about several crumbling colonial buildings that ringed the main plaza.

In the early hours of December 4, Tinio's four-hundred-man force— some with rifles and most with bolos—disembarked from their rafts on the Abra River in silence and stole into the town. The bulk assembled in Vigan's cathedral; others settled on the periphery. Just before 4:00 a.m., on a moonless night, an American army patrol challenged a party of the Filipinos in a wooded park off the plaza and was fired upon. Within moments, all hell broke loose. Insurgents spilled from the cathedral and took up strategic positions around the plaza. Rocked out of their sleep by gunfire, Parker's bleary-eyed men stumbled out of their palace quarters and into the pitch-black plaza, most still in their nightwear. They fired blindly at the muzzle flashes from the surrounding bushes and buildings. Rebels in the hospital, jail, and cathedral, with excellent lines of sight, fired mercilessly upon the disorganized Americans. Parker, sprinting toward the northwest corner of the plaza to give orders to his men, ran headlong into an explosive volley of gunfire. He threw himself to the ground, losing his revolver, and crawled to safety. Over the next three hours, fighting degenerated into hand-to-hand combat, moving from one building to another.

On the periphery of the plaza, Filipino soldiers swarmed Outpost Number 3 and fired wildly at the two sentries on duty. One was killed instantly; his comrade fell, wounded. The attackers moved on, bolting through the darkness.

The Americans retook the cathedral, capturing a number of Filipinos. At the hospital compound, however, rebel riflemen settled in behind a limestone balustrade, its upright carved columns spaced just about wide enough to provide portholes, capped by a lintel of solid masonry. From this perfectly defensible, bunker-like position, they were able to unload on the Americans. A squad of Americans at the compound's wall poured fire on the balustrade. The sharp reports between forces were no more than thirty-five yards apart. Despite an incessant barrage, the Americans were unable to dislodge the enemy.

As the fighting raged, ammunition ran low among the Americans at the hospital compound's wall. One soldier on the sick roster, twenty-nine-year-old Quartermaster Sergeant Norman M. Fry, volunteered to run boxes of rimmed Krag .30-40 cartridges out to the men. The lanky, dark-complexioned painter from Syracuse, New York, made a number of seventy-five-yard sprints to and from the wall with boxes of desperately needed ammunition tucked under his arms. As Fry frantically distributed the ammo among the soldiers along the firing line, a Mauser slug slammed through his neck, severing his carotid artery. He was killed instantly.

Elsewhere, just off the plaza, Private Joseph L. Epps, a former cowboy from Jamestown, Missouri, was ordered to keep watch over a house surrounded by a stone wall. Inside, the Americans were sure a band of enemy combatants was in hiding. Hearing movement inside the compound, Epps climbed the wall and trained his revolver on a startled group of seventeen rebel soldiers. The twenty-nine-year-old private ordered the fighters to drop their weapons and surrender, while yelling to his colleague to kick in the bamboo gate and cover him. Hearing that Epps required reinforcements, his commanding officer rushed back to find the two privates nervously holding the much-larger group of insurgents at gunpoint, their seventeen rifles neatly stacked in a pile.

Back at the plaza, another soldier on the sick roster, Private John A. Weimer, a twenty-year-old office clerk from Texas, was ordered to take a position by a stone coping nearest the hospital, and "to hold that position to the last extremity." Lying at the foot of a tree, partially exposed to the well-entrenched Filipinos, the farmer from Winfield, Kansas, held his own for more than three hours. With his blazing rifle at times overheating, and hundreds of empty cartridges piling up around him, Weimer single-handedly kept the rebels from flanking his comrades.

The Americans hammered away at the balustrade-protected riflemen, but were only able to pick off a few bolo men dodging about in the background. Nearby, Private James McConnell, a twenty-one-year-old, sandy-haired former laborer from Syracuse "fought for hours, lying between two dead comrades, notwithstanding his hat was pierced, his clothing plowed through by bullets, and his face cut and bruised by flying gravel." Finally, the Americans decided to rush the hospital balustrade, leaping up in unison and charging the enemy. In a storm of insurgent lead, seven American soldiers were quickly cut down. The Filipinos, however, were driven back and their position was finally breached.

As the bloody morning wore on, the Americans took the advantage and chased down pockets of the enemy. The bulk of Tinio's badly mauled force, however, slid away. In their wake, the battle's carnage lay strewn about the plaza: the bodies of forty Filipinos and eight Americans. Another three American soldiers lay seriously wounded. Over the course of the bloody morning, Parker and his men had captured thirty-two prisoners, including two badly wounded officers, and took eighty-four rifles into their possession.

On the trail to Tangadan Pass, on the same morning of December 4, 1899, Young and Howze were busy reviewing their fighting strength. The three companies of men at Young's disposal comprised 145 volunteer citizen-soldiers. Nearly all had signed up to fight in the Spanish-American War and had reenlisted for the Philippines. Young also had two companies from the 3rd Cavalry, providing another 115 men. The total fighting strength of his force: 260 men.

But beyond Howze, Young had only one other professional soldier with him, Major Julius Augustus Penn. Sporting a full goatee and

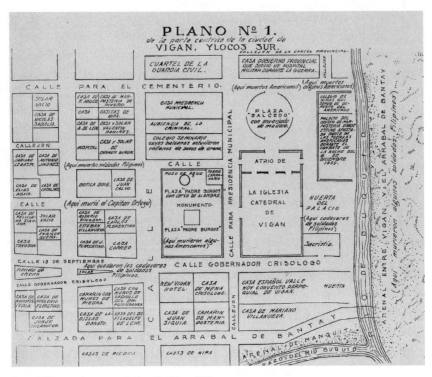

Juan Villamor's map of the Battle of Vigan.

handlebar mustache, the West Point graduate had served on expeditions against the Jicarilla and Mescalero Apache in New Mexico, followed by stints at posts in Indian and Oklahoma Territories. A valedictorian from the Army War College, where his thesis on mounted cavalry won accolades, Penn went on to help police the Butte Mine Labor Troubles in Oklahoma, fight the Bannock Indians in Wyoming and Idaho, and teach military tactics at West Point. Despite his rich experience, Penn never got past Tampa, Florida, during the Spanish-American War, where he oversaw troop transports bound for Cuba and Puerto Rico.

Young and Howze surveyed their core staff of officers and three companies. They had one professional soldier, while the rest possessed irrelevant if not completely useless skill sets for the military task at hand, including carpentry, sales, trade, and law. Would they be able to rise to the occasion, carry out an assault on the defenses at Tangadan, and hold the line under heavy fire—or would they cut and run?

Time would soon tell.

One of Howze's officers, Lieutenant Decker, with a squad of scouts, returned from his reconnoitering of Tangadan Pass. The news was not good. The enemy was strongly entrenched, burrowed in along a fortified ridge. Worse, their numbers seemed to be in the range of about eight hundred men, possibly more. Young's forces were outnumbered nearly three to one—and worse, they lacked the strategic high ground.

As Young and his officers debated tactics, the rest of the column halted along the sunbaked road to await orders. Some crawled under the few patches of shade to stretch out. Others gathered in groups to shoot dice, games of chuck-a-luck, high-low, and craps, where money quickly changed hands.

Ahead, Young's scouts captured a Filipino corporal and dragged him back to the command for interrogation. Under heavy duress, the unfortunate captive provided a wealth of intelligence regarding the defenses,

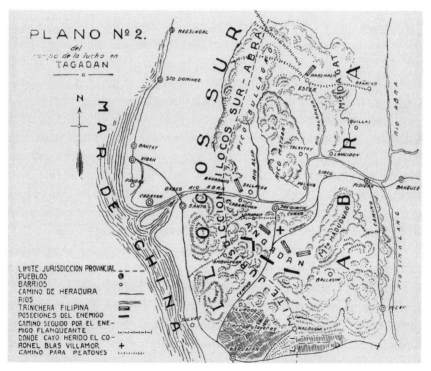

Juan Villamor's map of the fortifications at Tangadan Pass, Ilocos Sur.

location of troops, and weapons at the enemy's disposal. The Americans now had a better idea of the challenge they faced: The mountain had been fortified by tier upon tier of trenches. The highest point, a great bald knob, was a natural redoubt, strengthened by a large, circular trench. One crooked, steep trail led up to the ridge, making direct assault impossible. The only reasonable solution was to flank the defenses by climbing around the entrenchments and attacking from above. Far outnumbered, the brigadier general—a man of impulse and pluck—decided to attack. General Tinio, he reasoned, would not be expecting it.

The plan was put into motion. Major Penn and eighty men were ordered to run the flank. Decker, with his twelve scouts, was to hold the hilly terrain to the north. The rest of the men were ordered to occupy the front and low hills to the south, to cover Penn's flanking movement. Around 10:00 a.m., Penn's column moved out, crossed a small dry streambed, and climbed into the foothills. Narrow footpaths quickly gave way to straight climbing through dense, tropical thickets. After six hours of effort, the column reached the summit of the ridge. Here, they found what they had been hoping for: an open trail. They hustled along the deeply rutted path, through tall waves of cogon grass, and across to the southern side of the ridge. Then the trail dipped into a perfect defensive entanglement that had been created from a dense weave of scrub brush and branches, stopping the company cold. The men labored with bolos to hack through the barrier.

Down below, as if on cue, Colonel Hare's five companies of 33rd Infantry—another 270 men—arrived after their long march from San Fabian, bringing a much-larger contingent of officers and men to the impending fight. For Young, the unexpected reinforcements were a great relief. Hare's men took up positions on the threshold of Tangadan's defenses, a mix of former civilian officers, farmers, mechanics, lawyers, and businessmen, just as thin and inexperienced as Young's force.

Caught up at the time with the planning for a potentially brutal battle at Tangadan Pass, Young apparently gave little thought to the option of sending Hare's men to Tirad Pass, twenty-five miles to the south, to reinforce March's mountain pursuit of Aguinaldo. Instead, Young chose to direct every able man to the destruction of Tinio's Brigade at Tangadan. Once they broke through insurgent lines, he knew, they would be positioned to liberate Gillmore and his party of prisoners. Consciously or not, Young had just doubled down on Gillmore while giving Aguinaldo a pass.

⁓

As the sun began to recede from the tropical sky, one of the new arrivals from the 33rd Infantry's Company A, Private James A. Whalen, sprawled out for a catnap along the road. He never saw any of it: the tuft of dirt kicked into the air, the whizzing *ping* of a ricocheting Mauser bullet as it danced off the gravelly earth. Fired from the rebel trenches more than three-quarters of a mile away, the skipping bullet slammed into Whalen's left temple and lodged deep inside his brain. The unlucky private would live for another two hours, becoming the first casualty at Tangadan Pass.

More time passed. As the last minutes of daylight burned, Young was increasingly uneasy about Penn's long-delayed flanking column. Unknown at the time, out of sight on the ridge, Penn's men had just broken through the entanglement that had halted them on the trail. The payoff on the other side was grand: a vista across an impassable gorge that revealed a series of trenches below. In plain view, hundreds of bustling insurgents were painfully vulnerable and completely exposed.

Penn's eighty men stumbled into position along a firing line, taking a bead with their rifles on the mass of enemy activity below. On the major's signal, a first salvo exploded from the ridgeline, dropping scores of the exposed enemy. Cheers rang out across the waiting American lines. As Penn's company laid down waves of withering lead from above, their comrades below followed suit, unleashing a barrage of volleys against the trenches. When the return enemy fire slowed, small groups of American soldiers charged the Filipino positions, one after the other.

A few minutes before dark, Captain Russell, with his Company F, 34th Infantry, succeeded in gaining ground from which his men could fire directly into the rebel trenches. They opened up with a deadly barrage of rifle volleys that quickly cut up and demoralized the enemy. Around Lieutenant Colonel Villamor's command tent, three men fell dead and another was knocked to the ground, wounded. Exposing himself to enemy fire, Villamor was first grazed by a bullet along his cheek, drawing blood; a second round ripped across his shoulder—another flesh wound, but serious enough. Tinio, out of communication in the settlement of San Quintin several miles farther up the canyon, had no idea how badly his beleaguered forces were faring.

Unable to carry on, Villamor retreated, which in turn triggered a phased retreat of his men up the mountain, to the safety of higher trenches.

For the Americans, the sudden abandoning of the well-built trenches was an unexpected turn of events. Tinio's Brigade was falling back.

As the sun set, the 33rd Infantry's Company C moved against some trench works. Led by the fearless, if not slightly demented, 2nd Lieutenant Etienne de Pelissier Bujac, and under strong return fire, the eighteen-man column moved up a precipitous trail and into direct confrontation with the flaring muzzles from protected Filipino positions. Bujac advanced until an order was shouted from the trench ahead, in English: "Cease firing! You are killing your own men!" The command was echoed down the line, and the Americans' fire abruptly stopped.

Bujac, sensing a ruse, shouted back, "Cease firing, hell! That's some goo-goo speaking English; give them hell from the magazines!" A renewed barrage of lead erupted. Seeing a moment's opportunity, Bujac rushed the trench, his frighteningly insane yell nonplussing the enemy. Bujac sprang over the parapet with a column of men following closely behind. Elsewhere, others followed suit, spilling over the trenches.

Penn's men, meanwhile, kept up their rifle fire from above as succeeding trenches were taken. Darkness now gave way to a full new moon rising 10 degrees over the horizon, painting the scene with a cool lunar glow. The last charge was made up an almost-perpendicular slope. And then it was done. The flanking column on the ridge, Penn's men, ceased firing and let their overheated rifles cool. Tucked into the spur, they would bivouac in their position for the night. The echo of cheers below told of the trenches carried. The impregnable Tangadan Pass, Tinio's last line of defense, had fallen. Total American losses tallied two killed in action and thirteen wounded, with two later to die from their injuries.

By dawn, most of the Filipinos had managed a skillful withdrawal, taking most of their dead and wounded with them. Remaining pockets of insurgents were quickly dislodged. Found amid the bloody carnage and abandoned trenches were crates of ammunition—some three thousand rounds—and scores of Remington rifles that had been ditched during the panicked withdrawal. Filipino losses were estimated at thirty-five killed and eighty wounded, including ten officers.

The Americans had overrun the last and final defenses of Aguinaldo's army. Nothing separated them now from achieving their two primary objectives: the destruction of Tinio's remaining rear guard, and the liberation of the Gillmore party prisoners.

CHAPTER FIFTEEN

The Expedition

On December 5, 1899, flush with their victory at Tangadan, the two American battalions—one led by Colonel Luther R. Hare and the other by Lieutenant Colonel Robert Lee Howze—moved out at first light, advancing beyond the overrun fortifications of the Filipinos. Breaking over the mountain pass, the 350-man column dropped into the Abra River valley. Following orders from General Young, who had returned to Vigan to oversee operations with the balance of American forces, Hare and Howze's soldiers proceeded together up the wide expanse of the river course, torching insurgent barracks and food stores in their wake. By midmorning, a thick, heavy fog had rolled in, reducing visibility to just yards and casting an eerie pall over the march. The sun broke through in the late afternoon, moments before descending as a glowing red ball over the distant sea. After a ten-mile hike, the column reached the town of San Quintin where they camped for the night.

The next morning, while marching to the settlement of Pidigan, the Americans encountered several hundred starved Spanish prisoners who had been abandoned by their captors at Bangued. Brought before the command, the emaciated Spaniards excitedly explained that Lieutenant Gillmore and twenty-five other prisoners had been seen in the town just days earlier. The news grabbed the command's attention, and likely triggered wide-eyed glances among the officers.

Hare and Howze pressed the Spaniards for details. What they got were disheartening rumors. While the Spanish prisoners had been left behind, the Gillmore party captives, obviously more valuable, had been marched into the mountains. And then this, which the Spaniards had only heard secondhand: General Tinio had issued specific orders that under no circumstances were the Gillmore party prisoners to fall back into American hands. To ensure this did not happen, Tinio had commanded that Lieutenant Gillmore and his men were to be marched to a desolate location, deep in the mountains, and executed.

Runners were sent back to Vigan to share the grim news with Young. And now it dawned on Hare, Howze, and their officers: What had begun as an operation to capture Aguinaldo, and then shifted to the fight with his rear guard under Tinio, was about to become something else altogether. The forward advance of the northern campaign was no longer chasing the elusive rebel general or even focused on pacifying the country; it was now directed exclusively toward saving the lives of a navy lieutenant and his cutter crew taken at Baler. Hare had his own unspoken commitment to fulfill to his fellow veteran of the Indian Wars, Major Price, the brother-in-law of the captive lieutenant. He had given his solemn word that he would rescue Gillmore and the others if it were ever in his power.

As the expedition prepared to chase the American prisoners of war, Hare, as the ranking officer, assembled his fellow officers, rallying them around the probable challenges and possible payoff that lay ahead. And then, unable to contain himself, he punched the air, proclaiming, "I will find Gillmore if I have to follow him to hell."

Yet, with little more than unsubstantiated rumors in hand, it was unclear what route the Gillmore prisoners had followed into the Cordilleras. Trail upon trail cut into the mountains, an informal and age-old zigzagging network of foot-worn paths of mud, rock, and ruts that linked the lowlands to the uplands, towns to mountain villages, barrios to the Isneg *rancherias*. Had the Gillmore party prisoners gone south along the winding Abra River toward San Jose? Or north from Bangued toward La Paz and the high mountains of Ilocos Norte? No one knew.

The two commanders held differing opinions about the most likely route to follow. The discussion edged toward an argument as the senior-ranking Hare argued for the southern route, while dismissing Howze's views on the merits of going north. Hare summed it up: If Howze wanted to run off in another direction and waste precious time, that was just fine with the old colonel. The two American commanders, unable to reconcile, decided to split up and cover both scenarios. Hare's 33rd Infantry—with 220 men—would take the San Jose trail to the south, the most probable route, while Howze's 34th Infantry—with 130 men—would take the trail north toward Bangued and La Paz. Hopefully, one of them would pick up the route taken by the prisoners.

Howze, perhaps driven by a touch of competitive spirit, moved out at speed. By late afternoon, traipsing through rich, tilled land, he and his men could see the town of Bangued a few miles ahead. Along the rutted dirt road, a trickle of emaciated Spanish soldiers staggered toward them, warily at first, unsure if the Americans were liberators or about to become their new captors. Informed that they were free, the former prisoners burst into shouts of joy. The trickle grew by tens and scores until it was a large crowd, hobbling, limping, and being helped down the road, an unceasing stream of gaunt men that swamped the American column.

Inspired by their own elation, the Spaniards turned in their tracks and joined the American column heading to Bangued. "Never did a circus enter a town in the United States with a more enthusiastic and happy crowd of small boys than were the seven or eight hundred Spanish soldiers that almost overwhelmed us," recalled Penn. All told, roughly one thousand impoverished and ailing Spanish prisoners who had been abandoned by Tinio's forces came to the Americans over the course of the day.

The residents of Bangued greeted the mobbed American column with a brass band and the ringing of the church tower's bells. Howze marched into the town plaza to set up camp, and ordered his men to question residents about the American prisoners. The locals had little to share, but led Howze and a handful of his officers to the prison where the captives had been held. The officers poked about, kicking abandoned jars and cookware scattered about the yard, searching for clues. An officer ducked out of one of the cells and called for Howze to come have a look. Howze entered the dark chamber where his senses were assaulted by the lingering stench of the long-unwashed and ailing, a caustic mix of sweat, feces, and rot hanging heavy in the air. The officer pointed to the wall. Howze stepped forward, squinting to make out the words.

Crudely etched onto the wall with bits of charcoal was a list of names of the Gillmore party, similar to that found at San Isidro. But this time, the addition of a grim skull and crossbones suggested that a pall of hopelessness had fallen over the men. Howze may have reached out with a finger to trace the names, rubbing the charcoal residue into his fingers. This was palpable evidence that the prisoners had been here, and just days ago.

A chill raced through Howze. He would need to move at even greater speed, as soon as daylight offered the opportunity to resume the hunt.

Howze first needed to sort the Spaniards in his care. The first task the following morning was to secure boats and rafts to move the huge mass of Spaniards to the coast. The sick came first. Those still ambulatory were requested to march along the main road. Once freed from the responsibility of caring for the hungry former captives, an anxious Howze once again took up his pursuit of the Gillmore party, moving out at noon. Traveling north across the Abra River and east through San Gregorio to La Paz, nine miles distant, they hoped they might learn of the prisoners' movements. The column arrived at nightfall to little news, however. A few houses near the center of town were sequestered for the night, with strong outposts set and rotating patrols organized to guard against the remote chance that insurgents might double back from their retreat to attack.

Later in the evening, one of the American patrols came upon a Filipino who claimed to be a deserter from Tinio's Brigade. Upon close questioning, he advised that the Gillmore party had been taken north, with orders from Tinio to "dispose of them where the Americans will never find them." Howze and his command could only listen, frustrated at the turn of events. Time was of the essence.

Around 3:45 a.m., in the absolute dead of night, two weary guards on outpost duty heard rustling in the pitch-black brush. Two shadowy forms stumbled toward them. The guards raised their rifles and shouted challenges. The response could not have been more startling. The senior officer on duty raced back to the command to awaken Howze to the news: Two of the American prisoners had just staggered into the camp, and reportedly a third was close behind.

A groggy but excited Howze approached the rail-thin, bleary-eyed captives. Questions were rattled off in quick succession. Under the cool moonlit night, the prisoners began to recount their incredible escape.

~

Rushed out of Bangued three days earlier, the Gillmore party had been marched fifteen miles to a small mountain barrio called Danglas. Arriving just as darkness fell, they were quartered in a two-room bamboo shack lifted up on stilts. Most of the prisoners, including Gillmore, stayed in one large room of the hut; soldier Bruce, sailor Edwards, and civilian O'Brien occupied the small adjacent room. All three men were suffering from fever and dysentery, and believed that whatever was under way—most likely a protracted hike up into the mountains—was not survivable. They were slowly deteriorating, sliding toward death. The possibility of escape had been discussed among the group before, but Gillmore had angrily dismissed the idea each time with the same response: "Why man, that would be suicide, just like jumping off a bluff!" By now, Bruce, Edwards, and O'Brien felt they had no other choice but to act on their own. This time, they would not bring it up with Gillmore, knowing he would merely attempt to overrule them. This was no longer about following orders; it was about survival.

The three desperate men studied their accommodations for the night. On their side of the hut, leading from their room, was a second doorway, connected to a bamboo ladder to the ground. All agreed that this setup might just allow them to slip away once the guards fell into a slumber.

Lying awake with churning stomachs, the three prisoners listened to Tinio's soldiers straggling about the town and waited for the right moment. Unfortunately, too many people were up and about. If their escape was to be successful, the prisoners would need to rethink their plan. They needed to add the element of a ruse. It was agreed that Edwards would take an empty water jar, climb down the ladder, and ask the guards for permission to go to the river to refill it. Presumably, he would be escorted by a contingent of armed guards, as had happened in the past. Edwards was to make plenty of noise during all of this, to cover the exit of Bruce and O'Brien down the back ladder. The two would escape into the brush, quickly take the narrow trail through the tall canebrake to the river, and wait for Edwards and his escort. When they passed, Bruce and O'Brien would club the guards senseless, and Edwards would join his comrades to make their getaway to freedom.

The plan was put into motion. This time, to the great surprise of the prisoners, Edwards was sent to the river for drinking water without an escort. Bruce and O'Brien were nearly incredulous; there would be no need for violence. They slipped down the ladder and rushed into the brush. Breathless with adrenaline, hearts pumping, the three escapees regrouped and waded into the swift Abra River. They swam across, setting the water jug adrift at midstream. Reaching the opposite bank, they climbed out and stealthily made their way down along the riverbank. As the first rays of morning light broke over the horizon, they frantically searched for somewhere, anywhere, to hide. Out of time, they scrambled to the top of the promontory and wedged themselves among the rocks and brush. High and hidden from view, they had a sight line on the possible approaches by their guards from their camp. Sopping wet and chilled by the cool mountain air, the three ailing men dropped into fitful sleep, their stomachs gnarled with cramps caused by the dysentery. There they lay in silent agony until the sun rose completely, removing their cloak of darkness.

With the full morning light came the reverberating alarm of a gong, followed by excited shouts. The hunt was on. Rebel patrols moved out, searching the scrub brush and riverbanks. The three escapees lay as still as possible, until a gaggle of chattering crab-eating macaques swarmed the tree branches overhead, squealing in consternation at the intruders in their habitat. Convinced that the monkeys' din would attract a patrol, the prisoners tried to silence the excited primates with handfuls of thrown rocks. The assault only ratcheted up their volume. The men finally tried turning away and ignoring them, praying for silence. Thankfully, their novelty wore off and the monkeys settled.

Sunlight warmed the rocks throughout the day, and the three men lay completely still, wedged in place. But soon, thirst began to parch their throats. They berated themselves for not bringing water; to think they had even had a jug in their hands and discarded it in the river. Down below, the insurgent teams were busy patrolling suspected sections of brush, hoping to flush their prey. After a few hours, the frustrated search teams gave up their quest and returned to camp. The three prisoners remained silent, still.

Finally, the harsh tropical sun moved toward the horizon and began to set. The air cooled. The three men had survived the day. They made their way down from their rocky promontory, covering their tracks, and kept moving. Edwards and O'Brien were barefoot; Bruce had barely serviceable shoes that soon fell apart. They worked their way back to a tributary of the Abra River, slaked their severe thirst, and then quietly slid into the water. Carried along on the current, they half-floated and half-swam for about a mile, arriving at a rocky shoal, an ideal location to climb ashore without leaving any footprints.

Out in the night, again, wet to the bone, stomachs afire with infection, the three prisoners headed to the distant sea coast. As the trails became wider and more worn, they stopped worrying about the footprints they were leaving behind. At one point, moving at a jog, the prisoners froze at the sound of approaching horses. They dove into a muddy ditch just seconds before a Filipino cavalry patrol passed, their mounts snorting, possibly aware of the breathless forms hiding just yards away. To the Americans' amazement, the soldiers passed unaware of their presence. Within moments, the three escapees were again on the run down the dark road, barefoot, anxiously glancing over their shoulders.

Bruce, Edwards, and O'Brien finally arrived at the ferry crossing at Bangued and slipped back into the river. Holding hands, they fought the current together. But by mid-river, it was clear that it needed to be every man for himself. Separating, each called upon a final burst of energy, tapping unknown reserves for the very hope of survival.

"We landed almost a mile below where we started in, and climbed out on the bank looking like three drowned rats," Edwards recounted. "It was some time before we could go on, as we were all nearly exhausted by the long swim. It was only the thought of freedom and home that buoyed our spirits and gave us the strength to go on."

Sitting in the darkness, the three escaped prisoners assessed the decreasing menu of options before them. There was no place to hide, and in their current state of hunger, weakness, and pain, it was unlikely they could cover much more distance on foot. They needed to eat. The decision was made: They would risk going into town in search of food and, perhaps more importantly, information. They entered Bangued from the northeast, moving as quietly as they could through the unlit narrow streets toward the plaza. If American forces had bivouacked in the town, that's where they would be found. White flags of surrender hung from every house, though every structure they passed appeared deserted.

Stepping into the shadows of the empty plaza, the three escapees stopped to confer. They could move up into the mountains to hide and wait for the Americans, with the hope that they would come soon. Or they could gather up some bamboo poles, fashion a makeshift raft, and attempt to float thirty miles down the Abra River to Vigan, where they were sure Americans were encamped. Or, thirdly, they could try to find at least one friendly resident in Bangued of whom they could inquire about the location of American forces. They knew the local population had an uncanny ability to track the movements of American forces, and with a striking level of accuracy.

"Hunger got the best of the argument, and we decided to seek out the house of our former jailer, who had been friendly to us," recalled Edwards. They stumbled through the town's narrow, cobblestone streets to the house of Señor Mateo, the man responsible for their captivity for the past three months. A faint light danced in the window. Someone was home.

It was a huge gamble to approach the enemy for a hiding place and sustenance. It could easily go badly, and quickly—especially if American forces had passed through and caused any suffering to the town's residents. O'Brien pushed for a consensus, saying, "Let's take a shot at it." Bruce and Edwards agreed. They devised a plan: Edwards would go up the stairs and knock on the door. Bruce and O'Brien would stand guard at each end of the street. If it was safe, they would join him. Edwards made his way up the creaky wooden stairs, barefoot and still drenched from his swim across the river. He paused, took a breath, and rapped on Señor Mateo's door.

"*Quién está?*" came the response.

"It's Edwards, one of the American prisoners."

The door opened slowly. His former prison warden stood before him, smiling, graciously inviting him in. In the *sala,* the living room, several other men sat silently, barely illuminated by the flicker of candlelight. Edwards explained that he had two companions waiting down below. Bring them up, Mateo urged, and Edwards gave the signal. O'Brien entered slowly, surveying the room. Spying a large chest by the door with several bolos casually placed on top, he moved toward it and sat down, the weapons within reach in the event things went awry. With two bolos, O'Brien figured, he could surely dole out some damage.

Señor Mateo was effusive. He explained that a large American *El Kapitan,* on a huge horse—much larger than their native ponies—had ridden into town with more than a hundred American soldiers on foot. Mateo then turned his attention to the men, commenting in Spanish, "You must be hungry, and all I have is some cold rice and fish." The famished men smiled gratefully and were soon devouring the stale food as the warden continued his tale. That enormous horse—the sheer size of it was truly incredible, he gushed. More surprising, Mateo added, was that the Americans had treated the Filipinos well. They had arrived at noon, the same day the prisoners had been marched out to Danglas. After spending several hours in the town, the Americans—and that huge horse—had left for La Paz, heading northwest, in pursuit of Tinio and his prisoners. By Mateo's estimate, the American soldiers were now likely camped up the road, just a few miles from where the three men had escaped. The prisoners savored the irony: Had they stayed where they were, they would have reached the American forces long ago. Now, they would need to double back, covering thirty arduous miles in total, all of it unnecessary.

Mateo assigned a guide to lead Bruce, Edwards, and O'Brien through the night toward La Paz. They pushed forward with every ounce of their strength. As they neared the foot of the hill where it was believed the American forces were camped, O'Brien, the once-fearless world adventurer, simply quit. He lay down on the ground and refused to move. No more, not another step, he sighed. He was done; there was nothing left. Bruce and Edwards desperately encouraged him on. Go ahead, leave me, O'Brien argued. No, they responded, if they did that, he might be captured and killed. "What of it," he exhaled. "That would be a relief."

Left without much choice, Bruce and Edwards turned to the guide, who pointed to the crest of a distant hill. "You will find the Americans there," the guide said. "Now, I am going. Thank you." The guide disappeared in one direction and the two exhausted prisoners staggered in another, leaving O'Brien sprawled out on the ground between them.

Bruce and Edwards pressed forward, making one last push. Halfway up the hill, they were confronted by the startled American sentries settled behind a rock, rifles drawn. The soldiers demanded that the intruders halt and identify themselves.

<hr/>

And now here they were, telling their story.

Lieutenant Colonel Howze immediately sent a squad of five soldiers to bring in O'Brien, who quickly regained his will to live. The battalion commander then ordered everyone back to sleep for the few hours before daylight. In moments, under a blanket of stars and a half-crescent moon, the three exhausted, aching former prisoners of war slipped into deep, heavy sleep. Their ordeal was over.

<hr/>

Escape had come as a natural impulse to Bruce, Edwards, and O'Brien, who at great risk and against all odds had made their dramatic break from captivity. The balance of the prisoners, under armed guard, had at times conspired to make a similar exit, but had been either thwarted in their attempts or talked out of their proposed brash behavior by an ever-cautious Lieutenant Gillmore.

Back at Baler, though, life had settled into a different pattern for Apprentice Denzell G. A. Venville. Following the release of the Spanish prisoners, Lieutenant Colonel Tecson had withdrawn with his forces, leaving the town of Baler under the loose control of *Kapitan* Novicio and perhaps twenty-four soldiers. Presumably, with remote Baler out of the line of fire and under no immediate threat, it was better to focus on fighting the Americans as they pushed through central Luzon. Second-hand accounts, spun years later, suggest that Venville, after healing, almost enjoyed his time at Baler. He made friends with the locals and became an accomplished fisherman. In a shared living arrangement with the two priests, Lopez and Minaya—themselves inseparable since their youthful days at the monastery in Spain—the three prisoners became an established presence about town. Venville, hobbling about as a cripple, still cut an impressive figure, towering above the local residents with his shock of blond hair and smiling blue eyes.

There is no record that Venville made any effort to escape over the mountains or sail away on one of the many small fishing boats littering Baler's coastline. One can imagine that a relaxed tropical life, free of the rigid constraints and conventions found on board a navy ship, may have appealed to the impressionable boy. No doubt the two gentle priests, the sailor's constant companions, raised the bar of conversation above the expletive-laced sailors' tales of liquor, women, and raucous ports. And perhaps in this environment, the weak young man—the "girl sailor," as he had been called—found comfort.

All evidence suggests that Venville accepted his fate and settled into his captivity at Baler. Whether the separation and lack of communication with his family in Oregon caused him any distress, we do not know. His mother, Emily Mash, and his sisters, on the other hand, appear to have been consumed by the loss of their son and brother. Emily Mash's letters sent to the navy and army hierarchy would go unanswered for months, but she remained undaunted. In the interim, she anxiously pressed for answers through other channels, enlisting the support of the Republican senator from Oregon, German-born Joseph Simon. His telegram to

The rescue column marched along rivers and through canyons, climbing deep into the mountains of Apayao.

USAMHI

the navy seeking facts about the missing son of one of his constituents brought a response within a day:

> *The Bureau has no further information regarding Venville, but the Department believes the Commander-in-Chief of the Asiatic Squadron will use every effort and every means at his hands to effect the exchange of the prisoners captured by the insurgents.*

At daybreak on December 8, 1899, Howze's column and their three new additions were eating breakfast. Despite having only a few hours of slumber, Edwards remembered the meal as the best he had ever eaten—Swift's premium bacon, piping-hot coffee, and hardtack. The starved prisoners consumed all the bacon on hand and even tried to gnaw through some of the tough *carabao* meat the column had been holding in reserve.

After breakfast, the column marched on to Danglas, following a winding river for eleven miles into the mountains. Here, they encountered a community of long-haired, non-Christian tribal people who made the mountains of Abra their home. Dressed in loincloths, armed with spears, head axes, and shields, they appeared to the Americans as wild warriors from another world. The soldiers had heard tales from their native guides and scouts about these tribal people—tales of head-hunting and bizarre pagan rituals in the untamed Cordilleras. Now, meeting these fascinating warriors firsthand, the Americans gaped at them with a mix of caution and wonder.

Scattered about the settlement was indisputable evidence of a mad scramble into the mountains by Tinio's men. Eighty bull carts and sleds had been abandoned, while farther afield, where the trails grew narrow and more difficult to climb, other supplies had been dumped. Howze ordered the property burned and rallied his men to push on. They were close, right on Tinio's tail. But now they would also need guides to lead them through the uncharted territory they were about to enter. Arrangements were made with the native tribesmen, the Tinggians, for several guides. These hunters knew the terrain intimately and they could track; their knowledge and skills would be invaluable to the Americans.

With several Tinggian warriors on point, the column marched into the mountains, leaving smoldering piles of abandoned supplies in their wake. Over the next few miles, they stumbled across more ditched materiel: several hundred rifles, thousands of rounds of crated ammunition, reloading tools, cartridge presses, sheet copper, lead, and clothing. The rebels had jettisoned anything not absolutely critical for escape and survival. The retreat of Tinio's forces had become a rout.

By mid-morning, near the Tinggian village of Bandi, the Americans struck an element of Tinio's rear guard, nearly a hundred men. Decker and his scouts dispersed the soldiers in a running firefight. Edwards recalled with clarity how one of the scouts fired on a Filipino, sending him sprawling facedown in the dirt. The insurgent rolled over, arched sharply, and died. Taking advantage of the tragic outcome, Edwards stripped the dead man of his rifle—a Mauser in good condition—and an ammo pouch. The navy landsman was now armed and ready to join the fight. When the Americans regrouped after the skirmish, they counted seven insurgents killed and one wounded.

Two Aeta Negritos were among a number of Filipinos who joined the American rescue column as guides, runners, and *cargadores*.

Throughout the afternoon, the column followed a grassy trail along a knife-edged ridge. Their route gradually climbed into the main divide of the Cordillera mountain range and then spectacularly opened onto a richly forested promontory. Even at this altitude, the trail was still littered with abandoned pack animals and an odd assortment of jettisoned baggage. Penn recalled that the stunning old-growth forest, the inspiring vistas, and the chaos of a rout, "would have delighted a Remington or a Zogbaum," the two famous war artists of the day.

Before dusk, the American column passed through a stunning grove of majestic pine. In the crisp, biting air of high altitude, it was an environment of otherworldly beauty. Having covered more than twenty miles over rough, mountainous terrain, Howze ordered camp to be set in a deep canyon near the summit. As the exhausted column came to a halt, four more half-starved Spanish soldiers emerged skittishly from the surrounding forest. Like the piles of dumped crates and broken carts, they too had been abandoned by their fleeing captors.

Colonel Hare's column, leading the chase from another direction, was also in aggressive pursuit of the Gillmore prisoners. They had camped overnight in San Jose, traversed the Abra River outside the settlement the following morning, and hiked to the settlement of Dolores. Arriving before midnight, they had found three Spanish women left behind by Tinio's men, former prisoners who helpfully advised that the insurgent column had passed by just two days prior, with the American captives in tow. Their best guess: Tinio's rear guard and the remaining prisoners were now somewhere near La Paz.

This critical information confirmed for Hare that he and his five companies of 33rd Infantry had actually gone in the wrong direction. They now needed to catch up to Howze and his three companies of the 34th Infantry, who were on the right trail. The lives of Gillmore and the rest of the prisoners, he knew, hung in the balance.

Early on December 9, Howze's men broke through a steep, pine-covered slope and spilled onto a sunlit, grassy summit. Whipped by a fierce wind, the men paused to take in a stunning view of Laoag Valley and the glistening blue sea below. Ahead, they traced the trail, a winding path etched into the grassy ridge, which ominously dropped into another deep, thickly forested canyon. Into that abyss, Tinio's rear guard had disappeared.

USAMHI

Igorot *cargadores* preparing lunch on the trail. These mountain tribal people were pressed into service by both the Filipinos and the Americans.

They pressed on. At one point, the advance stopped and huddled around a rock. Howze and the officers were called forward. Before them, the advance pointed out the oddest of signs. Scrawled on a boulder was a slogan, an advertisement, chalked out in smudged white letters: DRINK PABST BEER—AGGIE DRINKS IT. It had to have been written by one of the prisoners, but which one? Howze's soldiers could not have known, but it was the beer merchant George W. Langford, leaving a trail, albeit half-erased by irritated insurgents who passed after him, to guide his rescuers. As the trail had become almost impossible to track, the inveterate marketer and salesman was making sure the American rescue stayed on course.

The terrain once again shifted from wooded forest to waist-high cogon grass land. Moving through the dry, golden field, the American column found more abandoned carts, rifles, ammunition, and several dead *carabao* that had collapsed under the duress of Tinio's forced retreat. The soldiers broke up the guns, bending their barrels and smashing their stocks.

Ammunition was scattered into the canyons. The freshly expired *carabao*, chilled by the cool mountain air, were butchered to augment the Americans' diminishing rations. In pockets of trammeled grass, the soldiers also stumbled over several bodies. Apparently, they were Filipino fighters who had died of their wounds along the way and were left behind. Without the time or inclination to pursue a proper burial for these unfortunate casualties of war, the Americans left the dead where they lay.

By the afternoon, at the western edge of the plateau, the American column dropped into a rocky draw that snaked into a deep canyon rutted by a creek. Ahead, they could see a handful of Tinio's rear guard, running from tree to tree, playing out a delaying action. Edwards was with Decker's advance, moving around a bend in the exposed creek bed, when the Filipinos opened fire. It was a clever ambush: Insurgent sharpshooters held a high ridge to the south and a hill to the north, hoping to create a gauntlet of triangulated fire through which the Americans would pass. Decker's scouts flanked the northern ridge, while Russell's company was sent through the underbrush to gain a firing position. A second company, led by Rollis, was sent up a steep slope to the south to gain the summit. Half of French's company was left with the pack train, while the other half took up positions along the ridge in front. Having encircled the Filipinos, the Americans were now in a position to retaliate with triangulating fire of their own, attacking the insurgents who had lost their cover. One by one, overwhelmed by the superior force, the Filipinos were pushed from their defensive cover, only to be shot down as they fled, arms flying awkwardly as they stumbled and fell. Recalled Edwards matter-of-factly, "It was a slaughter."

The American column lumbered on. As the sun began to set, they emerged from the canyon and descended into the foothills that overlooked the fertile Ilocos valley. In a final firefight at a large granary, they jumped a squad of twelve rebels, leaving one wounded and dispersing the rest. Howze ordered camp again to be set and the granary's rice divided among his men. Now near Banna, the exhausted column hunkered down to sleep, having covered another punishing twenty miles along the Cordillera's formidable mountain trails.

Some twenty-three miles to the southeast at the town of Dolores, Hare and his men had also pitched camp, after staggering in past midnight. The colonel surveyed his 270 men. Nearly all had worn through

The American soldiers encountered bloody skirmishes with General Manuel Tinio's rear guard along the way.

their footwear and were now barefoot, with some beginning to succumb to malaria, dengue, and dysentery. Hare knew his column was breaking down. If he was to catch Howze, his column would need to march at a forced pace, but less than half of the men were in any condition for such a march. It was time to cull his men. Hare ordered each company commander to select twenty men, who, in their judgment, would hold up under the rigors of the chase to come.

With the men chosen, a start was made the following afternoon, December 10, with one hundred men from the five companies, along with thirteen officers. Each soldier carried two days' worth of rations. The balance—some 150 men who were assessed to be either too sick, injured, or otherwise unable to press on—were ordered back to Vigan. The record of events for Hare's column becomes sketchy at this point. Along rugged trails, they skirmished with bands of insurgents. Like Howze's column, they came across arms, ammunition, and German-labeled medical supplies dropped by the retreating enemy. Challenged to catch his counterpart and still lagging several days behind, Hare rallied his men forward.

On the same day, farther north, Howze and his men were also forging on. Daylight had found them moving down the river, burning warehouses and barracks in their wake. Somewhere before the town of Banna, a group of ponies they had chanced upon were pressed into service for a number of the barefoot men.

To Howze's great surprise, one of Hare's privates, Squire Grose, Company C, 33rd Infantry, abruptly overtook the rear of his column, with several Filipino prisoners in tow. The confused thirty-one-year-old laborer from Lancaster, Missouri, was brought before Howze to explain himself and the insurgent prisoners in his possession. Separated from his company three days earlier, and thinking that his own regiment was ahead of him, the hapless private recounted how he had approached a local priest at Dolores for help. The priest found a Tinggian guide to take Grose into the mountains to the Americans. The guide, however, had followed the trail of the 34th Infantry, and not that of Grose's own 33rd Infantry.

With the fleet-footed Tinggian in the lead, the two had raced through the Cordilleras to catch the command. Along the trail, Grose—who was just shy of six feet tall and weighed a solid 175 pounds—surprised a group of twelve insurgents. Grose fought several, exchanging blows, and the rest quickly surrendered. The lost private then broke up their rifles and got back on the trail, taking along several of the more senior-looking captives as his prisoners and leaving the balance on the trail to ponder their fate. All told, the private had completed a nearly nonstop foot race over twenty-five miles of rugged mountain trails, all in the wrong direction, while single-handedly taking out a patrol of Tinio's rear guard. From here on, a visibly impressed Howze ordered Private Grose, an inspiration to his men, to stay with the 34th Infantry.

Howze's column marched out of the mountains, down into the town of Dingras, where they found a flood of Spanish prisoners. Among them, fifty-eight-year-old General Leopoldo Garcia Peña, the former Spanish commander of the province of Cavite, and about 750 Spanish soldiers—400 officers and 350 enlisted men—who had been taken captive on June 2, 1898. Held for more than eighteen months as prisoners of war, Peña and his men had been abandoned that morning by their Filipino captors. Howze sent them to the coastal town of Laoag, where he hoped they would find American forces who could deliver them to Manila.

Pushing on to the settlement of Solsona, Howze's men ran into another remnant of Tinio's persistent rear guard. This time, it was a company of Filipino soldiers camped by a large bamboo and *nipa* structure. As the Americans moved in, rifles at the ready to engage the enemy, the woven walls bulged out and collapsed, spilling a wave of more than a hundred exuberant Chinese into the sunlight.

Through interpreters, the anxious Chinese explained that they were all merchants and shop owners from the nearby towns of Laoag, Dingras, Vintar, and Batac. On Tinio's orders, their shops and warehouses had been ransacked and looted by rebel soldiers, who stripped them of cash, merchandise, jewelry, horses, cattle, stocks of local and European wines, and other provisions. The soldiers also divested their warehouses of several thousand bales of tobacco, a lucrative cash crop in the Ilocos region, after forcing them to sign papers under the threat of death that it was a voluntary donation to the revolutionary war effort. The bales were then cashed in with the Tabacalera Company's purchasing agent in Laoag. The insurgents even stole their supply of opium.

After these outrages, the Chinese explained, they had been rounded up and imprisoned, with the stronger members of their group separated and impressed into service by Tinio's men as *cargadores,* to haul equipment and supplies into the mountains. Howze ordered the gleeful band of liberated shopkeepers sent on to Laoag, where their demands for restitution could be heard.

By now, the day was done. As night fell in Solsona, having traversed another twenty-one tiring miles, the lieutenant colonel and his men collapsed into an exhausted slumber.

Unknown to Howze at the time, additional American forces had in fact landed at Laoag. They had failed, however, to move beyond the town to close off the unguarded mountain routes to the east. With these passes remaining open, Tinio's rear guard had easily retreated into the Cordilleras without resistance. It was later learned that Tinio, encircled at Solsona, had cleverly slid through enemy lines dressed as a peasant woman to make his way back to Banna.

With Hare and Howze's columns in aggressive pursuit and American forces holding the coast, the Army of Liberation had once again evaporated. General Tinio and his prisoners had simply vanished like smoke. Despite this setback, the Americans were not about to give up. At daybreak on December 11, Howze and his column marched from Solsona to Maananteng, a nearby barrio that stood vigil at the head of a yawning canyon leading into the Cordilleras. Latest intelligence suggested their quarry had fled through this steep, narrow canyon, a sharp wedge of geology carved over the millennia by the Cura River, a tributary of the Laoag River. If reports were right, Tinio's force had entered the canyon no more than twenty-four hours before.

Howze and his officers clustered around an old Spanish map. The canyon, they could see, led into the heart of the Cordilleras' wildest country, territory that remained uncharted and untamed. Now, it seemed, they might be in luck: If the frayed map was accurate, Tinio and his men were trapped, hemmed in by a ring of nearly impassable mountains. It was inconceivable that the insurgents could climb the near-vertical mountains, which peaked at over five thousand feet, and escape east across the range. Cornered into what the tattered map portrayed as a dead end, Tinio's forces could be chased down and the prisoners liberated.

With this news, excitement rippled across the American column. The end was in sight; they were close to completing their mission. But the short, hard morning march had demonstrated to Howze that his men were at the very end of their tether. The lieutenant colonel conferred with his officers. Their men had been marching and fighting from dawn to dusk, and rotating on outpost guard duty at night. Most were thoroughly spent following the 350-mile trek from San Fernando to Maananteng. Over the past six days, following the Battle of Tangadan Pass, they had covered a hundred miles that included an armed encounter with dogged bands of insurgents practically every day. The last two days covered a hard march through a wild, mountainous, uninhabited country over a narrow pack-trail. A count revealed just twelve pairs of shoes among the 130 bone-weary men. Even scrounging what they could from captured stores and the settlements they passed, the column had little food. If they were to go forward, it would be exclusively on foot. The trail through the mountains was known to be absolutely impassable for ponies or other pack animals. Every man who entered the canyon would have to be prepared to live off the land. Was it possible?

Howze and his officers were also fairly certain that Young and the 3rd Cavalry had continued up the coast to Laoag, which meant reinforcements and supplies were likely near at hand. If so, Howze's battalion, having already chased the enemy into the mountains where they were trapped, might as well wait for food and fresh troops. And wasn't Hare also on his way?

It was agreed: The battalion would wait. Messages were sent through the Spanish prisoners and by courier to Young, urgently requesting rations, footwear, and supplies. Sentries were posted at the mouth of the foggy canyon to ensure that none of Tinio's men backtracked and slipped back through their lines. If the enemy remained hemmed in by the unforgiving Cordilleras, they weren't going anywhere.

Howze again conferred with his officers. Like Colonel Hare had done, they decided they would need to cull their 130 men and take only the strongest forward. Howze had the men lined up and examined by the regimental surgeon. A quick medical inspection would determine who would proceed on the final dash after Gillmore and his band of prisoners; the balance would be sent to Laoag for much-needed medical care. The surgeon quickly made the cut, picking from among the cowboys and carpenters, mechanics and miners, blacksmiths and butchers, to select a fighting force that would continue the hunt.

Bruce, Edwards, and O'Brien, the three liberated prisoners who had made their desperate escape from captivity, surely should have been sent down to Laoag as well, to board a ship to Manila and get the medical care they needed. The three men were weak, undernourished, and had just emerged from extremely harrowing experiences as prisoners of war. In addition, they were not part of the formal US Army expedition; in fact, O'Brien was not only a civilian, but British as well. Nevertheless, their adrenaline was up, and they wanted in. Since joining the column four days earlier, they had performed admirably, and possessed some useful intelligence. With this, they made an impassioned case, and Howze relented. The troika was assigned to Decker's Company G.

As Howze's men sorted themselves at Maananteng, Hare's haggard column arrived on the scene, making good time but at a cost. Of the 113 soldiers who had started from Dolores, 18 had dropped out due to exhaustion or damaged feet. Hare now had a near-broken force of 95 men, and all were fast playing out. The colonel held council with his officers. It was agreed to cull the men once again, choosing from the eclectic mix of iron-workers and oil-mill operators, dairymen and druggists, bookkeepers and bridge men. The five companies were surveyed, and 74 enlisted men—the most physically able—were offered up for the job.

Together, the two joined columns comprised a force of men 151 strong, a fraction of the almost 400 soldiers who had started out together at Tangadan Pass just nine days earlier. Given Hare's seniority, it was agreed he would take the lead, with his force of 13 officers and 74 enlisted men. Howze and his column of handpicked men—6 officers, 59 enlisted men, and 1 Ilocano Scout—would follow, as soon as critically needed supplies arrived from the coast. On the afternoon of December 13, 1899, Hare marched his chosen contingent into the rocky canyon in a final push. Two of his men, too lame to keep up, dropped out after the first mile.

A few miles up the rock-strewn river, Hare's men were caught up in a light skirmish. They quickly scattered the insurgents, but the encounter put the column on edge. Rocks and boulders littered their path, a few defaced by George Langford's whimsical graffiti. Now the phrases took on a touch of biting sarcasm: In one place, DRINK PABST'S BEER—AGGIE DRINKS IT, and in another, GILLMORE AND PARTY—ON THE ROAD TO HELL. Hare and his men were closing in.

CHAPTER SIXTEEN

Cordilleras

NINE DAYS BEFORE COLONEL LUTHER R. HARE BEGAN A FINAL PUSH toward rescuing the American prisoners, the Gillmore party had begun its trek into the Cordilleras—Lieutenant Gillmore on horseback, twenty-five fellow captives on foot, and two pet macaques on the shoulders of Privates Huber and Honnyman.

The captives were now part of the chaotic retreat of Tinio's dwindling band of soldiers from Bangued, assigned their own guard under a Filipino officer, Lieutenant Yuson. Five miles to the northeast at the town of Tayum, Tinio's column was joined by another retreating force led by General Benito Natividad—crippled from a wound—and his family. "All about us were frightened native people," Gillmore recalled, "a jabbering, shouting rout of men, women, children, chickens, Natividad and his staff, crazy wooden carts, bellowing *carabao*, loads of ammunition and rifles carried in the arms of almost naked conscripts, sick and wounded men struggling painfully along and begging in vain for an ox or a pony." The prisoners fell into the procession, arriving at the small town of Dolores by late afternoon.

The logistics of the retreat were challenging, particularly feeding the five hundred–odd people of the eclectic column. In the center of each camp, large iron cauldrons were set up to prepare and distribute soup and rice. The prisoners soon learned they needed to muscle their way to the front of the hungry crowd if they wanted to eat; the Filipino soldiers, Chinese *cargadores*, and Tinggian guides were already in a scrum for their scant share. After a lean supper the march continued, a short three-mile jaunt to the settlement of San Juan, where they arrived around midnight.

The next day, the prisoners were marched without breakfast. Shortly after getting under way, a Filipino soldier galloped madly to the head of the column and presented Natividad with a message that seemed to bewilder him. The general held counsel with his officers and they decided to turn back. The huge column retraced its steps halfway to Dolores, and then cut across rice and cane fields into open country. The column pushed at pace over hills and across a number of small tributaries along a wide swath of riverbed until it finally reached the deserted settlement of La Paz by afternoon.

Gillmore had had enough. He requested rest, but Natividad would not permit it. The march needed to continue, and it did, for another fifteen miles over rough stony roads, up and down hills, until they at last came to the Tinggian village of Danglas. Faced with the arrival of the massive column, the local Tinggians had fled to the surrounding forest. After the prisoners had settled into their assigned bamboo hut, Yuson advised that if they wanted to eat, they would need to hunt down their own dinner. The hungry prisoners gave chase to abandoned Tinggian livestock and, after an hour, managed to club two pigs senseless and tackle six squawking chickens. They cooked up a fine supper, and Gillmore and his men went to sleep on full stomachs for the first time in days.

That was the evening, December 6, when Bruce, Edwards, and O'Brien had made their escape. The following morning, Tinio arrived, heard the news, and fumed. There was also word that just the day before, seven Spaniards had also escaped, but had been successfully chased down by their guards. Five of the men had been executed on the spot by Tinio's soldiers, one had drowned, and the last, presumably, had made it to freedom. Poor odds indeed.

But the search for the American escapees proved futile, and so the march resumed. Less than a few hundred yards on, the lumbering column met a steep trail and the weather warmed. Several of the load bearers, sixteen water buffalo, were hauling heavy sleds weighed down with Mexican silver. The burden was too much, and when the narrow path turned rough, the sleds broke apart. The bags of currency were shifted onto the backs of the *carabao*, but the straining animals refused to move. As a clutch of pack-train drivers discussed their dilemma, a small boy walked by with a stick in his hands. Unable to resist, he sharply punched one of the animals in the flanks. The *carabao* heaved up, kicked, and went scrambling over the bank. The bags burst open and their precious treasure—some $4,000 worth of dollar coins—scattered down the hillside and into the canyon. An infuriated Tinio arrived upon the scene, angrily unholstered his pistol, and shot one of the civilian pack-train drivers dead in his tracks.

From there, the hills grew steeper, the trail narrowed, and the river became treacherous. Yuson, his own horse tied to Gillmore's, led the way across the raging river. Suddenly, Yuson's horse was swept away, plunging Gillmore and the officer into the water in a blur of kicking, panicked animals. Both men managed to swim to shore, soaked and exhausted, half a mile downstream. Quartermaster William Walton recounted, with a touch of sarcasm, "One of the Spanish officers with us kindly lent him a spare horse, so he was able to continue his journey."

At dusk, the retreating column and their captives stopped to camp in a deep canyon. The prisoners slaked their thirst in a nearby cool stream, which would have to suffice for their dinner, too. Temperatures dropped, the high altitude delivering bitterly cold weather. By morning, all the men—prisoners and guards alike—were huddled around a small fire, trying to draw warmth into their chilled limbs.

At daylight on December 8, the march resumed, but by dusk, as they dropped into a valley near the present-day town of Nueva Era, Ilocos Norte, the last, seemingly endless miles had reduced the prisoners to a crawl. Staggering to a halt, they found several hundred more Spanish prisoners camped with their own guard. Since leaving Bangued four days earlier, Gillmore and his band of prisoners had traversed about forty miles, much of it over strenuous mountain terrain. Fearing they could not go another day without food, they summoned up the courage to slaughter one of the weaker horses. Gillmore and his men took the choice front- and hindquarters and passed the rest to the glum Spaniards. The gamey meat was cut up, threaded on wooden sticks, and roasted over an open fire. "If it was prime beef, I could not have enjoyed it any better," recalled Private Harry Huber.

As the men ate their roasted pack-animal supper, a rebel officer raced into camp on a wheezing gray horse, its nostrils foaming. The officer had orders for the entire column to move immediately; there could be no delay. The prisoners assumed this meant that an American rescue was near, so they stalled for time. The guards waved their bayonets about to get the prisoners moving. Pushed to their feet and poked along, dinner still in hand, the weary men stumbled into the night, Gillmore following on his horse. Guided by moonlight, they marched north, following a swift, ink-black river that snaked along the foothills of the looming Cordilleras.

For those on foot, the hike was as miserable as ever. They tripped over boulders, bruising shins and knocking knees. At midnight, the prisoners began to drop from exhaustion. Yuson had little choice but to stop and allow the men to rest. Four hours later, however, they were slogging through swampy, low country, and by mid-morning, they limped into a settlement where a long, hungry line of rebel soldiers and ragged Spaniards were already jostling for breakfast. Gillmore and his party elbowed their way into the pack to secure their handful of boiled rice.

Incessant marching and meager food continued as they made their way through Banna and Dingras. That night, Yuson announced that the men would need to push on, regardless of the hour. Gillmore and his men vigorously protested. They would not go any farther without a proper meal and rest. An argument ensued. The guards were assembled to prod the prisoners again, now seriously, at bayonet point. Yuson explained that the next town, their final destination, was only a short distance away. Seeing that resistance was futile, the prisoners got back on their feet. Outside of Dingras, however, their guard quickly lost their way and led the column into an impassable swamp. For two hours the weakened column marched in confused circles. Yuson, fed up with the incompetence, thrashed the lead guard with the side of his saber, bringing him to his senses and back on course.

In the absolute dead of night, the column finally made the lowland Ilocano settlement of Solsona, having covered an exhausting twenty miles over the previous twenty-four hours. The Gillmore party collapsed in a rice granary, while the rest of the weary column scattered themselves about the village. In just hours, the approaching dawn would reveal that they had reached the mouth of a canyon that led back into the jagged, dark peaks of the Cordilleras beyond.

On the morning of December 10, the men were hurried off into the canyon and marched along a rocky riverbed until noon. Gillmore and his sailors had hiked through the mountain domain of the Ilongots when leaving Baler, and the domain of the Tinggians when retreating from Bangued. Now, they were about to pass into the lands of the Apayao—known more accurately as the Isneg—who eked out a hard life among the steep cliffs overlooking the turbulent Apayao River. For nearly three hundred years, the Isneg had successfully thwarted attempts by the Spaniards to Christianize their people, resorting to punitive raids into the coastal lowlands to drive the point home. And, like the many other tribes of the Cordilleras, the Isneg were not just warriors and staunch defenders of their ancestral domain; they were also inveterate hunters of human heads.

An oblivious Gillmore party pressed on, unaware that Howze and his soldiers were on their trail, less than a day behind. But the increasing anxiety of their Filipino captors was surely evident. That afternoon brought a change in circumstances, when Gillmore and the twenty-two other prisoners were separated from Tinio's command, which itself had splintered into smaller groups, moving in different directions. The senior Filipino officer, Major Joaquin Natividad, the brother of the general—seeing his own forces starting to dissolve, and perhaps feeling the futility of their

The Tinggian and Apayao people, and their warring ways, deeply worried the Gillmore party prisoners as they moved higher into the Cordilleras.

retreat—approached Gillmore. "Don't be discouraged," he advised, saying they would all soon be free.

Separated from the massive column for good, Gillmore and his ragged, barefoot band broke off from the riverbed, turning up a narrow trail into the mountains, accompanied by several pack horses and a guard of four-teen armed soldiers, under the command of Yuson. Gillmore and Yuson still had their mounts. Just a short distance later, they struck a swift, chilly river. They followed it into another canyon, crossing it at every sharp twist and turn. Progress slowed to a crawl. The strong current tugged at the men's tattered clothing, in one instance tearing the legs off Huber's disin-tegrating pants. After an afternoon of hurried marching, they came upon an open gravel bed along the river and lay down for the night.

The constant effort to keep moving had left the column spent; they moved even more slowly after the sun came up. Before noon, one of the overworked pack horses collapsed from exhaustion. The prisoners and guards stopped to kill the animal, carve up the carcass, and roast the meat on wooden sticks. They packed all the remaining meat they could carry and trudged along trails until darkness. Again, they camped among the rocks of the same river, dining on the balance of the horsemeat under a brilliant canopy of stars.

On the morning of December 12, the prisoners moved out slowly, making a gorge by noon. As they climbed higher up a narrowing ravine, it was clear they would need to abandon the remaining animals. Yuson shot his own pony. The prisoners killed another two before letting the rest go. They cut up and bundled the flesh, each man carrying horsemeat on his shoulders.

Moving on, their advance brought them to steeper and rougher trails. In places, the prisoners had to crawl hand over hand, helping each other over the large boulders. It was now obvious that the rebel lieutenant had been ordered to take the prisoners to a location so wild and inaccessible that no sane American soldier would ever attempt a rescue. At times they had to cling to the rock walls with fingers and toes to inch themselves along. Gillmore later recalled, "The penalty of a single misstep [would have been] to dash to death into the rapids perhaps a hundred feet below." They had entered, he colorfully described, "a veritable devil's causeway." Just before dusk, they reached the head of the dark canyon and camped for the night, "more dead than alive."

The thirty-seven-man column consumed the last remnants of the rancid pack animals the next morning. At this point, Gillmore began to lose his sense of time. Their narrow, muddy trail climbed steeply up a pine-studded mountain. Now, Private Smith began to stumble and lag behind. And then he stopped. The guards forced Smith up, but he only walked another hundred yards before sinking again to the ground. Dragged onward, Smith eventually collapsed in a delirious heap. The guards circled, shouting angrily and kicking the catatonic soldier about the head. "I was so far gone that I do not remember I felt anything," Smith recounted. Yuson, fed up, called back to his men and motioned for them to come with their guns. At this point, another prisoner—his name was not recorded—fainted from fever.

The line of prisoners, watching the abuse, circled around the two collapsed men. They let Yuson see that if he shot the stragglers, he'd have an ugly fight on his hands. Yuson, not wanting to test his prisoners' resolve, stepped back to confer with his men. He then made a gesture with his hand, which the prisoners at first thought was a signal for the guards to begin their slaughter. In fact, it was the lieutenant motioning for help, as he too had begun to feel faint and needed some water. Yuson slumped to the ground and the moment passed. Obviously, everyone needed a little rest. "We looked so desperate that he was fairly frightened, and he gave orders for the guards to move slower," Huber recalled.

After a time, Smith collected his strength and they were able to stagger on. Toward evening, the column came upon three Isneg who had just finished their supper and were preparing to leave. The Isneg offered the little leftover rice they had, as well as some fermented sugarcane juice, for two pesos. As Huber recalled, "We also got some tobacco which gladdened the old sailors' hearts." The group stopped to camp for the night, despite the site offering nothing more than a few *nipa* huts. It was, however, near a freshwater stream that allowed the men to rehydrate. The pitiful purchase of food, however, wasn't enough, and the hungry men assessed other options. The ponies had been the first to go; now, they looked to the two pet macaques in the party. One belonged to Honnyman, the other to Huber. The monkeys had provided a source of continual entertainment and companionship for the men during their long captivity, but hunger now won out. It was decided to draw straws to select whose animal would die. A downcast Huber, having drawn the short straw, said good-bye to his friend, Maria, that night.

The night came on cold, and sleep was almost impossible. By morning, the hungry band of prisoners, along with their shivering armed hosts, awoke to find the mossy ground dusted with white frost. The prisoners were exhausted, and most of them were ill with fever, dysentery, and infection. They were completely out of food. Exposed to the elements, their situation was dire and deteriorating.

If this continued, they would surely die.

At Maananteng, Lieutenant Colonel Howze and his men waited impatiently for supplies. The delay paid an unexpected dividend, however; just after midnight on December 13, several 4th Cavalry soldiers arrived with an officer from Tinio's Brigade, Major Natividad, who had surrendered at Solsona just hours earlier. Exhausted from the chase, fearing death in the mountains, and having learned that his own brother, General Benito Natividad, was also planning to give it up, the major had slipped away from Tinio after being ordered to backtrack on the trail to find stragglers who had become disoriented in the night. Seizing the opportunity, the major had ditched his uniform, changed into civilian clothes, and beat a path to American lines.

Pressed by Howze, Natividad confirmed what everyone had feared: Tinio had ordered the Gillmore party prisoners separated and marched into the mountains. If the Americans attacked and the prisoners were not able to escape, Tinio had ordered his guardsmen "to kill them one by one, quietly and without the others knowing anything about it, only the officer to be saved." Seeing the faces of his inquisitors harden, Natividad emphatically added, "When I heard this barbarous order, I told the officers not to commit such an act of savagery . . . and they promised me they would not carry out the orders."

Howze knew he had to move. As if on cue, early on the morning of December 14, long-awaited supplies finally arrived. Howze pulled his men together and ordered them outfitted. Major Penn, Captains French and Russell, First Lieutenants Heaton and Decker, along with fifty-nine enlisted men, the liberated prisoners Bruce, Edwards, and O'Brien, and their faithful Ilocano scout Espino were each given five days' half-rations to pack. Most took advantage of the navy shoes that had arrived with the supplies. Edwards, his feet swollen, scabbed, and scarred, continued to go barefoot as he had done for the past several months. At 10:00 a.m., Lieutenant Colonel Howze ordered his column to enter the canyon. They were nineteen hours behind Colonel Hare.

Still at Howze's camp, Major Natividad, likely in awe of the American force arrayed before the canyon—oversized men, horses, and firepower—quickly drafted several letters to be conveyed by runners into the mountains. One was to his brother, pleading with the general to surrender with all the arms they held, and one to Captain Romero, another officer of the Tinio Brigade, conveying the same message. But the most urgent letter he drafted was to Lieutenant Yuson, whom he had placed over the Gillmore party prisoners. The lieutenant, he ordered, was to "present himself with all his forces to the nearest American authorities, bringing with him the American prisoners, whom he was to treat well." Natividad did not bother to write to Tinio; they had argued before about the possibility of surrender, if only to spare their men, and he knew the hardheaded general intended to fight to the bitter end.

At midday, Howze and his men came upon a small group of stragglers from Tinio's rear guard. A brief skirmish left one insurgent dead and drove the rest off. By late afternoon, Howze ran into the same difficult terrain as Hare had—the canyon bed had become too rough for the pack ponies to traverse. Howze ordered one killed for meat and the rest sent back. After an hour's halt for supper, they were back on the trail. The moon rose early, three days shy from full, illuminating the column as it navigated the canyon's rocky bed, scrambled over great masses of boulders, and wound in and out of the shadows of the sheer granite walls that enveloped them.

Four hours later, Howze's 34th caught up with Hare's 33rd at the point where the trail split off from the river and cut into the mountains. Combining their forces, the two commands agreed to alternate leadership each day. The united column of 152 American soldiers, augmented by a complement of guides, scouts, and *cargadores*, trudged on.

In the early morning of December 15, the rescue climbed a harrowing trail that weaved up an almost-perpendicular mountain face. Progress was tedious, compounded by the slick soles of their navy shoes, which made it nearly impossible to gain a foothold. The breathless men stopped frequently, but finally reached the summit—likely in the shadows of Mount Licud, at an elevation of 5,900 feet—which offered a magnificent view of the distant Laoag valley below. It was truly spectacular country. The trail then dropped down, and after ten miles on a steep, narrow path, they set up camp at the foot of a bluff, beside a dank, gloomy brook.

The column broke camp by sunrise, with Howze leading. The forest trail cut high in the mountains and later, led the men up, down, and along limestone cliffs of the oddest formations. Having crossed the principal range of the Cordilleras, the column came across the first human habitation they had seen since leaving Maananteng, where they once again ran into Tinio's rear guard. Several rebel soldiers were killed, a few captured, and two fled, abandoning their Mausers in a panic. The Americans assumed these soldiers would race ahead to warn their comrades that their pursuers were closing in. Every indication at this point suggested the rescue party was on track.

Farther on, they emerged from the forest and descended into a dense canebrake of weedy cogon. Across the deep ravine, Decker's advance spied a few Isneg huts nestled in a small clearing. Around them, a clutch of insurgents were cooking their midday meal. A sentinel, an Isneg armed with a steel-pointed spear, saw the Americans, gave a shout of alarm, and rushed out of sight.

Decker's men raced forward, their rifles raised. They called out for any men inside the hut to surrender. In response, they received a torrent of angry shouts in Tagalog. By now, the main body of the column had taken up positions and, in seconds, American rifles were blazing. Farther up the trail, several rebels ran back toward the cluster of huts to assist in its defense. Young Edwards set his bead on one. Just as the Filipino raised his rifle to shoot, the *Yorktown* landsman fired.

As Edwards struggled to comprehend that he had just killed another man, a large form crashed through the bamboo hut wall, falling seven feet to the ground while screaming, "Don't shoot. For God's sake, don't shoot!" The blurred figure dodged the bullets skipping about and landed on all fours, slicing one hand badly on some broken earthenware. It was one of the army captives, Frank McDonald, the escaped military convict.

Following McDonald's explosion from the hut, four rebels attempted to flee. The Americans' guns again lit up, killing one and wounding the others. Approaching the hut, Decker's advance found a prisoner of war lying flat on the floor amid the carnage, fully unscathed from the deadly barrage of lead. It was sailor Norman Godkin von Galen from the USS *Baltimore*.

As the Americans secured the clutch of huts and collected weapons, Fireman 1st Class John J. Farley from the USS *Urdaneta*, carrying four rifles in his arms, came up the trail. He quickly explained that he had been separated and held by four guards near a few huts not too far away. Upon hearing the rifle fire, his guards thought their camp was under attack by Isneg warriors. Once they heard shouting in English, however, they knew it was the American rescue, dropped their guns, and fled.

Howze learned that the three prisoners—Farley, McDonald, and von Galen—had escaped the previous day from the guard that was holding the Gillmore party, but they had not been fast enough in their escape and had been recaptured. Howze's men had stumbled right into them, just as lunch was being prepared. The final tally from the firefight was five insurgents killed, several more wounded, and twelve Filipinos taken prisoner, including three women, apparently the wives of some of the rebel soldiers. The Americans also took twelve *cargadores* into custody, along with a number of rifles, ammunition, and rice. Knowing now that Gillmore and his fellow prisoners were still ahead, Howze ordered the reenergized column to immediately move out.

Late that day, as the sun disappeared beyond the range, the trail descended to a stony riverbed carved in a canyon, where it was again impossible to determine the route taken by the prisoners. The men fanned out, searching for clues, poking about the brush, studying impressions in the earth, and following their instincts. One of the men ran back to Hare, holding a single sheet of yellowed paper, torn on one edge. He had found it fluttering in the wind. Hare studied the sheet, his eyes narrowing. It was a page from a US Navy memorandum book with a cryptic entry, written in Gillmore's hand.

It explained that Gillmore expected to be killed.

Hare folded the page, probably pocketing it, just as another soldier jogged out of the brush, pointing in the direction from where he had come. The men followed the soldier back and gathered around a set of large rocks that featured some of Langford's colorful graffiti: DRINK PABST BEER, ON THE ROAD TO HELL AND STILL GOING. Hare ordered the column forward, its way lit by the chalked slogans.

After making camp among a few Isneg huts, Hare scraped together enough provisions to send two guides back over the trail to Laoag with a message for Young: They had freed three prisoners and would continue the hunt. It was increasingly clear that the Cordilleras were, in fact, passable, and that meant the chase might continue east through the mountains and down into the heartland of Luzon. If correct, the rescue expedition might need to travel across the mountains into the Cagayan Valley and then up to the north-central coast of Luzon. In that case, a navy boat should be sent for them. As the two runners disappeared into the canebrake, the exhausted command consumed the last of its rations and stretched out on the ground for the night.

Daybreak on December 17 found the rescuers making slow progress. Their one map was poorly drawn and outdated, offering only a rough approximation of where they were. Again studying the ground for clues, the men found a fresh path and footprints along the banks of the river, and followed it until the trail came to an end. Here, they could see that a footpath turned into the river and continued on the opposite bank. The river would need to be crossed. A quick scouting of the area located, oddly, several abandoned bamboo rafts. The rafts were tied together with rope and assembled into a ferry. The soldiers stripped down, placed their clothes on the rafts, and waded across. On the northern bank of the river, they again found more of Langford's witticisms scratched out on the rocks, confirming they were on track. The first men over also found a message ominously etched into the sand: "Here we are, God knows where."

A day earlier, the Gillmore party prisoners had been on a relentless march through remote Isneg settlements, scrounging together, through purchase or theft, whatever sugarcane, sweet potatoes, and rice they could find. Then, they dropped down to a wide, turbulent river. The Filipinos, having earlier pressed several Isneg warriors into the role of guides, ordered the men to construct several bamboo rafts. Once completed, the column had floated across the frothy current in small groups. The rafts were then abandoned. That afternoon, the prisoners and guards followed the course of the river on foot, along its banks, until they were overtaken by darkness. At that point, the group of twenty prisoners and fourteen guards arrived at a small gravel bed along the riverbank, hemmed in by sheer, granite cliffs.

That evening, the guards moved off about fifty yards and camped by themselves among the rocks at a distance. Every night prior, they had camped together with the prisoners. Something, the prisoners sensed, was not right. The prisoners were sitting around a fire discussing their predicament when Lieutenant Yuson approached with a grim look. He stopped, stuttered for a bit, and then blurted out in Spanish, "General Tinio gave me orders to shoot you when we reached the mountains." The startling message was slowly translated by the bilingual men in the group. The prisoners stood in alarm, dumbfounded at the turn of events. Hospital Corpsman Huber recalled, "It was terrible to think we had marched all that distance and suffered such privations, only to be shot down like dogs in the heart of the wilderness of northern Luzon."

After a moment's silence, one that seemed to take an age to pass, the lieutenant continued, saying, "But I do not want the stain of your blood upon my head, so I will abandon you here."

The prisoners immediately began to reason with him. In broken Spanish and with frantic gestures, several theatrically explained that they almost preferred to be shot than left to starve or be killed by the Isneg. Yuson responded that American forces were on their trail and would arrive in days. He turned and started off. The prisoners called to him, begging not to be abandoned without at least a gun for their defense. Yuson stopped, said that he would check with his soldiers, and disappeared among the rocks. He returned a minute later on the run, breathlessly exclaiming, "My soldiers have left me and it is my duty to follow them." In a final gasp of desperation, Gillmore yelled out to the lieutenant, offering every protection and $500 in gold if he would stay to guide them to American lines. It was not to be. In this remote wilderness, where each man's survival hung in the balance, the offer was meaningless. "Adios!" Yuson called back, waving good-bye, and disappeared for good.

Enveloped in darkness, and having never felt more alone, the prisoners regrouped, sat down, and tried to make sense of events. Their main concern now was the Isneg head-hunters, who they believed would soon rush the defenseless men. To be sure, their column had raided Isneg settlements and abused their inhabitants along the way; retribution would be only logical. For now, to get through the night, they decided to divide the party. Half would stand guard while the others slept, and vice versa, in shifts. The only weapons at their disposal were two small axes and an old bolo, which one of the men had found at one of the *rancherias* and had concealed in his bundle. Each man collected a pile of stones for himself, which they agreed would serve as "formidable weapons in the hands of desperate men." Cold, hungry, and exposed to the elements, the twenty prisoners huddled together. Half of the men eyed the awful shadows, while the rest made their best effort to sleep.

At first light, the cold and weary prisoners awoke among the rocks on the riverbank, without their guard, alone in the unknown Cordillera wilderness. A weakened Gillmore convened a meeting to discuss their options again. Some spoke in favor of retracing the route back to the Ilocos coast, arguing that they already knew the country. Others suggested it would be better to build rafts and float down the nameless river; surely it had to bring them to the sea. The majority sided with taking rafts down the river. And while seniority and rank meant nothing in these mountains, the men still wanted structure and leadership. Gillmore, coughing, pale, and dazed, but still the only officer present, was elected their commander.

The abandoned prisoners began a march down the riverbank in search of a location to assemble a new flotilla of rafts. Several miles on, their trail terminated at a sheer rock face, which jutted into the swift, foaming rapids. Further passage was impossible. As the men searched for a way around this barrier, a group of Isneg arrived, armed with spears and bows and arrows. One let out a horrifying yell before retreating from view. Panicked, Gillmore and his men quickly took cover behind some rocks and tried to decide what to do.

Huber spied what looked like a grove of bamboo on the opposite bank and volunteered to swim over to scope it out. Gillmore agreed. Huber made the swim, confirmed his find, and motioned for the other men to join him. Ten more men swam over with the two axes and the dull bolo, cut a number of long poles, and pulled them back across the river. In time, they had a collection of one hundred poles, each about twenty feet long. Some quick math determined a raft composed of fourteen poles could accommodate three or so men. They would need at least six rafts.

The construction was laborious and slow. To their dismay, a full morning's effort resulted in a single raft. As the men rested, three unarmed Isneg appeared some two hundred yards out in the brush and began to make friendly signs. Gillmore suggested that Huber, who had picked up a few words of the Ilocano dialect, should parley and see what they wanted. Huber walked out to meet one of the Isneg, who cautiously came down to the bank. Huber motioned that they had been left by the Filipino soldiers with nothing to eat and would like to buy some rice. Huber offered money, but the Isneg man was not interested. Instead, he pointed to Huber's shirt. The hospital corpsman quickly pulled it off and handed it over. The man smiled and nodded. Behind him, another Isneg ran off, returning minutes later with a supply of rice and several more companions.

Huber, thinking the Isneg might help with the rafts, gestured for them to follow him. The group arrived at the camp, saw the number of rafts under construction, and began negotiating: one shirt per raft. A deal was struck. Soon, the five muscular Isneg men were busy building the remaining rafts with their sharp axes and, within half an hour, the task was done. More rice and a few coconuts were delivered to the group. The Isneg, content with their day's work and the bountiful trade, disappeared into the forested mountains.

The abandoned prisoners watched as night again fell, worried that the Isneg might return to divest them of the last pieces of their wardrobe. The same guard arrangements were put into place for the night, working in shifts, to ensure that any attack would at least be preceded by an alarm.

Shortly after daybreak on December 18, a few of the men tested their new rafts. They were buoyant, but each was in fact only good for two men, not three. More rafts would be needed. Huber and Sackett started out to try to find the Isneg to help them once again; they knew their settlement had to be close. A trail was located, but only a few steps along it, Sackett screamed and fell to the ground in agony. He had impaled his left foot on two sharpened bamboo stakes buried on the path. One razor-sharp stake had sliced into the ball of his foot and another into the heel, disabling him. Sackett had stumbled upon a typical Isneg defense set to protect their crops and villages. Huber carried Sackett back to camp, where the men were sitting around a small, crackling fire. Sackett's injuries, they felt, were an ominous sign, maybe even part of a trap to take them all down, one by one. It was decided they would immediately start down the river on what would be crowded, unstable rafts.

As the worried and weakened prisoners rushed to get onto the river, they heard the report of a revolver and loud shouts—an attack! Startled, the men instinctively closed together as a group, grabbing sticks and rocks to defend themselves.

Another yell, strangely familiar, and the men turned to one another in disbelief.

CHAPTER SEVENTEEN

Salvation

With Lieutenant Decker and his scouts leading the way, the men commanded by Colonel Hare and Lieutenant Colonel Howze were once again on the move. The steep terrain brought progress to a crawl. Shortly after 8:00 a.m., the advance returned to report that the Gillmore party was in sight. Hare and Howze moved to the front of the column to verify the news, surveying the horizon with their field binoculars. Sure enough, the trail following the riverbank ran through a patch of cogon grass, about eight feet tall, and emerged on a rock-strewn gravel bar. Ahead, the two commanders could count the twenty-odd prisoners, per-haps 150 yards away, building rafts at the water's edge. But something was clearly wrong. Tinio's soldiers were missing. A few large boulders hid the lower end of the gravel bar from view. They concluded that the prisoners' captors must be there, out of their line of sight.

Hare sent three details of soldiers to approach from the front and both flanks, and surround the group without being detected. On an agreed-upon signal—a shot from the colonel's revolver—every man was to simultaneously rush the prisoners' location, but hold their fire. The last thing they wanted was to shoot any of the prisoners by mistake. Once his soldiers were in place, Hare gripped his pistol and squeezed off a shot. Rifles up and ready, the three details rushed the party while shouting, "Get down, get down!"

Gillmore and his men did everything *but* get down. Upon hearing the American soldiers, they dropped their rocks and sticks and rushed toward them in an eruption of joy. The anxious soldiers, rifles still raised, clumsily raced past them, charging the harmless boulders beyond, slowing into confusion at the absence of an insurgent defense.

Huber ran to Hare with tears streaming down his face.

"Are you all here?" the colonel shouted.

"Yes!" Huber cried.

"Is Lieutenant Gillmore here?" the colonel asked. Huber nodded yes.

"Thank God!" Hare gasped, keenly aware of his triumph. Hobbling forward, the famed Gillmore, visibly confused, weakly approached Hare. Slowly, the dazed lieutenant realized that he was free.

The prisoners embraced their rescuers, laughing and crying, overwhelmed with emotion. The soldiers, in return, gave the prisoners a series of rousing cheers, the commotion reverberating against the canyon's sheer walls, echoing across the heart of the Cordilleras. Hare and Howze had pulled it off.

Once the initial excitement had subsided, Gillmore conferred with the rescue's command. He and his fellow prisoners had been abandoned two days earlier by their guards, he explained, who were under orders from General Tinio to march the men into the mountains and shoot them. The guards, however, had lacked the resolve to do so. Unarmed and without food, the footsore prisoners had decided to build rafts and proceed down the river, hoping to reach the sea. They had not the slightest idea where they were.

As the officers listened to Gillmore, several Isneg cautiously appeared on the opposite side of the river, a few hundred yards away, watching the strange events unfold. In all likelihood, they were gauging whether it was safe to return to work on the rafts, keen to earn more clothing. But it wasn't twenty men now with whom they would need to barter, but two hundred. As the Isneg assessed the situation, the liberated McDonald spied them. Armed with a rifle and consumed with an insane desire to square accounts with his captors, or with anybody for that matter, the army private had scrambled up a large rock and was scanning the countryside. Seeing the Isneg, McDonald squeezed off two shots before he could be restrained. Although he missed, the former deserter turned escaped convict foolishly frightened away the Isneg, whose priceless knowledge, food stores, and raft-building prowess were the key to the column's survival.

As the senior officer present, Colonel Hare assembled the men of both regiments, and with Howze and Gillmore by his side, began to speak. He recounted the hard marches and deadly skirmishes they had encountered, and praised the men before him, the handful who had the heart and fortitude, for their courage. It was a march that had succeeded in the face of impossible odds. And it was an honor to serve with such men. In midstream, with his nerves frayed, the old Indian fighter choked on his words, bowed his head, and fell into silence. It was a rare moment of overwhelming emotion for the colonel. The men broke into the raucous round of three cheers, first for Hare and then for Howze, and then for the men they had saved.

Among the rescuers was Lieutenant Lipop, carrying a small folding pocket Kodak (FPK) camera in his front shirt pocket. During the hike, for the past several weeks, he had been saving the last shot for just this moment. Lipop suggested a portrait of the Gillmore party for posterity's sake. They quickly scouted about for the best location and settled on a nearby rock. Gillmore and the nineteen liberated prisoners climbed onto the rock and jostled into a composition. Some of the injured men sat while others stood, in a single frame. Six other former prisoners were called to join—Bruce, Edwards, and O'Brien, who had escaped earlier, and Farley, McDonald, and von Galen, rescued two days earlier. Sackett hobbled to a front-row seat, his throbbing left foot wrapped in cloth. Honnyman sat with the one pet monkey not yet made into a meal; another prisoner climbed up next to him, a mongrel puppy from one of the Isneg *rancherias* in his lap. The incorrigible McDonald, still in a fighting mood, raised a bolo in mock defiance.

As the men arranged themselves, a small American flag appeared, one that had been fashioned from scraps of fabric by one of the prisoners during his captivity. The Stars and Stripes were handed to Gillmore, who triumphantly raised it above his head. The patriotic gesture triggered another mighty cheer. With 150 men looking on, Lipop snapped the picture, finishing the last shot on his last roll of film. He carefully placed the expended cartridge in his pocket for safekeeping; this, he knew, would be special.

The order was given for breakfast. The famished Gillmore party prisoners sat down to a meal of hardtack, bacon, and hot brewed coffee.

They were free.

Over breakfast, Lieutenant Gillmore and the army officers sat together and worked through their options, returning to the earlier debate among the prisoners. Should they backtrack over the trails they had just hiked, toward Laoag, or should they follow the river with the hope of reaching the sea? The return trip to the Ilocos lowlands meant at least four days without food, probably longer, as their column now included enfeebled prisoners and a number of injured and ill soldiers.

On December 18, 1899, at 8:30 a.m., Lieutenant Gillmore and nineteen other prisoners of war were rescued by elements of the US Army's 33rd and 34th Infantries, along a remote stretch of the Apayao River. Gillmore reported their captors had abandoned them two days earlier, leaving them to their fate. First row, sitting (left to right): William Walton, Harry F. Huber, Paul Vaudoit, Albert Peterson, Fred Anderson, Leland S. Smith, William Bruce, Elmer Honnyman, Archie H. Gordon, and George T. Sackett. Second row, standing (left to right): Ellsworth Pinkham, Lyman Paul Edwards, Silvio Brisolese, James C. Gillmore Jr. (holding the flag), David Brown, George W. Langford, James Curran, Norman Godkin von Galen, Albert O. Bishop, John W. O'Brien, Frank McDonald, Martin Brennan, and Frank Stone.*

USAMHI

* No known key to the photo exists for positive identification. The above key relies on partial identification made by participants in later years and cross-referencing with other photographs.

The officers again referred to their old, tattered Spanish map. Numerous Isneg *rancherias* dotted the length of an unnamed river that fed into the Pacific Ocean some ninety miles distant. If these communities were able to supply the huge column with food—they now numbered nearly two hundred men—they would be able to survive. It was agreed: They would take their chances on the river, aiming to cover twenty miles each day. With luck, the rescue expedition should be able to deliver the good news of the prisoners' liberation to their families by Christmas.

Hare ordered the construction of rafts for the river journey and a major production was soon under way. Using the soldiers' axes, a forest of bamboo stems was methodically chopped down for poles and tied together with vines and pegs. A small flotilla of rafts quickly materialized, adding to those that the prisoners had begun to build. The sick were counted off and assigned to the rafts; those still physically able would need to march on foot along the riverbanks.

With much of the day gone, Hare ordered the column to move out. The cumbersome group managed to travel just three miles to the next village, which they found deserted and bereft of food. Knowing that the Isneg hid their provisions, a diligent search was launched, and some rice and two pigs were found. Two more soldiers, however, ran sharpened bamboo blades through their feet during the hunt. Camping in the village, the command divided the rice and pork among the 148 soldiers, 26 former prisoners, and an odd assortment of local scouts, guides, and *cargadores*. Grossly insufficient, it was all the food to be had. The massive column of ragged men arose the next morning to continue their navigation along the river, the majority on foot, the rest on rafts. The river ran swiftly, forming a succession of rapids hemmed in by narrow canyon walls. At these points, it was necessary to swim and ferry the men across the river, from one gravelly beachhead to another. The ferocity of the rapids, however, quickly broke up the makeshift rafts, spitting the bamboo poles into the froth. Elsewhere, violent whirlpools upset the rafts, tossing men and equipment into the rushing water. If the column had been expecting a leisurely river cruise to the coast, they were sorely mistaken.

By the end of the first day, the column had covered less than five miles, far short of the daily target. A number of Isneg from the next village they passed were coaxed into helping to construct additional rafts, to replace those damaged or lost. In exchange, the Isneg were paid with clothes and trinkets.

Food was also bartered in exchange for Mexican silver, American gold, buttons, bits of gilt braid, and safety pins. After building some trust with the village chieftain, the Americans secured several Isneg as guides. By nightfall, the column had thirty-five well-made rafts, twenty-five feet long and five to six feet wide, each capable of carrying three or four men with their packs.

The following morning, the ragged flotilla of awkward bamboo rafts, manned by sick, injured, and exhausted men, began to navigate the stony rapids. Big boulders rose up in the center of the river, the seething waters drenching the men with spray. Arising from the jumble of rafts was a cacophony of shouted, anxious commands and an unceasing string of profanity as the teams worked their poles to avoid smashing into the rocks.

Lieutenant Lipop was dunked once, his precious FPK camera and film cartridges plunged into the cold, running river. The command raft, with Gillmore, nearly lost control several times, and at one point, the navy lieutenant's precious file of communications, orders, and a detailed diary he had carefully kept since the start of his captivity was swept away and lost forever. When a Chinese *cargador* was thrown into the river and dragged under, the 34th Infantry's regimental adjutant dove into the river and fished him out. At one point, one of the liberated prisoners, Frank Stone of the Signal Corps, leapt into the river and brought out a sergeant who had been stunned against a rock. Over the course of the day, eight rafts were lost, together with some thirty rifles, several belts of ammunition, and precious clothing. A weakened Gillmore spent much of the time on his back, watching the chaotic events unfold. "The scenery was so grand and imposing, [just] as the situation was appalling," he recalled.

After a third day of arduous effort in the turbulent canyon, and again, with only a few miles covered, Hare and Howze began to worry. According to their calculations, they should have been more than fifty miles downstream by this point, well beyond the halfway mark. Instead, they had gone less than twelve miles, and the river was only growing more treacherous. All rations were gone, while more men had joined the sick and disabled list. The situation was not sustainable. Progress at this pace would end in disaster for the column.

On Christmas Eve the men came to an abandoned Isneg village, where, hidden in the forest, they found unthreshed rice stores, a stash of coconuts, and two small pigs. Together, the bounty produced only a lean holiday supper, but as a sergeant major recounted, "We were well satisfied and thankful to get even this." A halt was made early in the afternoon so that more rice could be threshed. Turns were taken with the lone mortar and pestle, which was worked in shifts throughout the night.

The river itself should have been a source of sustenance for the expedition, but in these upper mountainous reaches of the fast-moving current, broken by cascading falls, little was to be had. They were accustomed to US Army rations and reliant on food stores that could be more easily bartered, purchased, or simply taken from local villagers. Perhaps they lacked the tools, know-how, and time to fish the river and therefore overlooked the mullets, carp, tilapia, and mudfish darting about below their rafts, and the freshwater shrimps, snails, and crabs lurking about the eddies and rocks along the riverbanks. While there is no record of the daily diet of the *cargadores* and guides on the march, we can assume they were more resourceful, benefiting from their intimate knowledge of the Cordilleras and more adventurous palates.

With a number of the rafts lost or dashed to pieces against the rocks and canyon walls, Hare ordered the men to devote the day to building more. Rather than going to the trouble of hunting for bamboo—cutting it down and hauling the poles back to camp—the men eyed an easier cache: the huts of the deserted Isneg villages they were passing through. Teams of soldiers tore down the vacant homes to salvage the long structural poles. When one village was demolished, the Americans moved to another. More homes were felled and a second Isneg settlement wiped from the map.

While the raft construction was under way, others in the column were ordered to pound out more of the rice husks from the store of unmilled rice. A scant Christmas dinner was pulled together, consisting of rice, sugarcane, and coconuts. A few of the men shared a can of corned beef, which had been carefully saved for the holiday. With scarcely a mouthful of food to eat for each man, the exhausted column collapsed into deep sleep with gnawing pangs in their bellies.

Time dragged on, drawn out by hunger, as the men pushed down the river. Another day passed, blurred by exhaustion. On December 27, Private Fred Day, a twenty-two-year-old farmer from Emporia, Kansas, came down with a violent bout of measles. A bed was rigged on one of the rafts to allow the feverish private to keep moving with the column. He joined the river-borne sick and lame, including a growing number of soldiers whose feet had been pierced by bamboo stakes placed along Isneg village paths.

Later in the day, the column struck another Isneg village. This time, however, the residents refused to part with their food. Tense negotiations with the village chief quickly became ugly. Finally, Hare ordered the soldiers to take what they could find at gunpoint and to force payment on the chief. Somehow, some of the soldiers also came into a quantity of locally distilled liquor, either purchased or stolen from the Isneg. Groups of the men, gaunt and undernourished in the first place, began drinking. Within hours, the already physically weakened Private Patrick Burke, Company I, 33rd Infantry—perhaps celebrating his twenty-eighth birthday that had passed three days earlier—was drunk. When confronted by an officer, the inebriated Burke, an English laborer with a penchant for disobedience, became belligerent. A fight broke out and Burke was restrained.

Thursday, December 28, marked the tenth day of their perilous journey through unknown country, with no sign of sea, civilization, or salvation. Already rescued once from a near-fatal dunking on the river and succumbing to stress, Private Frank Timbs, Company D, 33rd Infantry, mentally broke down and ran off into the jungle. The twenty-six-year-old teamster from Memphis was tracked down and also placed under guard. Meanwhile, Hare and his officers worried over their men's collapsing morale. The lack of food, illness, discipline problems—and now madness—suggested the worst.

On December 29, after repairing the rafts once again, the command determined that the river was taking a decided fall, causing it to run with terrific force. It was impossible to navigate, and everyone was ordered to make his way around the falls on foot. The rafts were set adrift to float beyond the rapids, where they were picked up downstream.

Late in the afternoon, a cheer rose out from the front. Everyone hurried forward to learn the good news. Ahead, around a sharp bend in the river, a vista through a narrow mountain pass embraced an expanse of lowland country. Studying the horizon, the men could see that the mountains suddenly terminated, the river dropping low and wide and snaking into the distance.

Their spirits buoyed, the column came upon a simple hut along the riverbank, a lame Isneg elder sitting by the door. Did he know where they were? The old man smiled, showing his chiseled, blackened teeth. It was a four-day journey to the sea, the old man explained, "which was anything but good news" for the exhausted and starved column. And what about this river, they asked; did it have a name? It was the Apayao River, the old man answered. And then he sold them some rice, coconuts, and much-needed salt.

Hare and Howze checked their progress, struggling to reconcile their location on the tattered Spanish map. After eleven days on the roiling river, they concluded that they had covered just less than fifty miles. The two senior officers looked grimly at one another: Nearly the equivalent distance remained before the river met the ocean on the northern coast of Luzon. Would they make it?

December 30 was again spent on the river, working the bamboo rafts, moving the column on foot, making more fords. There was no food to be found, and no settlements with which to barter. Racing against the clock, the column had little choice but to push on. Without nets, traps, or native fishing spears, the men passed on the chance to fish the river. As the haggard and worn column lay down to rest for the night, a slow drizzling rain began to fall, the elements once again mocking them.

Starting out without breakfast on December 31, the column undertook the longest march made on the river. They passed through a grove of wild plantains, but there was no fruit to be found. The desperate river trek seemed to have no end.

On the last night of the nineteenth century, on a desolate edge of the Apayao River, the beleaguered army column, the liberated Gillmore party, and its cavalcade of guides, prisoners, and *cargadores*, stretched out on a sandbar for the evening. The coast was still a hard twenty-five miles distant. Dinner for most was a heavy drink from the running river. Some of the Filipinos refused to go hungry, turning over rocks in the water and digging about the mud to scare up a meal of raw crawfish and snails.

The by-the-book Hare remembered that unless muster was held, there would be no monthly pay for the men. Battalion Sergeant Major Oscar Keesee, a former mechanic from Fort Worth, Texas, was sent to call the soldiers before the adjutant. The shattered column staggered forward. The ridiculousness of the procedural requirement evoked wise-cracks at the roll call: *Here. Present—for the most part. You tell me.* But it was more than just an accounting for the muster roll, and most knew it. This was Hare enforcing army routine and imposing structure on his men: muster, roll call, reveille. It was a critical tool to keep the grumbling men in line, and morale up, while pushing them to their limit.

Two hours into New Year's Day, 1900, Private Fred Day died following his battle with measles. The column awoke that morning to the gloomy news of his death. A chill rippled across the camp. Day's lifeless body was loaded on a raft, and the procession continued its way down the winding course of the Apayao. The river splayed and slowed as they approached smoother, more level land. Finally, the column discarded the rafts and resorted to marching along the riverbank, carrying those too weak or ill to stand themselves. At a branch, it was no longer the Apayao River now, but the Abulug, a fierce spigot of freshwater from the highlands of the Cordilleras that ran into the western Pacific. It was the course of this river—which spilled out into the Babuyan Channel of the Luzon Strait—that bridged the South China and Philippine Seas. The men hoped it would bring them home.

In the afternoon, the column noticed a streak of smoke staining the sky in the direction of the sea. Was it the boiler of a navy ship sent up the coast? An advance party rushed ahead. Howze, four scouts, and the liberated prisoner Edwards were met by a cutter from the USS *Princeton*. Unknown until now, their earlier message to Brigadier General Young had been received, and a gunboat had been sent to meet the rescue party.

The six men were ferried alongside the *Princeton*, where the ship's sailors helped them over the rails. Howze was taken to the wardroom to speak with the commander, and within the hour, a relief party, equipped with medical supplies and food, ventured up the river to meet Hare and the rest of the expedition. By late afternoon, the balance of the broken men had reached the coast.

The moment was surely magical for the prisoners. As Edwards recalled, he climbed aboard the *Princeton* in a pair of tattered pants, which barely covered his ulcerated legs. In the hours that followed, the bemused landsman was sent to the sick bay, deloused, bathed, shaved, given a haircut, and afterward, offered a stiff mug of grog. His filthy trousers were taken to the boiler room and burned.

On Tuesday, January 2, 1900, the Gillmore party rescue expedition had come to an end.

On January 4, the *Princeton's* steam launch, with her small boats in tow, transported the men to the *Venus*, a commercial steamship at anchor in the harbor. The *Venus* was ordered to land the 33rd Infantry soldiers at Vigan and continue on to Manila with the 34th Infantry soldiers and the liberated prisoners. She set sail that evening, arriving off the colonial Ilocos Sur city at daylight the following morning. Hare, Howze, and their men disembarked to be greeted on the beach by an exultant Brigadier General Young.

The general enthusiastically shook hands with the two officers and addressed the assembled soldiers. His heartfelt words of commendation struck the officers and enlisted men deeply:

> *God bless you, Hare. God bless you all. It was noble work; it was grand. And Hare, I have recommended you and Howze for brigadier-generals, and all the officers and men for Medals of Honor.*

There it was: a promise of promotions, medals, honor, and glory. The rescue party had exceeded every expectation; it had gone the distance, and prevailed. They were heroes. The men erupted into cheers. Little did they know at the time, but Young's glowing and generous promise would haunt many of the rescuers for years, offering, ultimately, little more than frustration in its pursuit.

A day later, on January 6, the ship dropped anchor in Manila Bay, escorted by a glowing sunset to the west. A navy tender, the *Barcelo*, arrived to transport the navy men to the USS *Brooklyn*, a new battleship that had arrived three weeks earlier. Here, they were to report to the commander in chief of the Asiatic Squadron, Rear Admiral John Crittenden Watson, the fifty-seven-year-old commander who had replaced Dewey.

The twelve sailors—Lieutenant Gillmore and the seven men from the *Yorktown;* three from the *Urdaneta;* and one from the *Baltimore*—clambered aboard the *Barcelo* and rode out to the massive *Brooklyn*. They recounted their ordeal to the admiral, who expressed his visible relief. The pressure on the army and navy to liberate Gillmore had been relentless, and now, finally, he could share the good news with Washington.

The following morning, Gillmore and his sailors again boarded the *Barcelo* for a ride to the Cavite Navy Yard. Some of the men were keen to collect their possessions in storage, while others had been ordered to report to the Cavite Naval Hospital for medical attention. Nearly all were wracked with dysentery, malaria, and infected sores and tropical ulcers. Quartermaster William Walton, sporting a nine-month growth of beard, was in the poorest shape, suffering from exhaustion, fever, and festering sores on his feet. He also had problems with his heart and vision, which he attributed to being struck in the chest by a rifle butt seven months earlier. Edwards had deep ulcers on his

Liberated soldiers and civilians outside the Governor-General's Palace in Manila on January 6, 1900. Front row, kneeling and sitting (left to right): Harry F. Huber, Martin Brennan, John W. O'Brien, and Leland S. Smith. Standing (left to right): Frank Stone, Frank McDonald, George T. Sackett, David Brown, William Bruce, Archie H. Gordon, George W. Langford, Albert O. Bishop, and Elmer Honnyman. Note that Private Elmer Honnyman, 1st Nevada Cavalry (far right), is handcuffed and chained, and presumably a guard stands outside the frame of the photo. Honnyman and several other liberated prisoners were arrested for desertion and other crimes upon their return to Manila.

Once back in Manila, Gillmore reported to Admiral Watson (center, front row) aboard the USS Brooklyn. Chauncey Thomas, the USS Yorktown's executive officer at the time of the ambush at Baler, is on Watson's left. The black armbands were worn in honor of General Henry W. Lawton, killed in action on December 19, 1899.

feet and legs, and a throat infection. Anderson was running a fever and fighting a bout of malaria. Apprentice Albert Peterson's heart was arrhythmic and palpitating, the result of nervous exhaustion and anxiety. Vaudoit and Woodbury were simply broken men. Lieutenant Gillmore was nothing more than a shell of his hearty, well-appointed self, weighing a mere 115 pounds of his original 180-pound heft. All would require months to get back on their feet.

The balance of the Gillmore party—eleven army soldiers, and civilians Brown, Langford, and O'Brien—were ordered to report to General Otis. Inside army headquarters, Otis interviewed the former prisoners and promptly dismissed their tales of hardship. They had been well treated, he had been told. Unspoken at the time was the fact that Otis knew at least one among the liberated prisoners was a convict, now back in chains; others were suspected to be deserters; and more than a few were known to have stumbled into captivity due to their own carelessness or inebriation. The general was jocular: "Well, you fellows have had a pretty good time. You've had a vacation and haven't suffered any. I think you can all go back to your outfits." Otis then wheeled around and walked out, leaving the men speechless.

Before returning anywhere, most of the men would spend a significant amount of time in the hospital. A number were crippled with fever, ulcers, and dysentery. All had dropped a frightening amount of weight.

Patient Ward, 1st Reserve US Army Hospital, Manila, where a number of the liberated prisoners of war were treated.

US NATIONAL ARCHIVES

Sackett was running a high malarial fever, wracked with diarrhea, and was fighting an infection in his right foot, a complication to the untended and filthy wound, caused by stepping on one of the Isneg bamboo stakes. Others battled what appeared to be psychological issues related to post-traumatic stress—anxiety, hypertension, and nervous system disorders.

Several soldiers and sailors, having been incorrectly declared deserters, had paperwork to sort. In subsequent court-martial trials, all were exonerated. McDonald, on the run following his court-martial conviction for theft, was transferred to Manila's Bilibid Prison, his original destination. Ironically, the troublesome private had been freed in the wilds of the Cordilleras only to be imprisoned again in Manila, under conditions that were arguably far worse.

The Manila papers provided the first details on Gillmore's arrival in the city. The *Manila Times* ran a banner headline on January 7, 1900:

LIEUTENANT GILLMORE'S PARTY ARRIVES SAFELY IN MANILA
All of the American Prisoners Held by the Insurgents in the North
Which Were Rescued by Hare and Howze
Are Back Again
Terrible Tales of Suffering and Hardship Told
Experiences are Recounted which Read
Like Romances of Adventure

The paper noted that all the men "are more or less sick, principally with sore feet received in their seven or eight months of forced marching through rough country, sparsely fed, without clothing, and suffering unspeakable treatment and hardship." At the Governer-General's Palace, the soldiers and civilians "presented a picture never to be forgotten by those who witnessed it," the men "bearded and barefooted, in every description of garment from a mere skirt or breech cloth and coolie hat, to slightly better but more respectable attire."

Recounting their various marches across Luzon, the reporter noted that "the sufferings on the trip are said by the men to be indescribable; tied together, marched barefooted over rocky roads in rainy weather, abused by their guards, and insulted by the populace of every town they came to, stones hurled at them, and cruel blows dealt, it is needless to describe the mental and physical torture of these unfortunate men."

To further manage the media, Gillmore astutely scheduled a press conference at the plush Hotel de Oriente, where his sister Clara was in residence. By taking control of the narrative, Gillmore was able to cast his tale of survival and salvation according to his own version of events, putting it in the best possible light. The story was widely distributed, running in major dailies in every American city, with variants of the headline:

LEFT AMONG SAVAGES
Lieut. Gillmore's Thrilling Experience with Gen. Tinio
Returns to Safety to Manila

The hyperbolic story began with Gillmore, hobbling with the help of a cane into the plush lobby of the luxurious hotel, where American officers and ladies were waltzing to the strains of "Aguinaldo's March." Around a table, he recounted to a captivated audience of fawning reporters "a remarkable story of his eight months of captivity, ending with his dramatic deliverance from a death that seemed inevitable." Described as tan and ruddy from exposure, but weak, nervous, and showing signs of long hardship, the navy lieutenant spoke "warmly of Aguinaldo," who had treated him "splendidly," but "very bitterly against General Tinio," under whom "he suffered everything." Abandoned by his captors and left without any rifles, Gillmore and his men had prepared to fight the "savages in war paint around us," armed with "cobblestones, the only weapons available to us."

"I was so weak myself," Gillmore added, "that I did not expect to get out, but I thought some of my men could." Gillmore went on to describe the grueling march into the mountains from Bangued, where "we lived on horse flesh for several days," and one day when he had been "reduced to chewing grass and bark."

It was a thrilling tale, spun largely from whole cloth for a gullible home audience.

Gillmore was now a national hero, publicly cleansed of doubt. His misadventure at Baler was now lost in a flood of positive press.

On January 27, 1900, Gillmore was detached to the USS *Solace*, a hospital ship, with some fifty patients in sick bay, for the cruise home. Among the passengers: Sailmaker's Mate Paul Vaudoit, with lumbar problems; Coxswain William Rynders, with his mangled fingers; and William Walton and Orrison Woodbury, each with a host of debilitating ailments. The easy-go-lucky Lyman Edwards, in remarkably good health, joined the contingent of bedridden patients aboard ship.

On Friday, March 9, 1900, after six weeks at sea, the hospital ship arrived at San Francisco, bringing the sailors home.

The liberated signal corpsman, Leland Smith, was back at work in his unit's photo lab when Lieutenant Lipop visited to drop off a roll of film. His Kodak pocket camera had weathered rain, mud, dust, and several unfortunate dunkings in the raging waters of the Apayao River. The odds that any image survived were remote, but Lipop wanted Smith to give it his best shot. Maybe something could be salvaged.

Smith retreated to his darkroom with the damaged film cartridge, carefully removed the spool of film, and attempted to process it. He lacked ice to keep the developer cool, and the roll of negatives began to loosen up. He put the roll into a hypo solution and then floated the negatives off the backing onto a clean glass plate. He then gingerly smoothed out the negatives and let them dry. Smith studied the images. Most were blurred or poorly exposed. Lipop was no professional, that much was obvious, and the little pocket Kodak had its technical limitations.

Only one image was any good—amazingly, the final one, of the Gillmore party prisoners posed on the rock on the morning of their liberation.

Smith began to run prints.

The triumphant news of the liberation of the Gillmore party brought little joy to the tumbledown shack nestled into a dirt patch at 1626 21st Street in Sellwood, Oregon. Emily Mash, struggling with her six children and dying husband, was at her wits' end. With her daughter Regina scratching out a surprisingly eloquent letter on lined school notebook paper, Emily begged the Honorable Secretary of the United States Navy for answers.

I am in great distress of mind concerning my son, D. G. A. Venville, one of the ill-fated Yorktown crew who was wounded and last seen at Baler on June 9th, 1899. Can you not tell me what has been done to find out what has become of him, whether he is living or dead?

She demanded that her son's personal effects be returned to her, declaiming it "a disgrace to the Navy that we have to plead for the things that our own dear boys have worked and paid for with their very lives." A brokenhearted Emily Mash concluded:

The loss of my son has made me at 40 a broken down woman not able to look after my little ones, for he was a good son and brother. The suspense is so great. If I only knew he was dead I would feel that he had died bravely for his country.

This anguished mother needed answers. The navy would take four months to craft a response, in which it offered nothing new.

Undeterred, Emily Mash continued her campaign. In her daughter's careful cursive, a steady stream of missives was fired off from Sellwood in search of the facts. Letters rained down on the White House, Washington politicians, and the military hierarchy, cascading into navy and army bureaucracy where they were duly logged, numbered, and processed for a response.

As she waited for answers, Emily Mash could only wonder: What in heaven's name would it take to find her missing son?

BOOK III

And for a moment it seemed to me as if I also was buried in a vast grave full of unspeakable secrets. I felt an intolerable weight oppressing my breast, the smell of the damp earth, the unseen presence of victorious corruption, the darkness of an impenetrable night.
—JOSEPH CONRAD, *HEART OF DARKNESS,* PART III

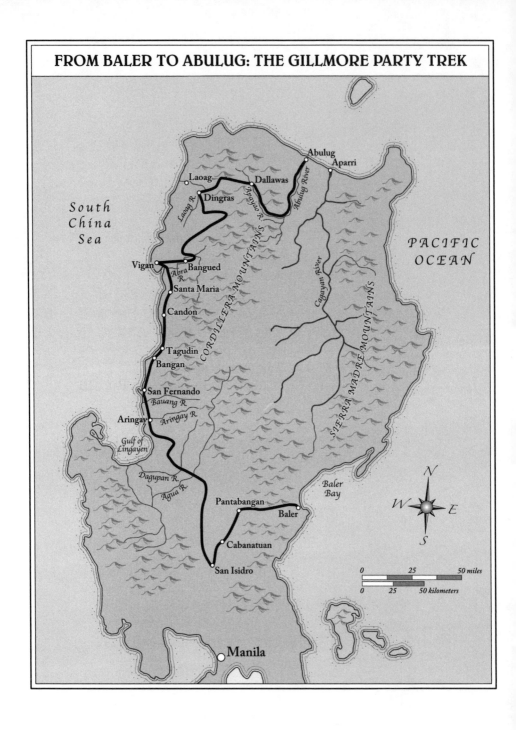

FROM BALER TO ABULUG: THE GILLMORE PARTY TREK

South
China
Sea

PACIFIC
OCEAN

Abulug
Aparri

Laoag
Dallawas

Dingras

Laoag R.

Apayao R.

Abulug River

Cagayan River

Vigan
Bangued
Abra R.

Santa Maria

Candon

CORDILLERA MOUNTAINS

SIERRA MADRE MOUNTAINS

Tagudin
Bangan

San Fernando
Bauang R.

Aringay
Aringay R.

Gulf of
Lingayen

Dagupan R.

Agua R.

Baler
Bay

Pantabangan
Baler

Cabanatuan

San Isidro

N
W   E
S

Manila

0   25   50 miles

0   25   50 kilometers

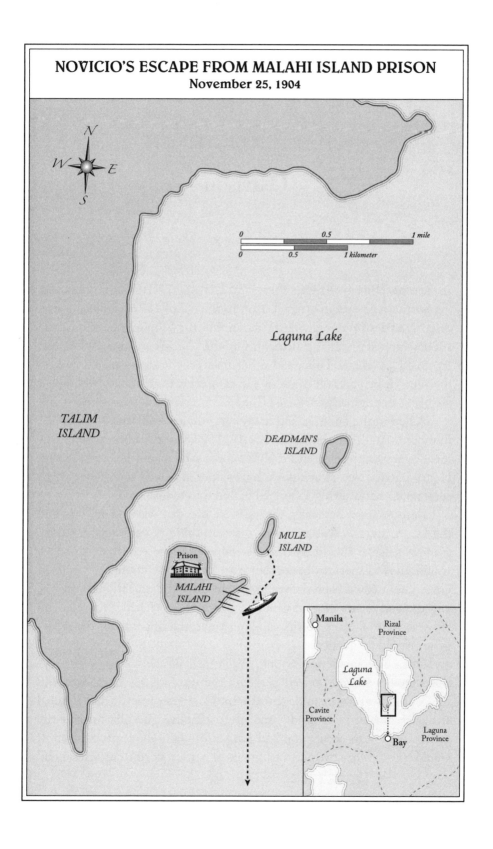

NOVICIO'S ESCAPE FROM MALAHI ISLAND PRISON
November 25, 1904

CHAPTER EIGHTEEN

Garrison

As far as United States General Elwell Otis was concerned, the northern campaign across Luzon in the fall of 1899 had been a success; it had destroyed organized resistance by the Filipino Army of Liberation, scattered remaining elements into the Cordilleras, and left General Aguinaldo, General Tinio, and other insurgent leaders isolated and on the run. To be sure, the costs of the campaign to date had been much greater than originally envisaged. The loss of American lives—officers and men killed in the fighting, and many succumbing to disease—continued to mount. And then, on December 19, 1899, while leading a "scout-in-force" against insurgents in a suburb outside Manila, the beloved General Henry Lawton was struck down by a sniper, shocking the military high command and throwing a stunned nation into mourning.

Despite these setbacks, the mission did not waver. For Otis and the US Army, the next step was to set up military garrisons in strategic towns across the archipelago. A stable and secure military presence would allow American benevolence to flow. A functioning system of government could then deliver police, health, and educational services, and the rudiments of infrastructure. Once these charitable works and reforms were in place, so the thinking went, the impetus for the insurgency would be quelled.

Otis's assessment was wrong. While half of the country's seventy-three provinces were indeed peaceful, the war was far from over, and the conflict was about to degenerate into a series of protracted regional struggles, waged with deadly and often-effective guerrilla hit-and-run tactics. American occupation had not yet brought about pacification. It would take another two and a half years of battles, skirmishes, arrests, and executions to extinguish the rebellion. By now, though, Aguinaldo was effectively neutralized and the Army of Liberation had lost its centralized command and control.

Facing superior American firepower, Aguinaldo's forces now focused on an irregular war of attrition. The aim: to prolong the war through the American presidential election in November 1900. The prospect of a William Jennings Bryan victory over incumbent McKinley offered hope for an anti-imperialist Democratic administration that would favor Philippine independence. Until then, the insurgency would grind on and American casualties would increase, erasing much of the progress achieved by the introduction of a civil government. Aguinaldo's forces ratcheted up their campaign of terror on the local populace, as well, targeting those who collaborated with the enemy. Over the course of the year, 350 assassinations and 442 assaults were recorded, primarily targeting municipal officials.

At the outbreak of hostilities in February 1899, a modest fifteen thousand American soldiers were in Manila; by January 1900, that number had nearly quadrupled, to some sixty thousand. They were deployed to garrison towns across the country on a campaign of pacification, policing, and development. Through 1902, American forces—augmented by some six thousand Philippine scouts drawn from successful experiments with Macabebe and Ilocano units—had established 552 garrisons across the islands.

Northern Luzon remained a hotly contested region. Several months into 1900, guerrilla activity spiked with daring attacks on convoys and telegraph lines. By mid-April, bloody raids on thinly manned American garrisons became the norm. On April 16, 1900, 800 insurgents stormed the garrison of Batac, Ilocos Norte, attacking in waves, resulting in 180 insurgents killed, 50 wounded, and 135 captured. A day later, a two-day assault on Laoag left another 300 Filipinos dead. The frontal assaults on better-armed American forces were a last-ditch defense against foreign colonizers, instigated by Tinio, who was running out of options, and Gregorio Aglipay, a fiery Ilocano lawyer turned Catholic priest and revolutionary. The stunning, near-suicidal attacks surprised even the battle-hardened Howze, who reported, "Much of the fighting hand to hand by fanatics worked up to a pitch by Padre Aglipay, and General Tinio's order. They were regular dervish charges. Slaughter terrible."

After a brief pause to extend an offer of amnesty—which was accepted by several hundred weary Filipino soldiers—the Americans went after the remaining rebels without mercy. Frustrated by the unceasing guerrilla war, the US Army instituted increasingly harsh measures, descending on target villages to destroy buildings and torch crops. Shoot-to-kill orders were issued against violators of the dusk-to-dawn curfew. The policy of benevolent pacification was quickly giving way to one of sharp reprisal, chastisement, and repression.

While these events unfolded in northern Luzon, a new set of challenges emerged in the east. As early as February 1900, according to newly surfaced rumors, towns along Luzon's porous, undefended east coast were becoming gateways of insurgent arms trafficking. A new town fell into American strategic sights: Baler. Intelligence suggested that not only were insurgent forces operating in the town with impunity, but they were also still holding one of the *Yorktown* sailors captive, along with several Spanish priests. Brigadier General Frederick Funston was ordered to lead several companies of 34th Infantry over the Sierra Madres to take control of the town.

On the morning of February 13, 1900, Funston saddled up and led his column out of San Isidro, Nueva Ecija. His command consisted of twelve headquarters scouts; Companies A, B, and D, 34th Infantry; one troop of mounted 4th Cavalry; a detachment with a Hotchkiss two-pounder mountain gun; and a sixty-three-mule pack train. The long column lumbered along the Pampanga River through Cabanatuan, Bongabon, and Pantabangan, and then tackled the narrow range of the densely forested Sierra Madres. At one point, they slowed to just four miles over a full day's march. Three mules either broke their legs or necks falling off the treacherous trail.

On February 20, after seven arduous days on the twisting mountain route, Funston's column rode into San Jose de Casignan, known more simply as San Jose. The settlement comprised little more than the small stone church that had briefly held the Gillmore captives and about twenty bamboo and *nipa* huts. During Funston's twisting 110-mile march, however, word had spread of his impending arrival. By now, the town was deserted except for a forgotten chicken and four forlorn ponies, the latter of which fled into the woods upon the Americans' approach. Funston's men pressed on to Baler, but it, too, was nearly devoid of life. Only two families remained.

General Frederick Funston, third from right, with Colonel Kennon to his right, on their arrival in Baler on February 28, 1900.

A US Navy warship, at anchor in the bay, had been sent to meet Funston with a three-month supply of rations for the new garrison. While Funston's men carted the provisions to the Baler church—the only structure capable of providing any protection from the elements—the ship's officers came ashore to greet Funston and his command.

Convinced that an insurgent force was nearby, Funston ordered his men to fan out and search the town. The effort turned up only an old brass cannon and a wagon of musket barrels, which were dumped in a swamp. After setting up camp, squads were sent to the surrounding farms to coax residents back. Over the following days, with the dawning realization that they would not be harmed, Baler's families cautiously trickled back to their homes.

The church at Baler as seen by the Americans when they arrived in Baler.

The rebels' absence stymied Funston, as the intelligence had been hard and compelling. Now, every resident claimed that the band of insurgents operating in Baler had departed the previous November and had not returned since. Furthermore, nothing was known about any *Yorktown* sailor or priests reportedly being held against their will. Several helpful residents did, however, guide a scouting party to the site of the ambush on Gillmore's cutter. There, mired in the muddy riverbank, sat the charred remains of the boat, which had been burned to its keel and stripped of its iron and copper work. A few of the American soldiers finished the job, cutting away small pieces and pulling out the remaining nails as souvenirs.

The Americans asked about the weapons aboard the cutter. Residents explained that insurgents had carried off the Colt Automatic and tinkered with it until it misfired, injuring several men. What about the dead sailors' remains? After the ambush, residents claimed, the bodies of those killed had floated down the river and were washed out to sea.

Finding insufficient excitement to keep him occupied—neither insurgents to fight nor captives to rescue—Funston and several officers took the opportunity to sail to Manila two weeks later. Left behind to establish the garrison was a team led by Major William A. Shunk.

Baler was now, for all intents and purposes, under American control.

Shunk, a West Point graduate with several decades of experience fighting Indians, began establishing the garrison under his command. He had served as chief engineer of the Second Division Army Corps during the War with Spain, and now, at forty-two, was known for his common sense and can-do attitude—just the right mix to build a new post from scratch. Shunk was assisted by a collection of competent officers. Captain Willard D. Newbill, a twenty-six-year-old Virginian, had served with a light battery in the Puerto Rico campaign under General Miles. Captain Clark Magwire Carr, raised in New Mexico and fluent in Spanish, was drawn from military lineage as prestigious as that of John A. Logan Jr. His father, Eugene Asa Carr, was the famed Civil War general known as the "black-bearded Cossack." Five lieutenants rounded out the command, a professional group with solid experience from service in the Spanish-American War. Among the remaining men were a contract surgeon and former family physician, Andy Hall, from Mount Vernon, Illinois, and two companies of the 34th Infantry.

Within weeks, Baler was buzzing with activity. One of the first tasks undertaken was the construction of a bridge across the Baler River, to connect the town to a beach, called Cemento, which was used for landing supplies. With lumber scavenged from the charred remains of the numerous homes torched in the hit-and-run arson attacks by the Spaniards during the siege, Carr, with a background in civil engineering, led the work, and a sturdy bridge was soon in place. An upgraded road quickly followed. At Shunk's direction, Carr also oversaw the construction of buildings to store the quartermaster's and commissary supplies. Assisting Carr was a local resident, the bright-eyed Feliciano Rubio, who lived several miles outside of town with his family. Conversant in Tagalog and Spanish, Rubio quickly became an invaluable go-between for the Americans and the townspeople.

The US Army garrison at Baler was aware of two primary threats: insurgent attack, and trouble with the warring Ilongots from the nearby mountains. Nevertheless, hunting and fishing expeditions were routinely sent out for fresh food—primarily deer, wild pigs, and an abundance of fish netted from the nearby rivers. The Americans also chased down rumors and vague reports that might help them get to the bottom of the Gillmore ambush, the reported killing of the four American sailors, the status of the inexplicably missing Apprentice Venville, and the alleged captivity of several priests. So far, no hard facts had materialized.

Finally, six weeks after their arrival, a report filtered up to Shunk that a certain Teodorico Novicio, posing as a civilian about town, was in fact a captain in Aguinaldo's rebel army. Shunk immediately ordered Carr to lead a party of men to arrest the rebel officer. That evening, after midnight, a detachment of American soldiers, with reluctant local guide Rubio in tow, arrived at the house of Novicio. There, they found some fifteen men gathered, along with Novicio's wife, who had just given birth. The Americans lined up the men outside the hut, and a deeply conflicted Rubio was ordered to identify the rebel leader. He nervously fingered Novicio.

Promptly arrested and detained in the garrison's guardhouse, Novicio denied everything at first, but by mid-morning the following day, he could not dismiss a landslide of incriminating reports from residents. The prisoner finally admitted, with pride and defiance, that he was in fact *Kapitan* Teodorico Novicio, an officer in the Army of Liberation.

After allowing the prisoner to languish for a week in detention, Captain Carr approached Novicio with a proposition, translated by Rubio. If he would sign an oath of loyalty to the United States and agree to turn in all the rifles and ammunition in his possession, he would not only be set free, but he would also be paid a reward for each weapon surrendered. Novicio knew a good deal when he heard one, and immediately agreed. On April 17, 1900, in front of Major Shunk and Captain Carr, the detained rebel forswore further violence:

> *I, Teodorico Novicio, a captain in the Philippine Insurgent Forces, a prisoner in the hands of US Troops, do hereby promise and declare that, in consideration of being set at liberty, I will do no further act of hostility toward the Government or Forces of the United States of America.*

With Carr as a witness, Shunk signed Novicio's parole. The town's insurgent leader walked out of detention and returned to his home, his wife, and his newborn child. A day later, on April 18, Novicio returned to the American command post to surrender four decrepit rifles, as he had promised. In return, he was paid $120. In US Army fashion, an official receipt was dated and signed in triplicate.

As the Americans kept up pressure to ferret out the truth about past events, a town-wide ruse began to falter. Several weeks after Novicio's parole, in the middle of the night, a visibly shaken Rubio appeared at Carr's residence to relate a stunning tale. All of the residents of Baler,

US NATIONAL ARCHIVES

Provisions from a US Navy warship at anchor in Baler Bay were stored in the church. As the only secure, stone structure in the town, the church became the commissary and storehouse for the new American garrison.

Rubio included, had been lying about the absence of insurgents and prisoners in the valley. On February 19, the day before the Americans had arrived, Novicio had been in command of forty armed insurgents stationed in Baler. At one time or another, he had held two Spanish priests, a Spanish schoolteacher, a Spanish hospital orderly, and an American sailor named Venville. The American, badly crippled as the result of wounds incurred during the ambush of the *Yorktown's* cutter, had not been sent across the mountains with the other prisoners. He had since partly recovered, and, along with two Spanish priests, was being held in the jungle outside Baler. Insurgent soldiers were still acting under the directions of Novicio, whose oath of allegiance to the United States had been a farce.

What triggered Rubio's change of heart? Earlier that same night, Novicio's men had come to his house to place him under arrest for collaborating with the Americans and escort him to the location where the other prisoners were being held for a court-martial. Realizing that Novicio intended to have him killed, Rubio knew he needed to escape. Prior to departing, he asked if he could first get his hat and coat, and was allowed to do so. Once inside his house, Rubio had jumped out the back window and hotfooted it to town. Now, he'd need protection.

The Americans quietly took Rubio into custody, but Shunk did not feel the information was actionable; in his opinion, running after loose, unconfirmed leads would only endanger any captives. He would first need to know where the prisoners were being held, and by whom. Hearing this, Rubio tasked his girlfriend to help. Weeks later, in late May, new information trickled in: a list of Novicio's alleged crimes with names, dates, and locations.

According to reports, during his control of the town, Novicio had been behind the murders of several suspected collaborators for the Spaniards, including Manuel Rodriguez, a former Spanish Army medic; Lucio Quezon, a Spanish schoolteacher and former colonel in the Spanish Army; and the schoolteacher's son, Pedro. The sailor Venville and the two priests, Juan Lopez and Felix Minaya, were still very much alive and were being held near the town of San Jose, about eight miles away. Most importantly, sources gave up the name of the lieutenant in command of the squad of Filipino soldiers holding the prisoners. The time had come to act.

On June 1, 1900, Captain Carr sent five groups of four men on hunting expeditions, a normal routine, with instructions to meet at the river at sundown for further orders. Hoping to throw off suspicions that might arise about the soldiers' movements, Carr, Surgeon Hall, and a native guide rode out to Novicio's house to invite him to join their hunt for wild pigs and chickens. Novicio declined. The Americans then rode out to the river and rendezvoused with the twenty men. The soldiers circled around Carr as he explained the real intent of the mission: They were on a hunt, all right, but not for pigs and chickens. They were hunting the lieutenant whom Novicio had placed in charge of three captives—Venville and the two Spanish priests. Once they found the lieutenant, reportedly at home in San Jose, he would surely be able to lead them to the prisoners.

As the sky darkened, Carr and his men followed the trail to the outskirts of San Jose. Two soldiers were ordered to enter the town and capture some residents. Two hapless locals were arrested, delivered, and forcefully persuaded to lead the squad to the house of the lieutenant. With their hands bound, the two impromptu guides led the American column to a settlement of several houses a few miles away. The lieutenant lived there, the residents advised. The soldiers surrounded the houses and ordered the inhabitants out. A surprised ten men and five women stumbled into the moonlit yard and were lined up. Candles were lit and the two residents were coerced into identifying the lieutenant. The exposed lieutenant, in turn, admitted that he had held the prisoners previously, but had turned them over to a fellow rebel soldier several weeks earlier.

The insurgent officer now became the Americans' new guide, while the rest of the group was held under guard to prevent them from sending warnings ahead. The column marched several more miles through woodland and jungle and deployed around a second house, only to have the new detainee anxiously explain that he, too, had passed on the prisoners to another individual. That man—Simaco Angara—could be found at a location fifteen miles to the west, along the bank of a small river. Carr again ordered several soldiers to guard the rebel lieutenant and other residents, and pressed their new detainee into the role of guide. The depth of a near-moonless night made it impossible to follow the trail, and the man declared he could not proceed without light. The Americans stopped, tied him up, and waited for dawn.

At first light on June 2, 1900, the column was again on the move. They trekked worn footpaths through the jungle, over hills, and across tilled fields, until they reached a handful of small bamboo shacks along a beautiful mountain stream. The men spread out around the camp, rifles raised, and moved in, only to find the site abandoned. Several large wooden crosses planted in the earth suggested the priests had been there recently. Carr and his men again angrily challenged the guide for a new location, fed up with his lying. Angara, the man explained, actually lived fifteen miles in the other direction. The frustrated column retraced its route, picking up the informants, residents, and soldiers it had left in its wake. It had become a wild goose chase.

The weary column rode back to San Jose and stopped at the church to sleep on its hard floor. At dusk, the column again started out with its unproven guide, fearing once again it was being led astray. Marching until midnight, they reached a deep river. After a grueling, nonstop escapade over the past twenty-four hours, the men were on the verge of collapse. Carr took the surgeon aside, seeking guidance. "Doctor, these men are very tired, very sleepy, and do not want to go any farther. What course would you advise?" Hall responded that with all the commotion the soldiers had stirred up, if they did not find Venville and the priests that night, the prisoners would almost surely be killed or moved deeper into the jungle and never found. Carr returned to his weary men and pleaded his case. Moved by the appeal, the aching soldiers agreed to press on. More than one wary eye was cast on their guide—no more games.

Wading across a river, the column was led to one house after another by its guides, only to learn that the ever-elusive quarry had been there earlier in the day but had moved on. Charging one location with a growing sense of skepticism, Hall fell into a ditch, soaking himself up to his arms. At another point, Carr lost his footing on a log that crossed a drainage canal and fell in, headfirst. Finally, at a fourth location, the Americans raced forward and found a man warming himself by a fire in front of his house. A startled Simaco Angara looked up to find some twenty rifles and revolvers pointed in his direction.

Angara rapidly exclaimed that he knew nothing. For the thoroughly exhausted Americans, this was not enough. They dragged the man to a nearby tree where a rope was strung up and a noose elaborately fashioned for his benefit. Once the rope was around his neck, Angara quickly admitted that he had been guarding the prisoners at a camp in the jungle about seven miles west, but that he had temporarily turned them over to a band of Negritos for safekeeping. The captives were now being held at a location beyond the Negritos' small village, opposite a large cornfield. It would be necessary to make a surprise attack, Angara added, as the Negritos were instructed to kill the prisoners if there was any danger that they might fall into American hands.

At dawn, on June 3, 1900, with a brilliant sun breaking over the bay, the Americans fanned through the sleepy Negrito village and stormed across the cornfield. Hall, armed with a revolver, and the guide were the first to stumble upon the prisoners. In a small, dark clearing in the forest, they found the first priest, bearded, severely emaciated, and wholly unguarded. Felix Minaya was standing in front of a small bamboo and *nipa* lean-to, washing his face over a washbasin with a coconut-shell ladle. The second priest, Juan Lopez, was asleep in the shelter, a structure barely large enough to accommodate two men lying side by side.

The shouts awoke the second priest, and suddenly both captives were recounting their travails in Spanish. They were survivors of the siege of Baler, they explained, but had not been allowed to leave with the detachment. Eight months earlier, they had joined a group of captives being held by Novicio—a schoolteacher named Lucio Quezon, a Spanish medical orderly named Manuel Rodriguez, and the American sailor Arthur Venville. One day when they awoke from their afternoon slumber, the medical orderly was gone. Later, the schoolteacher disappeared under similar circumstances. Finally, their friend Arthur was taken away.

The starved Spaniards rapidly related all they knew about Gillmore, the ambush along the river, and the death of the Americans, at least one of whom was buried alive. Novicio, they added, was the force behind these crimes. A furious Carr immediately dispatched a runner to Baler to advise Shunk to again arrest Novicio. The priests also shared that the man holding them, Angara, had a Mauser rifle and plenty of ammunition. When confronted, a sheepish Angara led several of Carr's soldiers on an eight-mile hike to retrieve the rifle and forty rounds of ammunition that he had hidden in the brush.

By the time the column and "two half-naked priests" returned to Baler late that night, Novicio had already been apprehended. The next afternoon, Carr, Hall, the two priests, and several soldiers located the gravesite of the buried Americans—a shallow depression along the river marked with a small cross. The soldiers began digging and quickly found the four skeletons, now a mangled mess. When the report reached the command, a livid Shunk had Novicio, in chains, marched to the gravesite under guard and roughly questioned. Standing before the decomposed remains in the exposed grave, Shunk demanded to know from the *kapitan* if it were true that one or more of the American sailors had been buried alive. A defiant Novicio met the cold, steely glare of Shunk and flippantly replied, yes, that's what he had been told—but he had had nothing to do with it.

The two priests, observing the events, scoffed at the response. Novicio was lying, and they could prove it—just go ask the grave diggers, who had confessed their awful deed to them. Lopez and Minaya, breaking their sacred bond of secrecy, offered up the grave diggers' names and where they could be found. One, Pablo Paulo, was living several miles south of Baler. Another, Tomas Gonzales, lived a few miles to the west.

As Novicio seethed in chains in the garrison's guardhouse, Shunk ordered the grave diggers brought in and deposed. The story of the *Yorktown* sailors killed during the ambush at Baler was finally coming together.

CHAPTER NINETEEN

Venville

THE LIBERATION OF FRANCISCAN PRIESTS JUAN LOPEZ AND FELIX MINAYA was an intelligence boon for the American garrison at Baler. The men provided information that led to raids on Novicio and other suspected insurgents, the capture of a cache of Remington rifles, and the retrieval of two Lee rifles taken from the *Yorktown's* cutter following the ambush nearly a year earlier. With Novicio confined, residents worked up the courage to come forward with more bits and pieces: a wristwatch and keepsakes that had been stripped from the dead sailors, the cutter's compass, along with its oars, anchor, and chain. Angara and the two grave diggers were taken under American protection, the latter two providing nearly identical stories. Now that Major Shunk and his men had pieced together events subsequent to the ambush, the military wheels of justice began to turn.

The story surrounding Apprentice Denzell G. A. Venville remained murky. Lopez and Minaya provided extensive depositions—a chronicle of events, names, and implications levied against Novicio and the Gutierrez clan of San Jose in the sailor's disappearance. From what Shunk and his men could gather, Venville had been severely injured during the ambush and held behind with other wounded sailors after the balance of the Gillmore party was marched over the mountains. When the besieged Spaniards finally capitulated in June 1899, and began their trek to Manila, Venville was again held back, and as Tecson's forces were withdrawing, he was turned over to Novicio's smaller force of about thirty men, along with the two priests. The prisoners were moved to a house owned by Novicio's aide, and then relocated to a second house within the town proper three months later. Finally, on February 16, 1900, when it was reported that "600 Americans all mounted on big horses" were descending on Baler,

Novicio ordered the three captives moved again, this time to the guard-house in front of his own residence.

Novicio, panicked that the Americans would rescue his prisoners, knew he needed to act. On February 19, a day before General Funston's arrival, Novicio ordered a guard of soldiers to march the captives to San Jose, where they were placed in the custody of the town's *presidente*, Francisco Gutierrez. Warned that the arrival of American forces was imminent, the town's *presidente* packed up his extended family and fled to the forest with his new charges.

Five days later, the priests explained, their circumstances had changed. The six guards who had accompanied them were relieved by two men from Novicio's command, Querijero and Marguerito, who marched them deeper into the forest, to a hardscrabble Ilongot settlement. Then, oddly, the two escorts abandoned them. Left among a band of humorless, well-armed tribal head-hunters, Venville and the priests quickly grew deathly afraid, sensing their lives were in imminent danger. Before the situation deteriorated, the unguarded prisoners elected to hike back to the previous camp, to rejoin the Gutierrez clan. Two days later, Novicio's two men reappeared, along with the *presidente* of San Jose. They explained to the prisoners that their absence had been due to a need to attend an Ilongot wedding ceremony a few miles away. They then fell into a huddle for some serious talk with the rest of the Gutierrez men. To the prisoners, the ever-shifting guard arrangements, locations, and orders were perplexing. Surely something was afoot.

The following morning, on February 28, the two soldiers abruptly left again, to report back to Novicio. Strangely, the daughter of the *presidente*, unprompted and for no apparent reason, prepared a grand breakfast for Venville. The hefty serving of venison and plate of steaming rice was a rare luxury. As Venville enjoyed his breakfast, four members of the Gutierrez clan casually approached to ask if he would like to join them on a fishing excursion to the nearby Diatt River. It was a regular ritual and, in fact, Venville had become quite an expert with his net and weights, often bringing home a decent catch. While scraping his plate clean, Venville agreed. The group gathered up its fishing nets and bows and arrows, and disappeared down the trail.

By 10:00 a.m., Lopez started to wonder aloud where the fishing group had gone. Normally, they would return early, before the heat of late morning. Sitting in one of the camp's small *nipa* huts, Lopez inquired of the *presidente*, "Where is Venville?"

The *presidente* replied, "Oh! He is all right; he has gone with them to the mountains."

By noon, as lunch was being served, the priests' worry turned to fear. Lopez again asked, "Why hasn't Venville come back?" The *presidente* ignored him. The priest repeated the question three more times, aggressively pushing for an answer.

The *presidente*'s brother angrily broke in, "*Na dispacha na* [He's gone.]"

"Why?" Lopez cried. "What has Venville done?"

The *presidente*, irritated by the interrogation, responded, "He is a bad man, and Novicio did not want him to be with you two priests. Didn't you notice last night he tried to escape? He left the house and we found him in the woods."

The priest was incredulous. He rejected the explanation. "No, we were sleeping, all three of us together. He was in the middle and didn't try to escape."

Lopez walked out of the hut and went to join Minaya, who was discussing Venville's absence with the *presidente*'s wife, Brigada, at her small bamboo and *nipa*-thatched hut.

The anguished woman, in the midst of her own confused confessional, questioned, "Was it wrong for my husband to harm Venville?"

"Yes," responded Minaya. He explained that it was not the way to treat prisoners. She then began to cry.

Lopez shared what he had heard from the *presidente* and concluded that Venville had been taken out and murdered. The two priests began to fret about their own fate.

Around 1:00 p.m., two members of the sham fishing party returned without Venville, without any fish or game, their fishing nets dry and unused. The priests angrily confronted the men, demanding to know, "Where is Venville?" The men were silent.

The daughter who had cooked Venville his bountiful breakfast entered, assessed the uncomfortable silence, and asked the men, "Have you really done that awful thing?"

Not responding, the two men looked at each other and grinned.

The priests' deposition to Major Shunk suggested the worst. They explained further, that on March 2, a new guard, Simaco Angara, was placed in charge of them. Armed with a rifle, Angara was ordered to guard them closely, and, if there was any chance they were about to fall into American hands, to kill them.

And then this: Several days later, an Ilongot delegation from a nearby tribal settlement arrived at the camp, bearing three large bales of valuable tobacco. It was a gift, they said, for the Gutierrez clan. For an Ilongot marriage festival, the priests understood, it was necessary to take a human head. The tobacco was likely a payment in gratitude to the *presidente* for facilitating this bloody cultural requirement.

The priests' implication: There had been a trade—the boy Venville for a lucrative cache of tobacco. Outsourcing the murder to the Ilongots also offered Novicio and his cohorts plausible deniability for their crime.

Finally, a week later, a worried *presidente* isolated the two priests from his family and sent them deeper into the woods, with Angara as their lone guard. "Novicio orders that I separate you two from the rest of the party," he nervously explained, "to the place of an old man who will be good to you." There they lived, in a dark, gloomy patch of forest, far from any settlement, until their rescue by the Americans three months later.

As the Americans dug for information, an uglier and uncorroborated version of events arose. Several Baler locals, either stating the facts as they knew them, or, quite possibly with an ax to grind against the priests, "asserted that [Venville] had been 'killed to close his mouth' as to the homosexual practices of the priests." One of the American soldiers would later recount how, upon arriving in Baler with Funston, they heard that "the Padres took [Venville] away with them," that he and three of Funston's scouts stumbled across the priests, and through forced questioning, learned that Venville "had been the personal slave of his captors [the priests!], all this time," prior to his then-recent disappearance. One later published account salaciously referred to Venville as "a body slave" of the priests.

⚊⚍⚊

The two Spanish priests also offered up information not related to Venville. A third priest, Father Mariano Gil, was being held captive in the town of Casiguran, fifty miles north along the coast. Embracing another opportunity for a boredom-breaking adventure, the Americans launched another rescue, which reunited the three joyous priests in Baler. Their pathetic appearance compelled the post commander to issue clothing "in

Preparing to undertake the rescue mission of the Spanish priest being held by Army of Liberation forces at Casiguran, around June 10, 1900.

value not to exceed $5.00" to "each of the three destitute Spanish Friars recently liberated from the enemy and now at the post."

And yet, despite this success, the mystery of Venville's disappearance confounded the garrison. To date, all they had was hearsay, rumors, and secondhand reports about what may or may not have happened. After all they had heard, was it remotely possible the naval apprentice was still alive? Or, if not, would it be possible to recover his remains?

On the other side of the world, a worried mother kept up a relentless letter-writing campaign on behalf of her missing son. Emily Mash, Arthur Venville's remarried, illiterate mother, turned again and again to her teenage daughter Regina to carefully craft each letter. Among the many missives, one was sent to General Arthur MacArthur Jr. on May 24, 1900. In it, Mrs. Mash explained that one of her son's shipmates from the *Yorktown*, the liberated Orrison Woodbury, had written to her, explaining that her son could not have died from his wounds. The words of comfort buoyed her spirits; it was likely that her boy was still alive.

Father Mariano Gil, days after his dramatic rescue from Casiguran, posing with his liberators on their arrival at Baler.

Oh dear Sir, think of my son's feeling if he saw that boat going away and leaving him still in the hands of the enemy. Oh Sir, can you not send soldiers there to demand my son or find out his fate. I will be so relieved when I learn if he is dead. The long strain of 13 months and more will be over, if he comes back alive God only knows my joy. I have waited so long for news that the suspense is killing me. My poor son has only his brokenhearted mother to plead for him . . .

On August 2, 1900, Major General Loyd Wheaton responded to one of Mrs. Mash's letters, recounting the facts as the army knew them at the time. He concluded that it was understood the boy had been turned over to "Elongots (mountain Savages)." It was therefore impossible to determine whether or not Venville was still alive. "Novicio is now in confinement at Baler," the general advised, and "every effort has been made to capture Gutierrez," his coconspirator. If he is taken, the general promised, "he will also be brought to trial."

A day later, Mrs. Mash wrote Navy Secretary Long, rejecting the official doublespeak and demanding action.

> *I received notice from Rear Admiral Remey that my son D G Venville was alive as late as May 18th, 1900 but reported to have been murdered since then, but Dear Sir, I do not think they would keep him and be kind to him for thirteen months and then murder him, but I do think they want to get money for his return and I write to beg you to send $200 to the Army Officer stationed at Baler and to have some notices printed in English, Spanish, Tagalog, with the picture of my boy on it, stating that the $200 Dollars in gold would be paid for his safe delivery into the hands of the Americans.*

In the envelope, Emily Mash included a cherished photograph of her sailor son.

A week later, the navy formally rejected Mrs. Mash's plea for a ransom to be paid. "The money earned by an enlisted man is his, and cannot be disposed of by any but the man himself. . . . The Bureau therefore has no authority to grant your request; however, you can rest assured that every effort will be made for the recovery of your son if he is alive, although there are unauthenticated reports that he was murdered by savages in February last."

Undeterred, Emily Mash continued to fire off letters across the military and political hierarchy, with ever-greater frequency and anxiousness. Convinced her boy was somehow still alive, Emily came upon a new idea: Despite her own poverty, she would raise a ransom herself in order to pay the rebels to release her son. Around Portland, a ransom-raising campaign was soon under way, led by the local newspaper, collecting a nickel here and a dime there from concerned citizens.

～～

On July 21, 1900, Major Shunk reported the latest information on Venville to US Army headquarters, converging the disparate facts to a likely conclusion, and it was not good.

After a diligent five-month search, it was positively known that Venville had been turned over on February 20, 1900, the day the Americans had arrived in Baler, to the *presidente* of San Jose, reportedly "to be by him made away with." The *presidente* had been a fugitive ever since. Novicio had ordered the disposal of Venville, according to Simaco Angara's testimony, who also added that the *presidente* of San Jose had told him the boy had been killed. Further, Novicio's orders were that the two Spanish priests in Angara's care should also be killed "if the soldiers got near them." Shunk reported that Venville "was well known to and much liked by a great many natives in the Baler Valley, and it is a common report among them that Venville has been murdered."

Shunk concluded, "Captain Novicio is a prisoner in our hands, and we have sworn depositions of witnesses who saw him compel the burial of a wounded sailor who was still alive, and the deposition of an executioner who, by the same Novicio's orders, murdered a Spaniard, a brother-in-law of said Novicio. We have abundant evidence of other barbarities of Novicio, and from all of the foregoing, it is believed that Venville has certainly been murdered."

Father Gil was reunited with fellow priests Juan Lopez and Felix Minaya, both of whom were held captive with *USS Yorktown* Apprentice Venville by Novicio's men.

And with that report, the American garrison concluded its hunt for the sailor Venville, and the case grew cold.

◆～◆

The bad news trickled down the military chain and made its way to a heartbroken Emily Mash. The unlikelihood of her son's survival arrived on the heels of an article by the *Portland Oregonian* newspaper, on August 18, 1900, of its progress to raise a ransom:

RAISING A RANSOM
Nearly $100 Contributed for Arthur Venville
Money Will Be Sent to General MacArthur
Who Will Publish Reward throughout Luzon

The article continued, "If this brave boy still lives he cannot receive a higher service than rescue from his savage captors. Lt. Woods is confident that within another day or two he will see the full amount collected. The sum of $250 is deemed necessary to offer a suitable reward."

With receipt of the tragic news of Venville's presumed death, Emily Mash's campaign had hit a wall. With great sadness, she agreed to have the collected funds—some $300 at final count—diverted to finance a gleaming, white marble shaft to mark her boy's empty grave outside Portland, at the Milwaukie Pioneer Cemetery near Sellwood.

On September 23, 1900, a funeral service was held for the sailor. A photographic portrait took the place of a casket. The marble shaft was inscribed:

D. G. A. VENVILLE, BORN JAN. 8, 1881,
WHO WAS WOUNDED AND CAPTURED WITH LIEUT. GILMORE [*SIC*],
OF THE U.S. NAVY,
ON APRIL 12, 1899, AT BALER, LUZON, P. I.,
AND WAS TREACHEROUSLY MURDERED BY ORDER OF NOVICIO,
AN INSURGENT GEN'L, SOME TIME AFTER FEB. 20, 1900

The inscription concluded, "We know not where his body lies, but his spirit is with God."

CHAPTER TWENTY

The Trial

WHILE EMILY MASH SOUGHT ANSWERS ABOUT HER MISSING SON, Apprentice Denzell G. A. Venville, US forces chased an increasingly desperate General Aguinaldo. On the run deep in the Cordilleras, and cut off from news and his soldiers, Aguinaldo was still issuing directives to his guerrilla leaders and urging on their campaign against the Americans.

On June 27, 1900, from his hidden command in Tierra Virgin, Cagayan, he issued Order No. 202:

> *As I have previously ordered that all the Leaders of the guerrillas are free to attack any detachment or enemy post, harassing them continually, I reiterate the same order, all the more during these days because it is very important to do so to favorably influence the cause of Filipino Independence in the next Presidential election in the United States of America. . . . We [must] deliver strong blows to the Americans which will redound in our favor in all parts, and will bring the downfall of the Imperialist party that is working for our enslavement.*

Aguinaldo hoped that a presidential election of anti-imperialist candidate William Jennings Bryan would result in the Americans' relinquishing control of the Philippines and recognizing its sovereignty. Crucial now were military successes that might demonstrate the revolutionary government's commitment to the cause of independence and its capability for self-rule. Aguinaldo continued:

> *Aside from this, you must endeavor with all urgency and in coordination with Señores Calixto Villacorte and Teodorico Novicio, [to]*

attack the towns you believe are most convenient . . . carrying out the attacks in such a way as to achieve the expected results. After this operation, you will proceed with all your respective columns to the province of Isabela, immediately sealing off the entrance to the Caraballo Mountains to prevent the entry of the enemies.

It was to be another stalling action to hold the line, similar to the attacks, ruses, and retreat employed at Vigan, Tangadan Pass, and Tirad Pass the previous December. Little did Aguinaldo know, the enemy had already arrived across the mountains. Novicio, for that matter, was languishing under lock and key at Baler and was about to be brought to trial in a fight for his life.

In an endless bustle of activity, Major Shunk expanded the garrison at Baler. Security was the first concern, addressed by the construction of sentry posts around the town. New buildings sprouted: offices for the command, barracks for the men, a hospital, cookhouses and mess halls, a commissary and storerooms, stables for the horses and mules, a blacksmith shop, and harness shed. Most were cobbled together from remnants salvaged from the many wooden structures burned during the earlier siege; when that supply of wood was exhausted, the soldiers turned to the dense primary forest that surrounded them.

In a very short time, the Americans were embedded in the town's life, transforming it completely. The garrison became the town's biggest employer and consumer of the nearby farms' produce and livestock. Inevitably, the soldiers sought out the laundresses and female vendors who had become regular staples around the camp. Led, informally, by a fiery, quick-witted woman named Dominguez, matchmaking became something of an industry. Soon, a number of the garrison's soldiers were living with a subset of the town's single women, an arrangement to which the military hierarchy turned a blind eye.

Preparations for Novicio's trial were undertaken with a striking level of seriousness. Officers from other regiments were detailed to Baler to serve on the military commission, with an aim to infuse some level of impartiality into the proceedings. President of the commission was forty-three-year-old Lieutenant Colonel John H. Beacom, 42nd Infantry, an Ohio native whose exploits included commanding an Indian Scout company in the Dakotas in the 1880s and a stint with a British expedition to the Sudan. Captain Frank D.

US NATIONAL ARCHIVES

Dominguez, designated the "Belle of Baler" by the American soldiers who arrived to establish the Army garrison.

Webster of the 20th Infantry, a Missouri native and West Point graduate in his early thirties, who had been posted in the Philippines with his wife and two daughters, was designated the prosecutor.

Lieutenant Colonel Beacom convened his first meeting at Baler on the afternoon of September 25, 1900, with the first order of business being the appointment of counsel for the accused. Major Shunk assigned Captain Willard Newbill, Shunk's subaltern, to defend Novicio. After a translator was sworn, Novicio was arraigned on two specifications of murder—for ordering the *Yorktown* sailor Ora B. McDonald to be buried alive, and for ordering his own brother-in-law, Manuel Rodriguez, to be bludgeoned to death. Insufficient evidence was in hand to charge Novi-cio for Venville's murder, but his complicity was suspected. The insurgent *kapitan* pleaded not guilty to both counts.

The prosecution called its first witness, grave digger Tomas Gonzales. The local resident was quizzed about whether he knew the accused, his recollection of the capture of the Americans, and how he was fetched by one of Tecson's soldiers and taken to the Baler River around 9:00 a.m. on the morning in question.

"What did you see there?" Webster asked.

"Americans," responded Gonzales.

"What condition were those Americans in?" Webster continued.

"They were lying on the ground; two of them were dead," testified the grave digger.

Overseen by a contingent of Tecson's soldiers, Gonzales had joined three fellow grave diggers—Balbino Sindac and Pablo Paulo, and his own brother, Luiz Gonzales. Together, they were ordered by Novicio to dig a hole to bury the American sailors.

Webster focused his question: "What did you do when the captain, Teodorico Novicio, said, 'Bury them'?"

"We lifted them and put them in the hole."

"How many did you put in the hole?" Captain Webster clarified.

"Three," came the response.

"What was done with the fourth man?" Webster continued.

"We asked each other what we should do with this one; he is still warm yet."

"Was he dead or still living?" Webster prodded.

"His body was warm yet and his eyes were open," the witness explained matter-of-factly.

Gonzales then began to describe the process of burying the wounded McDonald, who had been shot through the thigh. The sailor, still visibly alive, was moved to the grave and soil heaped upon him.

Webster focused his attention on the subject of the dying sailor. "Did you call anybody's attention to the fact that this man's eyes were open, or moving about, at the time you laid him in the hole? If so, whom did you address?"

"I called to Captain Novicio," Gonzales responded, " 'What about this man—he is alive yet?' and Novicio said, 'Bury them,' and we had to obey . . ."

Lieutenant Colonel John H. Beacom, 42nd
Infantry, presided over Novicio's trial. The rebel
leader was charged with burying alive *USS
Yorktown* sailor Ora McDonald following the
ambush of Lieutenant Gillmore's cutter.

Novicio's counsel, Captain Newbill, stepped forward for cross-
examination.

"You stated that you put three into the hole; were all of these three
dead?" Newbill began.

"Yes."

"Is it not probable that the fourth had died as well, during the digging
of the grave, and that the warmth of his body was not necessarily a sign
that he lived, and that the working of the muscles of the face might have
been due to contraction rather than an absolute evidence that this man
still lived?" argued Newbill.

Gonzales thought for a few seconds and responded, "While we were
digging the grave the third man died. I think the fourth man was still
alive, because if he was dead he would have been cold."

Newbill rephrased the question, suggesting that the warmth of McDonald's body did not mean he was alive. He then questioned under what authority Gonzales had to obey Novicio.

"Being the head of the town, although we are not soldiers, we have to obey him," admitted Gonzales.

Newbill probed at various other points: the movement of McDonald's eyes, then whether Novicio had even understood whether the man was perhaps alive. Finally, he inquired about the relationship Gonzales had with Novicio.

"How long have you known him previous to the burial of these Americans?"

Gonzales smiled. "I knew him for many years; we were boys together."

On September 27, the second grave digger, Pablo Paulo, was called and sworn as a witness for the prosecution. Over the course of more than five hours of direct and cross-examination, Paulo explained in detail the course of events surrounding the burial of the dead and dying sailors. As with Gonzales, the testimony focused on McDonald. Paulo confirmed that the fourth sailor was weak but still alive when he was placed in the grave. Paulo described how he had heaped dirt on McDonald, covering the sailor up to his chest.

"Did you notice any movement of this man at this time, [and] if so, what?" Webster pressed.

"There was no movement of the hands, for they were laid across the breast and covered up; only his eyes were moving," Paulo responded.

At Webster's direction, he stood up from his chair, walked to the middle of the court, and stretched out on the floor. With his hands across his breast, he mimicked the dying man, his eyelids fluttering. With the court hanging in silence, Paulo then emitted a low, exhausted moan, deep from his gut, the final, tormented gasp of the sailor's agony. For a moment, the courtroom froze.

On the third day of the trial, the commission traveled from Baler along a difficult trail to the house of a third grave digger, Luis Gonzales, who was gravely ill. The post surgeon, David Hogan, physically examined the ailing man and confirmed a diagnosis of pulmonary phthisis—tuberculosis—concluding, "[T]he said Luis Gonzales will not live over two months." Presented as a witness for the defense, the dying man, coughing bloody sputum between his words, contradicted his fellow grave diggers. His testimony was emphatic: The sailors were all dead and gone well before they were placed in the grave. No man had been buried alive.

In succeeding days, the trial ground on. The defense presented the fourth grave digger, Balbino Sindac. He described the digging of the grave, and likewise stated that all four sailors were dead before they were buried. McDonald's eyes were open, but he was not moving.

The prosecution then called its final witness, Simaco Angara. The farmer-turned-rebel-guard explained that while he was not a soldier, he had been directed by Novicio to take charge of the two priests, who had, days earlier, been held with Naval Apprentice Venville. Newbill objected. The prosecution was introducing new charges and issues that were wholly irrelevant to the proceedings. The Judge Advocate explained that the question was asked to prove that Captain Novicio had authority in and around Baler that was recognized and obeyed. The objection was overruled.

The line of questioning for Angara continued. Orders were given to him from Novicio, through the *presidente* of San Jose de Casignan, to guard the prisoners, he testified. Novicio personally gave him a Mauser rifle and fifty rounds of ammunition, a week after the Americans arrived.

"What were the rifle and ammunition given to you for? What were you to use them for?" Webster asked in closing.

"In case the priests tried to escape, to shoot them, and as protection against the *Illongotas*," Angara responded.

The defense attempted to undermine the lack of official authority present behind the orders. Newbill challenged the witness: Why did he follow the orders of Novicio—why would one obey his orders?

The answer was direct: "Because I was afraid of him," Angara nervously admitted.

Another portion of the military trial was devoted to the alleged murder of Novicio's brother-in-law, the Spaniard Manuel Rodriguez, on March 1, 1900. Prosecution witness Tomas Carillo, an insurgent soldier, readily admitted that he had clubbed the man to death, as it was feared that if left alive, the hospital medic would provide information to the Americans regarding their cache of hidden weapons. Carillo offered up a handwritten note, allegedly signed by Novicio, which contained instructions to kill Rodriguez. The defense contested its authenticity. They produced Novicio's sister Manuela, the victim's wife, who argued that her own husband might have simply left town. The biggest weakness in the case, however, was the lack of a body. In the defense's view, the prosecution lacked evidence that a crime had even occurred.

After nearly forty hours of testimony over six days, the prosecution rested its case. Novicio declined to be sworn as a witness in his own defense, but requested time to present a written statement.

The following morning, Newbill presented a seven-page spirited defense for Novicio, countersigned by the accused. For the first charge of murder, the defense outlined the contradictory testimony and the open question regarding whether McDonald was still alive prior to being buried. Even if it did happen, Newbill reasoned, "the defense does not see fit further to dwell upon the question since were it now granted that one American was buried alive, the offense would lie at the door of Quicoy, the officer present who represented the authority of the Commanding Officer of this Valley. That Quicoy was the adjutant of Tecson is born [*sic*] out by the testimony of Valenzuela, as well as that of Don Fabian Hernandez, a former judge, and the nearest approach to a gentleman among the natives of these parts."

For the second charge, the murder of Novicio's brother-in-law, Newbill argued that without a body, it could not be proved he was dead. Newbill concluded: "The defense is not prepared to admit that he has more than disappeared."

The commission deliberated and came to a consensus. On both specifications, Novicio was found guilty. And then it handed down its recommendations for sentencing:

And the Commission does therefore sentence him, Captain Teodorico Novicio, to be hanged by the neck until he is dead . . .

In the commission's view, Novicio had indeed ordered an American prisoner of war to be buried alive, and then ordered his own brother-in-law murdered to eliminate the potential risk that he might aid and abet the Americans. As per standard procedures, the court's findings and recommendation that the penalty of death be imposed were sent to US Army Headquarters for review and approval. The Judge Advocate was recalled and, there being no further business before it, the commission adjourned *sine die*.

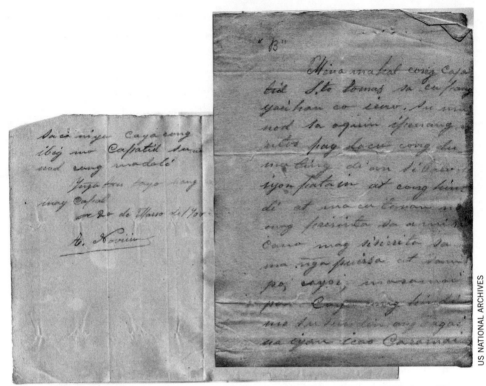

US NATIONAL ARCHIVES

In a US Army military tribunal held in September 1900, Novicio was charged with two murders. Evidence included handwritten instructions allegedly issued to a subordinate, Sergeant Tomas Carillo, to kill a Spanish medic named Manuel Rodriguez. The victim was Novicio's own brother-in-law.

Within weeks, the story broke in newspapers across America. The *New York Tribune* ran the headline:

FOUND GUILTY OF BURYING ALIVE AN AMERICAN SEAMAN
Other Atrocities Charged To Him

"The rebel Captain Novicio has been tried by a military commission at Baler, Northern Luzon," the story reported, "charged with burying a seaman named McDonald, of Lieutenant Gillmore's *Yorktown* party. Novicio was found guilty and sentenced to death. The Commission's sentence is now in the hands of General MacArthur for approval."

While not a part of the formal charges, the news story linked Novicio to the missing Venville, weaving together a story loaded with inaccuracies: "Testimony was also produced at the trial showing that Novicio also caused the death of Venville, another member of Lieutenant Gillmore's party, by delivering him into the hands of native tribesmen, known as Ilongotes [*sic*], who under the pretext of going fishing, lured Venville into the woods and murdered him, with two Spanish friends who were fellow captives with him." The story then went into the realm of spun-from-whole-cloth fiction, reporting that "the tribesmen bound Venville, opened his veins, and sucked his blood until dead."

A similarly sensationalized wire story pulsed across the country, with colorful headlines from the *San Francisco Call, Richmond Dispatch, Nebraska State Journal,* and *Salt Lake Herald*:

SENTENCED TO DEATH FOR BURYING MAN ALIVE
Findings of the Military Court in the Case of Insurgent Captain Novicio

FILIPINO SENTENCED TO DEATH
Terrible Atrocities against Americans—Fiendish Murders

BURIED AN AMERICAN ALIVE
Death Sentence Pronounced on a Filipino Savage

MUST DIE FOR BLOOD SUCKING

When the ghastly account ran in the local papers in Portland, it struck Emily Mash like a thunderbolt. Huddled with her dying husband and anguished children, she no doubt wept as the stories were read to her. That her son, their brother, after being brutally ambushed and held captive for so many months, could then meet so horrendous a fate was beyond comprehension. In the weeks that followed, the Mash family carefully tracked the local papers for further news, desperate for details. Surely the US Navy would write her to either confirm the tale, or perhaps, against all odds, provide a fresh sliver of hope that her boy was still alive.

Two months passed without a word. On December 28, 1900, Emily sat with her daughter and again wrote Navy Secretary Long, enclosing a clipping of the gory report. All she wanted back was her boy.

Dear Sir:

The newspapers of October 28, 1900, report the horrible manner in which my son D. G. A. Venville met his death. I have waited all these weeks hoping to have the report denied or confirmed by the Navy Department. Will you please let me know if it is true or false. If true, if they have found his grave, for I can't help but think if the natives saw the way in which he was murdered they must know where they laid his body.

Respectfully,
E. Mash
Sellwood, Oregon

That same week, there was progress in the Novicio case, but perhaps not what Mrs. Mash wished to hear. After a careful legal review, General MacArthur issued his findings on the commission's recommendations and Novicio's death sentence. He tackled the two specifications in reverse sequence, beginning with the charge of murder of the Spanish medic Rodriguez: "A single witness relates how, in obedience to the orders of the accused, he enticed Rodriguez from his home and beat him to death with a club, and he produced what he purports to be a written order of the accused to do this murder," MacArthur noted. A comparison of the writing samples and the alleged order written by Novicio "reveals an unlikeness between them, while not precluding the possibility that the accused wrote the order to kill Rodriguez, yet leaves a strong impression that he did not in fact write or sign it." That the commission did not make any attempt to verify the presence of a body was viewed as sloppy work and thoroughly undermined the case. "The disappearance of the deceased and the unsupported word of his confessed murder is all there is to show that the deceased may not be living." In view of the serious doubts that a murder had occurred, MacArthur concluded, "the finding upon the 2d specification is disapproved."

A day after Christmas, 1900, Teodorico Novicio was gifted with exoneration on the charge of murdering his brother-in-law.

MacArthur then tackled the other specification, recounting Lieutenant Gillmore's ambush at Baler that left four American sailors dead or wounded on the banks of the Baler River, the detailing of the accused and a detachment of insurgent soldiers as a burial party, the digging of the grave, and the long, slow wait for the last two men to die. As McDonald was moved to the grave and partially covered with earth, MacArthur recounted, the grave diggers questioned what should be done with him.

> *That dissolution was close at hand and the victim nearly, if not quite, unconscious is probably true; that he was still alive when the earth was finally heaped above his head cannot be doubted. Some of the party may have thought he was dead, but the accused had notice to the contrary, and there is no evidence that he made in person, or caused to be made, any examination to ascertain whether the fourth man was actually dead when under his orders the burial was completed.*

MacArthur now addressed the issue of the chain of command: "Although the accused is thus shown to have given commands for the burial of one of these sailors while yet alive, it is also shown that the said Quicoy was present as the representative of his chief—an officer superior to the accused—and that the latter was executing such commands as were given by Quicoy." But that didn't let Novicio off the hook. "An order so inhuman could operate to the protection of no one executing it," MacArthur reasoned. Quicoy may have initiated the crime, but Novicio carried it out.

The general concluded, "There is no reasonable doubt that the last of the four sailors placed in the grave was buried alive and that the accused at least transmitted and saw carried out orders to accomplish the result." But with more powerful principals behind the crime, "the reviewing authority, while confirming the sentence adjudged, is constrained to mitigate the extreme penalty imposed to imprisonment at hard labor for life."

❧

On a clear, bright morning in early January 1901, Baler's residents convened at the plaza. The Americans had announced that the verdict would be passed on the notorious Novicio, still being held at the garrison. Scores of townspeople under bowler hats and umbrellas stood along the periphery of the plaza in nervous anticipation. Uncompromising American military justice was about to be served.

Novicio was collected from the post's guardhouse by nine soldiers of the 22nd Infantry and marched to the front of the Baler church. Five paces before the stone structure, the security detail stood at attention, rifles at their sides. The diminutive rebel *kapitan*, dressed in a light linen jacket and summer hat, stood alone before the new post commander, Captain George A. Detchemendy. Novicio stood perfectly still, awaiting the consequences of his actions.

Detchemendy began, with the post translator following along in Spanish: "Charge: Murder, in violation of the laws and customs of war. Specification One: In that Teodorico Novicio, of the insurgent army of the so-called Filipino government, did willfully, feloniously, and with malice aforethought, kill and murder a wounded American soldier, one McDonald, ordinary seaman, by burying or in person causing the said McDonald to be buried alive, whereof the said McDonald then and there died. This at or near Baler, Luzon, P.I., on or about April 12, 1899, in time of insurrection."

Detchemendy's voice boomed with finality: "On the first specification—guilty." The translator repeated the words in Spanish. The gravity of the words hung in the air. The crowd murmured knowingly.

The officer continued: "Specification Two: In that Captain Teodorico Novicio, of the insurgent army of the so-called Filipino government, did willfully and feloniously and with malice aforethought, by use of his military authority, kill and murder a Spanish prisoner, one Manuel Rodriguez, by causing and compelling men under his command to shoot the said Rodriguez, inflicting wounds whereof the said Rodriguez then and there died. This at or near Baler, Luzon, P.I., on or about March 1, 1900, in time of insurrection."

The post commander continued with authority, "On the second specification—not guilty."

Not guilty? Excited chatter rose up from the assembled crowd. Everyone knew that the commission had earlier recommended Novicio's execution, death by hanging until dead. He had killed one of the American sailors and surely he would pay. And they all knew of his other crimes: the murder of Manuel Quezon's father, Lucio, and brother, Pablo, and his orders for Venville to be dispatched. Would he get away with these crimes too?

Detchemendy then read out the penalty: For his crimes, Teodorico Novicio is sentenced to a life term in prison at hard labor. The translator shared the striking news in Spanish, which sharply tugged at the breath of those looking on. The incredible conclusion slowly dawned on the townspeople: The *kapitan*'s life would be spared.

In January 1901, Captain Detchemendy, in front of the church at Baler, announced the verdict to Novicio. General Arthur MacArthur Jr. had commuted Novicio's death sentence to life in prison, noting weak evidence in a mismanaged trial.

CHAPTER TWENTY-ONE

Bones

JUST AFTER SUNRISE ON APRIL 23, 1901, SOME THREE MONTHS AFTER *Kapitan* Teodorico Novicio's conviction, the *El Cano*—a civilian ship on an ambitious mission—dropped anchor in Baler Bay. On board was the fifty-year-old landscape gardener of America's national cemeteries and superintendent of the United States Burial and Disinterment Corps, David H. Rhodes, and his crew of fourteen morticians, embalmers, and grave diggers. Their task: to disinter and ship to the United States the remains of US Army, Navy, Marine Corps, and civilian contractors who had died during their service in the Philippines. The American military establishment placed a premium on the recovery of human remains; it was noble work that honored sacrifice and helped to relieve the anguish of the bereaved.

Rhodes had sailed from San Francisco with a load of shovels, pick-axes, spades, screwdrivers, hammers, white lead, disinfectants, and twelve hundred metallic California caskets and wooden shipping crates. After stops to exhume bodies in Hawaii and Guam, Rhodes's team had tackled Manila, where gangs of contracted day laborers had helped to dig up the bodies of 275 men at the Malate Cemetery, another 89 at the Paco Cemetery, and, with some extra caution, two possibly still-infectious bodies at the city's Smallpox Hospital Cemetery. By December, Rhodes and his men had visited a list of gravesites around Manila and Laguna Bay, exhuming 102 sets of remains for shipment home.

Rhodes's Burial Corps expedition had then moved on to northern Luzon. Caskets and materials were shipped by railroad to Dagupan, which served as a staging ground for their grim operations. Beginning in

January 1901, the party focused on the exhumation of bodies at the large post cemeteries, and once completed, sent smaller teams to other far-flung sites—either by bull carts and wagons, or, if along the coast or on a river, by steam launch or large native *bancas*. For nearly a month, Rhodes, his assistants, and a pool of laborers crisscrossed the island, relentless in their pursuit of the bleached, fragmented bones of Americans who had died by violence or succumbed to disease. They scoured the provinces of Pangasinan, Zambales, Tarlac, Nueva Ecija, Pampanga, and Nueva Vizcaya, unearthing and crating another 250 sets of remains, which were casketed and loaded onto railroad cars for transport to Manila's port for eventual shipment home to the United States.

Once back in Manila, Rhodes had set out to locate a suitable ship that could take his team on the next leg of its somber expedition, to the coastal towns of Luzon. After much effort, the *El Cano* was secured from the Compania Maritima Line. She was coaled, watered, and loaded with supplies, including several hundred caskets. Sailing from Manila Bay on February 27, 1901, Rhodes spent the next three weeks circumnavigating southern Luzon, stopping at a string of sleepy coastal towns to retrieve remains—nineteen at Lucena, twenty-four at Legaspi, and thirty-two at Nueva Caceres. The *El Cano* visited the island of Catanduanes and then doubled back to sail up the east coast of Luzon.

By the time Rhodes arrived in Baler, his ship already had 189 sets of remains stacked in caskets in the hold. Based on information provided by the garrison, retrieval teams proceeded to two known gravesites. In a boat much like Lieutenant Gillmore's cutter, one team went up the Baler River to the shared riverside grave of the *Yorktown* sailors Ora McDonald, Charles Morrissey, John Dillon, and Edward Nygard. Another team hiked into town to retrieve the remains of three other American soldiers who had died over the past year at the garrison—one by violence and two by disease.

Along the banks of the murky, green river, the first Burial Corps team located its assigned gravesite and broke out the shovels, turning over the sandy earth that Novicio's men had tossed over the dead and dying sailors. Soon they hit the tangle of bones.

Decomposition had occurred slowly and in stages, beginning with the process of autolysis (self-digestion) within minutes of each man's death.

In this harsh, tropical environment, had the bodies of these sailors been left unburied aboveground, invertebrates alone would have reduced the fully fleshed corpses to clean bones in as little as two weeks. Burial in this instance, following Casper's Law of Decomposition, had slowed the process by a factor of eight. Still, the team members knew they were likely to find only skeletonized human remains.

As Rhodes's crew hollowed out the grave, they discovered that the four bodies had been buried in such a manner that it was impossible to identify one set of remains from another. Everything was dug up and placed in a single casket, an indistinguishable collection of brittle bones stripped clean by highly efficient waves of ravenous insects and microbes. Had the bones been left undisturbed to allow the full cycle of human decomposition to complete itself, they would have been broken down further, into proteins, carbohydrates, sugars, collagen, and lipids, a biological reduction to the simplest building blocks of the natural environment.

At Baler's town cemetery, a mile down the road from the church, the three other sets of remains were also exhumed and processed. With work completed at Baler, the four newly filled caskets were transported back to the *El Cano*. By 5:00 p.m., both teams were back on board.

Just over two years after their deaths, through the laudable efforts of Rhodes and his Burial Corps team, the four sailors killed during the ambush of Lieutenant Gillmore's cutter—their skeletonized remains sharing a single casket—were finally going home.

❦

When time permitted, Major Shunk had continued to hunt for the missing naval apprentice during his eight-month tour of duty at Baler, but by November 30, 1900, the day he was to be relieved by his replacement, he had run out of time. As a final act, the post commander wrote to update army headquarters: "After many months of diligent search, I have been unable to get any clue in regard to Venville of the USS *Yorktown*." He recounted that he had announced a standing $100 reward for any information, and had even offered to exchange Novicio, who was facing the death sentence at the time, for the missing sailor. "As the relatives [of Novicio] were making appeals that his life be spared, every few days, it

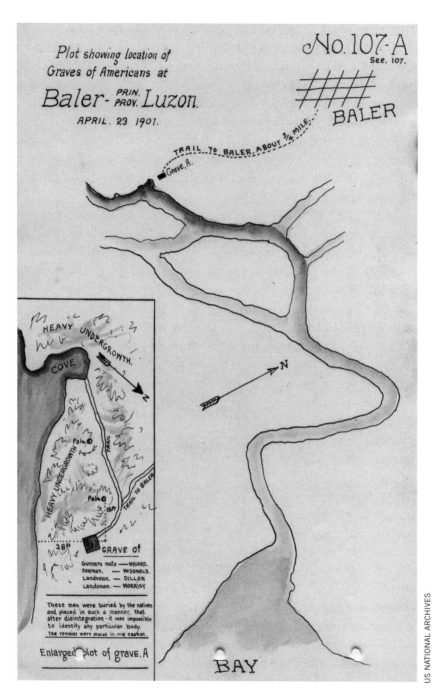

David H. Rhodes, US Army Burial Corps, mapped the hundreds of his team's exhumations in the Philippines, including the remains of the four *USS Yorktown* sailors killed at Baler during the ambush of Lieutenant Gillmore's cutter on April 12, 1899.

would seem that the two offers combined ought to have procured Venville's return, if he were alive; but nothing resulted from the operation of dozens and dozens of searching parties that were sent out day and night." Shunk continued, "Novicio and his family say that Venville is still alive. All the other natives say he is dead, and I regret to say that the latter statement is almost certainly the correct one."

The exasperated major offered a sliver of hope: "The only remaining chance is that Venville may have been taken elsewhere and may still be held a prisoner; but this has never been suggested, nor is it in accordance with their practices."

The arrival of forty-one-year-old Captain George Augustine Detchemendy brought a dramatic change in leadership to the Baler garrison. The St. Louis native carried more than two decades of army experience to the job, and had been commended for gallantry at San Juan Hill; however, the last few years had been marked by increasingly erratic, unstable behavior. By late 1898, prior to his posting to the Philippines, Detchemendy was on leave with a surgeon's certificate, his marriage in collapse, living in a San Francisco hotel as a recluse. The army coaxed him back with a new assignment at a Butte, Montana, recruiting station, but by then, ill-tempered and confrontational, Detchemendy had run into new problems, including charges that he had publicly berated a citizen. By November 1899, the captain was embroiled in an urgent, obsessive campaign: He was at war to correct a misspelling, having the "e" added back into his family name officially on file, "Detchmendy."

Detchemendy was an odd one, indeed, but it would be his fanatical behavior, if not overt insanity, that would produce results in the distant tropical archipelago of the Philippines.

Soon after his arrival at Baler, Captain Detchemendy began receiving copies of the anguished letters that Emily Mash had sent across the military and political hierarchy. Holed up in his own quarters, between moments of lucid garrison leadership and bizarre fits of rage provoked by the most inconsequential of events, Detchemendy was moved to action. Despite—or likely due to his questionable mental stability—the captain immersed himself in what amounted to an unceasing eleven-month obsession to resolve the mystery of the boy Venville.

Captain George A. Detchemendy was the garrison commander at Baler. Suffering from paranoid delusions and rarely venturing out of his quarters, Detchemendy was obsessed with finding the remains of *USS Yorktown* Apprentice Venville and bringing his murderers to justice.

In one of many lengthy, typed reports, Detchemendy described the case as an "exceedingly sad affair," detailing how he was "often spoken to on the subject by numerous soldiers of [his] company, who always displayed nothing but the greatest reverence and respect for the brave dead sailor and an intense desire to lessen the great sorrow of his mother.

"From the start," explained Detchemendy, "I always believed that the capture of Francisco Gutierrez, ex-*presidente* of San Jose, was most important." All they could learn, however, was that Gutierrez had fled before the arrival of the Americans at Baler in March 1900, and had been a fugitive ever since. After an initial two months with little progress, Detchemendy raised Major Shunk's initial reward to $250, for any information that might assist them in finding Venville alive, or, if he was already dead, $50 for the whereabouts of his remains. Furthermore, informants would be protected and the reward "cheerfully" paid. Without a printing press available at the garrison, Detchemendy ordered the reward notice copied and recopied by hand, by scores of soldiers, in English and Tagalog, and distributed throughout the valley. Search parties, averaging two to three each month, were sent out on his orders to scout for information.

Meanwhile, Novicio languished at the guardhouse at Baler, waiting for his life sentence at hard labor to be imposed. Finally, on March 19, 1901, he was transferred to Manila's notorious Bilibid Prison. Novicio's wife appealed to Detchemendy frequently, "and seemed to be in great distress." The captain "allowed her every possible privilege," adding, "To her and to her sister, I gave several copies of the Venville notice of reward, besides explaining to her how unhappy was the mother of 'Bembio' [the name of Venville in the Tagalog dialect] and how anxious I was for any information concerning 'Bembio.'" While Emily Mash's letters had a profound effect on the driven captain, the continued lack of information was frustrating and suggested the worst. "There being absolutely no word concerning Venville from Mrs. Novicio and her relatives was positive proof to me that the lost one was dead," wrote Detchemendy at the time in an official report.

Since his narrow escape at Tirad Pass on December 2, 1899, Filipino general Emilio Aguinaldo had fled east, traversed three provinces of the Cordilleras, and dropped into the Cagayan Valley in the heart of northern Luzon. He celebrated his thirty-first birthday on March 22, 1900, while on the run with a force of 168 men. In April, the general reconnected with Tinio, but the pressure of the advancing Americans kept both leaders on the move. Tinio returned to his command in Ilocos, and Aguinaldo climbed into a second range of mountains, the Sierra Madres, in search of safer refuge. Finally, on September 6, 1900, Aguinaldo arrived at the eastern coastal town of Palanan, assured that his isolation would be his salvation.

He would be right for the next six months. But the garrison at Baler, constantly chasing reports of rebels, arms, and insurgency, stumbled over Aguinaldo's guard on the trail to Pantabangan. In an engagement during the night of February 5, 1901, a scouting party from Baler led by Lieutenant Parker Hitt killed one insurgent, scattered the rest, and captured documents that suggested Aguinaldo's presence at Palanan. By sheer luck, the wall of secrecy surrounding the rebel general's hideout had been breached. The Americans plotted.

It took another month for a new drama to unfold. On the evening of March 14, 1901, just as the sun sank behind the Sierra Madres, a surprised Baler garrison watched the 1,026-ton USS *Vicksburg* steam across the bay on a mysterious run. The ship returned that night to Baler, and the story leaked from no less than her commander, Captain Edward Buttevant Barry: They had just landed General Funston, four other officers, and a force of seventy-seven Macabebe scouts forty-five miles north at the town of Casiguran. Funston and his men were undertaking a bold ruse. With the Americans posing as prisoners of war, the Macabebe force intended to march north, enter Aguinaldo's stronghold, and capture the insurgency's center of gravity alive.

The *Vicksburg* quickly left Baler, anchoring itself off Casiguran. Eleven days later, on March 25, she again steamed across the bay of Baler in a plume of dense, black smoke, stopping long enough to share news of the mission's success. The ruse had been brilliantly executed. Funston and his men had marched into the camp under guard and had taken the rebel general captive with surprisingly little violence. The priceless prisoner, along with his command, was now en route to Manila.

The news of the dramatic capture splashed across banner headlines in America. The *Washington Post* exclaimed:

AGUINALDO TAKEN
Filipino Chief Brought to Manila as a Prisoner
Captured by Gen. Funston
Most Dashing Achievement in the Career of the Little Kansan
Betrayed by His Own People

After fifteen months on the run since the battle at Tirad Pass, the diversion of American forces to Lieutenant Gillmore's rescue, and the resulting grand failure that had allowed Aguinaldo to slip away, the war's center of gravity had been removed. The insurgency—or, more accurately, the war for independence for a sovereign and self-ruled Philippine nation—would soon stutter and stall.

⸻

Three days after the news of General Aguinaldo's capture broke across America, on March 31, 1901, Emily Mash was back at it. It was an extreme long shot, but perhaps Aguinaldo knew about the fate of her son. Having exhausted every other possible lead, Emily again sat with her daughter Regina and drafted a letter to the captive rebel general, who, according to the newspaper reports, was being held on the grounds of Manila's Malacañang Palace under the watchful eye of the US Army. Emily dictated the strongest appeal she could muster, pleading for any help to ease her loss. She begged Aguinaldo for assistance, for his compassion, for the sake of God, as a son to a mother. Emily included a picture of her son, a formal naval portrait of Apprentice Venville in uniform, handsomely sporting a cap from the USS *Adams*, one of his earlier ships.

Three months later, when a small tattered envelope arrived at the Mash home in Sellwood in early July, it almost certainly sparked great hope. Addressed simply in matter-of-fact cursive to "Mrs. Emily Mash, Sellwood, Oregon, US of America," its two-cent George Washington stamp postmarked Manila, the envelope offered absolutely startling contents in the form of an elegant two-page letter, handwritten in Spanish. Unable to decipher its contents, Emily Mash sought out a foreign language instructor from a nearby university, who provided a typed translation in English.

Manila, 9 June 1901
Malacañang
Mrs. Emily Mash

Dear Madam:

For some time I had in my Possession, and with me in my prison, your favor of the 31st of last March, which I now answer. Its contents filled me with sorrow, for, expressive as it is of the sentiments of a mother, the anxiety and grief that you naturally suffer are not beyond my comprehension.

What I most regret just now is, that I cannot set your heart free from the doubt by which it is tormented, knowing only this much about the matter, that the men of the "Yorktown" were captured by the troops of the Revolution in Baler, whence they were taken to another place for their imprisonment. I also know, as you yourself admit, that the said prisoners were well treated by the troops of the Revolution. But I am not informed as to the sad end which you say befell your unfortunate son. I unreservedly tell you that I have no knowledge of that fact. However, in order to please you, I shall try—within the limits of my relative freedom I enjoy in my prison—to inquire and investigate what you so much desire. It would be my greatest pleasure if I could give you any information concerning the matter, and if that information were of the most satisfactory character, such as I would like it for my own mother.

Eagerly profiting by the sad opportunity which procures me the honor of communicating with you, I offer myself, from this my prison, as your most devoted and most respectful servant.

Emilio Aguinaldo

Along with the letter, the former rebel general returned the picture of Emily's beloved son.

Following his capture by the Americans, General Emilio Aguinaldo wrote Arthur Venville's mother, advising her that while he knew nothing of his fate, he would make inquiries. In his letter, Aguinaldo returned to her a photo she had sent him of her son.

Back at Baler, ignited by Emily Mash's steady stream of appeals, Detchemendy was relentless. "I questioned probably a thousand or more Tagalogs in a kindly way concerning the whereabouts of 'Bembio' (or Venville) without the least response excepting from Feliciano Rubio and Benito Aguilar, friendly Tagalogs. I am now satisfied that this dearth of knowledge was due mostly to the great fear of the Ilongots (head-hunters)."

In early July 1901, Detchemendy received information that the former *presidente* of San Jose, Francisco Gutierrez, had returned to the valley. He immediately sent a detachment of soldiers to investigate. After more than six months, Feliciano Rubio, the post's trusted guide and translator, finally gave up the remaining facts. Gutierrez, he explained, was responsible for arranging the boy's murder. Rubio also identified, for the first time, the names of the Ilongots behind the assault. They belonged to the band led by Nut Gai, who had previously befriended the American detachment.

Detchemendy knew he was close to solving the case. He ordered scouting parties sent out day and night, chasing down every lead. The *presidente*'s son, Protacio, who reportedly had been with the group that murdered Venville, was arrested and interrogated. Under extreme duress, Protacio was forced to lead a nighttime raid to capture his father in the surrounding jungle. Detchemendy and five soldiers, a roped Protacio in tow, burst onto a location only to find that the elusive father had once again fled.

Under unceasing pressure, new intelligence trickled in: "Gutierrez is said to be a half-breed Tagalog and Ilongot . . . and is believed to be hiding among the Ilongots. 'Augustin,' a well-known full-blood Ilongot of Nut Gai's band, is said to be the half-brother of Gutierrez." Information about where they were likely hiding came to light. Unwavering in his pursuit, Detchemendy ordered his men to keep digging, and launched a series of raids. The narrow focus on the hunt for Venville was now a full-time preoccupation for the garrison, and for the captain, a salve to his mental imbalance.

By August 1, Detchemendy's incessant pressure and armed raids had severely strained relations with the surrounding Ilongot community. Reporting to headquarters, Detchemendy advised, "[I]t is considered that a war by the Americans upon a band of Ilongots under Nut Gai is very likely to occur at any moment. Up to present I have had very friendly relations with Nut Gai and his people and their conduct in this respect has been only such as to cause their horrible crime to be more revolting.

It was some of Nut Gai's men who had assisted Gutierrez to murder and decapitate Venville, and the whole band have been deceiving me in the most perfidious manner and at the same time continuing their diabolical practice of head-hunting with fiendish delight."

The final straw for Detchemendy was the cruel news that the head of "a defenseless old woman" had been taken recently by Nut Gai's Ilongots. Despite professing great friendship for the Americans and declaring that they were "reformed," having abandoned their behavior, old customs apparently died hard. Detchemendy was prepared to deliver retribution one way or another: "Every effort will be made to avoid unnecessary bloodshed by an attempt to make prisoners of the guilty men, but a failure in this should result in an attack upon the entire male portion of Nut Gai's band, all of whom are more or less guilty and deserve severe punishment."

It was now all-out war. In another raid on August 31, 1901, Nut Gai and two others Ilongots were captured. The tribal chieftain, however, would not be held for long. In days, he made his escape from Baler's guardhouse and disappeared into the surrounding jungle. Shortly thereafter, another of the imprisoned Ilongots assaulted and killed an American sentry in a murderous bid to escape, but was shot down himself. Death came quickly for others. An American detachment was sent out to arrest "several other implicated Ilongots, but in the ensuing attack by a band of Ilongots, two of the prisoners were killed." Of those being pursued for Venville's murder, three were dead and one was on the run.

Finally, the garrison was given a break: Benigno Bitong, an alleged member of the hunting party that had led Venville to his death, was caught. Taken by Detchemendy and a squad of soldiers to the camp where the priests had been rescued, Bitong was forced at gunpoint to lead them to the site of the murder.

Early on September 1, the party proceeded northwest up a dry creek bed of the Diatt River. At a distance of about three and a half miles, Bitong abruptly stopped in his tracks. Here, he indicated, was the spot where Venville had been killed.

The party began a diligent search of the area, digging along the riverbed and among the high grass. Little was found beyond a piece of an outsole of an old shoe and a few strips of blue US Navy clothing the size of a dollar bill. But that was enough. The party marked the site where it believed the murder had occurred with stones from the riverbed, creating a large horizontal cross, ten feet long and six feet wide. Immediately on their return to Baler, Detchemendy ordered a larger party to prepare to reexamine the site.

Two days later, on the morning of September 3, 1900, Lieutenant Parker Hitt, twenty-one men, Rubio, and Bitong marched back out to San Jose, under Detchemendy's orders to locate the grave and any remains. This time the soldiers brought Campana, one of the surviving Ilongot prisoners still in their custody who had been implicated in the killing. At first, Campana "denied even that he knew of the crime, but, on being placed at the head of the column, he proceeded without hesitation and without prompting to a point on the Diatt River, about three miles above San Jose, previously visited and marked by [Detchemendy]." The soldiers spread out to scour the surroundings. Convinced that the Americans already knew everything, Campana called Rubio over. Together, they walked to a small clearing nestled between three trees. The Ilongot prisoner stopped and pointed to the ground. *Here.*

The soldiers fell to their knees and began to dig up the site with their bare hands, an area about two and a half feet deep and three feet across. Every handful of earth was sifted, each clump of dirt broken up in their fingers and studied. First, a soldier held up a small piece of blue cloth. A second soldier called out another find, an indistinguishable mud-caked object, followed by another. Scraping off the wet earth, prying at their finds, the objects took shape, revealing fragments. Bone fragments. As the men worked, a small pile took shape.

Once they were convinced all the remains had been retrieved, the American soldiers added to the stone cross and pyramid that had marked the murder site. On a tree near the exposed grave, one of the men carved out a rough inscription with his knife, mangling the young sailor's initials:

G. D. A. VENVILLE
FEB. 28, 1900

Lieutenant Hitt wasn't happy with the makeshift memorial. "The size of the tree and brittleness of the bark prevented the cutting of a more elaborate inscription," Hitt recounted. Under the circumstances, it was the best they could do.

COURTESY OF THE UNIVERSITY OF MICHIGAN

Lieutenant Parker Hitt, who first located Venville's grave along the Diatt River.

With the discovery of the remains, a confession now flowed freely from Campana. Yes, he admitted, he was one of a band of about twenty Ilongots under the command of Nut Gai. They had been hunting deer along the Diatt River when they heard men approaching. It was a Filipino and an American. They hid, lying in wait. Just as the other men passed, Nut Gai and another warrior each shot an arrow at the American, killing him. The Filipino ran away. The Ilongots then pulled out their bolos and carved up their bounty. They cut off the American's head and chopped off his hands and feet as souvenirs. They lazily tossed the remaining torso into a small depression, covering it with a bit of earth and some nearby stones.

Days after the killing, Campana had passed the area with his dogs and saw the pelvis, leg bones, and other remains ripped apart and scattered about the riverbed, some thirty feet from the site of their incomplete grave. He supposed the remains had been dug up and carried off by the packs of wild pigs and feral dogs that roamed the forest.

The mystery of Denzell George Arthur Venville's disappearance—his murder, dismemberment, and partial burial—was now solved.

Back at the garrison, the collected bits and pieces of the *Yorktown* apprentice were turned over to post surgeon David Hogan for examination. The surgeon laid out the excavation's bounty: thirteen small fragments that hardly resembled the boy sailor. But they were indeed human. Two of the bones were cervical vertebrae, pieces from the top of Venville's spinal column, which formed the flexible framework of the boy's neck and supported his skull. Another six fragments were dorsal vertebrae from the middle of his spinal column. Hogan was quickly able to identify these bones by their faceted sides, where the heads of the ribs were joined. The doctor noted two clavicle bones, parts of the apprentice's shoulders, as well as his manubrium, a flat, dagger-shaped bone from the middle of the chest that formed part of the sternum, and which on better days would have been connected to the first two ribs of Venville's torso. As Hogan scraped the dirt off the manubrium, the fragment revealed what appeared to be a cut, a sharp slice by a bladed instrument. His conclusion: the strike of a bolo, and confirmation of death by violence.

Moving on, Hogan studied a prism-shaped artifact, the longest of all those recovered. This was a radius bone, from the boy's forearm. Finally, the surgeon studied a singular phalanx, a segment from one of the boy's fingers. The surgeon wrote up his findings, cataloged the remains, and placed them in a cloth sack inside a small box that was then tinned, soldered shut, and placed inside an unnecessarily large casket. The surgeon's job was done.

On Friday, September 6, 1901, religious services with full military honors were conducted for Venville in front of a large wooden cross on the plaza of Baler, in the shadows of the church that had witnessed so much tumult and violence. The American garrison turned out in its entirety for the occasion, as did a number of Filipinos who had befriended the wounded sailor during his tormented stay in the town.

Detchemendy, his mad obsession finally paying dividends, made a short address to those gathered. He gave thanks to those who had devoted many months to the hunt for the boy's remains. Paperwork was processed, cables sent, and approval was granted to ship the casket to the Manila morgue on the next boat from Baler. The bleached sack of fragments, sealed inside a box inside a casket, began its solemn journey home.

On September 22, 1901, the *New York Times* picked up the story, head-lined GHASTLY RELIC OF GILLMORE'S PARTY.

With a Manila byline, the piece explained that Captain Detchemendy had recovered a portion of the body of the ill-fated apprentice of the *Yorktown,* and that the remains were being shipped home. True enough, on December 5, the casket arrived at the port of San Francisco. From there, it was forwarded to Portland, Oregon, to the funeral home desig-nated by the family.

The prayers of Emily Mash had been answered. Her many missives, dictated to her daughter Regina, scratched out on ruled pages of a school notebook, and sent around the world to presidents and generals, had finally brought closure to a mother's broken heart.

A ceremony was held on December 15, 1901, at St. John's Episcopal Church in Sellwood, the only structure large enough for the overflow-ing crowd of mourners. The funeral brought together a near-prostrate Emily Mash; Venville's three sisters, Ruth, Regina, and Grace; four step-siblings, Percy, Sarah, Charlie, and Neita; and nearly the entire Sellwood community.

One woman who attended the funeral as a little girl later recounted, "All of the schoolchildren of Milwaukie were there, but I don't know why." Another attendee recalled the oddity of pallbearers carrying not a typical casket, but a small metal box. The long procession returned to the empty memorial that had been constructed more than a year earlier, in September 1900, and where an earthen grave had now been dug. The thirteen bone fragments—all that remained of the Mash family's murdered brother and son—were buried with military honors and rifle salute.

With the full story now known, the resolute marble shaft that had been bought with funds collected for a ransom, was etched with an update:

THE BODY OF D. G. A. VENVILLE

WAS FOUND 12 MILES FROM BALER AND

WAS LAID TO REST HERE

DEC. 15, 1901

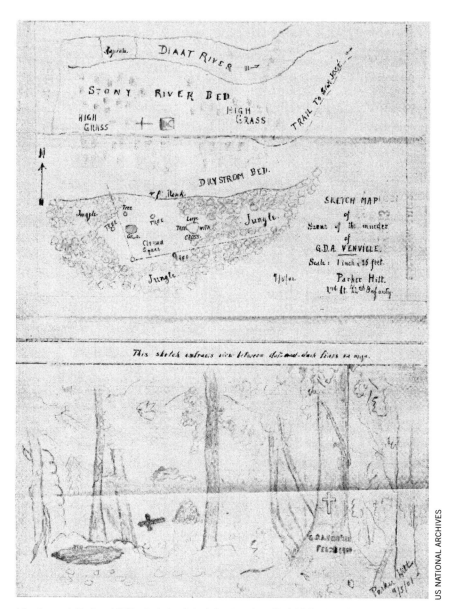

Lieutenant Parker Hitt's sketch, dated September 5, 1901, showing the location where Venville's remains were found along the Diatt River. Only a handful of bones were recovered.

It was, of course, inaccurate. There was no body, just a handful of bones, notched by bolos and plundered by beasts of the forest. For the grieving, world-weary Emily Mash, it would have to suffice. Her boy was finally home.

On December 24, 1901, John David Long, Secretary of the Navy, wrote a highly unusual letter to Elihu Root, Secretary of War, commending the conduct of Detchemendy, Hitt, and the garrison at Baler, for the "zeal and perseverance" with which they had prosecuted the search for the remains of Venville. Often at odds, this was one military branch of service paying tribute to another. Secretary Long enthused: "The fact that the loss of one naval apprentice in the multitude of fatal and other casualties which have occurred during the insurrection in the Philippines could have inspired such unselfish and hazardous service as was involved in the search for the remains of D. G. A. Venville, is a high tribute to the character of the soldiers of the United States Army and will tend to unite the Navy to it in closer bonds." The Secretary closed, "I have the honor to request that you will transmit to the officers and enlisted men above mentioned the grateful appreciation and commendation not only of the Navy Department, but of the officers and enlisted men of the entire Navy for their act, and for the thoughtful remembrance of the family of the boy who was so cruelly murdered."

Justice would be slow in coming to Baler, and may not have arrived at all. A reclusive Detchemendy, cloistered in his quarters, continued to push his men on an unceasing hunt for the Gutierrez brothers. But the post had trouble even holding those men they had caught. Bitong took advantage of a violent typhoon that ripped across eastern Luzon in October 1901 to slip from the guardhouse, like Nut Gai, who had escaped the previous August, and his fellow Ilongot, who was killed during an escape attempt. And then, after fifteen months of increasingly bizarre, obsessive-compulsive behavior, Detchemendy completed his tour of duty and spiraled out of control. Diagnosed as medically unfit and suffering from "delusions of persecution and paranoia," the former garrison commander was found to be in a "very excitable" condition, and "markedly lacking in self-control."

On the obelisk:

D.C.A.
VENVILLE
BORN
Jan. 8, 1881,
WHO WAS WOUNDED
AND CAPTURED WITH
LIEUT. GILMORE,
OF THE U.S. NAVY, ON
APRIL 12, 1899
AT BALER, LUZON, P.I.
AND WAS TREACHER-
OUSLY MURDERED,
BY ORDER OF NOVICIO,
AN INSURGENT GEN'L,
SOME TIME AFTER
FEB. 20, 1900.

WE KNOW NOT WHERE
HIS BODY LIES,
BUT HIS SPIRIT IS
WITH GOD.

THE BODY
OF
D.C.A.
VENVILLE
WAS FOUND
12 MILES FROM
BALER,
AND WAS LAID
TO REST
HERE
Dec. 15, 1901.

Denzell George Arthur Venville's grave at Milwaukie Pioneer Cemetery outside Portland, Oregon.

It was believed "the trying service at Baler undoubtedly accentuated his aberrations." Baler, it seemed, had broken the man.

By 1902, a number of the alleged participants in Venville's brutal murder had been captured by the Baler garrison, but by then it was too late. Despite the tremendous amount of time and energy devoted to arresting those responsible, the US Army was hesitant to try them for their crimes. In fact, military commissions were about to be curtailed as the US Army prepared to exit from the business of dispensing justice in the Philippines. After nearly three years of warfare, the near collapse of the revolution, and their growing success with pacification, civil and military authorities in the Philippines were shifting their focus to amnesty and reconstruction. Desperate to wipe the slate clean and heal the wounds of war, the Americans simply wanted to move on.

On April 17, after nearly eight months in captivity and legal limbo, Campana and Protacio became lucky beneficiaries of this policy shift. The army turned over the two prisoners to civilian authorities for a review of their cases, which would lead to their eventual release. A third conspirator also being held was similarly transferred from the Baler guardhouse five days later.

Despite the startling setback, the garrison remained committed to bringing the principals behind the crime to justice. The manhunt shifted to those directly implicated in ordering and overseeing Venville's murder: the three Gutierrez brothers, Francisco, Luis, and Jose. On July 13, 1902, new intelligence led to their capture. Each man was charged with ordering the murder of Venville, trials were held, and convictions meted out.

But on November 21, before the convictions could be confirmed, the Baler post was again ordered to turn over the prisoners, and all their papers, to the civilian constabulary. The outcome of the civil cases against the Gutierrez brothers has been lost to history, though one credible reference suggests that at least two of the men were publicly hanged at Baler. Equally likely, given the already-murky and convoluted case, a lack of witnesses, and the passage of time, it would have been difficult if not impossible to prosecute these men. And with a broad amnesty just months away, it seems more probable that the charges were dropped and the men set free.

In tandem with the handover of control to Filipino civilian authorities, American garrisons were being vacated across northern Luzon. From June 1901 through June 1902, US Army posts in seventy of ninety-eight towns were withdrawn in the provinces of Bataan, Nueva Ecija, Morong, Pangasinan, Bulacan, Pampanga, and Rizal. With this sharp scaling down, US Army Headquarters requested feedback from their remaining posts, where unstable conditions meant that withdrawal was not obvious. In each case, a decision had to be made: Should the Americans maintain the post, or close it down? Among the garrisons facing this question was the post at Baler.

To gauge public sentiment, the post commander asked the *presidente* of Baler to gather his citizens' views. The core question: Should the Americans stay or go? The *presidente* convened the equivalent of a town hall meeting, attended by all 249 heads of households present. The pros and cons of the Americans' presence were discussed, likely with some spirited debate. Grievances were surely aired, the economic impact assessed, and prospects for peace and order in the future weighed. Once all the views were on the table, a vote was taken, and a proclamation drafted to share the results:

United States of America
Philippine Islands
District of Principe

In the official residence of the Presidente of Baler, District of Principe, Don Tomas Amasona, Presidente of the said town, in the presence of his council and all the men of legal age of the town, in compliance with the verbal order of the Military Commander of this department inquiring as to the wishes of the people in regard to keeping American troops in this town; asked people present, who unanimously informed him of their desire to have a detachment of soldiers stay in this town in order that the peace and tranquility which has marked it since the arrival of troops in this district may remain—still they submit themselves to the orders from higher authority. There being no further business this document was signed by the Presidente and the persons present. 10 April 1902. The Secretary certifies to it. Signed by the Presidente of the town and 248 others.

On April 11, 1902, the day before the third anniversary of Gillmore's debacle at Baler, the proclamation, including eight pages of the townspeople's signatures—some flowery, regal, and elaborate, others in careful if not labored penmanship—was delivered to the garrison commander.

The Baler post commander could only marvel at how far Filipino-American relations there had come.

CHAPTER TWENTY-TWO

Dead Man's Island

KAPITAN TEODORICO NOVICIO MAY HAVE ESCAPED THE IGNOMINY OF a public hanging, but he did not escape punishment. Arrested in April 1900, tried at Baler by a US military commission from August to October 1900, and advised that his sentence was commuted to life imprisonment in January that year, Novicio languished in the post's jailhouse for another three months. All told, by April 1901, the rebel officer had been locked up behind bars for nearly a year.

The post commander was keen to have Novicio relocated; his presence was a distraction, and agitated the locals. Finally, he received permission to transfer the prisoner to Manila's Bilibid Prison. On April 3, 1901, Corporal Frank Hanson, 22nd Infantry, a twenty-three-year-old former laborer from Buchanan County, Iowa, was placed in command of a detail of six guards to escort the shackled Novicio on a three-day steamship excursion to the capital city. The trip completed without event, the squalid, overcrowded confines of the country's national penitentiary became Novicio's home for the next eighteen months.

By every account, Bilibid was a hellhole of pestilence and disease. In harsh and unsanitary conditions, inmates suffered dysentery, dengue, malaria, smallpox, and plague. Bilibid's residents also faced the scourge of beriberi that had affected the Spanish garrison under siege at Baler. During a six-month period in 1902, some two thousand prisoners contracted the disease. They fell, one by one—first with heart problems, followed by edema and swelling legs, staggering gait, mental deterioration, and paralysis. For seventy-seven of Bilibid's inmates, death followed. And in one unfortunate instance, disease came not by chance but rather by mistake: Army surgeons, testing a vaccine, inadvertently injected a luckless group of prisoners from a batch of cholera plague serum that had been tainted with deadly bubonic plague. Ten prisoners who received the serum fell violently ill and subsequently died.

As Novicio began his life as a military convict, the Americans were bringing the insurrection to a close. One month after Aguinaldo's capture by General Funston at Palanan, Isabella, on March 23, 1901, the Filipino leader issued a proclamation of formal surrender. He appealed to his comrades to lay down their arms against an irresistible force and pursue a path of promised liberties and peace. "By acknowledging and accepting the sovereignty of the United States through the entire Archipelago, as I do now without any reservations whatsoever, I believe I am serving thee, my beloved country." Aguinaldo closed: "May happiness be thine!"

The rebel general's eloquent appeal was more powerful than expected. A broken, demoralized force of remaining holdouts surrendered in quick succession, including Colonels Juan and Blas Villamor at Bangued on April 27, General Manuel Tinio at Ilocos Sur on May 1, and the rebel priest Gregorio Aglipay a day later. Within months, Aguinaldo's military generals from provinces across Luzon had surrendered, turning over their arms and, for the most part, signing statements of allegiance to their new colonial masters. Recalcitrant "incorrigibles"—senior officers and administrators of the revolutionary government who refused to swear fealty to their new colonial masters—were deported to the remote backwater of Guam, where they could do no harm.

On July 4, 1902, President Theodore Roosevelt formally declared the Philippine Insurrection over.

~ ~

Bilibid Prison quickly became an embarrassment to the civil administration that lauded itself on good governance, quality infrastructure, and improved social services. Declared a "hotbed of tuberculosis and contagion," Bilibid's decongestion was set in motion. Those prisoners with sentences of less than ten years—largely for crimes ranging from larceny, arson, and robbery, but also manslaughter, rape, and murder—were released, with time off for "good conduct in confinement." Convicts looking at imprisonment of more than ten years were ordered to start serving the "hard labor" to which most had been sentenced, and were sent off to build roads and railway lines around the archipelago. And the worst offenders were to be sent to a new facility on Malahi Island, a twenty-seven-hectare spit of an islet situated in the middle of Laguna Lake, the largest inland body of water in the Philippines. Here, some thirty miles south of Manila, the country's hard-core prisoners were to be assembled to toil in hot, dusty rock quarries, hammering rock into gravel for road construction in nearby Fort McKinley, headquarters of the US Army. A sentence of hard labor now actually meant a lifetime of unceasing physical toil.

Malahi Island, nestled off the southern tip of dagger-shaped Talim Island, was a tropical Alcatraz of sorts, an inaccessible garrison surrounded by the 900-square-kilometer brackish Laguna Lake. The prison, separated from the larger military post, comprised three *nipa* barracks, a small hospital, a wooden mess hall, and a corrugated-iron building with ten cells for solitary confinement, all nestled on a half-acre of land. Wrapping the prison compound were three barbed-wire fences, six feet apart and eight feet high, each with thirty-six strands of razor-sharp barbed wire. Seven watchtowers, manned by rifle-wielding sharpshooters, circled the prison, along with rows of streetlamps to illuminate the perimeter at night. The post's rock-crushing machine, fed with an unceasing flow of rocks quarried by the prisoners from surrounding islands, stood off by itself. Banging and clanging away, the deafening machinery created a steady stream of gravel, which in turn was carried off by the dust-choked and sweat-drenched prisoners, sacks on their sunbaked backs, to awaiting barges.

Beyond the imposing prison and its chain gangs of prisoners, views in every direction revealed hundreds of fish pens in the shimmering waters, staked out by the residents of nearby lakeshore communities, which raised tons of milkfish (locally called *bangus*), tilapia, and carp for Manila's voracious wet markets. Amid this waterborne bounty, the country's worst offenders and highest-risk prisoners toiled for eight hours per day, six days a week—Sunday was a rest day—under the careful armed watch of their US Army guards.

In September 1904, after three years and five months at Bilibid, Teodorico Novicio was delivered in chains to Malahi Island and put to work. The routine was quickly set. Each day, he and his fellow prisoners were shackled and delivered to the post's one steam launch, the *Denver*, for transport to nearby Talim Island. Novicio swung sledgehammers and pickaxes against boulders, fed the insatiable rock crusher, wrangled weighty sacks of gravel, day in and day out. The shift from the mind-numbing idleness of Bilibid to chain-gang labor in dust-choked rock quarries, without respite, undoubtedly shocked Novicio's system.

After several months of exhausting labor, a physically depleted Novicio knew the score. The island hellhole and relentless, bone-jarring work would surely kill him. It had killed many others already, as evidenced by the graves of forty-four inmates located just a few hundred yards to the north of Malahi, on a second islet called Bunga, given a more-appropriate name by the Americans: Deadman's Island. By November 1904, the number of graves represented an annual prisoner mortality rate of nearly 26 percent. Novicio's imprisonment at Malahi was a death sentence, and he knew he would need to escape if he was to survive.

On yet another interminable day in captivity devoted to the mindless manufacture of gravel—it was Friday, November 25, 1904—Teodorico Novicio decided to act.

As Novicio's workday was about to begin on that November morning, on the other side of the world, in Washington, D.C., the US president and his family, like the rest of America, were wrapping up Thanksgiving Day festivities. President Theodore Roosevelt was in a celebratory mood, having been reelected earlier in the month in a Republican landslide victory over his Democratic challenger, Alton B. Parker. The two candidates had shared a largely common platform—support for the gold standard, labor unions, and, to some degree, fair treatment for the inhabitants of their new possession, the Philippines. Both Roosevelt and Parker held forth an aim to grant eventual independence to the Filipinos, if and when their capacity for self-government had been demonstrated.

America's foray into colonial expansion in the Philippines remained a hot-button political issue. In his fiery campaign speeches, candidate Parker had railed against the Republican policy of imperialism, which he considered a peril to America's democratic traditions and a burden to its treasury. On October 15, 1904, Parker exhorted, "The Republican Party stands for the subjugation of defenseless foreign peoples. Democracy stands for freedom. We relieved Spain of this thorn in her flesh, only to plunge it into our own. We have paid, and are paying, enormously for the privilege."

Arguing against the proposition that the guarantee of Filipino independence would only promote further insurrection among the restive population, Parker responded that the path of imperialism left only two choices for Filipinos: either submission or violence, two "fearful alternatives." He prayed that Americans themselves would never be saddled with such a choice. "Shall we forbid the Filipinos to hope for independence?" Parker questioned. "Shall we prevent their building up of their own civilization and try to force ours upon them?" Parker's speech concluded with a plea:

> [O]ur work should be to guard the foundation on which our Government rests. Its basis is that of declared ideas—ideas that are stronger than battleships and armies—ideas which for more than a century have stimulated our development, and which have given promise that our "world mission" shall be not to seize the territory of distant peoples and rule them with a scepter of iron, but to establish truth, honor, justice, and peace among the nations. We must choose whether within our borders the basis of government shall continue to be this idealism, or a materialism which is a sure precursor of dissolution, for no nation can endure upon a basis of materialism, however splendid. Prudence requires that the choice be made in time. The time is now.

Parker, a lawyer and judge, was no match for Roosevelt—a Rough Rider at Cuba, and a national war hero whose exploits and ambition were as expansive as America itself.

On November 8, 1904, the American electorate chose Teddy Roosevelt—a war president who lived by the tenet, "Speak softly and carry a big stick"—by a nineteen-point margin. The hugely popular Roosevelt won thirty-two out of forty-five states, taking every northern and western state, and 56.4 percent of the popular vote.

Roosevelt's Thanksgiving Day had been spent working in the office in the morning and horseback riding with his wife and children in the afternoon. That evening, the president sat down for a family dinner at the White House, joined by his friends, Massachusetts senator Henry Cabot Lodge and his wife. It was planned as a quiet respite before an impending journey.

While the conversation was not recorded, the forty-six-year-old Roosevelt looked to Henry Cabot Lodge, eight years his senior, for concurrence on his positions and worldview. A Harvard-educated lawyer and noted historian, Lodge represented the conservative Republican faction in the Senate. He strongly supported American intervention in Cuba, and called for the annexation of the Philippines, arguing that it was a moral obligation of the United States to lead the world. America was destined to be, drawing on Jefferson, an "empire of liberty." Having studied the ancient Germanic origins of Anglo-Saxon government, Lodge was a strong proponent of the superiority of the Anglo-Saxon race. He pushed a hawkish platform over the years, anchored on self-professed patriotism, and felt strongly that America was the "world's best hope."

After dinner, the bags and trunks of the president and his entourage were sent ahead to the train station. At midnight, the president, along with his wife, Edith, his outspoken and fashionable twenty-year-old daughter Alice, a cortege of officials, and a battalion of newspaper reporters, boarded a special train of the Pennsylvania Railroad for an excursion to St. Louis, Missouri, symbolic gateway to the West. Excitement and anticipation rippled among the jostling, lighthearted party. They were off to a celebration of the world's technological advancement and superiority over the past hundred years, a "golden milestone in the highway of human progress and a coronation of civilization." They were on their way to the grandest exhibition ever held to date: the 1904 World's Fair.

◆━

President Roosevelt had opened the World's Fair remotely, by telegraph, from the White House on April 30. Not wanting to use the popular venue for partisan political purposes during the campaign, he had not yet visited. Now, with his reelection in hand, none of that mattered, and the reports about the fair were glowing. The dazzling spectacle, an electrified city built on twelve hundred acres in the heart of St. Louis, celebrated the centennial of Thomas Jefferson's Louisiana Purchase. Constructed at a cost of $20 million, it offered fifteen hundred purpose-built, temporary buildings on lavishly landscaped grounds, each designed to run throughout the seven-month exposition. On display was an extravagant showcase of the cultural, economic, and technological progress of sixty-two foreign nations, the United States federal government, and forty-two of the country's then forty-five states. It was an opportunity for America, a new global economic and military power, to show off and flex its impressive might. Not surprisingly, the World's Fair was hugely popular and a stunning commercial success.

As President Roosevelt knew, the sheer scale and diversity of the fair was mind-boggling. More than thirty-six thousand visitors could be accommodated at a time, flooding into the grounds, the palaces, and the pavilions to be informed and educated about the latest developments in technology, fine arts, manufacturing, science, civics, foreign policy, and education. At different exhibits, visitors were enthralled by experimental flying machines, a forty-horsepower automobile, a wireless telephone, an X-ray machine, an electric typewriter, a telephone answering machine, and a number of newfangled kitchen appliances—a coffee machine, bread machine, tabletop stove, and dishwasher. Bright electrical lights, installed under the guidance of inventor Thomas Edison, ensured that the exposition literally shimmered in an excess of brilliance.

It took no less than a week for a visitor to adequately cover the enormity of the World's Fair, and perhaps a month to study it at any level of detail. President Roosevelt and his party would have but a day.

—◦—

As Roosevelt's presidential train barreled through the night toward St. Louis, just off Malahi Island, in a time zone half a day ahead, Novicio's risky plan was being put into play.

As morning broke, Novicio and thirty-four other inmates assembled for their daily work detail. On this day, they were ordered to nearby Mule Island, some three hundred yards off Malahi, to build targets for a firing range, which, when completed, would be used for practice by the three companies of 7th Infantry stationed at the prison post. Starting out at 6:00 a.m., the gang of laborers was prodded onto the post's steam launch, the *Denver*, under the guard of three soldiers, for transport to the worksite. On this day, the guard included an overseer, Private Harvey H. Herman, of Nazareth, Pennsylvania, armed with a .38 caliber revolver; and two sentinels, Private Abraham Owens, who had left his wife behind at Jefferson Barracks, Missouri, and Private John Tummet, from Menasha, Wisconsin. Both Owens and Tummet were armed with rifles. Also on board was a local civilian crew, along with their wives, who were responsible for operating the launch.

The work detail contained a mean bunch of hardened convicts. Of the thirty-five prisoners, seven were incarcerated for life and fifteen were serving sentences from ten to thirty years. The majority of the inmates were serving time for murder, followed by the crimes of theft, violating the laws of war, assault, highway robbery, banditry, drunkenness, kidnapping, and for one, insurrection. Also on board, scattered about this posse of misfits, murderers, and freedom fighters, were the tools for their work: pickaxes, shovels, crowbars, and axes.

Once at Mule Island, the prisoners collected their gear and got to work. They toiled under the searing sun throughout the hot morning, taking a short break for lunch. At 5:00 p.m. their workday was done. Typically, when loading onto the sixty-foot-long, ten-foot-wide *Denver,* the prisoners were ordered to assemble in the stern, while their guards watched over them from the bow. Between them, prisoners and guards were separated at some distance by the engine-room hatch and deckhouse. Stepping onto the launch this time, however, the prisoners casually spread out across the deck, in both the stern and the bow, intermingling with their guards, Privates Herman, Owens, and Tummet. In their hands, the prisoners still held the tools of their trade.

Moments after shoving off from Mule Island, prisoner Venancio Cueto, a former *Katipunan* leader, called out to his colleagues in the crowded bow, "Be ready!" In seconds, several prisoners grabbed Private Herman by the neck and relieved him of his revolver. Startled, the private cried out, "What are you doing? What are you doing?" Other prisoners, led by Novicio, descended on the second guard, Private Tummet, who squeezed off a shot and then violently swung his rifle in his defense. The stock of the swinging rifle split Novicio's skull, sending the former rebel *kapitan* reeling. The prisoners relieved Tummet of his weapon as a blur of pickaxes chopped the sentry to the ground.

Elsewhere on deck, one of the prisoners shouted, "Hold the engineer!" In a violent scrum, the engineer was beaten and thrown overboard. A full-scale riot ensued in the bow of the launch. The prisoners stabbed the guards with their own bayonets and descended on them with axes, hatchets, and shovels. The wives of the civilian boat crew screamed in horror as the captain and his deckhand son were hacked to death. Private Owens, also able to fire one round, was attacked with shovels and axes before his mangled body was thrown overboard. Four prisoners stormed the engine room with a revolver and bayonets and took control of the launch. Ringleader Cueto seized the boat's steering wheel and pointed her south, to his hometown of Bay, Laguna. There, once on his own turf and among his supporters, he planned to make a run for the mountains of Taal.

Cries of anguish from the deck of the *Denver* carried on the wind. On nearby Malahi Island, a company of 7th Infantry soldiers marching up to parade could see the riot in progress and people in the water. They double-timed into position and deployed along the shore, firing at will at the launch. The soldiers stood on the shore and took careful aim with their rifles, methodically squeezing off shots at Cueto, who was visibly in command of the launch. One shot tore through the ringleader, then another, and finally a third, sinking him to the deck, wounded but alive. The launch, unmanned, swerved crazily across the water until another prisoner took control of the wheel.

The stack of American rifles unleashed wave after brutal wave of hot lead. Expending all the ammunition from their belts and a full box of new ammunition, the company fired 1,740 rounds at the launch from an initial distance of six hundred yards. Four other companies on Malahi fell into position—the entire garrison, in fact—and commenced firing at the escaping launch.

As the breathless inmates struggled to steer the launch toward the distant mainland shore, a hail of lead from the soldiers on Malahi rained down on the small craft. Prisoner Hipolito Bautista, a thirty-year-old member of a notorious gang of bandits, was killed outright. Another, Justo Gabriel, was knocked overboard and drowned. Round after round slammed into the hull, while others shredded the launch's tarp and reduced the steering wheel to splinters.

Novicio, his shattered head seeping blood, likely lay propped up against the launch's railing, helplessly watching the escape go awry. As bullets whizzed by, at least one rifle round, possibly more, slammed into his weakened form. As he struggled to control the bleeding—he had been shot before in the raid on Baler in 1897, and was familiar with the pain and damage from a rifle round—other inmates struggled to maneuver the launch away from the deadly American rifle fire. Falling out of rifle range at 2,500 yards, the launch steamed at eight knots toward the town of Bay, where escape to the mainland, and the mountains of Tagaytay beyond, was possible.

The eight-minute barrage from the American garrison had shattered the launch, punching more than seventy-five rounds into the hull alone.

Novicio lay bleeding on the deck, with two American soldiers—the dead overseer Private Harvey Herman and the mortally wounded Private John Tummet—sprawled about him. Beyond them, Novicio could surely see the silent, crumpled form of inmate Bautista, torn apart.

The rich irony of his predicament must have struck Novicio. He now found himself in a situation strikingly similar to the *Yorktown* sailors who had suffered his ambush on the Baler River more than five years earlier. His loss of blood was surely alarming; the rebel *kapitan* may have known his time was near. Maybe, looking over the dead and dying sentinels, he savored the moment, knowing he had wrought a final price on the American occupation he so desperately despised. Maybe he smiled, witness to the band of inmates in flight, aiming for freedom in the distant mountains, where they might lose themselves under their dense and impenetrable protection. One prisoner, thinking of the race to liberty ahead, stripped the sturdy leather boots from Private Herman's feet.

The broken launch reached the mainland shore some fifty minutes later, just as the retiring sun splashed a blood-orange glow across the lake. Ringleader Cueto ordered all the prisoners out of the boat; at least one refused and was thrown overboard. The bulk of the escapees quickly jumped from the launch and disappeared toward the vastness of the mountains to the south. Reports later suggested that they dragged along the two women on the launch—the wife of the dead civilian captain and her mother—for their physical entertainment, but the women were abandoned a few miles later. Left behind on the launch were five prisoners who refused to flee, most with light sentences nearly served in full, and in the case of one, prisoner Jose Lacson, whose near blindness limited his options.

Night arrived to find Teodorico Novicio slumped on the deck of the beached launch, abandoned by his comrades, awash in a pool of his own blood. Beside him, a fellow inmate lay dead or dying. How long either lived is not known. In those final hours along the lake's shoreline, Novicio may have recalled his troubled, adventurous life, formed by his childhood in Baler, where he first brewed an irrepressible anger at the Spaniards who lorded over his town and his people. And from there: His introduction to the secret revolutionary society, the *Katipunan*, while at his studies in Manila; his enlistment in Aguinaldo's forces as a trusted lieutenant; leading the first bloody assault on the Spanish garrison at Baler. Laying siege to the town's church, and eyeing the approach of the *Yorktown* in

Baler Bay. Ambushing Gillmore's cutter on the river. Burying Nygard and Dillon. Watching Morrissey die. Ordering the still-struggling, half-dead McDonald into his earthy grave. Deceiving Funston, Shunk, and Newbill as they sought to establish a garrison and impose their occupation on his people. Ordering the Gutierrez brothers to deliver the boy Venville into the hands of the Ilongots to be beheaded. Standing trial, receiving a death sentence, and then—against all odds—winning a reprieve. Languishing for three years in prison, first at the guardhouse at Baler, and then in the dank, infectious confines of Bilibid, and finally, on the deadly hard-labor nightmare of Malahi Island.

From Novicio's perspective, he had accomplished great things. And he knew that unlike so many others, he had never given up. He had never surrendered. Yet, now Novicio understood. This was the end. And maybe he smiled with a final thought: *Freedom was at hand.*

Teodorico Novicio, inmate number 469, died on the blood-drenched deck of the launch. The sheer amount of blood was evidence, the military investigators later concluded, that a considerable number of inmates had been shot by the garrison of soldiers firing from Malahi's shore. Records are scant, but it is known that an autopsy was never performed on Novicio. Death was noted as "probably gunshot wound or wounds, presumably inflicted by sentries while prisoners were attempting to escape from Malahi Island on launch *Denver.*" The report added, with typical military brevity, "Body was not inspected by a medical officer. Sentries were killed. Not in the line of duty."

The following day, Saturday, November 26, 1904, the *Denver* was retrieved and returned to Malahi. The bodies of Novicio and Bautista were brought to Deadman's Island for burial. A glum collection of inmates in chains were pressed into service to haul the shattered bodies off the launch, dig simple graves, and wash down the mess on the decks. The two prisoners' bodies were unceremoniously dumped in nominally marked earthen pits. Novicio's corpse, already in a rapid state of tropical decomposition, was tossed into grave number 46.

～

On the very day Novicio was buried, Roosevelt spent a glorious day touring the St. Louis World's Fair. A twenty-carriage procession swept up and delivered the presidential party to the fairgrounds, led by two battalions of 8th Cavalry and a platoon of mounted police. Roosevelt was first taken to a vantage point on the summit of Festival Hill, which afforded a panoramic view of the lagoons, palaces, and grounds. He was rushed through a selection of the national pavilions, beginning with France and an obligatory toast of champagne, followed by visits to those of Mexico, Holland, Great Britain, Cuba, Belgium, Austria, Italy, China, Brazil, Japan, and Germany. The visit to Great Britain's pavilion, for all of eight minutes, was the longest stop. The president's intensive schedule, arranged down to the minute, did not allow time to linger.

Following a luncheon reception, Roosevelt visited his former log home that had been relocated to the fair, replete with a buffalo hide on display—from the first buffalo he had ever killed, he explained to his daughter Alice. Afterward, the president visited the one exhibition he truly wanted to see: the Philippine Reservation. While arrangements for the trip to the World's Fair were being planned, Roosevelt had signaled in advance that he wanted to spend as much time as possible at the Philippine exhibits. And how about a parade on its grounds? The president loved a good parade.

The forty-seven-acre site, home to one hundred buildings and more than seventy-five thousand objects on display, was cleared of visitors. The president's tour began with a walk over the replica Bridge of Spain, not over Manila's Pasig River, but a man-made lagoon called Arrowhead Lake, past a replica of the Magellan Monument, to a faux version of Intramuros, Manila's Walled City of the Spanish Colonial era. From there, the president and his entourage entered pavilions that highlighted the educational services being delivered to the Filipinos, prospects for commerce and trade, and the islands' history and diverse ethnology. The tour visited the most popular exhibits: the collection of tribal villages, populated by some of the thousand or so Filipinos drawn from some ten ethnic groups across the archipelago and shipped to the fair.

The presidential party proceeded to a grandstand to watch the much-anticipated military drill of Philippine scouts and the constabulary band. The scouts were the talk of the St. Louis Exposition: four companies of battle-hardened Filipinos drawn from Macabebe, Ilocano, Tagalog, and Visayan units, renamed the 1st Battalion Philippine Scouts. Serving as the escort to scores of dignitaries, the scouts had entertained over a million visitors with their exquisitely timed marching and precision drills since the opening of the fair seven months earlier. And today they were about to perform for the president.

True to form, the scouts shined. Since their arrival, they had been outfitted with new full-dress uniforms: olive-drab flannel shirts, russet leather waist belts, and the latest cartridge belts with suspenders. More importantly, the aging rifles that they had brought along from Manila had been taken away, destroyed, and replaced with brand-new US magazine .30 caliber carbines—ironically, advanced weaponry they had not been allowed to use for combat operations in the Philippines.

On perfect cue, the scouts stepped forward to perform the manual of arms for the president, "with merely a preparatory command from their officers," reporters noted. Then in open order, one news account enthused, using the typical language of the day, "the little brown soldiers executed intricate calisthenics with their rifles, keeping in time with the strains from the horns and the tap of the drum." A special drill with glistening steel bolos followed, thrilling the rapt audience.

The president was beside himself with delight. In his exuberance, he called out to the commanding American officer, Major William H. Johnson, on assignment from the 16th Infantry, to request that the band play "Garryowen." It was a martial favorite, an eighteenth-century Irish drinking song that had become the regimental march for a number of US Army units, including the 7th Cavalry. Reportedly, it was also the last song played for General Custer and his men before their last stand and annihilation at the Battle of the Little Bighorn. The Philippine Constabulary Band was only too happy to take the request, and fired up a spirited rendition. Roosevelt enthused to his entourage gathered in the viewing stand that the song was "the greatest fighting tune in the world."

The hurrah for our brave commanders!
Who led us into the fight.
We'll do or die in our country's cause,
And battle for the right.
And when the war is o'er,
And to home we're goin',
Just watch your step, with our heads erect,
When our band plays Garryowen.

President Roosevelt clapped heartily, completely taken by the precision of the drill and quality of the marching. He requested then and there that the Philippine scouts march in his inaugural parade in Washington, D.C., scheduled in a few months' time. Here at the World's Fair, the parade and drill now came to a close. Major Johnson raised his hat and called on his Filipino subordinates to cheer the beaming president.

The Filipino scouts and constabulary responded with a hearty, joyful cheer: "Hip hip hooray! Hip hip hooray! Hip hip hooray!" They cheered their new commander in chief and they cheered America, their new colonial masters. They cheered their benevolent assimilation into a foreign culture, and they cheered its awesome military might. On that blustery autumn afternoon, echoing across the parade ground, their hearty celebration electrified the audience.

It was obvious to President Roosevelt, and to all in St. Louis that day, more than eight thousand miles from the Philippines: Pacification was complete.

CHAPTER TWENTY-THREE

Empire's End

FROM A PURELY MILITARY PERSPECTIVE, THE AMERICAN CAMPAIGN IN the Philippines ultimately can be viewed as a striking success, anchored on a counterinsurgency strategy that delivered civic action and benevolent treatment, tempered with the tools of chastisement. By 1904, American colonial administration of the Philippines was under way. A war-weary local populace begrudgingly accepted the promises of civil government. Those unwilling to cede a desire for national sovereignty quickly faced imprisonment, deportation, or death on prison scaffolds. Policing soon fell to the indigenous population, allowing American troop levels to wind down. Garrisons were ordered shut. The troops, by and large, came home. The war was over.

In short order, American business interests rapidly expanded across the islands. Exports in sugar, copra (dried coconut meat yielding coconut oil), and lumber spiked, and the economy grew. Supporting this growth was a massive program of education that targeted a population that was only 40 percent literate. Major investments were made in Manila's water supply and sewer systems. Noted American architect Daniel Burnham, the creative force behind the urban planning for Chicago, Cleveland, San Francisco, and Washington, D.C., arrived in 1905 to master-plan the capital city of Manila, which in turn encouraged an avalanche of investments in new roads, highways, and residential neighborhoods. More than four hundred thousand acres of land held by the Spanish friars was purchased from the Vatican by the US government for $7.2 million, and redistributed for development. The English language soon became the currency to unite a country divided by geography and ethnicity. Over the several decades that followed, the port city of Manila emerged as the preeminent "Pearl of the Orient," proudly crowned the "Queen of the Pacific."

During the ensuing decades, powers were incrementally conferred on local leaders and the government leadership "Filipinized," with vague rhetoric from Washington on the prerequisites for the eventual grant of independence. In 1916, the Jones Act abolished the Philippine Commission that lorded over the country and provided for an elected Senate, greatly increasing national autonomy. The first elected Senate president— a Spanish *mestizo* and son of Baler known for his flamboyant fashion, fiery oratory, and explosive temperament—was Manuel Luis Quezon, whose father, the schoolteacher Lucio, and brother Pablo had been murdered on Novicio's orders.

Political wrangling, both internally and with Washington, continued for another two decades, until the passage of the Tydings-McDuffie Law by the US Congress in 1934. The law set out terms for commonwealth status for the country, mandated a constitutional convention, and outlined terms for trade and immigration. Most importantly, however, Tydings-McDuffie committed to the granting of independence after one final decade of American rule. In the first national presidential election in 1935, Quezon battled against his two main rivals, former rebel general Emilio Aguinaldo and Bishop Gregorio Aglipay, the former rebel priest. The son of Baler prevailed, and was generally accepted to be the second president of the country following Aguinaldo's brief reign at the turn of the nineteenth century.

The Commonwealth decade staggered forward, suffering "maldistribution of political power, slow and uneven economic development, and military insecurity." Then came the cataclysm of World War II, the invasion and brutal occupation by Imperial Japan, followed by the liberation of the country by the Americans. The devastating war left the country in a state of ruin and economic collapse. Once a jewel of the Orient, Manila was reduced to a sprawling, hellish slum, its grandeur and elegance shattered beyond recognition.

With America's attention diverted to other priorities in the world, political rhetoric pushed for a promise to be fulfilled. On July 4, 1946, against the backdrop of a battle-scarred city, a stream of dignitaries and officials gathered around a flagpole to read speeches. The US Army Band played the American National Anthem. The fastidious, white-haired, fifty-five-year-old American high commissioner, Paul Vories McNutt, a former Democratic governor from Indiana and Harvard-trained lawyer, with a pensive General Douglas MacArthur by his side, lowered the American flag. The ebullient Philippine president, Manuel Roxas, then raised the Philippine flag. The Philippine Army Band played a stirring rendition of the country's national anthem, "Bayang Magiliw." Spectators wept. In Manila Bay, the cruisers from the US Navy's 7th Fleet unleashed a twenty-one-gun salvo, followed by gun reports from scores of other ships from other nations that had assembled to witness the momentous occasion.

A month shy of forty-eight years, America's imperial adventure in the Philippines had come to an end.

Epilogue
The Cost of Conquest

THROUGHOUT TIME, GREAT MINDS—LEADERS WITH WISDOM AND INSIGHT, inventors and scientists, philosophers and thinkers, even geniuses of evil—have influenced the course of world events. But what of minds less great, perhaps even mediocre, and their actions and decisions, seemingly mundane, that remain unexamined in the bin of history? Is it possible that one reckless decision, fueled by misplaced ambition, could trigger a cascade of consequences that then alters the course of a war?

Wrought in privilege and steeped in arrogance, a defiant Lieutenant Gillmore elected to break from his official orders, to travel up the river at Baler in a risky and vainglorious attempt to seize the accolades and recognition he believed were his due. That singular action ignited a debacle of ambush, death, and captivity that in turn gripped the imagination of the American public. It led to the diversion of critical resources—two United States Army battalions—from their primary task at hand: the capture of the elusive center of gravity to the Philippine-American War, General Emilio Aguinaldo. Concern that one of America's own naval officers languished in the hands of "savages," as the story was spun, trumped the hunt for the rebel general.

To be sure, when Aguinaldo was finally captured in March 1901, hostilities quickly wound down and the conflict came to an end. His generals surrendered, arms were turned in, and a weary Filipino people got on with their lives. Arguably, Gillmore's recklessness at Baler unnecessarily prolonged an increasingly bloody and repressive pacification campaign by as long as eighteen months.

Gillmore's since-forgotten debacle left a costly trail of death. We can begin with the loss of the sailors at Baler and the deaths among the rescuers from disease and exhaustion. The numbers from there become theoretical, but striking in their magnitude. The United States ultimately deployed some 126,000 soldiers, unleashed in successive waves, to subdue the country, with a sacrifice of 4,234 American and 16,000 Filipino Army of Liberation lives. The civilian population bore the brunt, as they always do in times of war. As many as 200,000 civilians may have died during brutal back-to-back epidemics of plague and cholera that swept across the islands.

We cannot lay this at Gillmore's feet, but consider this: From January 1900, when Aguinaldo slipped through the US Army's hands and disappeared into the Cordilleras, through June 1901, after he had surrendered and called on his followers to lay down their arms, some 326 Americans were killed in action and another 654 wounded. During this same time frame, 5,280 Army of Liberation fighters were killed in engagements with American forces, with an equal number wounded. Put another way, 33 percent of the total 16,000 Filipino fighters to die over the course of the entire conflict occurred *after* Aguinaldo's escape in January 1900. Arguably, all of this carnage may have been, in fact, unnecessary, had Aguinaldo been swept up in the claws of the US Army's pincer movement in December 1899, and the military campaign brought to a timely close.

Instead, an inordinate focus on Gillmore's rescue resulted in more death and far greater pain for a country in transition, for better or worse, from one colonial master to another. As the campaign for pacification dragged on, increasingly oppressive measures were instituted, ranging from scorched-earth policies to executions to exile, which, while effective, tainted the stated objectives of American benevolence and its "empire of liberty."

The story of Gillmore is more than a tragic tale of one man. It is a study of impetuous decisions and misused privilege, of arrogant attitudes and failed leadership, all on a desperately human scale, and which came to embody one nation's anxious grasp at empire at the end of the nineteenth century. Through that lens, it was at the terminus of Baler, during Gillmore's failed push up the river, where that grasp at expansion stuttered and then stalled.

Incredibly, Gillmore escaped censure and the consequences of his actions by working the media to manage the fallout of his disastrous decision at Baler. A tale of hardship and martyrdom, eagerly fed by the press to the American public, tied the navy's hands. Who could criticize the lieutenant now, after all he had gone through? As a result, not a single official—at least in public—questioned the lieutenant's decision to defy orders and stumble into an ambush for his own purposes. Nor had anyone bothered to tally the tragic consequences for the many men involved in his captivity and rescue. The costs, in fact, were heavy, and borne by many.

Of the fifteen crew members aboard the *Yorktown*'s cutter on April 12, 1899, at Baler, five were killed in the Philippines. The lucky ten who survived, a rather hardy bunch, faced lasting damage to their health.

Chief Quartermaster William Walton was discharged in 1902 after eleven years of service, and, in deteriorating health, returned to his thirty-year-old wife in Vallejo, California. Despite hiring a lawyer to assist with a disability claim, Walton's application was rejected with finality in June 1905. He died less than three years later of heart disease, on February 4, 1908, at the age of forty-four.

French-born Sailmaker's Mate Paul Vaudoit, reenlisting in the navy and rising to the rank of chief master-at-arms, died suddenly two years later, in 1910. Found dead in his bunk aboard his ship at anchor in Subic Bay, Philippines, the fifty-two-year-old sailor was buried outside the US Naval Base, in the hillside Olongapo City cemetery.

Apprentice Albert Peterson, discharged in 1902, went on to work in California's oil fields until a chronic case of dysentery and gastroenteritis completely disabled him in 1920, at the age of thirty-eight. Unable to support his wife, Emma, and teenage daughter Henrietta, he argued for a disability pension, which, after years of effort, was finally granted in 1925, and then later reduced. In poor health and dire financial straits, Peterson saw his marriage dissolve. A debate with the veterans' pension office ensued for years, with Peterson writing in 1933 to explain, "I do not think any man can go through what that little bunch of men went through without paying a future price." After a series of fainting spells and a bad fall, the bedridden and impoverished sailor died at the age of fifty, with his sister at his side.

Several of the other *Yorktown* sailors fared better. Seaman Silvio Brisolese, the Italian son of a pastry maker, returned to San Francisco to work as a ship rigger, residing cheek by jowl with his parents and extended Italian family. He drew a small navy pension and died on January 6, 1942, at the age of sixty-two. The hard-drinking, foul-mouthed Coxswain Ellsworth Pinkham stayed in the navy until his retirement in 1919 at the rank of chief boatswain's mate. He died at the age of fifty-six. Seaman William H. Rynders, who lost the tips of three of his fingers in the ambush at Baler, went on to serve aboard a number of ships until his discharge from the navy as gunner's mate, with a monthly retirement pension of $15. He died in Solano, California, on May 17, 1946, at the age of seventy-seven.

Landsman Frederick Anderson also continued on in the navy, rising to the rank of chief gunner's mate, and settled in Buffalo, New York, with his wife, Florence. He died on December 20, 1950, from stomach cancer, at the age of seventy-one. Following his discharge, Ordinary Seaman Orrison W. Woodbury went on to marry and divorce, and then settle as a lodger in Brooklyn, New York, where he worked in a shoe factory. After an extended petition process, Woodbury was awarded a Purple Heart in 1943 for the injuries he received at Baler more than four decades earlier. He continued to attend encampments with the Spanish-American War Vets, until his death on January 18, 1958, at age seventy-eight.

Not surprisingly, the one sailor who outlived them all was known for his upbeat, optimistic attitude: Landsman Lyman Paul Edwards. Following his early discharge, he returned to his family's farm in Missouri to pursue an enterprising career in dry goods and groceries, until failing eyesight forced his retirement. To honor the Filipino doctor who saved his life in Vigan, Edwards named his oldest son Castro, after Dr. Jose Gabino Castro. In his later years, Edwards labored over a narrative about his captivity, *Prisoner in the Philippines*, assisted by his daughter Virginia Lee, which was privately published in 1969. Edwards died of heart disease on January 26, 1977, at the age of ninety-nine.

The balance of prisoners who joined the Gillmore party over the course of their captivity faced a similar mix of early death and long, fruitful lives.

Private William Bruce, diagnosed with acute diarrhea, was hospitalized on the day of the prisoners' arrival in Manila. Tragically, the attending army physician rejected the soldier's repeated complaints, noting his "appearance and hospital records do not corroborate" his statements, "none of which are true." Declared "sound and well," the ailing private was quickly mustered out on January 26, 1900. Keen to stay in the Philippines, Bruce returned to Bangued to set up a small saloon, where he died of chronic dysentery just three months later, on May 2, 1900, at the age of twenty-three. Private George Sackett was also in and out of army hospitals battling a pernicious array of infections and disease until his discharge at Fort Brayard, New Mexico, in May 1902. By then, the once-healthy, 143-pound former printer from Indiana had wasted to ninety-seven pounds. Wracked with coughs and chills, and spitting blood, Sackett was diagnosed with incurable tuberculosis. He died on February 15, 1903, at the age of thirty-three.

British civilian John O'Brien, the hopeful gold miner who had joined the daring escape with Bruce and Edwards, went on to set up a trading company in Manila, while battling a case of chronic gastroenteritis. Business waned, and O'Brien finally washed up in Los Angeles in May 1908, penniless, heartbroken from a failed romance, and at his wits' end. On July 27, in a run-down room in an apartment house on Grand Avenue, O'Brien once again surrendered, just as he had in the cold, dark mountains of the Cordilleras during his brazen escape from Tinio's men. This time, O'Brien pulled up a chair in front of a mirror, and with a dime in one hand and a revolver in the other, determined to decide his fate with the flip of a coin. The dime spun into the air and landed tail's up. He lost. O'Brien raised the revolver to his broken heart and pulled the trigger, killing himself instantly. Left unclaimed in the city morgue, O'Brien's body was buried in the city's potter's field for the indigent. He was thirty-eight.

Private Elmer Honnyman returned to Reno, Nevada, in July 1900, wracked with a post-traumatic stress disorder and uncontrollable anxiety. Despite an enlarged heart that raced at 120 beats per minute, he was denied a disability pension. To raise money for his care, Reno's business community rallied around the ailing veteran. Back on his feet, Honnyman worked briefly as a forage master, shipping horses to Honolulu and Manila, until a series of paralyzing strokes and epileptic episodes left him disabled and destitute. A massive outpouring of public concern followed, resulting in a resolution by Congress, in March 1908, to grant the bedridden and mute soldier a $20 monthly pension. Honnyman died in 1912 at the age of forty-one.

Other Gillmore party captives suffered equally premature deaths, and at least one was murdered.

Fireman 1st Class John James Farley was discharged on October 21, 1901, and died in Newark in March 1914, at the age of forty-one. Private James Curran, tagged by his superiors as a "professional gambler," reenlisted in the Coast Artillery in Honolulu in 1902 after having been rejected by his own 16th Infantry. He died at the age of forty-four in 1918. Army Private Frank Stone settled with his wife and raised a family in Vallejo, California, passing away on November 22, 1926, at age fifty.

American civilian prisoner George Langford, the happy-go-lucky Pabst beer salesman whose chalked slogans guided the US Army rescue, stayed on in the Philippines to manage business interests in fishing, logging, and pearl farming. He settled in Zamboanga, established a family, and oversaw his plantation on the island of Basilan. On the morning of September 17, 1917, at his beachfront property, an irate Langford confronted two local men, brothers, for stealing lumber. An argument ensued, and Langford pushed one of the men to the ground. The man rose, with his bolo drawn, and Langford shot him in the neck, which just made matters worse. Both men descended on Langford with their razor-sharp machetes, hacking him to death. Dead at forty-five, Langford was buried at Zamboanga, leaving behind a wife and three children.

Civilian quartermaster Albert Sonnichsen, whose escape to Vigan provided crucial intelligence to American forces, struggled to publish his book, *Ten Months a Captive Among Filipinos*. The raw, poorly written text attracted little interest. Sonnichsen's father approached the anti-imperialist society, hoping to land a patron given the book's scathing critique of America's foibles in the Philippines. Noting that his son "arrived at his home in this city, half-starved and hollowed, a veritable pauper," he spelled out the marketability of the book: "As to the conduct of Lieut. Gillmore, it richly deserves criticism. From the surviving members of his boat's crew, all of whom have been to visit my son, I find them unanimous in stating that at Baler, after firing one shot from his revolver, the Lieutenant fell into the bottom of the boat, crying 'I am hurt,' where he remained until firing ceased." The senior Sonnichsen concluded, "[A]ltogether, Mr. Gillmore, during his imprisonment, proved himself a parsimonious, peevish and selfish person, always pining for privileges on account of his rank, and for whom his own subordinates had no respect." Only his son's book told the truth, the father boasted, as all others, constrained by their service in the army and navy, were "not able to say anything on account of evil consequence."

Whether the letter helped broker a deal is not known, but publisher Charles Scribner acquired the work of the budding author in November 1900. Like Edwards, Sonnichsen credited Dr. Jose Gabino Castro, the Filipino medical doctor at Vigan, for saving his life, and dedicated the book to him. Selling fairly well, the book concluded with the only known public indictment of Gillmore's behavior in captivity:

Some of the hardships endured might many a time have been greatly ameliorated, had the men been made to feel in the only officer present among them more of the moral influence of a leading mind and of a spirit better befitting the situation in general, and if less efforts had been made in obtaining those personal "rights" and individual "privileges," the claims to which not only had the tendency to embitter them against him, but even frequently caused the most disrespectful bickering and undisguised ill-feelings, undisguised at times even among those who for reasons of their own felt that loyalty and silence might someday be gold.

Ten Months a Captive Among Filipinos initiated a lifelong career as an author for Sonnichsen. He married, raised a family, and continued writing until his death on August 15, 1931, at the age of fifty-three.

Edward Burke, the scrappy man from Dorchester, Massachusetts, who had survived both the attack on the USS *Urdaneta* and his subsequent captivity, reenlisted to face a series of alcohol-fueled incidents that earned him a string of court-martial punishments, and finally, for assaulting a fellow sailor, an eighteen-month term in prison. Settling in Seattle, Burke lived to the age of sixty, passing away on October 6, 1938.

The twice-deserting, convicted scoundrel William Duff Green, who had enlisted in the army under the alias of Frank McDonald, was marched in chains to Bilibid Prison following the arrival of the Gillmore party at Manila. Months later, he was shipped to Alcatraz Island to serve out his three-year sentence at hard labor. On arrival, he wrote Gillmore to seek his help: "I believe you know my character sufficiently to believe me not quite as 'bad' as painted. I appeal to you for your immediate aid." Gillmore took pity and penned an endorsement on April 9, 1900, stating:

As far as I know this is a very deserving case. McDonald joined my party as a prisoner of war in November 1899. He shared in our hardships, when we were sent to the mountains. Escaping in the mountains from that party, and after meeting many hardships from the savages, was again captured by the insurrectos, and then rescued with two others by Colonel L. R. Hare's party. He then joined, and fought, with that party, and was with them when Colonel Hare rescued my party. I have frequently noticed him, and called Colonel Hare's attention to him as being a hard worker and good soldier.

A day later, Texas senator Charles Allen Culberson, a staunch anti-imperialist, sent his own letter, together with Gillmore's glowing recommendation, to the adjutant general in Washington. On May 15, 1900, after serving less than four months in prison, Green was once again liberated, with the unexecuted portion of his sentence remitted.

Green skipped about, apparently serving more prison time in California on a drug charge. In 1932, he was found wandering the streets of Los Angeles in a half-crazed and half-naked state. Admitted into the veterans' hospital, he repeatedly attempted to pass off falsified discharge papers for an army pension, for which he was unqualified. When his claim was rejected with finality, Green wrote to the Pension Review Board that it was a "complete outrage," given that he had "served his country as faithfully ... with distinguished service, suffering hell and facing death every day as a member of the lost Gillmore landing party, with my health impaired ever since, and for the last three years a complete wreck depending on charity, being picked up by the police as a wanderer in rags, starved to the bone, dazed of mind, unable to hold my bodily excretions, put in a hospital, etc." Green died in Santa Clara County on March 31, 1942, at the age of sixty-nine.

And finally, there were some prisoners who enjoyed normal, if not mundane, lives.

Samuel Tilden Herbert, the ordinary seaman who, like Burke, survived the assault on the *Urdaneta,* continued his life on the seas as a merchant marine, plying routes of the northeastern seaboard. Herbert succumbed to coronary thrombosis on May 30, 1945, at the age of sixty-eight.

Hospital Corpsman Harry Huber attained brief fame with a full-page, illustrated story of his captivity published in April 1900, by the *San Francisco Call,* entitled "Held Prisoner for a Year by the Filipinos." In a collegial competition with his friend and former schoolmate, Albert Sonnichsen, Huber also wrote a manuscript about his captivity, but it was never published. Huber stayed active in veterans' affairs, serving as state commander for the United Spanish War veterans. He died on October 25, 1949, in Alameda County, California, at the age of seventy.

Impressively, Signal Corpsman Leland Seymour Smith, the photographer from Council Bluffs, Iowa, outlived all his army colleagues. Following his liberation, he returned to his photo lab in Manila after a brief hospitalization for swollen feet and tropical ulcers, and by July 1900, was shipped out to China to photograph the Boxer Rebellion. Discharged in

June 1902, Smith settled in Berkeley, California, giving occasional interviews to the media about his experiences. Smith died on July 4, 1975, at the age of ninety-seven.

Other prisoners in the Gillmore party either vanished into the woodwork or left behind limited documentation, their full stories lost to history. Civilian David Brown, the Canadian criminal, was briefly pilloried in newspapers across America once his tales of deception and deceit became known. Typical was the story that ran in the *Macon Telegraph* as the prisoners arrived in Manila: "Preacher Brown had better change his name and emigrate to the Fiji Islands. There is no room for him in the land of Stars and Stripes." It appears that Brown again got himself into trouble in Manila, was arrested for his involvement in a robbery, and sentenced to five years in Bilibid Prison. No further evidence of his travails has been located.

The US Army rescuers fared no better than the prisoners that they had liberated. The grueling months-long march through northern Luzon and subsequent mountain rescue expedition in the Cordilleras took its toll, leaving the weakened men vulnerable to disease and early death.

Corporal Elmer Deming, Company G, 34th Infantry, had been on the march continuously for two months and fell sick on January 14, 1900, while on a reconnaissance mission. The soldier from Bonner Springs, Kansas, died from smallpox eight days later in Laoag, at age twenty-six, and was buried in the military cemetery at Laoag, Grave No. 1. Private Neal Brogan, a clerk from Fort Smith, Arkansas, died in Bangued four days later, also from smallpox, at age twenty. His effects were burned to prevent contagion, and he was buried in Grave No. 1 at Bangued's "native cemetery." Less than a month later, Private Bert W. Hayden, H, 34th Infantry, a twenty-five-year-old miner from Colorado, died from spinal meningitis, and he too was buried at Laoag. Three other soldiers from the 33rd Infantry who dropped out early in the rescue—Privates Frank D. Hawes, William A. Holt, and William Sisk—all died of disease in mid-January 1900. One of the soldiers wounded during the raid on Vigan, twenty-one-year-old William H. Bostwick, an electrician from Michigan, died of disease on July 2, 1900. Another soldier committed suicide. Death for the men in these two regiments, many ground down from the exhausting march after Gillmore, was relatively commonplace.

Other soldiers on the Gillmore party rescue expedition died in the years that followed. The former undertaker from Ohio and trumpeter Walter B. Rose, Company D, 33rd Infantry, was dishonorably discharged and sent to Alcatraz Island for a fifteen-year sentence, for "assault with intent to kill." He died while in prison from chronic dysentery and gastritis on June 12, 1901, at the age of thirty-three. Private George Strauss, Company G, 34th Infantry, who had been recommended for but not awarded a certificate of merit for his "gallant and meritorious service" while serving on the rescue with Decker's Scouts, returned to Ohio with a case of chronic bronchitis and diarrhea, and died of pulmonary tuberculosis on March 20, 1902, at the age of thirty-one. Another private, Carl Burrage, Company C, 33rd Infantry, died at age twenty-five in 1903.

Like the liberated prisoners, many of the soldiers suffered from long-term health maladies. Sadly, nearly all were drawn into extended arguments with the Bureau of Pensions to prove their ill health and causal linkage to their military service. Most failed to make their case to an indifferent army bureaucracy.

Private John Thomas, Company F, 34th Infantry, survived the rescue to face months of hospitalization during the succeeding year and a half, fighting malaria, dysentery, a liver abscess, and a ruptured bowel. He returned to Phoenix, Arizona, to work as a cook and waiter in a hotel, but by November 1905, his ill health compelled him to file a disability claim. Thomas died five months later, on March 28, 1906, at the soldiers' home in Los Angeles. The army belatedly rejected his pension claim a full year later, noting that Thomas had not proven his ill health was the result of his service in the Philippines.

Private Norman L. Knibbs, Company F, 34th Infantry, fought chronic dysentery, malaria, and a host of other maladies. In May 1902, he filed a disability pension claim with the army, was examined by a doctor at Los Angeles, and was found to have heart problems, malaria, stomach and bowel trouble, blood poisoning, and total disability of his left thumb and hand. Embroiled in a messy divorce and remarriage at the time, he abandoned his claim and deserted military service after reenlistment. He died of pulmonary tuberculosis in 1909 at the age of twenty-seven.

Sergeant Peter R. Lavick, Company F, 34th Infantry, had the same complaints—diarrhea, malaria, and chronic inflammation of the liver—and applied for a disability pension following his discharge in 1901. He was rated for an $8 per month pension. However, just seven months later, three new examining physicians rejected the findings. With "no evidence he is now suffering from chills and fever; skin clear and normal; no evidence that digestion formations are not properly performed; no malaria; stomach normal in size, nothing abnormal," Lavick's pension claim was repeatedly rejected. As Lavick suffered during the final throes of tuberculosis, special congressional legislation in June 1910 approved a $30 monthly pension. Lavick enjoyed the long-denied benefit for exactly one monthly payment before he died on November 13, 1910, at the age of thirty-three.

Scores of other enlisted men who joined the rescue slowly deteriorated, succumbing to various ailments and disease over the years, and dying, on average, just under the age of fifty. The officers, due to their better education, diet, and access to quality medical care, had far greater longevity: The average age of death for an officer who had participated in Gillmore's rescue was around seventy. General Samuel Young, for example, died peacefully at home in Helena, Montana, on September 1, 1924, at age eighty-four. Lieutenant Colonel Robert L. Howze died from surgical complications of sepsis following a cholecystectomy—surgery on the gallbladder—in 1926, at age sixty-two. Colonel Luther Rector Hare died at Walter Reed Hospital in 1929, at the age of seventy-eight. The majority of other officers from the 33rd and 34th Infantries went on to complete full military careers through retirement, or returned to civilian life to pursue opportunities in business, law, and other endeavors.

Official recognition for the soldiers involved in the rescue was long in coming. General Samuel B. M. Young's initial commendation at Vigan, on January 5, 1900, had been glowing. He called the work of the rescue unparalleled, and recommended that every man be awarded the Medal of Honor. When the recommendation was not acted upon, he pushed again:

I renew my recommendation made in my despatch of January 5th, 1900 . . . that all officers and men accompanying Colonel Hare and Lieut. Colonel Howze . . . be given medals of honor, for exceptionally gallant, meritorious and hazardous services in a heroic pursuit of the superior forces of the enemy under the insurgent General Tinio, in Northern Luzon, P.I., from Dec 5th to 18th, 1899, through a most dangerous and difficult country, through hardships and exposure, without sufficient supplies of clothing and without food save for what little rice could be found in a wild country, thereby forcing the enemy to liberate twenty-two American prisoners held by him, including Lieutenant Commander Gillmore, US Navy, and his party, December 18th, 1899.

The US Army's Medals Review Board disapproved Young's recommendations. General Otis's refusal to support the brigadier general reportedly caused a deeper rift in their already-strained relationship.

Colonel Hare also pressed for recognition for his men. In his report, he wrote:

I call special attention to the cases of life saving by Pvt. Frank Stone, Signal Corps and Corp. John A. Morris, Co. B; 33rd Infy. I recommend a suitable medal in each case. I saw Stone rescue Lavick myself, and it was at the imminent risk of his own life. The stream was a torrent. Dr. Hadra witnessed Morris' rescue of Timbs, and I passed over the place myself on a raft shortly afterwards and fully appreciated the difficulty of making the trip without an upset. I was amazed, as well as pleased, at what I would have pronounced an impossible feat, i.e., pulling a man out, after the raft had been turned over, at that particular place. My Adjutant, Capt. James M. Burroughs, pulled a drowning Chinaman [cargador] out after he had gone down three times. He was entirely underwater when he reached him, and was going down the stream in a millrace current. Burroughs was on a native banca made for one, and his skill and coolness in pulling the Chinaman [out] was a fine exhibition of presence of mind.

Hare's request for special medals was also denied.

Similar requests were made for the men of the 34th Infantry. On June 26, 1902, Lieutenant Colonel Robert Howze followed up on an earlier request to the War Department, this time with the support of a senator, asking that all of his officers and enlisted men of the 34th Infantry be granted a special campaign medal for the hardships endured during the Gillmore party rescue, through special legislation to Congress. That request, again, was denied.

Raised expectations haunted many of these soldiers for years. A number of veterans tried independently to pursue the medals they had been told were their due, unaware of the formal rejection years earlier. It was not until 1924 that the first wave of Silver Stars was issued to an initial batch of the veterans engaged in the rescue. These awards were limited to those men who had been earlier recommended for certificates of merit mentioned in orders, or wounded. A second batch of Silver Stars was issued five years later, in 1929, many posthumously by then, to the remaining US Army rescuers who qualified.

A number of the veterans never received the recognition, as the US Army did not bother to hunt them down. George Hindman of Terrell, Texas, a corporal with the 33rd, received his Silver Star on November 11, 1929, the very day he died.

And what of the catalyst for all of this?

Following his liberation, Lieutenant James C. Gillmore Jr. arrived in San Francisco, traveled by rail to Washington, D.C., and was placed on sick leave for another two months. In August and September 1900, *McClure's Magazine* published Gillmore's two-part illustrated account of the assault at Baler and his captivity. It was a continuation of his repackaging and spin: "The story of his boat-battle with Filipinos on the east coast of Luzon, his capture and narrow escape from execution, his extraordinary experiences during eight months of captivity, his journeys for hundreds of miles through the interior of Luzon, and his rescue by American troops just after he and his six comrades had been abandoned by their guards in the mountains, and when their murder by the savage tribes seemed imminent."

When General Aguinaldo was captured in 1901, the media sought out Gillmore for his views. He again spun a tale, waxing political:

> *I was with Aguinaldo's family while in the Philippines, and they impressed me as above the ordinary in intelligence, so that it can be readily seen what a task it was to apprehend Aguinaldo, the smartest man of his tribe. I say Funston is a hero, every inch of him. I am inclined to believe his capture will end the war, as the insurgents now are without a head.*

In May 1902, while tasked to the USS *Cincinnati*, Gillmore found himself in the center of another small adventure. He had been sent to retrieve the remains of United States Consul Thomas T. Prentis, who had been killed during the devastating eruption of Mount Pelee on the island of Martinique, the most deadly volcanic event of the twentieth century. The cataclysm had obliterated the city of St. Pierre, the "Paris of the West Indies," and incinerated some thirty thousand people with a hurricane-force pyroclastic cloud that swept through the city.

By 1905, Gillmore's marriage had failed, and he divorced his wife, the former Mary Ball, in April of that year. At the same time, he was drinking heavily. He was censured twice by his commander for being under the influence of liquor while aboard ship, leading to another suspension from duty. Again, a disingenuous Gillmore claimed that he was "surprised" and "completely thunderstruck" by the accusations.

As Gillmore battled to keep his record clean, his abandoned ex-wife went into a tailspin. On June 28, 1905, the forty-five-year-old, blonde-haired, blue-eyed Mary S. Gillmore, with a "dull facial expression, sallow skin, and contracted pupils," was admitted into Washington, D.C.'s, Government Hospital for the Insane in the throes of a psychotic break. The doctors diagnosed her as a chronic alcoholic with evidence of a ten-year history of drug use and a case of venereal disease, most likely passed on by her seafaring former husband. She appeared frightfully nervous, with marked tremors in her voice and hands, and in the grips of deep hallucinations. She was treated with bromides and sedatives as her family sought to head off the mandatory commitment hearing. In a flurry of activity, Mary was released a day before the hearing, narrowly avoiding a forced stay at the institution.

Despite his travails, Gillmore finagled a promotion to commander and took charge of the USS *Rainbow*, followed by an assignment on the USS *Helena*, in the Philippine Squadron of the US Asiatic Fleet. While he was at sea, however, more trouble was brewing at home in Virginia: Gillmore's fifteen-year-old son Stuart, in a mysterious late-night hunting incident, somehow managed to shoot his boarding-school classmate with a .22 caliber rifle, in the back. The boy, Philip Edelin, had been walking ahead and heard a bullet zing by his head. Just as he was turning around, the second shot hit his body. The local newspaper was filled with speculation about whether the shooting was accidental or intentional. In any event, the boy recovered and charges were not filed, though the incident suggested deeper troubles within the Gillmore family. While Gillmore was at sea, Mary left her son with relatives and moved to Denver, Colorado, to rebuild her life and start anew.

By March 1908, after a stint running the Cavite Naval Yard in the Philippines, Gillmore was ordered stateside to serve as post commander of the Navy Recruiting Office in New York City. He was soon promoted to captain, and in July 1909, took the command of the Pacific Fleet's Pennsylvania-class armored cruiser, the USS *Maryland*. In 1910, during an annual battle practice competition, the 13,680-ton, 504-foot warship, with its 830-man crew under Captain Gillmore's command, attained the highest final merit among the twenty-six vessels of her class. She was awarded the gunnery pennant in recognition of the high state of efficiency of her personnel.

On July 1, 1911, Gillmore was ordered home to Washington, D.C., bringing to a close a thirty-five-year naval career, and placed on the retired list with the rank of commodore. The rank, as obsolete as the man on whom it was being bestowed, had been retired as well, and was nothing more than an honorary title. But for Gillmore, it was a star on his sleeve, a final elevation in a surprisingly uneven career that brought him close to the rank of a rear admiral. It also notched him up for a higher retirement pension. Yet for Gillmore, it was surely not about the money. Keenly aware that many of his peers and underlings had rocketed past him over the years, Gillmore embraced his title as a welcome salve. The empty commodore label was recognition, albeit long overdue, of his years of service and his contributions to the navy. It was a moniker he would wear proudly for years to come.

❦

There would be one final adventure, albeit brief, for Gillmore. How the commodore secured the invitation is not known; perhaps it was thrown down by an army officer as a collegial challenge, or, perhaps it was a test of the resolve and courage of a sailor who had just celebrated his fifty-eighth birthday two weeks earlier. Whatever the catalyst, a nervous Gillmore arrived at US Army Airfield at College Park, Maryland, on July 23, 1912, game for a test in the clouds above.

Newspaper reporters turned up to cover the event, assured of a story their editors would love: A lauded naval hero, a former prisoner of war who had faced down near-certain death, was about to climb into a largely unproven contraption and courageously tempt fate once more. At his impending execution by an insurgent firing line some thirteen years earlier in the far-flung Philippines, the story went, Gillmore had demanded that his blindfold be removed so he could die like an officer and a gentleman. How would this aging hero, an artifact from a bygone era of sails and steam, react to a terrifying flight into the skies above?

Opened only a year earlier, the US Army's aviation school at College Park was on the cutting edge of experimental flight. The flight trials drew huge crowds, thrilled at the spectacle and daring. But the high-risk aerial acrobatics came at a cost. Just five weeks before Gillmore's arrival, Lieutenant Leighton W. Hazelhurst, a seasoned army airman, and Al Welsh, a civilian pilot, had climbed into a new Wright "Army Flier" to conduct one of a series of technical tests. Loaded with 125 pounds of gunshot, the biplane had just left the ground and was rounding a turn at a mere thirty feet when it suddenly "pitched forward and fell like a plummet." The aeroplane crashed into a crumpled mass of debris on the airfield, breaking Hazelhurst's neck and crushing Welsh's skull and leaving both men dead.

This Gillmore knew: Aeronautical flight was in its infancy, and it was deadly. The country's newspapers kept a breathless body count of the many pioneering aviators whose machines had exploded and crashed into the earth with alarming regularity. Hazelhurst had been the fourth US Army aviator killed since the first fatal accident four years earlier. That first fatality was followed by scores of other pioneering military airmen from across the globe—French, German, Italian, and Russian—whose experimental flights brought tragic and often spectacular death.

A far greater loss of life was being experienced at county fairgrounds, aerial exhibitions, and high-stakes races across America. At these events, showboating aviators dazzled the crowds with perilous spiral glides, ocean rolls, and dips-of-death, with often-catastrophic consequences. In fact, since the delivery of the first Wright machine to the US Army in 1909, to the day of Gillmore's flight in 1912, a total of 166 aviators had been killed around the world. This wasn't a casual joyride for the pompous old commodore; it was a high-risk stunt for an old naval officer with something to prove. For the sake of posterity, Commodore Gillmore had arranged to have both newspaper reporters and a portrait photographer present to document his date with destiny.

Gillmore's pilot for his flight, 2nd Lieutenant Thomas DeWitt Milling, 15th Cavalry, on aeronautical duty with the Signal Corps, represented a new generation of warriors. Trained by the Wright brothers a year earlier, the twenty-five-year-old Milling was now one of the school's flight instructors, pushing the machines to their limits, testing their ability to carry and fire machine guns and drop bombs from thousands of feet in the air. Their plane on this day: a new Curtiss biplane trainer that had been delivered to the school only a few weeks ago.

Stable, rugged, and maneuverable, the two-seater Model D trainer was a variant of the popular Curtiss "pusher," named after the rear-mounted propeller that literally pushed the aircraft through the air. The fuselage was constructed out of nothing more than spruce, bamboo, wire, and doped linen. To fly the plane, full body engagement was required. The pilot operated the wing's ailerons, small, hinged control surfaces attached to the trailing edge of the wing, with a yoke attached to his shoulders. Working like a sort of seat belt, the pilot twisted his torso to achieve a turn. The front elevator and rear rudder were controlled by the steering wheel that the pilot gripped with his hands. Powered by a 60-horsepower Curtiss V-8 engine and maneuvered by the pilot's own contortions, the aeroplane had a maximum speed of fifty miles per hour.

A visibly uncomfortable Gillmore donned one of the army flier's stylish black leather coats, tan leather gloves, a pair of flying goggles, and a heavy aviator's helmet. He climbed into the aeroplane's passenger seat, beside Lieutenant Milling. Immediately, there was a problem: At just five-foot-two, the diminutive commodore was too short to settle his feet on the plane's struts. A rope was quickly scared up and installed to provide Gillmore with a way to anchor his feet while in flight. Once strapped in, pilot and passenger posed for famed Washington, D.C., society photographer George W. Harris. A relaxed Milling smiled, his cheeky youthfulness on display. Gillmore gripped his seat and forced a grin.

As preparations for the flight began, several young army officers gathered around Gillmore to wish him well. A *Washington Post* reporter joined in. It was all in good fun, mocking the famed naval hero. "Good-bye, Commodore; have you written your last will and testament?" one soldier asked. The army was about to put the esteemed navy officer to the test. How would the old man fare?

US NATIONAL ARCHIVES

On July 23, 1912, following his retirement from the US Navy after a thirty-five-year career, Commodore James C. Gillmore Jr. (left) took the opportunity to fly as a passenger in a newfangled Army biplane at College Park, Maryland. Having lived through the ages of sail and steam on the world's seas, the commodore was able to experience, albeit briefly—for his daring escapade lasted just five minutes in duration—the age of flight, the advent of which transformed the very nature of war.

The aeroplane's noisy, eight-cylinder gasoline engine was turned over, and the aircraft ran the length of the airfield, its unwieldy thirty-foot wings struggling to lift the fuselage into the sky. The engine coughed and sputtered. Lieutenant Milling shakily climbed higher, the bamboo frame of the seven-hundred-pound contraption shaking wildly. The safety of the ground rapidly fell away to reveal a panorama of the city of Washington some eight miles distant. Then, partly to test the limits of the aircraft, but more likely to send the old commodore's heart into his throat, Milling sharply leaned his shoulder into a few violent turns and dipped the plane like a roller coaster in free fall. A wind-thrashed Gillmore held on for dear life. Milling eased up the wheel and roared back into the clouds. He banked the Curtiss again; the biplane shuddered.

If Gillmore experienced the proverbial "life flashing before his eyes," his focus would have been on the Philippines, circa 1899. It was here that the naval officer, then a lieutenant, had gambled with his life, and the lives of others. The result was a fiasco—captivity under Filipino revolutionaries for eight arduous months. Gillmore's grasp for heroics was ridiculed inside the navy hierarchy. His own men, in fact, were his most caustic critics. But a savvy Gillmore had managed it: Once liberated, he had spun a tale of his own captivity to suggest transcendent bravery and gallantry in the face of certain death. For the general public, this made him a hero, while saving him from official rebuke. Now, it had also brought him to the pickle he was now in: barreling through the sky, risking life and limb, to prove himself once again.

In five short minutes, the near-death experience was over. The aeroplane dropped wildly from the sky and its spindly tripod of wheels bounced across the airfield, the ashen yet thankful naval officer reconnected with solid ground. The newspaper reporters leaned in for comment as spectators gathered around. Gillmore carefully collected himself; this was his moment. "It is a pleasant sensation when one is used to it," the passenger professed, "and when you know when the driver is going to make one of those fast turns . . ." Gillmore continued the jocular banter: "[B]ut I'll have to admit I felt like asking for a transfer when Lieutenant Milling made that first dip. After that everything was lovely." Here was Gillmore spinning at his vintage best, playing to the media, spouting off with boasts and braggadocio. He knew the world wanted its heroes, and he would kindly oblige.

Unbuckled from his seat and untied from the struts, Gillmore climbed out of the Curtiss, flashing a smile of relief. Once again, Gillmore had survived. And now it was time to head back to the club for a drink and to share his latest adventure.

The following day, the *Washington Post* ran the story prominently, recounting how Lieutenant Milling had carried Commodore Gillmore in his new training aeroplane, "but was not able to thrill him in the least." Old Gillmore was of tough stock, the reporter implied, hewn from another generation of hardship and heroics. A man who had stared down death at the barrel of an insurgent's gun, who had been starved and beaten, who had emerged from hardship even tougher. What fear could some newfangled aeroplane stir in such a man?

Settling into retirement, Commodore Gillmore idled away his time at the New York Yacht Club in Manhattan and the Army and Navy Club in Washington, D.C., served as an elected officer on the Washington Corral, Military Order of the Carabao, and at one point, was elected Patriarch of the Herd.

A catastrophic stroke in 1924 sent Gillmore to the US Naval Hospital in Washington, D.C., where his condition degenerated and his mental faculties failed. By April 1926, psychotic, and suffering from organic brain disease, a thrombosis of a cerebral artery sank him into a vegetative state. Incontinent and ridden with bedsores, the impaired commodore became a burden to the naval hospital and was transferred to St. Elizabeth's, the sprawling Government Hospital for the Insane that overlooked the Potomac and Anacostia Rivers in the southeast quadrant of the city. It was the same facility where his former wife had narrowly avoided commitment two decades earlier.

Bedridden, helpless, and unable to express himself beyond inarticulate cries, Gillmore languished at the hospital for another fourteen months. On June 13, 1927, at 5:10 a.m., the old sailor finally gave in, at seventy-two years, eleven months, and three days of age. The official cause of death was general arteriosclerosis and terminal acute bronchopneumonia. With an autopsy refused by the family, the cadaver was sent to Lee's Crematory in Virginia. A burial was held at Arlington National Cemetery with full military honors.

The Secretary of the Navy wrote to Gillmore's son Stuart to express his condolences: "We regret and deplore his death and desire to express to you our heartfelt sorrow at his loss. We share with you in the sense of personal bereavement and trust that you may be comforted and your grief assuaged by God who holds the eternal destiny of man in His hands."

Gillmore's page-nine obituary ran the next day, riddled with factual errors, a victim of the commodore's long-term massaging of his exploits:

COMMODORE GILLMORE DIES; RENOWNED FIGHTER
*Received Congressional Medal of Honor
for Gallantry in Spanish War
Evaded Filipino Death*

The story recalled that Gillmore, described inaccurately as a "possessor of Congressional Medal of Honor," had been captured by Filipinos. It colorfully recounted that "during their captivity their execution was at one time decided, but Commodore Gillmore delayed it by refusing to die with his hands tied behind him, declaring it was not the way for an officer and a gentleman to die. While his captors were debating his protest, word came that an American rescue party was approaching and the Filipinos fled to the hills with their prisoners."

Two weeks later, *Time* magazine latched onto the heroic anecdote: "Died. James Clarkson Gillmore, 72, last Commodore in the US Navy (rank became extinct in 1899) in Washington, D.C. When Filipinos took him prisoner during the Spanish-American War he was lined up to be shot, refused to have his hands tied, said, 'It is not a fit way for an officer and a gentleman to die.' His captors debated, were interrupted by a rescue party, finally released him."

The legacy of James Clarkson Gillmore Jr. was now forever etched into the record: gallant American naval commodore, hero to a thankful nation, savior to his comrades, and, above all, an officer and a gentleman. What had eluded him in life, the old commodore had secured in death.

APPENDIX A: LIEUTENANT GILLMORE'S CUTTER CREW

Name	Rank	Place of Birth	Date of Birth	Age (at capture)
GILLMORE Jr., James Clarkson	Lieutenant	Philadelphia, Pennsylvania	July 10, 1854	44
WALTON, William	Chief Quartermaster	Mannheim, Germany	September 3, 1864	34
VAUDOIT, Paul	Sailmaker's Mate	Saint-Servan, France	June 12, 1857	41
PINKHAM, Ellsworth	Coxswain	Kittery, Maine	July 29, 1866	32
RYNDERS, William Henry	Ordinary Seaman	Amsterdam, Netherlands	July 6, 1868	30
BRISOLESE, Silvio	Ordinary Seaman	San Francisco, California	October 27, 1879	19
WOODBURY, Orrison Welch	Ordinary Seaman	Lynn, Massachusetts	June 15, 1879	19
EDWARDS, Lyman Paul	Landsman	Peru, Indiana	October 1, 1878	20
ANDERSON, Frederick	Landsman	Buffalo, New York	September 25, 1879	19
PETERSON, Albert	Apprentice 3rd Class	Oakland, California	November 28, 1881	17
Killed April 12, 1899				
DILLON, John	Landsman	Galway, Ireland	May 5, 1859	39
McDONALD, Ora Butler	Ordinary Seaman	Carmel Valley Village, California	August 15, 1877	21
MORRISSEY, Charles	Landsman	Columbus, Nebraska	February 21, 1879	20
NYGARD, Edward John	Gunner's Mate 3rd Class	Warsaw, Poland	April 1, 1870	29
Killed February 28, 1900				
VENVILLE, Denzell George Arthur	Apprentice 2nd Class	Dudley, England	August 1, 1881	17

Appendix B: The Gillmore Party Rescue Expedition

Name	Rank	Place of Birth	Age (at rescue)	Occupation
Staff	**33rd Regiment, US Volunteer Infantry**			
HARE, Luther R.	Colonel, Commanding	Noblesville, Indiana	48	Soldier / USMA
CRONIN, Marcus D.	Major	Worcester, Massachusetts	34	Soldier / USMA
BURROUGHS, James M.	Captain, Regimental Adjutant	Houston, Texas	30	Lawyer
CAMPBELL, Tilman	1st Lieutenant, 1st Battalion	Augusta, Arkansas	25	Bookkeeper
SHERBURNE, Thomas L.	1st Lieutenant, 3rd Battalion	New Orleans, Louisiana	21	Student
KEESEE, Oscar	Sergeant Major, 1st Battalion	Fort Worth, Texas	22	Mechanic
GEBERT, Albert E.	Sergeant Major, 3rd Battalion	Indianapolis, Indiana	25	Bookkeeper
HADRA, Frederick	Surgeon	Alamo, Texas	32	Physician
TWISS, John C.	Hospital Steward	Amherst, New Hampshire	31	Soldier
ROSE, Walter B.	Trumpeter	Coshocton, Ohio	31	Undertaker
Company A				
BUTLER, James S.	Captain	Yazoo City, Mississippi	21	Farmer
FISHER, Thomas L.	Sergeant	Fayetteville, Texas	30	Oil Mill Operator
TATE, Robert F.	Sergeant	Yazoo City, Mississippi	29	Merchant
CRANFORD, John W.	Corporal	Nashville, Tennessee	25	Druggist
HINDMAN, George	Corporal	Dallas, Texas	33	Railroad Man
JACKSON, Edward C.	Corporal	Cincinnati, Nebraska	19	Cowboy
ANDERSON, Charles	Private	Leroy, New York	32	Laborer
BENTON, Lawrence	Private	Coldwater, Michigan	28	Cook
BUNSTINE, Roy Neil	Private	Stonington, Illinois	18	Farmer
CHAPPELLE, James L.	Private	Algiers, Indiana	33	Farmer
CLARK, John B.	Private	Holmes County, Mississippi	25	Carpenter
DALLAS, George B.	Private	Chicago, Illinois	25	Miner
DRUMMOND, Willard S.	Private	Pierce City, Missouri	24	Longshoreman
GALLAGHER, James	Private	Ayrshire, Scotland	27	Timberman
McCAMMAN, Willie J.	Private	Ivarea, Pennsylvania	19	Soldier
O'RODDY, Patrick	Private	Bruckless, Donegal County, Ireland	25	Miner
ROBERTS, Collins	Private	Versailles, Indiana	23	Farmer
WILSON, Charles W.	Private	Waynesboro, Tennessee	22	Farmer

Company B

Name	Rank	Residence	Age	Occupation
VAN WAY, Charles	Captain	Shelbyville, Indiana	26	Mechanic
LIPOP, John J.	Lieutenant	Charlottesville, Virginia	27	Clerk
HUMPHREY, Lamar G.	Sergeant	Hot Springs, Arkansas	23	Express Driver
KELLER, Roger I.	Corporal	Dayton, Ohio	24	Soldier
MORRIS, John A.	Corporal	Brashear, Missouri	29	Bridgeman
NEWBERRY, Joseph J.	Corporal	Selma, Alabama	31	Soldier
WEST, Erasmus G.	Corporal	Birdville, Texas	22	Farmer
ARNOLD, Carroll B.	Cook	Dayton, Ohio	23	Carpenter
BEALL, Walter T.	Private	West Station, Mississippi	21	Baker
HARNDEN, John D.	Private	Allerton, Iowa	23	Farmer
HARNOIS, George C.	Private	Saint Joseph, Missouri	28	Teacher
JACKSON, Herbert L.	Private	Douglasville, Texas	21	Timberman
SIMMONS, George W.	Private	Meridian, Texas	23	Laborer
McIRVIN, Arthur H.	Private	Ottawa, Kansas	26	Lumberman
O'BRIEN, Frank	Private	San Francisco, California	31	Bridgeman
THROCKMORTON, Charles T.	Private, Co. L, attached	Kansas City, Missouri	21	Laborer

Company C

Name	Rank	Residence	Age	Occupation
LOWE, William L.	1st Lieutenant	Shreveport, Louisiana	30	Clerk
SCOTT, Walter F.	Sergeant	Brownsville, Tennessee	21	Dairyman
CHAPMAN, Harry	Corporal	Richmond, Virginia	35	Farmer
SCRUGGS, William E.	Corporal	Chattanooga, Tennessee	24	Farmer
ADDINGTON, Emmett	Private	Helena, Texas	22	Waiter
BEASLEY, Talmadge	Private	Jasper County, Missouri	25	Farmer
BROGAN, Neal	Private	Fort Smith, Arkansas	20	Clerk
BURRAGE, Carl J.	Private	Pittsburg, Texas	21	Painter
HORNER, Edgar A.	Private, Co. D, attached	Bogata, Texas	29	Carpenter
KELLEY, Thomas	Private	Milan County, Texas	21	Farmer
LANE, Louis A.	Private	Switzerland	27	Cook
POWELL, Charles M.	Private	New Albany, Mississippi	22	Laborer
SWEET, George W.	Private	Hartford, New York	28	Farmer

Name	Rank	Place of Birth	Age (at rescue)	Occupation
33rd Regiment, US Volunteer Infantry				
Company D				
HULEN, John A.	Captain	Columbia, Missouri	28	Real Estate Agent
WILLIAMS, Hugh	2nd Lieutenant, Acting QM	New Orleans, Louisiana	33	Bookkeeper
COX, John R.	Corporal	Waldron, Arkansas	27	Telegraph Operator
CROCKETT, George B.	Corporal	Boston, Massachusetts	32	Motorman
FREIMUTH, Ferdinand	Corporal	Bochum, Germany	27	Engineer
CLEAVES, William A.	Private	King George County, Virginia	20	Hostler
HOCKER, Oak	Private	Jackson Township, Monroe County, Missouri	24	Laborer
LAMBERT, George J.	Private	New Orleans, Louisiana	27	Cooper
MESSNER, Charles L.	Private	Morrow, Ohio	29	Farmer
ROBINSON, Joseph T.	Private	Columbus, Texas	21	Barber
TIMBS, Frank	Private	Memphis, Tennessee	26	Teamster
WALKER, Jessie Edwin	Private	Paris, Texas	27	Mechanic
Company I				
ELLIS, Richard J.	Captain	Youngstown, Ohio	29	Treasurer
ARMSTRONG, Edgar A.	Sergeant	Steubenville, Ohio	22	Bookkeeper
BALLARD, Samuel H.	Sergeant	Vanceburg, Kentucky	22	Soldier
BEST, William D.	Sergeant	Brookston, Indiana	23	Laborer
BURGSTALLER, Vincent	Sergeant	Graz, Austria	21	Gardener
CALDWELL, Milton	Corporal	Lottridge, Ohio	33	Farmer
RODDY, Theodore J.	Corporal	Burleson County, Texas	22	Laborer
BRAMMER, Robert	Corporal, Co. H, attached	Vanceburg, Kentucky	23	Railroader
BURKE, Patrick	Private	Rhymney, Monmouthshire, Wales	27	Laborer
DAY, Homer W.	Private	Vigo County, Indiana	22	Miner
HALEY, William J.	Private	Lafayette, Indiana	35	Laborer
MORRIS, Bert	Private	Shelburn, Indiana	19	Farmer
SHARP, Robert J.	Cook	Harrisburg, Pennsylvania	27	Teamster
WALTON, Jobe C.	Private	Elizabeth Township, Lawurence County, Ohio	20	Miner
WESTLAKE, Fred	Private	Lafayette, Indiana	21	Ironworker
WHITE, David A.	Private	Bellaire, Ohio	23	Railroader

			Officers	13
			Enlisted Men	72
			Total:	**85**

34th Regiment, US Volunteer Infantry (1st and 3rd Battalions)

Name	Rank	Residence	Age	Occupation
Staff				
HOWZE, Robert L.	Lieutenant Colonel, Commanding	Overton, Texas	35	Soldier / USMA
PENN, Julius A.	Major	Mattoon, Illinois	34	Soldier / USMA
JERNIGAN, Frank A.	Hospital Steward	Wharton County, Texas	27	Railroader
Company E				
CHRISTIAN, George W.	Private	Shelby County, Missouri	33	Cook
Company F				
RUSSELL, Frank G.	Captain	Pembroke, New Hampshire	36	Carpenter
HEATON, Wilson G.	Lieutenant	Glasgow, Iowa	31	Salesman
CLAPHAM, John T.	Sergeant	Mifflinburg, Pennsylvania	34	Mechanic
LAVICK, Peter R.	Sergeant	Roscoe, Goodhue County, Minnesota	22	Student
STRONG, George O.	Sergeant	Olcott, New York	26	Mechanic
STOLPE, Brady	Corporal	Gothenburg, Sweden	22	Farmer
FLETCHER, Edward S.	Corporal	Toronto, Canada	25	Miner
BUCKLEY, Hyrum S.	Private	Brigham City, Utah	26	Laborer
BROWN, Joseph	Private	Belleville, Illinois	36	Laborer
CLINE, Thomas A.	Private	China Grove, North Carolina	20	Cook
FRAKES, Frank B.	Private	Adel, Iowa	27	Plasterer
HAAN, Peter G.	Private	Grand Rapids, Michigan	30	Laborer
HALL, Warren F.	Private	San Saba, Texas	20	Rancher
HULL, Ezra A.	Private	Martinsville, Missouri	23	Laborer
KLEINER, Eugene	Private	Germany	21	Mechanic
LOW, John	Private	Franklin County, Iowa	26	Laborer
KNIBBS, Norman L.	Private	Dansville, New York	21	Plumber
POWELL, William H.	Private	North Landing, Indiana	21	Laborer
THOMAS, John	Private	Guntown, Mississippi	32	Cook
TROWBRIDGE, George	Private	Buffalo, New York	28	Sawmill Hand
WORMELL, Roy A.	Private	Arizona	17	Laborer

Name	Rank	Place of Birth	Age (at rescue)	Occupation
Company G				
DECKER, Stewart M.	Lieutenant	New Florence, Pennsylvania	42	Attorney
HENDRICKSON, Benjamin	Sergeant	New Denmark, Wisconsin	26	Carpenter
CRANEY, James G.	Corporal	New York City, New York	22	Farmer
DEMING, Elmer L.	Corporal	Lenape, Kansas	25	Farmer
HOGAN, James C.	Corporal	St. Clair, Michigan	27	Teamster
MERIDITH, George W.	Corporal	London, England	30	Laborer
BALDWIN, Arthur R.	Private	Hamburg, Iowa	26	Laborer
BOWEN, William	Private	Uvalde, Texas	22	Farmer
DAY, Fred D.	Private	Emporia, Kansas	22	Farmer
FORBING, Frank J.	Private	Fort Wayne, Indiana	23	Blacksmith
HALEY, William H.	Private	Blooming Prairie, Minnesota	21	Farmer
LAUGHLIN, Jerry H.	Private	Fond du Lac, Wisconsin	28	Railroader
LEONARD, Frank	Private	Rudolfswerth, Austria–Hungary	24	Miner
McMAHON, James	Private	Chicago, Illinois	30	Teamster
MEEHAN, Thomas	Private	Troy, New York	29	Miner
MILLER, Jacob H.	Private	Russia	25	Laborer
O'NEIL, John J.	Private	Duncannon, Ireland	30	Carpenter
STRAUSS, George A.	Private	Cleveland, Ohio	28	Laborer
VAN CUREN, Isaiah	Private	Illinois	23	Cowboy
WILDES, Arthur K.	Private	Maine	23	Fireman
WILSON, Claud T.	Private	Iowa	23	Laborer

Company H				
FRENCH, Frank L.	Captain	Sparta, Wisconsin	37	Merchant
BIRD, William	Sergeant	Shelbyville, Kentucky	29	Bill Poster
BYRNE, James E.	Sergeant	Brooklyn, New York	34	Clerk
BYRNE, John	Corporal	Jersey City, New Jersey	34	Laborer
CUPER, Martin	Corporal	Nordhausen, Prussia	31	Butcher
LONGWELL, Fred M.	Corporal	South English, Iowa	26	Farmer
PRATEL, Henry J.	Corporal	New York City, New York	23	Salesman
ROOS, Carl	Corporal	Karlstad, Sweden	27	Engineer
BENBOW, Edward A.	Private	Cleveland, Ohio	21	Miner
CONNELLY, Thomas P.	Private	Washington, D.C.	31	Miner
DOWNIE, Frank L.	Private	Adrian, Michigan	28	Lineman
GEARIN, Joseph	Private	Dublin, Ireland	34	Laborer
HAYDEN, Bert W.	Private	New Jersey	25	Miner
KENNEDY, Michael	Private	Indiana	24	Laborer
NORTHRUP, Marvin A.	Private	Houston, Minnesota	22	Engineer
OGLE, Homer B.	Private	Newark, Ohio	30	Railroader
SHANAHAN, Michael	Private	Missaukee County, Michigan	33	Laborer
WICKBOLDT, Albert	Private	Germany	22	Laborer
CAMPAGNOLI, Nicholas	Musician	Santa Fe, New Mexico	18	Painter
Attached				
ESPINO, Eugenio	Private	Candaba, Pampanga, Philippines	34	Lepanto Scout
		Officers	6	
		Enlisted Men	60	
		Total	**66**	

Appendix C: Report of the US Burial Corps, Expedition to the Philippines

November 14, 1900–June 24, 1901

Over the course of seven months, the US Burial Corps expedition to the Philippines, led by Superintendent David H. Rhodes, covered a large swath of the archipelago to retrieve the remains of American officers and enlisted men of the US Army, Navy, and Marine Corps, and civilian employees connected with the military service. Their steam transport, the *El Cano,* often arrived at remote locations without deepwater ports or piers, forcing Rhodes and his men to contract native boats, or, when those were not available, to simply wade ashore with their tools and caskets in hand. On land, travel entailed the use of army wagons, bull carts, pack mules, *carabao,* and ponies, and more often than not, a fair amount of hiking on foot. An escort of armed troops accompanied the men into hostile areas. Special precautions were required when handling remains still infectious with smallpox. And given the time of the year, Rhodes's expedition encountered typhoons, incessant rains, and rough seas, making the work of transferring bodies and caskets from one point to another, or from land to steamer, "an extremely hazardous operation for the safety of the dead, as well as the living."

By the end of the expedition, Rhodes's burial corps had traveled nearly eight thousand miles by land and on water in the Philippines—covering twelve islands from Luzon to Jolo—to disinter 1,375 sets of remains.

Rhodes's disinterment report provides a fascinating glimpse into the risks faced by the Americans while campaigning in the Philippines. Of 1,263 individual names and locations listed in one record, comprising about 30 percent of the 4,234 total American deaths during the conflict, 308 were killed in action or died subsequent to gunshot or bolo wounds, around 24.4 percent of the total. The greatest threat, however, was disease, which claimed some 771 lives, or 61 percent of the total. Dysentery and diarrheal disease killed 326 men (26 percent), followed by typhoid, 166 men (9.2 percent); smallpox, another 107 (8.5 percent); and variola, or measles, 76 (6 percent). If one survived an armed encounter or dangerous accident, new risks were posed by postsurgical infections and shock (12 deaths) or poorly managed anesthesia (chloroform narcosis, 2 deaths).

Nearly 10 percent of the men were killed in accidents, around seventy-six men, and a disproportionate number, fifty-three, due to accidental drowning in raging rivers and deep seas. Eleven accidental deaths were due to gunshot wounds, including one incident in which an approaching soldier was killed by a sentry. One soldier was killed by the kick of a mule, another jumped off a racing locomotive, and a third fell to his death while sleepwalking. Three men died of accidental skull fractures or concussions; one was gored to death by a *carabao*.

There were also self-inflicted deaths: nine suicides, eleven deaths due to alcoholism, and one death due to "vino poisoning," a toxic overdose of the potent local brew. Three deaths were due to drug abuse: one from opium poisoning, and two from overdosing on morphine. One man died from untreated syphilis and another from ptomaine poisoning. The brutal tropical climate also took its toll, with heat prostration and sunstroke responsible for the deaths of nine men. Beyond the enemy, disease, accidents, and self-inflicted damage, Rhodes also noted nine deaths by murder, as well as three deaths attributed to being "killed by comrade."

Incredibly, only 11 of the 1,375 sets of remains exhumed during Rhodes's expedition to the Philippines were declared "unknown"—less than 1 percent. Of these, 6 names were in fact known, but their individual remains could not be separated from the remains of the others with whom they had been buried. Included in this unfortunate tally of unknown dead were the four USS *Yorktown* sailors—John Dillon, Edward Nygard, Ora McDonald, and Charles Morrissey—killed on the banks of the Baler River on April 12, 1899, and buried in a common grave.

Author's Note

I ARRIVED IN THE PHILIPPINES IN 1983, FRESH OUT OF COLLEGE, READY to change the world. A Peace Corps tour of duty brought me into the Cordilleras of northern Luzon, to work and live among communities of tribal Igorots and Aetas. And when I thought the adventure could not get any more thrilling, I found myself front-row to a peaceful "People's Power" revolution that overthrew a dictator. Soon based in Manila, I moved up the organizational food chain of international development, working as a documentary filmmaker, urbanist, and agent for reform across sprawling urban slums and impoverished rural backwaters of the developing world.

By happenstance, and notably in reverse, I was following in the footsteps of my grandfather and his family, who, having fled the tumult of the Russian Revolution, arrived in the Philippine Islands in 1920. My grandfather went on to work at a brewery, developing fruit-flavored soft drinks, and died unexpectedly in 1937. His citizenship: Filipino. By 1939, my grandmother and my father, still a boy, were again on the move, migrating to America to escape the looming clouds of war. And who would have imagined: Proof of their former citizenship, discovered in faded documents of naturalization and coming into my possession years later, would ultimately seal the deal with my prospective father-in-law, who had vowed his daughter would never marry outside her culture.

As an immigrant family in constant motion across time and space, much of our family history simply disappeared, save for one thing: a tattered family photo album of my grandfather's life in colonial Manila. Sepia portraits of a rather dashing man in a fine white linen suit on the verandah of the Army and Navy Club, cigar and cocktail in hand, suggested the country had, for a time, lived up to its moniker of the Pearl of the Orient.

A search into my family's history segued into a decades-long exploration of the rich history of my adopted country. I soon found myself struggling to understand fully America's arrival in the Philippines at the turn of the century, a bloody event that had been relegated to a footnote

334

in history. I worked through books on the Philippine-American War, yet most seemed partial and incomplete, providing either a broad-brush treatment or a rehash of tired anecdotes. Other accounts were colored by political perspectives of their times. The more I studied, the less that seemed clear, and the more I wanted to know. How did the United States stumble into an experiment with empire on faraway shores, and become embroiled in a bloody campaign of pacification? How did America manage to quell a restive nation on the verge of achieving a hard-fought victory for independence? And what were the lessons in all of this, for the Philippines, America, and the rest of the world?

My armchair research into these questions led me to the tale of the nearly yearlong siege of a town called Baler. A careful read of the first-hand narrative of events by the Spanish garrison's commander, Lieutenant Cerezo, suggested a self-serving construction that did not add up. Further research led to nothing more than derivative accounts that regurgitated the same tale, with little analysis and fewer facts. But most of all, a critical incident within the siege drama—a failed US Navy rescue in which men had lost their lives—remained largely untold. No one, it seemed, had invested the time or resources to go back to primary sources. Further research, I decided, was necessary.

That fateful decision initiated an exhaustive five-year odyssey to find answers across three continents, at a score of libraries and manuscript vaults, and in private collections and ancestral attics. And then this: In the midst of my research, in the vast, dim expanse of the United States Army Archives in Carlisle, Pennsylvania, long tucked away in an envelope in a folder inside a box on a shelf, I found the photograph. It was no larger than a playing card, depicting a group of twenty-three ragged men posed on a rock. The photograph had no key save for a singular reference, "The Rescue of Gillmore." There it was. For well over one hundred years, the men remained unnamed, unknown, and forgotten. Challenged, I vowed to identify these survivors, learn their stories, and tell their tale.

I assembled a team of researchers to help retrieve individual military service records for every member of the Gillmore party and the two battalions of US Army soldiers involved in their rescue. In the Philippines, Spain, and the United States, I hunted down primary accounts by survivors, some buried in official files, others in the form of unpublished manuscripts shelved by their authors. A veritable treasure trove of personal letters between sailors and soldiers involved in the events—painstakingly assembled over three decades, starting in the 1920s, by a driven US Army regimental historian, and later scattered across rare manuscript collections—was retrieved, reassembled, and sifted through to fill in the blanks. I made contact with descendants of the American prisoners and their Filipino captors, whenever they could be found, and they kindly shared family documents and stories they had been told.

Slowly, begrudgingly, the grainy image of those men on the rock gave up its secrets, revealing a tale of debacle and despair, of heroism and heart, that framed America's brief foray into colonial conquest. And when it was clear what had transpired, I felt compelled to retrace Lieutenant Gillmore's route across Luzon. I explored the Baler riverbank where his cutter had been ambushed, men killed, and others buried alive, sifting the loamy soil in my hands. I tracked the prisoners' march across villages, towns, and into the majestic Cordilleras, and drove my bare feet into the sandy coastline where the broken rescue column emerged at Abulug, more dead than alive. And on the threshold of the awe-inspiring Sierra Madres, I hiked the rocky banks of the Diatt River where head-hunters had cut down Naval Apprentice Denzell George Arthur Venville, pausing where I imagined he may have met his brutal demise. On my desk while I assembled this account, a collection of river-worn stones, some that may have been witness to that sad affair, have stood vigil.

As I tabulated the cost of the Gillmore folly that began at Baler, I found myself drawn to the individual stories of death, heartbreak, and despair that followed. Each new document revealed one incredible backstory after another—of American soldiers and sailors, most mere boys at the time, sent to fight in a distant war on a faraway shore. My writing, I found, grew to become a trust: to tell their stories, to recount their tale, and to help these men find their rightful place in history.

The result is *The Devil's Causeway* narrative. The story is completely true. All text appearing in quotation marks has been taken from primary source material, including diaries, memoirs, letters, trial transcripts, news articles, and original military service and pension files. Lost to turbulent times, the story of the *Yorktown*'s debacle at Baler, and the events that followed, are pieced together here, for the first time, in their entirety.

Acknowledgments

The unearthing of the long-buried Gillmore party tale was assisted by many along the way, and to all, I remain deeply indebted and forever thankful.

First and foremost, this story would not have been told without the research expertise and sheer genius of Jonathan Webb Deiss at Soldier Source in Washington, D.C. Over the course of some five years, he and his team of "stack rats" assisted me in scouring the National Archives, chasing one curious lead to the next, to retrieve a priceless trove of documents and photographs that form the core of this narrative. Hats off to Jon, Amanda Morrison Jain, Anne Musella, Briana L. Diaz, and Susan Strange.

At the US National Archives in Washington, thanks to Cyndi Fox, and to Trevor Plante and Miriam Kleiman, who extended wonderful support as well as a rare and memorable behind-the-scenes tour for the family into the catacombs below. The team at the Navy Historical Foundation at the Washington Navy Yard—Todd Creekman, Glen Helm, Laura Waayers, John Reilly, Timothy Pettit, Regina Akers, and Joel Westphal—provided a wealth of rare archival gems. Special thanks as well to Jennifer Bryan for her kind assistance at the Nimitz Library at the US Naval Academy in Annapolis, Maryland. Research at the US Army Military Institute at Carlisle Barracks, Pennsylvania, was ably assisted by Clifton Hyatt and Isabel Manske. My great thanks to Betsy Rohaly Smoot at the National Security Agency for her generous sharing of Parker Hitt's unpublished papers.

Access to a number of special collections and archives at libraries proved instrumental when it came to adding meat to the story's bones. In the United States, thanks to Edward Fields at the Davidson Library at the University of California, Santa Barbara; Bruce Tabb at the University of Oregon's Special Collections; Juan Gomez and Laura Stalker at the Huntington Library in Pasadena, California; Maury York at the Joyner Library's Special Collections Department at East Carolina University; and Maurice Klapwald at the New York Public Library.

Great help was extended by Nan Card at the Rutherford B. Hayes Presidential Center in Fremont, Ohio; Scott Anderson at the Sharlott Hall Museum in Prescott, Arizona; Mike Jones at the John A. Logan Museum in Murphysboro, Illinois; David Henry at the Missouri Historical Society in St. Louis; Teresa Coble at the Kansas Historical Society in Topeka; and Katelyn Wolfrom at the Drexel University Archives in Philadelphia. I am deeply indebted to Dolly Macken-Hambright of the Milwaukie Pioneer Cemetery Association and to Cheryl Aussman-Moreno, for their generous assistance, and for allowing me to bring the Venville tale full circle.

In the Philippines, I am deeply thankful for the enthusiastic assistance from Engracia Santos at the American Historical Collection of the Rizal Library at Ateneo de Manila University in Quezon City; Elvie Iremedio, Mercy Servida, and Mark Manalili at the Lopez Museum and Library in Pasig City; and Teresita Ignacio at the National Archives in Manila. My thanks to several noted historians at the University of the Philippines, Jaime Veneracion and Augusto de Viana, for their guidance and support, and to Maria Luisa Garcia for her expert Spanish translations. I am also deeply indebted to Dr. Jaime Laya for his wonderful support, and at the National Museum of the Philippines, Jeremy Barns, Erwin Sebastian, and Benigno Toda III. In Spain, my special thanks to Father Cayetano Sanchez at Madrid's Archivo Franciscano Ibero-Oriental, for making the original handwritten Minaya diary available.

For the helicopter excursions across Luzon and into Baler, my warm thanks to Butch Jimenez, Butch Meily, Quirino Tangonan, Arnold Picar, Jennifer Salonga, Donna Hernandez, and Odette de Guzman. Thanks also to Baler-born Senator Edgardo Angara, his always-helpful executive assistant Olive, security aide Bong, and on the ground in Baler, Noel Dulay. During our research forays to Baler, I would have been far less effective without my trusted research assistant, Samantha Westfall, who took copious notes, wrangled the film, and added the most intriguing pieces to my rock collection. A big thanks to Eric Sales, for his keen and ever-artful eye.

To the descendants of the Gillmore party adventure who graciously shared their family archives and stories—Virginia Lee Edwards, Luis Tecson, and Sonny Tinio—words cannot express my gratitude. Special thanks as well to Charles W. Van Way and Gordon Ovenshine, who generously shared information about their grandfathers' tours of duty in the Philippines.

On the production side, my great thanks to the digital magic conjured up by the Design Muscle team: Billy Villareal, Mike Kalaug, Jan Carlo Dela Cruz, Karla Redor, and Mark Bryan Salle. My thanks as well to all those who helped at critical junctures, including Juan Miranda, Albert Atkinson, Fernando Zobel de Ayala, Carlos Reyes, Julieta Azanza, Zaide Revalo, and Krip Yuson, among many others. I have been overwhelmed by the steadfast support extended by Menardo and Kay Jimenez, Butch and Tricia Jimenez, Joel and Gidget Jimenez, Carmen and Jay Ong, and my sister, Meredith Westfall. My warm thanks to Brian McAllister Linn, one of the country's leading experts in military history, for sharing his insights and valuable time.

For those who volunteered to slog through early drafts of the narrative, I am especially grateful for the astute insights and valuable critique that immeasurably improved the storytelling. Those brave souls: Steve Groff, Darius Teter, Basil Zavoico, Brian Cady, and my late, great father, Michael Westfall.

Against all odds, I am blessed with a terrific literary agent, Jason Allen Ashlock at Movable Type Management, whose strategic insights and boundless enthusiasm allowed this book project to break through to the other side. My sincere thanks to Keith Wallman at Lyons Press, whose deft editorial hand brought a bright polish to the tale, and to Janice Goldklang and the rest of the Lyons Press team who has made this all possible. Special thanks to Meredith Dias, Shana Capozza, John Spalding, Vicky Vaughn Shea, Justin Marciano, Mary Rostad, Melissa Hayes, Steve Talbot, and Candace Hyatt.

My greatest debt of gratitude is owed to my wife, Laurie, and our three daughters, who patiently suffered my extended absences without complaint as I toiled away at long-lost history in our "den of pain" below, and to my co-time-traveler, Magnum, who snored soundly at my feet, until, as was often the case, the sharp rays of morning light arrived to gently nudge us back to the present.

Notes and Sources

A number of first-person accounts informed the details of the *Yorktown* cutter's ambush at Baler. The most important were those by then-lieutenant James C. Gillmore Jr., in his two-part *McClure's Magazine* article, and in his official account to Admiral Watson following his liberation in January 1900; Chief Quartermaster William Walton, as published in *Leslie's Popular Monthly,* and what appears to be his unpublished diary (though unattributed); Seaman Lyman P. Edwards, in a privately published manuscript graciously provided by his family; and a wide range of official reports written by key figures involved in the incident. These reports include Ensign William H. Standley's detailed narrative to Commander Sperry following his reconnaissance mission to the mountaintop at Baler, and a second write-up following the ambush; a similar report by Executive Officer Chauncey Thomas Jr.; and formal statements submitted to the navy by individual sailors following their liberation, including those by Seaman Orrison W. Woodbury, Seaman William H. Rynders, Coxswain Ellsworth E. Pinkham, and Naval Apprentice Albert Peterson. Also providing excellent insights into the debacle were the private letters of Commander Charles S. Sperry to his wife, Edith, as events unfolded, and an unpublished memoir by William H. Standley.

A major source for the events at Baler and the prisoners' subsequent captivity and rescue were three collections of the papers of Charles F. Manahan, an army veteran and regimental historian for the 34th Infantry, who spent nearly three decades chasing the Gillmore tale. While publishing an army veterans' newsletter, Manahan toiled from 1927 to 1955—twenty-eight years!—in an ultimately futile effort to piece together disparate events, starting with the ambush at Baler to the liberation in the mountains of Apayao eight months later. Manahan painstakingly hunted down accounts, one letter at a time, from the *Yorktown* survivors, their relatives, other involved naval officers, and a number of soldiers attached to the mountain rescue. Manahan's astounding archive of research, left to languish following his death and scattered across the rare manuscripts rooms of UC-Santa Barbara and the Huntington Library in Pasadena, California, and in the US Navy's archives, has served as a wellspring of information. Also important was Woodbury's formally transcribed account provided in May 1940, in response to prodding by the naval historian, Captain Dudley Knox—who served with him on the *Yorktown* at the time of the ambush—to sit with a navy stenographer and recount his experience.

The eight-month captivity of the Gillmore party prisoners was additionally informed by a number of accounts by army and civilian prisoners who joined the group of captives over time as they slogged across Luzon. The most well-known is Albert Sonnichsen's book, *Ten Months a Captive among Filipinos,* in wide circulation when first published in 1901. Other important accounts include those written by Hospital Corpsman Harry Huber, Sonnichsen's close friend, who struggled with his own unpublished manuscript, a copy of which can be found at the American Historical Collection at Ateneo University in the Philippines; and an excellent account by Private Leland Smith of the Signal Corps.

Important first-person accounts of the US Army's rescue expedition, which I drew upon heavily, include Brigadier General Julius Penn's privately published forty-seven-page narrative, written eleven months before his death, and an unpublished account by Sergeant Albert E. Gebert, collected by Manahan, which includes useful information on the death of Major Logan at the battle of San Jacinto. Also quite helpful was Juan Villamor's two-part chronicle on the Philippine-American War in northern Luzon, which provides rare insight into the Filipino perspective and the battles at Tangadan and San Jacinto, battles that are, sadly, otherwise poorly documented.

Direct descendants of General Manuel Tinio and Lieutenant Colonel Simon Tecson, Sonny Tinio and Bobot Tecson respectively, provided excellent unpublished and detailed biographies of their grandfathers.

Important works that documented the siege at Baler and subsequent events include the detailed account by the surviving leader of the Spanish detachment at Baler, Saturnino Martin Cerezo, *Under the Red and Gold: The Siege at Baler,* and the massive three-volume personal diary of Father Felix Minaya, sourced from the Archivo Franciscano Ibero-Oriental in Madrid and translated from the original handwritten Spanish. Accounts of the subsequent events at Baler, including Venville's captivity, murder, and the hunt for his bones, and the liberation of the three Franciscan priests, again go back to Manahan, who collected first-person accounts from Surgeon Andy Hall, Colonel Harry Newton, and Major Willard Newbill. Also helpful were the first-person recollections by various veterans of the Philippine-American War in the military veterans' journal, *American Oldtimer,* which saw publication in Manila from the 1920s up to the start of World War II.

The eclectic assortment of first-person accounts helped me make sense of the vast amount of primary source material scoured from the US National Archives (in Washington, D.C., Maryland, and St. Louis, Missouri), the Library of Congress, Navy Historical Center, and Army Historical Center at Carlisle, Pennsylvania. Over the course of five years, many thousands of pages of material were accessed, scanned, and studied, ranging from the Organized Military Personnel Files (OMPF files) of the *Yorktown* crew and key naval officers involved in the events, and the Compiled Military Service Records (CMSR files) of most of the 168 soldiers of the 33rd and 34th Infantry involved in the rescue, covering their enlistment papers, carded medical records, and communications. Astoundingly, a number of military records appeared to have remained unopened since they had been filed more than a century ago. Where possible, incredibly informative pension files were pulled.

To gain context, lock down timelines, and confirm facts, the hunt continued into related records of unit histories, regimental communications, and the extensive records relating to the establishment and operation of the US Army garrison at Baler. Focused themes drove the research effort, drilling more deeply when required, into specific records groups relating to the northern Luzon campaign in the fall of 1899 through 1900; American and Filipino prisoners of war; the battles at San Jacinto, Vigan, and Tangadan Pass; the role of native scouts; communications and operations of Bilibid Prison in Manila and the prison post at Malahi Island; the trial of Teodorico Novicio and other insurgents; and the relentless hunt for Apprentice Venville's grave *and* remains. Hundreds of records were pulled on the USS *Yorktown* ship itself, relating to its construction, equipment, layout, armaments, cruise reports, muster rolls, deck logs, and communications. Also sourced were the quite fascinating operations of the US Burial Corps under Rhodes, and the details of his grim expedition across the Philippine archipelago to retrieve and repatriate the remains of fallen American soldiers, sailors, and civilian contractors.

A critical angle of the research focused on defining the catalyst to the entire tale—James C. Gillmore Jr. himself. The work started by delving into his naval career, through his OMPF, and a review of communications, orders, and the various ships on which he served. We then went back in time, to explore his tenure at the United States Naval Academy, which revealed his court-martial trials, expulsion, and restoration as a cadet. The exhaustive files, containing details such as his own lengthy handwritten exams, were further informed by the communications of others—specifically, a number of prominent citizens from Philadelphia—who had intervened on the wayward cadet's behalf. These were traced back to Gillmore's childhood home in Philadelphia, to triangulate his privileged upbringing, and to city records and newspaper articles that revealed the Gillmore family's tragic past.

All told, more than a hundred disks of digital material were pulled from various archives, comprising more than two hundred gigabytes of data, nearly all of it primary source documents and records, to guide this work.

Abbreviations Used in Notes and Sources

AAG	Assistant Adjutant General
Adj	Adjutant
AG	Adjutant General
AGO	Adjutant General's Office
CM	Court(s) Martial
CMSR	Compiled Military Service Record
8AC	8th Army Corps
E	Entry or Series Number
GCM	General Court Martial
LS	Letter Sent Number
LR	Letter Received Number
LRB	Letter Received Book
M	Microfilm
MDLC	Manuscripts Division, Library of Congress
MHI	Military History Institute, US Army War College, Carlisle, PA
NACP	National Archives at College Park
NARA	National Archives and Record Administration, Washington, D.C.
NHF	Naval Historical Foundation, Washington Navy Yard, Washington, D.C.
NPRC	National Personnel Records Center, St. Louis, Missouri
OMPF	Organized Military Personnel File(s)
PIR	Philippine Insurgent Records, National Archives
R	Roll
RG	Record Group
SecWar	Secretary of War
SO	Special Orders
T	Telegram
USNA	William W. Jeffries Memorial Archives, United States Naval Academy
USVI	United States Volunteer Infantry

PROLOGUE: THE BOY VENVILLE

XIII. Venville was one of eight: Denzell George Arthur Venville, Service Number 1574247: OMPF, Correspondence RG 24, E 88, 170702, 225693, 248025, 283529, 294283, 218876, 225693, 226620; RG 94, E 530, RG 15, E 19, Pension, and Census.

XIII. "They call me a 'girl sailor': "Monument to Arthur Venville Unveiled," *Portland Oregonian,* September 23, 1901.

BOOK I

CHAPTER 1: BALER, 1897

5. As the first-quarter moon: The account of the first attack on the Baler garrison in 1897 is drawn from two sources: (1) *Defensa de Baler,* a 187-page handwritten diary by Franciscan priest Felix Minaya, translated by the author from Spanish, Part I, Chapters 1–3, 1–57, presumably written circa 1900; and (2) *El Sitio de Baler (Under the Red and Gold), Antecedentes,* by Lieutenant Saturnino Martin Cerezo, published in 1904 in Spanish, and republished in English in 1909. Note that this latter edition, translated and edited by Major F. L. Dodds, US Army, lacks the antecedent section recounting the first attack on Baler.

5. While only distantly related: Teodorico Novicio's genealogy remains sketchy, and little is known about his family background. Cerezo's account of the siege implied "Teodorico Novicio Luna" was a Luna, related to the painter Juan Novicio Luna, but he did not provide details; most likely, it was on the maternal side and at some distance, and the inclusion of "Luna" in Teodorico's name was a mistake, accepted as fact and repeated by subsequent writers and historians. A variety of documents confirm that "Teodorico Novicio"—sans any explicit reference to "Luna"—was an Ilocano raised in the town of Baler as a child, who later married and settled in the town. Father Minaya's diary also refers simply to a "Teodorico Novicio," as well as a cousin named Ricardo Novicio. Teodorico apparently had several siblings. US Army records from the Baler garrison refer to a sister, Manuela, who married a Spanish medical orderly, and Luis, a brother. Luis also appears to have been fighting for the Filipino Army of Liberation, and possessed a similar streak of hotheadedness. The US Army's post commander at Baler, Captain Detchemendy, noted on September 18, 1902, that *"the brother of Teodorico is charged with having cruelly murdered the Spanish commanding officer and his wife at Palanan."* An earlier reference provides further support: While with General Aguinaldo's command at Palanan, Dr. Simeon A. Villa writes in his diary about a military trial held on January 16, 1901, wherein Luis Novicio was charged with *"committing abuses under menace of arms,"* and sentenced to six years' imprisonment.

The most compelling evidence regarding Teodorico Novicio's correct name is provided through his own actions: In court testimony, depositions, signed documents, and communications, the captain consistently refers to himself as "Teodorico Novicio" without the addition of "Luna" at any time. It would appear that Cerezo simply had his facts wrong; unfortunately, poor genealogical records for this time period make further clarity unlikely. See: Cerezo, 47; Minaya, Part I, 26–36; Detchemendy to Army Division Headquarters, September 18, 1902 (for reference to Luis); Courts Martial transcript, Trial of Teodorico Novicio, RG 153, E15, 23994 (for reference to Manuela and trial exhibits D, E, and F written and/or signed in Novicio's own hand); and Diary of Dr. Simeon Villa, Philippine Insurgent Records (for reference to the trial of Luis).

10. They were greeted: For background on the Franciscan priests assigned to the Baler, two lengthy and informative articles have been published in the Spanish Franciscans' bimestral historical journal, *Archivo Ibero-Americano*: (1) "Cronica: Muerte de un heroe espanol del destacamento de Baler," *Archivo Ibero-Americano,* No. 58, July–August, 1923, Madrid, which notes the passing of Father Juan Lopez and recounts his ordeal at Baler; and (2) "Los ultimos de Filipinas: Tres heroes franciscanos," written by Father Lorenzo Perez, OFM, *Archivo Ibero-Americano,* No. 63, Madrid, July–September, 1956, which summarizes the Minaya diary and provides additional details on the Franciscan priests.

11. "Brothers . . . we will embark: Minaya, Part I, 36.

11. In his excitement, Novicio appointed a mayor: Novicio designated two captains, Moises Sison, and a certain Miguel, a native of Binangonan, who was also appointed to serve as *cabeza de barangay,* or mayor of the town. Two lieutenants were also named: Ricardo Novicio, presumably a brother or relative, and Norberto Valenzuela. Minaya, Chapter XI, 104–15.

11. "If any of you fail: Minaya, Part I, 38.

12. "To arms, infantrymen: Minaya, Part I, 44.

13. Whether Mota borrowed the priest's gun: Father Minaya suggests that Lieutenant Mota borrowed the priest's revolver, lamented all was lost, and committed suicide, but then spends significant time in his diary refuting recurrent claims that the commander was inadvertently killed by Father Carreño. Cerezo's *Under the Red and Gold* account skips over the incident in its entirety.

13. "Come up, my sons: Minaya, Part I, 48.

14. Disbelief hung in the air: Minaya, Part I, 53.

14. "Go back on board: Minaya, Part I, 59.

Chapter 2: A Defense to Madness

The account of the siege of Baler is composited from two sources, Felix Minaya's unpublished handwritten diary and Lieutenant Cerezo's detailed first-person narrative, *Under the Red and Gold.*

16. The detachment, the bulk of whom: Cerezo was quite prolific, reworking and expanding his narrative in subsequent years. In a subsequent Spanish-language version published in 1934, detailed appendices provide a map of the region; plan of the town; layout of the church and its grounds, including the location of the graves; a detailed floor plan of the church building and its defensive entrenchments; a list of all those besieged by name, title, age, occupation, and how they fared during the siege; a detailed accounting of food rations and stores; and various commendations and news articles issued after the event.

19. Drawn from an established family: Simon Tecson's brothers, Alipio and Pablo, were also officers in Aguinaldo's army; Pablo, in fact, had been a close friend to the nationalist Jose Rizal, the intellect who sparked the very notion of Filipino consciousness. An unpublished biography of Simon Tecson was provided to the author by Luis Zamora Tecson, the lieutenant colonel's grandson. See also: Quennie Ann J. Palafox, "Simon Tecson and the Siege of Baler," National Historical Institute, Manila.

21. In September 1895, Lopez and Minaya: For a biography on Juan Lopez, see "Cronica: Muerte de un heroe espanol del destacamento de Baler," *Archivo Ibero-Americano,* No. 58, July–August, 1923. For Felix Minaya, see "Los ultimos de Filipinas: Tres heroes franciscanos," by Father Lorenzo Perez, OFM, *Archivo Ibero-Americano,* No. 63, Madrid, July–September, 1956.

21. "So you have not seen: Minaya, Part II, 35–36.

21. "Absolutely none: Minaya, Part II, 36.

21. "So, everything is a pure lie: Minaya, Part II, 36–37.

22. "Felonies such as the ones: Minaya, Part II, 38.

23. Almost purpose-built vectors: Fitted with sponge-sucking mouthparts incapable of chewing solid food, the flies regurgitated their putrid stomach contents on whatever surface they had landed in order to liquefy their food. This contaminated soup was then sucked back into their mouths, leaving behind the beginnings of deadly dysentery among the starved, weakened soldiers. See: White, Graham B., *Filth Flies: Significance, Surveillance and Control in Contingency Operations* (Washington, DC: Armed Forces Pest Management Board, 2006).

23. "Little Henry! Little Henry!: Cerezo, 53.

24. In short, these men were: Beyond the immediate physical effects of beriberi, the compounding problem for the thiamine-starved men was Wernicke-Korsakoff syndrome, a severe memory disorder. The disorder was first identified by a German neurologist and psychiatrist, Karl Wernicke, in 1881, who noted key symptoms in patients: mental confusion, eye movement disorders, poor motor coordination, deteriorating to delirium, somnolence, stupor, and then death. Six years later, a Russian neuropsychiatrist, Sergei Korsakoff, described a startling syndrome of retrograde amnesia—an inability to form new memories—and confabulation, referring to the practice of filling gaps in memory by fabrication, in alcoholics deprived of thiamine. "This mental disorder," Korsakoff wrote, "appears at times in the form of a sharply delineated irritable weakness in the mental sphere, at times in the form of confusion with characteristic mistakes in orientation for place, time and situation, and at times an almost pure form of acute amnesia, where the recent memory is well preserved. . . . Some have suffered so widespread a memory loss that they literally forget everything immediately." See: Maurice Victor et al., *The Wernicke-Korsakoff Syndrome and Related Neurological Disorders Due to Alcoholism and Malnutrition*, 2nd Edition, Contemporary Neurology Series (Philadelphia: Davis, 1989); *Diagnostic and Statistical Manual of Mental Disorders*, 4th Edition (Washington, DC: American Psychiatric Association, 2000); H. E. DeWardener and B. Lennox, "Cerebral beriberi (Wernicke's encephalopathy): Review of 52 cases in a Singapore prisoner-of-war hospital," *Lancet* 1, 11–17, 1947; Charles F. Lewis, Merle M. Musselman, A. D. Thompson, and E. J. Marshall, "The Natural History and Pathophysiology of Wernicke's Encephalopathy and Korsakoff's Psychosis," *Alcohol and Alcoholism* 41(2), 151–58, 2006.

25. One rumor gaining traction: Spanish- and English-language newspapers carried the rumors of internal division and fratricide within the walls of the Baler church. See: "Lo de Baler," *El Noticiero de Manila*, June 3, 1899, as republished in Cerezo, 263; and "El Destacamento de Baler," *La Epoca*, July 9, 1899. The rumors were repeated upon the Spaniards' arrival in Manila in July 1899, forcing Lieutenant Cerezo to specifically deny that he struck down Alonso with his sword when his fellow officer attempted to surrender. See: "Welcomed as Heroes," *Washington Post*, July 8, 1899.

CHAPTER 3: ARRIVAL

26. Other powers—the Germans above all: Joseph L. Stickney, *Admiral Dewey at Manila* (Philadelphia: Moore, 1899), 87–88; Henry Watterson, *History of the Spanish-American War* (New York: Werner, 1898), 453–465; James A. Le Roy, *Americans in the Philippines* (Boston: Houghton Mifflin Company, 1914), 210–231; Thomas A. Bailey, "Dewey and the Germans at Manila Bay," *American Historical Review* 45, No. 1 (October 1939): 59–81.

27. The United States was forged: Thomas Jefferson, writing to James Madison from Monticello, April 27, 1809: "We should have such an empire for liberty as . . . never surveyed since the creation: & I am persuaded no constitution was ever before so well calculated as ours for extensive empire & self government . . ." Thomas Jefferson Papers, Reel 46, MDLC.

27. Through treaties, purchase: Walter Nugent, *Habits of Empire* (New York: Knopf, 2008), 265–73.

27. Dewey's squadron incurred: The lone fatality at the Battle of Manila Bay was Chief Engineer Francis Randall of the US Revenue Cutter *McCulloch*, a coal carrier, which had been ordered to keep well out of range of the fighting. See: Stickney, *Admiral Dewey at Manila*, 41; Leon Wolff, *Little Brown Brother* (London: Lowe & Brydone, 1961), 57; and *Bounding Billow*, Vol. I, No. 7, November–December 1898, a newsletter published on board the USS *Olympia*.

28. 323 Spaniards killed: Winfield Scott Schley, *Forty-Five Years under the Flag* (New York: D. Appleton, 1904), 323–31; David F. Trask, *The War with Spain in 1898* (New York: Simon & Schuster, 1981), 265.

29. In a few days, Gillmore would report: Admiral George Dewey, Commanding US Naval Force on Asiatic Station, aboard flagship USS *Olympia* to Lieutenant James C. Gillmore Jr., US Navy, aboard the USS *Solace*, April 3, 1899. RG 24, E 88, General Correspondence 173341.

When the USS *Yorktown* arrived in Manila Bay on February 23, 1899, she joined an American armada at anchor: the Asiatic Squadron's flagship, the USS *Olympia;* the USS *Culgoa,* a refrigerator ship; the USS *Buffalo;* the USS *Monadnock;* the USS *Helena;* the USS *Concord;* the USS *Petrel;* the USS *Callao;* a number of Spanish ships captured by the Americans; and many transports and merchant ships. Letter from Lyman Paul Edwards to his parents, February 26, 1899, in which he asked them to "excuse the dirt, we are coaling ship." Letter provided to the author by Edwards's granddaughter, Virginia Lee Edwards.

29. As was his custom, he had left: The Gillmore residence was a four-level, eleven-room, three-bath townhouse, 4,320 square feet in size, located at 1922 Sunderland Place, NW, Washington, D.C. See *Washington Post*, April 28, 1901. The house later sold for about $11,000 in 1908. See *Washington Post*, February 12, 1908. For the list of Gillmore household help, see Census, 1900, District of Columbia, Washington City, June 12, 1900. See also: Building Permit issued to Lieut. Gillmore, Lot 78, 1922 Sunderland NW, September 18, 1897, Washington, D.C., NARA M T1116, R 218, Permit 401.

30. Gillmore had been stalled: James C. Gillmore Jr., Service Number 4644: Dead File, NPRC, St. Louis. See also: Acting Chief of Bureau, Supplies and Accounts, responding to request that Lieutenant Gillmore's monthly allotment of $160 to his wife continue during his captivity as a prisoner of war, July 16, 1899. RG 24, E 88, General Correspondence, 181933.

31–32. In less than a year, more than four hundred saloons: An American commission of Protestant church leaders, led by former Army Secretary Peyton, visited Manila in October 1899, and determined there was no chance for Methodist, Presbyterian, or Episcopalian missionaries to gain any traction; Manila, he was told by a fellow minister, was a "hellhole" overrun by American soldiers, who were nothing more than "45,000 drunkards, rakes and gamblers." "Bad Report from Manila," *New York Times*, October 4, 1899.

32. "two whole streets filled: William T. Sexton, *Soldiers in the Sun* (Harrisburg, PA: Telegraph Press, 1934), 56–57. One report suggested over eight hundred prostitutes had flooded into Manila during the first year of American rule, each requiring a $50 bribe to the port authorities; another report, that a single ship delivered three hundred girls. See Ken De Bevoise, *Agents of Apocalypse: Epidemic Disease in the Colonial Philippines* (Princeton, NJ: Princeton University Press, 1995), 85–93. A head count of prostitutes working in forty-two brothels in the Sampaloc district of Manila on November 4, 1901, found a mix of 14 American, 1 Spanish, 12 Russian, 3 Romanian, 1 Hungarian, 2 Italian, 1 Australian, 1 Turkish, 72 Filipino, and 124 Japanese women at work. See report from Brigadier General George W. Davis, Provost Marshal General, US Army, Commanding, to Secretary of the US Military Governor in the Philippine Islands, May 29, 1901. RG 94, E 25, 368853.

33. The USS *Yorktown*'s designation: Among the supplies in the *Yorktown*'s hold were 428 pounds of bolts, nuts, rivets, screws, washers; thirteen different kinds of brushes and brooms; 120 quarts each of rubber and marine cement; 450 pounds of Portland cement; 435 pounds of nails; and a year's supply of assorted wood: 1,550 linear feet of ash, cedar, mahogany, oak, pine, sycamore, and walnut. Also included were 1,300 pounds of steel, iron, lead, tin, and solder; 165 pounds of spare rubber sheets, gaskets, and packing flax; an array of oils, varnish, paint, shellac, and grease; calcium phosphide for illuminating purposes, bathtub white enamel, and a package of gold leaf. There was also every conceivable plumbing pipe, elbow, and valve; replacements for every hook, lens, plug, toggle, and cleat; and a formidable set of over four hundred tools ranging from anvils to axes, mallets to saws, pliers to tongs. Records of the USS *Yorktown*'s retrofit and gunnery, Bureau of Construction and Repair, US Navy. RG 19, E 92, 4586e; RG 19, E 92, 4665e. See also: History of the USS *Yorktown*—Gunboat No. 1, Naval Historical Center, Department of the Navy, DANFS.

33. Raised by an older uncle, Sperry: References written on Sperry's behalf were sent to the Secretary of the Navy by a number of prominent citizens from Waterbury, Connecticut, including Dr. Alexander C. Twining, a scientist and educator who is credited with inventing refrigeration, and Frederick J. Kingsbury, a noted banker and historian. When Sperry needed support to remain in the Academy despite his physical deficiencies, Connecticut governor William A. Buckingham and a number of leading businessmen came to his aid. See United States Naval Academy Records. Midshipman Charles Stillman Sperry. RG 24, E 403, jacket 530.

33. Dismissed twice for medical deficiencies: Sperry suffered a loss of hearing in his left ear, and excessive varicocele, an enlarged vein in his scrotum. With the help of a number of his uncle's influential friends, he was able to convince the US Naval Academy administration that his medical ailments did not pose a risk to his naval career. United States Naval Academy Records. Midshipman Charles Stillman Sperry. RG 24, E 403.

34. Sperry had been promoted: Joseph Anderson, editor, *The Town and City of Waterbury, Connecticut from the Aboriginal Period to the Year 1895* (New Haven, CT: The Price and Lee Company, 1896), Volume III, pages 1235–36.

34. While away at sea, Sperry wrote: Charles S. Sperry Papers, Family Correspondence, MDLC.

34. She stood out at the harbor: RG 24, E 118, Yorktown Decklog, 17/11/1898-27/05/1899.

36. Most were skilled seamen: The lowest-paid enlisted crew member, Apprentice 3rd Class, earned $9 per month; the highest-ranking petty officer, the Chief Master-at-Arms, William Crosby, $65 per month. The highest-paid officer, of course, was Commander Sperry, who earned a handsome $291.66 per month.

36. Fifteen others—Chinese cooks: See: Recapitulation of Muster Roll, USS *Yorktown*, March 31, 1899; Census, USS *Yorktown*, July 19, 1900.

36. Black anthracite coal: In 1892, the US Navy was burning 116,903 tons of coal at a cost of *$621,131.* By 1901, that amount would triple, to 382,040 tons. As important as coal was the availability of coaling stations at strategic points along a ship's route. See: "Fuel Accounts for Uncle Sam's Navy," *New York Times*, December 21, 1902; "Navy Used $621,131 in Coal," *New York Times*, October 24, 1896; "No Coal, No Navy," *New York Times*, January 15, 1899; "Our New War-Ships," by Benjamin Tracy, Secretary of the Navy, *North American Review*, June 1891.

37. Of course, the ship also had: The *Yorktown* was not the pinnacle of energy efficiency. A quick set of calculations: A typical short ton (2,000 pounds) of coal has 20.754 million Btu. A barrel of crude oil has 5.8 million Btu. The *Yorktown* gulped 2,730 pounds of coal an hour at maximum cruising speed, or the equivalent of 4.88 barrels of oil an hour. A barrel of oil is equal to about 19.5 gallons of octane 87 gas at the pump. Working it another way, the *Yorktown* needed about 95.16 gallons of gas an hour to operate at her full-power natural draught speed, consuming about 7.72 gallons per knot. Working it into statute (road) miles (12.32 x 1.15 = 14.16), she needed 6.72 gallons of gas to stagger a mile equivalent at sea, or put another way, she got 0.14 miles to the gallon—that's 739 feet per gallon of gas equivalent. See: Report on full-power natural draught trial for the USS *Yorktown*, December 19, 1902; Bureau of Construction and Repair, US Navy, RG 19, E 92, 14597e.

37. Firefighters and soldiers battling: Philippine War, Linn, 60.

CHAPTER 4: A GENEROUS MISSION

39. "The Holy Father wishes: Telegram from Cardinal Rampolla, Secretary of State, Vatican to Monsignor Martinelli, Apostolic Delegate, Washington, D.C., July 31, 1898. RG 94, E 25, 79350.

40. "fire, sword and wholesale executions: Frank Charles Laubach, *The People of the Philippines, Their Religious Progress and Preparation for Spiritual Leadership in the Far East* (New York: George H. Doran Company, 1925).

40. "A sad day has dawned: Extract of proclamation issued by Archbishop Nozaleda, May 6, 1898, in Charles S. Sperry Papers, MDLC.

41. On March 23, 1899, a letter: Archbishop Nozaleda to Admiral Dewey, March 23, 1899. Charles S. Sperry Papers, Baler File, MDLC.

43. "[Admiral Dewey] has laid out an 'interesting cruise': Commander Sperry to his wife, Edith, April 1, 1899. Charles S. Sperry Papers, Family Correspondence, MDLC.

44. "If the soldiers do not wish: Admiral Dewey to Commander Sperry, April 4, 1899, No. 1227-S, Charles S. Sperry Papers, Correspondence File, MDLC.

44. Another 506 pounds of fresh beef: Deck log, USS *Yorktown*, April 5, 1899.

45. "We have been filling up: Sperry's estimate of forty Spaniards still holed up in the church at this point, presumably based on what Admiral Dewey had told him, was, in fact, incorrect. Fifty-two Spaniards initially took refuge in the church, and were later joined by the priests Minaya and Lopez, for a total of fifty-four men. Fifteen men had since died, and two had deserted, leaving thirty-seven men remaining in the church. That Dewey had such near-accurate intelligence, presumably provided to him by Archbishop Nozaleda, suggests that a steady stream of information was indeed making it out of the church and back to Manila. Sperry to his wife Edith, April 6, 1899, MDLC. Charles S. Sperry Papers, Correspondence File, MDLC.

45. "Of course, they will not come: Ibid.

45. "quite an expert: Woodbury to Manahan, June 26, 1940. Charles F. Manahan Papers, NHF.

45. Lieutenant Gillmore, however: Ibid.

45. On Tuesday, April 11, at exactly 11:40 a.m.: Ibid.

CHAPTER 5: RECONNOITER

46. taken under Sperry's wing: William H. Standley Collection, Vital Statistics, Miscellany Folder, MDLC. For a biography of his father, Harrison Standley, see *History of Mendocino County, California* (San Francisco, CA: Alley, Bowen & Co, 1880), 615–17.

46. Sperry ordered him to take: This account of the reconnoiter at Ermita Hill, Baler, is drawn from Ensign William Standley's report to Commander Sperry, April 11, 1899. Charles S. Sperry Papers, Spanish-American War File, MDLC.

46. Standley was also tasked: Ibid.

47. The sole Filipino rifleman: Ibid.

47. Four more men armed: Ibid.

47. This was *Kapitan* Teodorico Novicio: Father Felix Minaya confirms that Novicio was present at the initial parley with Standley. Minaya, Part III, 111–13.

48. What the officers on the deck: Ensign William Standley's report to Commander Sperry, April 11, 1899. Charles S. Sperry Papers, Spanish-American War File, MDLC.

48. Otherwise, the Americans could not: Ibid.

49. A skeptical Novicio: Ibid.

49. He was, in fact, exactly: Ibid.

49. As the confused discussions: Ibid.

49. The two boat crews: Deck log, USS *Yorktown,* April 11, 1899.

50. Until the town could be located: This account draws on two sources: (1) Commander Sperry's report on the Baler incident to Admiral Dewey, April 20, 1899; and (2) Executive Officer Chauncey Thomas Jr.'s report to Commander Sperry on the mission preparations, April 13, 1899. See: Accounts of the capture and rescue of Lt. Gilmore [*sic*] and a boat crew from the USS *Yorktown* near Baler, Luzon, RG 45, E 464, hj182; and Charles S. Sperry Papers, Spanish-American War File, MDLC.

50. He volunteered to climb: Ensign Standley was referring to a well-known geographic feature in Baler, called Point Baja at the time, and later renamed Ermita Hill.

50. A landing party: Commander Sperry's report on the Baler incident to Admiral Dewey, April 20, 1899. Charles S. Sperry Papers, Spanish-American War File, MDLC.

51. Sperry assigned Quartermaster: Ibid.

51. "check any disposition to rashness: Sperry to Admiral Dewey, April 20, 1899, page 9. Charles S. Sperry Papers, Spanish-American War File, MDLC.

52. "I can think of no point: Ibid.

52. The soldiers scrambled: Cerezo, 94.

53. The heavily tattooed, German-born: Born in Mannheim, Germany, Walton had signed up as a merchant mariner at age twelve. His life at sea was immediately obvious from the seventeen different tattoos inked across his chest and arms—of women, ships, daggers, and "Young America"; bracelets drawn on both wrists; and faux rings etched on his fingers. Walton started his naval career at Mare Island, California. Since then, he had married his sweetheart Katherine, settled with his in-laws in nearby Vallejo, and had decided the navy was for him. In 1896, his third reenlistment was accomplished at the port of Chefoo, China, without a second thought. Records consulted for William

Walton, Service Number 1472421, include OMPF, RG 15, E 19, Pension, Correspondence, RG 24, E 88, 78849 and 199889.

53. "one of those excitable Frenchmen: Commander Edward E. Capehart to Chief, Bureau of Navigation, April 2, 1908. OMPF, Paul Vaudoit.

53. Sperry had him charged: Born in Saint-Servan, France, along the Brittany coast, Vaudoit joined the French Navy at age twelve. Three years later, during the Franco-Prussian War, he helped defend Mont-Valerien's fortifications during the siege of Paris. Vaudoit later made his way to California to join his brother Frank, who ran a men's clothing store. After ten years of selling suits and fedoras, however, his former adventurous life on the high seas again beckoned. Vaudoit, sporting scars on the left side of his jaw, nose, chin, and the back of his scalp, plus a missing set of incisors, bicuspids, and molars from his upper jaw, was on his second enlistment and eighth ship. Paul Vaudoit, Service Number 1072879: OMPF, Correspondence RG 24, E 88, 264174, and Census.

53. His operation of the ship's steam cutter: Pinkham—aboard the *Yorktown* under an assumed name, John Ellsworth—was on his fourth enlistment and eleventh ship. A life on the world's seas and rough ports had left him with a deformed nose, a deep scar across his right eye, and a gallery of ink: stars on the back of each hand; a coat of arms, a fierce eagle, crossed flags, and several ships on his chest; a FREE TRADE motto across one forearm; a ship, sailor, hula girl, and hut on the other; a dragon on one leg; and snake and bird on the other. The alias was Pinkham's dark secret: He had been dishonorably discharged from the navy in September 1897 after a series of convictions for drunkenness while on duty, fighting, and "using profane and abusive language to the sentry on brig post." Pinkham walked off the USS *Boston* at Chefoo, China, reportedly married a Hawaiian woman, and for a time, served as a captain on a local island steamer. A year later, the war with Spain lured the seasoned sailor back into the navy, where he had surreptitiously reenlisted under his new name. Ellsworth Everett Pinkham, Service Number 1533070: OMPF, and Census.

53. The two other petty officers: Rynders was a seasoned merchant mariner who had spent a decade at sea before joining the US Navy. The hazel-eyed sailor displayed far less of his past across his body, with only a single W.H.R. etched into his right forearm. And like Pinkham and Vaudoit, he too encountered trouble on the sail over. For some unknown infraction, he was called before Commander Sperry, found to have demonstrated "inaptitude for rating," and demoted in rank. This was generally a temporary punishment, invoked to correct errant behavior. For Rynders, it appears the point had been made, as his performance quickly improved but the disrating rank held until the end of his naval career. William Henry Rynders, Service Number 1267098: OMPF, Correspondence RG24, E 88, 199889, 201096, 209302, 213513, 213827, and Census.

53. As the gunner's mate: Born in the city of Warsaw, Nygard first enlisted seven years earlier at Mare Island and was now on his seventh ship. Since then, the tall, blue-eyed Pole had performed well and moved up through the ranks after passing the gunner's mate exam the previous December. Edward John Nygard, Service Number 1066760: OMPF, RG 15, E 19, Pension, Correspondence RG 24, E 88, 199889, 206726, 200420, 235190, and Census.

53. Among the three seamen: The 130-pound, blue-eyed Woodbury, a graduate from Massachusetts Nautical Training School—later known as Mass Maritime Academy—had been found missing from his station one night while sailing to Manila and had been charged with neglect of duty. He was sentenced to a reduction in rank to Ordinary Seaman 4th class for a month. Orrison Welch Woodbury, Service Number 1074334: OMPF, Correspondence RG 24, E 88, 201540, 205204; RG 94, E 530, 217193, 231383, and Census.

Brisolese joined the *Yorktown*, along with Lieutenant Gillmore, after being detached from their hospital ship in Manila Bay. Silvio Brisolese, Service Number 1552376: OMPF, Correspondence RG 24, E 88, 216799, 221021 (which includes his nine-page account of captivity, dated May 3, 1900, Manila), 259356, and Census.

Ora Butler McDonald, Service Number 1663205: OMPF, Correspondence RG 24, E 88, 199899, 239711, 246334, and Census.

54. Three landsmen included: Records for Frederick Anderson, Service Number 1039557: OMPF; also, a detailed entry on Anderson regarding his background and list of punishments can be found in the "Conduct Book and Duplicate Shipping Articles of the USS *Manila,* April, 1899 to June, 11, 1902," 99, RG 24, E 358. From these entries, we can discern he enlisted on December 31, 1898, at New York City, and had first served on the USS *Monterey.*

Lyman Paul Edwards, Service Number 1556687: OMPF, Correspondence RG 24, E 88, 211673, 170701, 211673, 212837, 215049, and Census. Edwards also wrote an account of his captivity, an unpublished manuscript entitled *Prisoner in the Philippines.*

Charles Albert Morrissey, Service Number 1263980: OMPF, Correspondence RG 24, E 88, 172881, 199889, 201258, 201464, 205541, 207824, 210907, 212121, 320054, RG 45, E 210, Box 5, and Census.

54. The cutter's crew was rounded out: Albert Peterson, Service Number 1366400: OMPF, Correspondence RG 24, E 88, 221021 (which includes his nine-page account of captivity, dated May 3, 1900, Manila), RG 15, E 19, Pension, and Census.

54. "damned landing party business: Frank C. Pinkham, brother of Ellsworth, to Manahan, August 15, 1938. Charles F. Manahan Papers, NHF.

54. A replacement was quickly: Dillon had done a stint in the navy more than a decade earlier as a coal heaver, and had spent the last decade alternately working as a merchant marine, which had left his short, stocky, 170-pound frame riddled with tattoos, and a barber, when work as a sailor was scarce. Attracted by the crew's positive reports about the newly refurbished ship, Dillon happily came aboard as a landsman. Lacking other good opportunities for work at sea—he was getting a bit old, and admittedly, there was always a crop of younger muscle willing to work for less—it would be an opportunity for stable work with a decent wage of $16 per month. John Dillon, Service Number 1757002, OMPF.

54. Stepping belatedly into the cutter: Lyman Paul Edwards, *Prisoner in the Philippines* (unpublished manuscript), 27. Frank C. Pinkham to Manahan, August 15, 1938. Charles F. Manahan Papers, NHF.

55. Under muffled oars: Report on Landing, Standley to Sperry, April 12, 1899. Charles S. Sperry Papers, MDLC.

55. Any firing, then, meant: Ibid.

55. In the forward bow, Apprentice Venville: That the lead line was marked in feet—and not fathoms, as per standard procedure—is not a minor point. Seaman Orrison Woodbury suggests that, given the lead line was prepared aboard the *Yorktown* before departing, and was oddly marked in feet with the assumption they would be sounding very shallow depths, it is evidence that Lieutenant Gillmore had official orders to proceed up the Baler River. Official accounts by Commander Sperry and other officers contradict this assertion, and in a later communication, following a discussion with Captain Knox (who was an ensign aboard the *Yorktown* at the time), Woodbury states his earlier perception was wrong. See: Woodbury to Manahan, April 21, 1940, Charles F. Manahan Papers, UCSB; Woodbury to Manahan, June 26, 1940, Charles F. Manahan Papers, UCSB.

55. It was 5:50 a.m.: Deck log, USS *Yorktown,* April 12, 1899.

56. As the men searched: Report on Landing, Standley to Sperry, April 12, 1899. Charles S. Sperry Papers, MDLC.

56. As Standley settled down to sketch: Ibid.

56. It was increasingly clear: Ibid.

56. *"Mira este hombre:* Ibid.

56. It was now twenty minutes: Ibid.

57. Thomas quickly dispatched: Executive Officer Thomas to Sperry, April 13, 1899. Charles S. Sperry Papers, Spanish-American War File, MDLC.

Chapter 6: Trouble

58. "Not a sound was made: Gillmore, *McClure's,* August 1900, 292.

59. Anyone on the receiving end: Reference—Colt Automatic.

60. Gillmore ignored him: Minaya, 113.

60. "Trouble was coming: Gillmore, *McClure's*, August 1900, 294.

60. An insurgent force let fly: Minaya, 114.

61. He fell back: Minaya states that Novicio was the Filipino who both ordered the cutter to halt, and fired the first shot at the cutter, which killed Morrissey and in turn triggered the insurgent fusillade that followed. See: Minaya, Part III, 111–13.

61. Several sailors pushed Dillon: The details of the ambush at Baler have been reconstructed from the following: published accounts by Gillmore in *McClure's* and Walton in *Leslie's;* Edwards's unpublished manuscript, *Prisoner in the Philippines;* official statements to the US Navy provided by Gillmore, Woodbury, Peterson, Brisolese, and Pinkham; a contemporaneous diary attributed to Anderson; Woodbury to Knox, June 9, 1940, and his dictated statement, May 4, 1940; communications from Woodbury and Frank Pinkham to Manahan; and Minaya's diary, in which he recounts what he had been told directly by Novicio.

61. Others desperately grappled: Woodbury to Knox, June 9, 1940. RG 45, E 464, hj182.

61. "Damn you, I hope you get: Frank Pinkham to Manahan, August 15, 1938. Charles F. Manahan Papers, NHF.

62. For Pinkham and several others: The naval historian Dudley Knox, who was an ensign on the *Yorktown* during the incident at Baler, prodded Woodbury, who was visiting his office in Washington, D.C., to sit with a stenographer and provide his account of the ambush as an important contribution to the historical record. His report, dictated to one of Knox's secretaries on May 4, 1940, was rather thin. His memory jogged, and perhaps realizing the importance of his own knowledge, the sailor wrote to Knox a month later, on June 9, 1940, providing a far more detailed account of the ambush. Woodbury to Captain Knox, June 9, 1940. Charles F. Manahan Papers, NHF.

63. "It is useless for us to try: "Report of Capture, Captivity, and Rescue" by Silvio Brisolese, May 3, 1900. RG 24, E 88, 221021.

63. Pinkham, disgusted, threw: Charles B. Pinkham to his mother, *The Herald*, January 9, 1900.

63. "Gillmore behaved like an old woman: Woodbury's letter to the editor, *Chicago Tribune*, May 18, 1901.

64. Gillmore's gold Annapolis graduation ring: Walton, *Leslie's*, 421.

64. A firing line: Edwards, 29.

64. He was an officer: Walton, *Leslie's*, 421; Gillmore, *McClure's*, 298.

64. Breaking the dark moment: Edwards, 29. The senior officer arriving on the scene was most likely Lieutenant Colonel Simon Tecson, the only person of superior rank in Baler at the time who would have been in a position to berate Novicio in front of his men.

64. It was Lieutenant Colonel Simon Tecson: Lieutenant Colonel Simon Tecson's intervention in the execution is related in reports of the ambush conveyed to 34th US Infantry forces arriving at Baler in March 1900. See: Captain Newbill's report to Adjutant General, Manila, P.I., July 31, 1900. RG 395, E 2140.

66. Along the way, Brisolese tore: Woodbury to Manahan, April 21, 1940. Charles F. Manahan Papers, UCSB.

66. Filipinos were civilized: Edwards, 30.

66. It was exasperating: Ibid; Walton, 422.

66. All the Filipinos wanted: Ibid.

66. The *Yorktown* would then: Walton, 422.

67. The only thing the Filipinos: Ibid.

67. With this basic information: Ibid.

67. He should announce: Ibid.

67. He carried the cutter's Stars and Stripes: Edwards, 29; Edwards to Manahan, March 18, 1933. Charles F. Manahan Papers, NHF.

68. They then surmised: Cerezo, 98.

68. When Vaudoit quickly complied: Ibid. The apparent confusion and disorientation on the part of the Spaniards suggest that the long-term nutritional deficit had impacted their ability to reason and make sense of the events unfolding around them. Their inability to differentiate the Frenchman Vaudoit from the Spaniard Olmeda, the latter whom they all knew from recent interactions, and their inability to connect events to the obvious evidence of a ship in the bay (whose guns and searchlight they had seen), as well as their own apathy to their situation and lack of interest in rescue, suggest severe mental problems related to thiamine deficiency—significant memory loss that impairs memories of all but the distant past. The Spaniards were confabulating among themselves, making up stories and unable to admit to an inability to remember. They wove nonsensical stories of events before them, rooted in fact, using fragments of memory and sensory information.

68. Parley over: Walton, 422; Cerezo, 98.

Chapter 7: Off Beach and Bar

70. The contorted bodies: This account of the grave digging and burial along the bank of the Baler River is drawn from the seventy-page verbatim transcripts of Novicio's trial by military tribunal, held at Baler from September 25–October 2, 1901. Courts Martial transcript, Trial of Teodorico Novicio, RG 153, E 15, 23994.

71. "Captain, are we going to bury: Ibid, 7.

71. "Bury them: Ibid, 7, 11.

71. *"Agua, Amigo:* Ibid, 12.

72. "Have pity on the man: Ibid, 22.

72. "What about this man: Ibid, 8.

72. "Go on burying him: Ibid, 9.

72. Standley's report: Report by Commander Sperry to Admiral Dewey, April 20, 1899.

73. As a blood-orange sun dipped: Deck log, USS *Yorktown*, April 12, 1899.

73. "Boats waiting off beach: Sperry to Dewey, April 20, 1899, 11–12.

73. They missed every time: Ibid, 12.

74. The shots would confirm: Cerezo, 95.

74. If the Spaniards meant: Deck log, USS *Yorktown*, April 12, 1899.

74. The Spaniards climbed: Cerezo, 96.

74. The men set out: Edwards, 32.

75. The cutters were rowed: Deck log, USS *Yorktown*, April 12, 1899.

75. Both reports, delivered: Thomas to Sperry, April 13, 1899; Standley to Sperry, April 12, 1899. Charles S. Sperry Papers.

75. "The plain truth is poor Gillmore: Sperry to his wife, Edith, April 21, 1899. Charles S. Sperry Papers. Commander Sperry also expressed discomfort over the whole Baler affair, which in his mind didn't add up: *"There is something a little queer about the whole business. I do not see how the Spaniards could hold out comfortably for eight months unless they had friends and the means of outside communication. The admiral was not at all certain that they would accept deliverance by our hands. The insurgents said they had put pickets around the church but had not fired on it, though the Spaniards killed anyone who came within 60 yards."* Ibid.

75. "the most trifling assistance: Sperry to Dewey, April 20, 1899, 13. Ibid.

76. "To land eighty or ninety men: Ibid, 16.

76. Once in open water: Deck log, USS *Yorktown*, April 14, 1899.

BOOK II

Chapter 8: Sierra Madres

82. The prisoners were: Edwards, 32; Gillmore, 297; Walton, 424.

82. "swift as a mill race: Walton, 424.

82. Prodded along, the column: Edwards, 34.

83. Moving into a steeper canyon: Gillmore, 298; Walton, 424.

83. After a thoroughly unsatisfying dinner: Edwards, 33.

83. So attired, an Ilongot: Renato Rosaldo, *Ilongot Headhunting 1883–1974: A Study in Society and History* (Stanford, CA: Stanford University Press, 1980); Laurence L. Wilson, *Ilongot Life and Legends* (Manila, Philippines: Bookman, Inc., 1967); *National Geographic*, September 1912.

84. "Under other circumstances: Edwards, 33.

84. Along the trail: Lawrence R. Heaney and Jacinto C. Regalado Jr., Vanishing Treasures of the Philippine Rain Forest, The Field Museum, Chicago, Illinois (www.fieldmuseum.org).

84. Gillmore and his sailors: When the Spaniards arrived in 1521, it is estimated that 92 percent of the country's total land area was forested. Nearly four centuries of logging, using primitive and laborious techniques for lumber—at first for shipbuilding, to serve the galleon trade, and later, as vast areas were cleared for commercial crops such as abaca, a banana-like plant called "Manila hemp" and used for making rope, tobacco, and sugarcane—reduced the cover to around 70 percent by 1900. The arrival of the Americans led to new markets and the introduction of more modern and mechanized technology. By 1901, the Philippines' precious hardwood lumber commanded fourteen cents per cubic foot, triggering major investments in new logging concessions. American efforts through the post–World War II period reduced forest cover by another 10 percent, to about 60 percent. In the five decades that followed, in part driven by large timber contracts with Japan under the War Reparations Act following World War II, the granting of vast logging concessions under the Marcos regime, unsustainable clear-cutting techniques, and rampant illegal logging, the remaining forest cover was reduced by more than half, with the country's forest cover plummeting to just 25 percent total land cover. Primary, virgin, old-growth forests areas, like those found in the Sierra Madre range, were decimated to perhaps 3 percent of total land area. See David M. Kummer, *Deforestation in the Postwar Philippines* (Quezon City: Ateneo de Manila University Press, 1992); Marites D. Vitug, *Power from the Forest: The Politics of Logging* (Manila: Philippine Center for Investigative Journalism, 1993).

For a summary of the incredible biodiversity found in Luzon's rain forests, see: Cutler J. Cleveland, Ed. *Encyclopedia of Earth* (Washington, DC: Environmental Information Coalition, National Council for Science and the Environment, 2007).

85. "I sat on a boulder: Gillmore, *McClure's*, 298.

86. Within a year, Gillmore was remarried: Augustina had been raised in Trinidad, Cuba, amid the luxury of the expatriate community, whose profitable enterprises fed America's growing appetite for sugar. Her merchant father, William V. Hagner, was perhaps the grandson of Valentine Hagner, a Revolutionary War patriot and the first Treasurer of the United States.

86. Sister Annie was then born: A fairly complete picture of James C. Gillmore Sr. and his family has been reconstructed through a detailed review of the following records: Federal Census, City of Philadelphia—1850, 1860, and 1870; property deed for the Chestnut Hill residence, dated July 9, 1954; State of Pennsylvania tax assessment for James C. Gillmore, Division 7, District 2, City of Philadelphia, September 1862; United States passport certificates for James C. Gillmore, October 10, 1851, and June 30, 1870; births and deaths in the city of Philadelphia, various; James Gillmore's will and probate court reporting on the disposition of his estate; proceedings from the orphans' court on Gillmore children, May 2, 1862, through November 27, 1876; published obituaries, and site visit to Gillmore gravesites and review of burial plot map of the South Laurel Hill Cemetery, Philadelphia.

86. Supported by three Irish servants: Deed of sale for Chestnut Hill, Germantown estate to James C. Gillmore, July 1, 1857. *Smedley's Atlas of the City of Philadelphia,* (Philadelphia: J. B. Lippincott, 1862), Plate 20.

86. Three days later: Physician's certificate, Return of a death, City of Philadelphia, James C. Gillmore, February 2, 1863; Obituary, *Philadelphia Enquirer,* February 5, 1863.

87. On March 3, 1863: Physician's certificate, Return of a death, City of Philadelphia, Augustina J. Gillmore, March 3, 1863; Obituary, *Philadelphia Press,* March 6, 1863.

87. Augustina was interred: Report on Burial Lot for a Fund for its Perpetual Care, Gillmore Family, Laurel Hill Cemetery, Philadelphia, Pennsylvania. Laurel Hill Cemetery Records.

87. The family plot: Physician's certificate, Return of a death, City of Philadelphia, Florence Gillmore, August 24, 1863.

87. Luckily, their father's estate: James C. Gillmore's will; Report on accounts by Edmund Yard, administrator of the estates of James C. Gillmore and Augustina J. Gillmore, both deceased, March 6, 1863, and October 25, 1864, respectively.

87. The two older Gillmore daughters: Clara Gillmore married Lieutenant Butler Delaplaine Price on October 18, 1866. Price mustered into military service in 1861 with the 2nd Pennsylvania Volunteers, at age sixteen, and served under the command of his father, Colonel R. Butler Price, in the defense of Washington, D.C., against Confederate forces. By the time of his wedding to Clara, the twenty-one-year-old army officer was a five-year army veteran, with a bright career ahead of him that would arc with a promotion to the rank of brigadier general in later years. See: CMSR and RG 15, E 23, Pension, Butler D. Price; RG 94, E 297, 4688acp1873; RG 94, E 26, 245214.

87. Common among those of privilege: Obituary, James C. Gillmore Jr., *The P.M.C News,* Vol. 9, No. 13, June 1927.

88. Each cadet was groomed: Pennsylvania Military Academy, Chapter 6: Curriculum and Faculty 1865–1887, 117–40. See also: (1) Theodore Hyatt, President, PMA, to William Belknap, Secretary of War, regarding Articles of Assembly, October 13, 1874. PMA, RG 94, E 297, 4507acp1874; (2) PMA Academy and Chester Academy, History of Delaware County, 350–51.

88. "jabbered angrily and threw nuts: Gillmore, *McClure's,* 299.

88. "to see the terrible Americans: Walton, 424.

89. The ship dropped anchor: Deck log, USS *Yorktown,* April 17, 1899.

89. "*Couchera repecchino:* Sperry's Larrabee-coded cable to Dewey, April 17, 1899. M 625 R 369, NARA.

89. "The *Yorktown* visited Baler: Dewey cable to Washington, April 18, 1899. M 625 R 369, NARA.

91. "The Tennessee regiment here: Sperry to his wife, Edith, April 23, 1899. Charles S. Sperry Papers.

91. "Dewey's Bad News: *Washington Post,* April 19, 1899.

92. "That the capture should have been: Ibid.

Chapter 9: San Isidro

93. "all manner of names: Gillmore, *McClure's,* 301–2.

93. "Our sailormen: Ibid, 302.

94. This time, their thin charade: Albert Sonnichsen, *Ten Months a Captive among Filipinos* (New York: Charles Scribner's Sons, 1901), 8–10; Harry Huber, Personal Diary, 1–4.

94. William Bruce and Elmer Honnyman: William Bruce, born and raised in Kentucky, lived an itinerant life with his siblings as they followed their mother, Bertha, from one textile mill job to another. Saddled with a dead-beat husband, "cruel and brutle [*sic*], a heavy drinker who drank up what should have went to his familys [*sic*] support," Bertha's difficulties were compounded when he ran off to Indian Territory to marry an Indian woman. Young William Bruce moved on as soon as he could, working the mines of Coal City, Illinois, until he was caught up in the stampede west in search of a far more lucrative type of mine. Settling in a dusty little gulch in Ely, Nevada, Bruce joined a hard-scrabble band of dreamers and schemers, hoping to strike gold. At twenty-one, Bruce was engaged to a girl at the camp, but the patriotic call to "Remember the *Maine*" trumped their marital plans. See:

RG 15, E 23, Pension, William Bruce; Elmer Honnyman: CMSR, 1st Nevada Cavalry; RG 15, E 23, Pension, Correspondence, RG 94, E 25, 304377.

94. Rousted from sleep: Albert O. Bishop. RG 94, E 638. See also: Correspondence, RG, E 25 253624, Census 1880, Des Moines, Polk County, Iowa, 1885.

94. Arriving in Malolos on February 3, 1899: Sonnichsen, 71–79; Huber, 18–20; Edwards, 35.

94. There was a fifteenth man: David Brown's real name is genuinely unknown to this day. One newspaper refers to an investigation into previous charges against William for sexual assault in Minnesota: *Duluth News Tribune*, June 16, 1900. See also: "Echo of an Old Story," *Macon Telegraph*, January 9, 1900.

95. The bleary-eyed, cotton-mouthed: Sonnichsen refers to Brown as "Arnold" in his narrative, as in Benedict Arnold, for his traitorous behavior. See: Sonnichsen, 35; Huber, 9.

95. Keen to win favor: Huber, 26; Sonnichsen, 55.

95. The men quickly learned: Edwards, 40; Sonnichsen, 57.

95. "We all felt pleased: Huber, 43.

96. To secure an appointment: Those writing on behalf of Gillmore's application to the Academy included Colonel John Weiss Forney, a politically connected owner of the *Philadelphia Press* newspaper, and Pennsylvanian congressman Alfred C. Harmer, a fellow businessman. United States Naval Academy Records, James C. Gillmore Jr., RG 24, E 403, jacket 2107.

96. His oldest sister: Physician's certificate, Return of a death, City of Philadelphia, Ella Pearce, June 21, 1871.

96. An appointment letter: United States Naval Academy Records, James C. Gillmore Jr., RG 24, E 403, jacket 2107.

96. Errant behavior: Graduating first in one's class, for example, allowed a cadet to receive a promotion five years ahead of a cadet graduating in tenth place.

96. The first weeks: "Negro Cadet Issue," *New York Times*, April 9, 1922.

96. "hazing, or encouraging the hazing: US Naval Academy Register of Delinquencies, R 10, Volume 376–377, 1871–1873, M 991, NARA.

96. An investigative panel: The Board of Inquiry was headed by Lieutenant Commander Winfield Scott Schley, head of the Naval Academy's Department of Modern Languages. Ibid.

97. The ten demerits: Ibid.

97. "inattentive at dress parade: Ibid.

97. "skylarking: Ibid.

97. On November 29, 1874: United States Naval Academy Records, James C. Gillmore Jr., RG 24, E 403, jacket 2107.

99. Other letters arrived: The corrupt Cattell would later be implicated in skimming points off navy supply contracts and providing the navy secretary with a beach cottage in trendy Long Branch, New Jersey, the summer capital of Washington's leadership at the time. "The House Enquiries, The Naval Investigation," *New York Times*, May 24, 1876; "His Connection with Cattell Explained—He Knew Nothing of His Percentages Received from Contracts," *New York Times*, June 2, 1876.

99. "Mr. Gillmore lost both: James W. Paul to George Robeson, Secretary of the Navy, December 4, 1874. United States Naval Academy Records, James C. Gillmore Jr., RG 24, E 403, jacket 2107.

99. With the resulting revisions: US Naval Academy Register of Delinquencies, R 10, Volume 376–377, 1871–1873, M 991, NARA.

99. loitering in the washrooms: Ibid.

99. In 1876, Gillmore graduated: United States Naval Academy, Semi-Annual and Annual Examinations and Deficiencies, 1872–1876, James. C. Gillmore Jr., RG 24, E 406, vols. 1–3.

102. "concerning the fate of Gillmore: *San Francisco Examiner*, April 23, 1899.

102. "both the army and navy: Ibid.

102. Filipino rebel forces: Edwards, 37; Huber, 45; Sonnichsen, 182.

103. In parallel, a second division: Linn, 104–16.

103. Brevetted twice for bravery: Following decades of advocacy and campaigning, Arthur MacArthur Jr. was retroactively awarded the Congressional Medal of Honor in the 1890s for his role in "seizing the colors of his regiment at a critical moment and planting them on the captured works on the crest of Missionary Ridge" during the Civil War.

103. Despite a rather smug bearing: Linn, 208; Sexton, 37–38.

103. "every ounce of his 210 pounds: "General Lawton Killed by Filipino Bullet," *New York Times*, December 20, 1899.

103. Enlisting in the Civil War: Henry Lawton saw action at the Battle of Shiloh during the Civil War. Rising in rank to lieutenant in the 30th Indiana Infantry, Lawton won the Congressional Medal of Honor for his bravery at the Atlanta campaign, "for distinguished gallantry in leading a charge of skirmishers against the enemy's works" on August 3, 1864, and by the end of the war was a brevet colonel.

104. It was his last chance: Linn, *The Philippine War, 1899–1902*, 101–2; Sexton, *Soldiers in the Sun*, 122–24; Trask, *War with Spain in 1898,* 235–38.

104. "laden with all manner: Gillmore, 302.

104. Gillmore again opted: Sonnichsen, 182.

105. The procession tramped: Ibid, 186.

105. For the time being: Linn, 117–138; Sexton, 129–49.

107. "the same daily ration: Edwards, 38.

CHAPTER 10: A RAY OF LIGHT

109. On May 19, disease carried off: Cerezo, 104, 110.

109. As a final act: Ibid, 121.

110. All extra arms: Ibid, 123.

110. A firing line: Ibid, 124.

111. Only Cerezo knew: Ibid, 126.

111. "defended even to madness: Cerezo, 126.

111. "a ray of light: Cerezo, 127.

111. Finally, it was agreed: Ibid, 127.

111. The dazed Spaniards: Ibid, 129–30.

112. With the later addition: The number of survivors emerging from the church has been inaccurately presented in a number of sources. This math is based on an accounting that tallies with Appendix I, List of the Besieged, as provided in Cerezo, 1909.

112. An infuriated Cerezo: Minaya, Book II, 138.

113. Since Venville would not: Woodbury to Manahan, April 21, 1940, Charles F. Manahan Papers, UCSB; Statement of Orrison W. Woodbury, dictated May 4, 1940. Dudley Wright Knox Papers, MDLC.

113. "made most welcome by: Woodbury to Manahan, July 15, 1940. The startling meeting of the two American sailors and the Spanish soldiers in the church was never referenced in Cerezo's carefully constructed memoir. It begs the question: What else did Cerezo leave out of his account of the siege, and why?

113. "Here's a little unimportant thing: Woodbury to Manahan, July 15, 1940. Woodbury relates this incident to Manahan in an earlier letter as well: *"Old Bill could have given you the dope as well as I but I will give you my yarn of it. On June 6 Rynders and I were taken to the church and put up for the night with the Spanish soldiers—I think there were 20 or 30 of them. Venville, Rynders and I before this had been separated and assigned to 3 different [Filipino] families."* Woodbury to Manahan, April 21, 1940, 8. Charles F. Manahan Papers, UCSB.

114. As a result, during their march: Cerezo, 132.

114. The angry Spaniards: Ibid, 132.

114. "worthy of the admiration: Cerezo, 219.

115. Yet, despite the accolades: Cerezo provides one such article in the original Spanish version of his book, in the appendices of *El Sitio de Baler*, 263–70: "Lo de Baler," *El Noticiero de Manila*, June 3, 1899.

115. Those seeking answers: Cerezo vehemently rejected any and all doubts raised by skeptics about the siege and embarked on a four-decade-long campaign to establish his version of events as fact.

First printed in 1904, and expanded and republished thrice thereafter, through 1946, Cerezo's tome, *Under the Red and Gold,* still left many questions unanswered.

115. In the weeks that followed: A raft of news articles lauded the Spaniards' pluck and valor. Among them: "Welcomed as Heroes, Survivors of Baler Feted by Spaniards in Manila," *Washington Post,* July 8, 1899; "Honor to Baler Heroes; Spanish Club Gives Them a Banquet"; "Feast of Good Things and Patriotic Toasts," *Manila Times,* July 16, 1899; "A los de Baler," *El Imparcial,* September 6, 1899; "El Destacamento de Baler," *Le Epoca,* September 2, 1899; "Le defensores de Baler (The Minister of War lauds the survivors' valor)," *El Imparcial,* September 10, 1899; "El Medico de Baler (Dr. Vigil honored)," *El Imparcial,* September 10, 1899; and "Spaniards Brave in War," *New York Sun,* July 29, 1900.

115. "Baler was consecrated: Cerezo, 141.

Chapter 11: Prison

116. The entreaties fell: Sonnichsen, 217; Huber, 70.

116. "This, together with the ragged: Sonnichsen, 214.

116. "Help yourself: Sonnichsen, Ibid.

117. For good measure: Sonnichsen, 215.

117. Tinio's military force: Juan Villamor, *Unpublished Chronicle of the Filipino-American War* (Manila, Philippines, 1924), Part I, 37–58.

118. Dysentery, typhoid, and malaria: These prisoners probably didn't realize that in war, often more men died of dysentery than in battle. Untreated, it was deadly. During the Russo-Turkish War six decades earlier, among the 34,198 soldiers with epidemic dysentery, some 9,534 died, a mortality rate of almost 28 percent; and in the Sino-Japanese War five years earlier, the 38,094 deaths from dysentery (among 155,140 cases) represented a mortality rate of nearly 25 percent. Closer to home, 44,558 soldiers died of dysentery in the Civil War, over 4,500 alone at the Andersonville Prison in Georgia.

118. "In the daytime we had: Walton, 422.

118. Sonnichsen was the first: Typhoid was another health threat facing the prisoners, a highly contagious disease transmitted through infected feces and filth flies. It had proven to be a major killer in the Spanish-American War, debilitating 20,738 recruits, killing 1,590 men in contaminated national camps before they ever set foot on a battlefield. Starting with a prolonged fever, diarrhea, abdominal pain, and rashes, the typhoid bacterium, *B. typhosus,* could prostrate a man, push him toward delirium, and then to death. Vector-borne diseases also posed great risk, including malaria and dengue. Malaria, caused by a microscopic parasite carried by the *Anopheles* mosquito, was widespread among the prisoners, destroying blood cells and causing chills, fever, weakness, and anemia. Left untreated, it was deadly. Dengue, known as "break-bone fever," was transmitted by the *Aedes* mosquito, causing intense headaches, skin rash, and severe muscle pain, and in the worst instance, death.

118. All the men suffered: Dhobie itch, also known as jock itch, crotch rot, or by its proper medical name, *Tinea cruris,* is a fungal infection of the groin. The hot, humid environment found in the Philippines ensured that this condition was widespread in soldiers and prisoners of war alike.

118. Finally, around July 2: Sonnichsen, 217.

118. The Filipino doctor: Ibid, 220.

119. On arrival, the sailor: Ibid, 228.

119. Over the course of his two-month stay: As Sonnichsen recuperated, it must have struck him as the oddest of coincidences that he was, in fact, a second-generation prisoner of war. His father, Nicholas, a Confederate soldier with the 27th Regiment Mississippi Infantry (CSA), had been captured and incarcerated at Rock Island Prison in Illinois where he weathered the brutal winter of 1863 with twelve thousand other gaunt, starved prisoners. By the time of his release in 1865 at the war's end, having survived on rat pies and slaughtered dogs, the prisoner population was whittled down by nearly 16 percent from the ravages of influenza, smallpox, dysentery, and war wounds. See: Nicholas Sonnichsen, *Account of Imprisonment at Rock Island Prison,* Albert Sonnichsen Papers, NYPL.

120. "If that man got: Huber, 75.

120. The opportunity for sunshine: Huber, 75.

120. At Bangued, the capital: Huber, 79; Sonnichsen, 264

121. The monkey brought: Huber, 71.

121. "as he was very vain: Edwards, 40.

121. "He was a more or less: Ibid.

122. Gillmore then started: For her first years at sea, the USS *Hartford* had sailed the Cape of Good Hope and the Far East, as the flagship of the East India Squadron. At the height of the Civil War, she was known for running a gauntlet of Confederate defenses, including an assault by the ironclad ram *Manassas* and a fire-raft that nearly swept her up in flames, to help take New Orleans and Vicksburg.

122. Today, five small spits of land: Various geographical features were named after Lieutenant Commander Rockwell, Lieutenants Symonds and McClellan, Masters Hanus and Guertin, Ensigns Katz and Minett, Surgeon Ferebee, Paymaster King, 1st Marine Lieutenant Smith, Boatswain Gunner Stuart, Carpenter Martin, and Sailmaker Fassett. South of Sitka lies a deep natural port called Jamestown Bay. Their map of Sitka was published by the Coast Survey, and further data in Captain Beardslee's report was published by the Forty-Seventh Congress in 1882.

122. On May 12, 1882: Mottram Dulany Ball was a graduate of Virginia's College of William and Mary and a former Confederate colonel with the 11th Virginia Cavalry (CSA).

122. After a brief honeymoon: The USS *Iroquois,* a pre–Civil War sloop-of-war that had been recently overhauled, was notable for her participation in the massive search for the Confederate raider *Shenandoah,* which brought the 1,106-ton, 199-foot three-masted ship on a chase around the world.

122. It was largely uneventful: While at sea, Gillmore may have become aware of the ugly turn of events in Philadelphia for Edmund Yard, his father's former business partner and executor and trustee for his father's estate. Much to the surprise of the business community, Edmund Yard & Company declared bankruptcy in July 1884, with outstanding liabilities over $1 million. Among the debts: $12,522.73 borrowed by Yard from the Estate of James C. Gillmore. After thirty-two years of milking the cash cow, and amassing a fortune himself, Yard had handed over the business to his two sons, Edmund Jr. and William, who drove the enterprise—previously generating $2 million to $3 million in annual sales—directly into the ground. "With a Million in Debts," *New York Times,* July 17, 1884.

122. At the port of Colon: The Panama Railroad project was dreamed up by William H. Aspinwall, who was running the Pacific mail ships, as a scheme to manage the great uptick of traffic generated by the California gold rush in 1849. The forty-eight-mile railroad took $8 million to build, required over three hundred bridges and culverts, traversed mountains and swamps, and resulted in the loss of twelve thousand lives—workers from the United States, the Caribbean, Europe, and China—to cholera, yellow fever, malaria, accidents, and other causes. The loss averaged nine lives per day for over forty-four months of construction. The rail link at Colon was the precursor to the famed canal that would be completed in 1914.

123. Between assignments at the Bureau of Equipment: The *Vesuvius,* with a seventy-man crew, carried three fifteen-inch pneumatic guns, all mounted forward, which required the ship to be aimed, like a gun, in order to lob its five-hundred-pound nitroglycerine shells toward the enemy. The *Vesuvius* ran along the Atlantic seaboard, participated in holidays and festivals, and showed off her big, noisy, experimental guns. Ultimately, the experimental ship was deemed a failure. The pneumatic guns in her main battery had too short of a reach, at two hundred yards to one and a half miles, while the method of aiming her guns, which were not swivel-mounted, involved actually turning the ship, which was both crude and inaccurate. Worse, she was completely defenseless in retreat.

123. "rare wines, excellent brandies: "On the Slopes of an International Volcano," *New York Times,* November 11, 1906. For a description of the Shanghai Club, see: C. E. Darment, *Shanghai: A Handbook for Travellers and Residents* (Shanghai: Kelly and Walsh, 1911).

123. In a fit of cursing and invective: The officer whom Gillmore slapped was Captain Ernest Gordon of the SS *Sundra.*

124. "I must call attention: Lieutenant Gillmore to Commander Houston, USS *Machias,* November 28, 1895. Fitness Report, James C. Gillmore Jr. (Part 1, 35–36).

124. "I must plead ignorance: Lieutenant Gillmore to Commander Houston, USS *Machias,* June 30, 1896. Fitness Report, James C. Gillmore Jr. (Part 4, 7–12).

124. "the disgrace brought by: Navy Department, General Court-Martial, Order No. 77, Washington, July 29, 1896. Copy of published records in Fitness File, James C. Gillmore Jr. (Part 4, 7).

125. An exasperated Houston: Ibid, 25.

125. The *Terror* took a direct hit: Captain Charles D. Sigsbee wrote a letter to John Long, Secretary of the Navy, on August 25, 1898, favorably mentioning the officers, including Lieutenant Gillmore, who served with him on the deck of the USS *Saint Paul* while it was under torpedo attack. RG 24, E 88, 135349. Prior to this incident off San Juan, Puerto Rico, Sigsbee served as the captain of the USS *Maine,* which sank at Havana harbor following a devastating blast on the evening of February 15, 1898.

125. Gillmore, at this stage of his career: Abstracts of Service Records of Naval Officers, James C. Gillmore Jr., R 5, Vols. 8–9, M 1328, NARA.

126. The *alcalde* announced: Gillmore, *McClure's,* 402; Huber, 84; Sonnichsen, 273; Ref—Bangued relaxed confinement.

126. Within days, fourteen children: Gillmore, *McClure's,* 402; Huber, 85; Sonnichsen, 281–82, 291.

126. Suddenly, Bangued was the country's epicenter: Sonnichsen, 291.

127. "The ginger ale: "A Spanish Refugee Brings Bad News of Lieut. Gillmore and Party, Captured at Baler," *Boston Daily Globe,* September 16, 1899.

127. The rest had been waylaid: Huber, 82.

127. Dividing the provisions: Ibid, 83.

128. "But for whatever little comforts: Sonnichsen, 286–88.

128. "*But let us all be merry:* Ibid, 289–90.

129. In the early evening: Huber, 85.

129. "Clings to Prisoners; *Washington Post,* October 31, 1899.

130. The coded communication: Sonnichsen in a letter to his mother and father, November 26, 1899. Albert Sonnichsen Papers, 85 M 19. New York Public Library. Also: Sonnichsen, 305–6.

130. Alone, Sonnichsen stumbled: Sonnichsen Letter, November 26, 1899, ASP, NYPL; Sonnichsen, 309–37; Huber, 87.

131. The civilian quartermaster: Sonnichsen letter, November 26, 1899, ASP, NYPL; Sonnichsen, 338–44.

131. Slipping out of the hospital: Ibid.

131. Then, as suddenly as it had begun: Sonnichsen letter, November 26, 1899, ASP, NYPL; Sonnichsen, 354.

131. It was a message from Lieutenant Gillmore: "Report on the Capture of Vigan, P.I.," Lieutenant Alex McCracken, Commanding Officer, USS *Oregon.* RG 24, E 88, 195893. See also: Sonnichsen letter, November 26, 1899, ASP, NYPL; Sonnichsen, 355–57.

132. That night, during a hearty dinner: Sonnichsen letter, November 26, 1899, ASP, NYPL; Sonnichsen, 358–66.

132. "slept as if I had: Sonnichsen letter, November 26, 1899, ASP, NYPL.

132. "a toast to the hope: Sonnichsen letter, December 3, 1899. ASP, NYPL.

132. A fine fatted goat: Huber, 89.

133. Three men were sailors: Insurgents had raked the gunboat with enfilading gunfire, killing five men, including the ship's youthful commander, Naval Cadet Welborn Cicero Wood. The attackers took five of the crew prisoner, stripped the ship of her armaments—a one-pounder gun, a Colt Automatic, and a Nordenfeldt twenty-five-millimeter gun—and burned the ship where she lay. Separated from their comrades, the three sailors arriving at Bangued included Seaman Samuel Jones Tilden Herbert, a twenty-three-year-old from La Plata, Maryland; and two scrappy, scarred firemen who worked the ship's boilers: ruddy-faced Seaman Edward Burke, a veteran of the dockyards of Boston; and Fireman 1st Class John J. Farley, from the mean streets of Newark, New Jersey. Samuel Jones Tilden Herbert, Service Number 1765403: OMPF; Edward Burke, Service Number 1852481: OMPF; John James Farley, Service Number 1757852: OMPF.

133. A fourth sailor: Landsman Norman Godkin von Galen, from the USS *Baltimore*, had already lived a storied life. At age nine, while playing on Seattle's docks, he was unwittingly taken out to sea. Before long, the boy was put to work as a member of the crew, holystoning decks with pumice and rigging sails. The novice sailor visited Hong Kong and rounded the fierce waters off Cape Horn before returning to Seattle a year later, a seasoned mariner. He walked home and entered his house to greet his speechless parents, who were sure their ten-year-old boy was dead. As a teenager, Norman watched as his father, Otto, attempted to reclaim what was purportedly an Austrian title of nobility and a family castle worth millions. Allegedly, Otto's father was the illegitimate son of a count and had been denied his share of the family wealth. Whatever the tale, it amounted to nothing. Having tasted life at sea, von Galen later enlisted as a cabin boy in the Revenue Cutter Service, the forerunner to the modern Coast Guard, serving aboard the USS *Bear* on Bering Sea patrol. Nearly a year later, von Galen had had enough of the frozen north and enlisted as a private in the 4th Cavalry, and was discharged in Manila one year later. After kicking around the city, von Galen reenlisted for service at Cavite in August 1899, this time choosing the navy. Unpublished account of Norman Godkin von Galen's life, written by Gloria C. Morrisette, his daughter. See also: OMPF, Norman Godkin von Galen; RG 24, E 88, 206087; "Seattle Has a Family That Belongs to Nobility," *Tacoma News*, October 8, 1894.

133. The other prisoners: Private Frank Stone, Signal Corps, an articulate salesman from Sacramento, California, was jumped along the railroad tracks in a suburb of Manila after being asked for a light for a cigarette. Knocked unconscious from behind, the athletic, six-foot-one, twenty-four-year-old private was taken without a struggle. See: Frank Stone, Physical Exam of Recruit, RG 94, E 638; Enlistment Papers, RG 94, E 91b.

It was much the same for Private Archie H. Gordon, 3rd Infantry, from West End Avenue, New York City. While on duty in Baliuag, Bulacan, the stout, twenty-five-year-old, blue-eyed soldier ventured out of camp to warn nearby residents, who were seen passing signals the previous evening, that if "they didn't stop monkeying with the lights, they might get a volley some night." While returning from his foray to give this helpful advice, he was knocked on the head with a blunt instrument, rendered unconscious, and taken captive. See: Archie H. Gordon, RG 153, s18311. See also: Archie H. Gordon, Enlistment papers, RG 94, E 91b; RG 94, E 94; Archie H. Gordon, Physical Exam, RG 94, E 638.

Private James P. Curran, 16th Infantry, a semiliterate gambler and lumberman from Sheboygan, Michigan, was somehow "snapped up by a party of these sneaks within 20 yards of his own outpost." See: Gillmore, *McClure's*, 400. See also CMSR, James P. Curran, 34th Michigan Infantry; Enlistment Record; Physical Exam, RG 94, E 638.

Corporal Leland S. Smith, Signal Corps, a former lumberman from Council Bluffs, Iowa, had been tasked with photographing General Lawton's advance north. Hauling three large-format cameras and their heavy glass plates out to the front lines, Smith was fortunate to always be on the edge of the action. On one unlucky day in mid-October, however, he was caught up in the crossfire between American and Filipino positions, turned around in the ensuing confusion, and captured. See: Leland Seymour Smith, CMSR, 35th Michigan Infantry; Quarterly Return, Michigan Military Academy, RG 94, E 73; AGO 162607, which includes a nice letter from Smith's mother, Mrs. A. C. Foster, to President William McKinley, dated November 15, 1898, requesting an officer's commission for her son in order to help their financially distressed family; Physical Exam, RG 94, E 638; Enlistment Papers, RG 94, E 91b.

At least one captive had managed to wander into his own predicament: Private Martin Brennan, also with the 16th Infantry, a former miner from Mahoney Township, Pennsylvania, had joined a group of Filipinos for a drinking session while on patrol with his colleague, Corporal Calvin O. Baker. Both men soon passed out, dead drunk from the strong "vino" being served. When they awoke amid a band of insurgents, Baker panicked, attempted to flee, and was killed on the spot. Brennan, too groggy to run, survived. See: Martin Brennan: CMSR: 1st Florida Volunteer Infantry (Spanish War); Company K, 16th USVI. See also: RG 94, E 638 (physical exam); RG 391, E 1568 (history of Company K, 16th Infantry, with an account of Brennan's capture); RG 94, E 25, box 2375, 353612 (relating to the charge of desertion placed on Brennan's record following his capture); and RG 94, E 501, 660731 (statement of his military service).

Several interesting records relate to similar abductions of soldiers in Brennan's unit (some while intoxicated), and the heavy use of "vino" being sold to the men by local vendors around their camp; these records can be found in RG 391, E 1066 (Commanding Officer, Company D, 16th Infantry, requesting permission to close local liquor shops in the town of Meycauayan, Bulacan, due to the "unusual amount of drinking among the men" and the sale of the same on credit in the run-up to payday); and RG 391, E 1566, LR, with a report by Captain Lewis, 20th Infantry to Adjutant, summarizing the events behind the capture by insurgents of three 16th Infantry soldiers—Sergeant James Boyle, Company K, and privates William H. Miller and Thomas J. Daley, both Company D— who were later released. Boyle would be dead two years later, at the northern Luzon post of Aparri, due to "chronic opium poisoning."

133. As records later showed: Six generations earlier, John Sackett arrived in America as a colonist sometime around 1630, and founded the community of Westfield, Massachusetts. He oversaw its transformation from untamed wilderness to a thriving community. Three generations later, in 1779, George's great-grandfather, Buell Sackett of Sheffield, Massachusetts, was a volunteer in the 5th Regiment Continental Infantry that fought in the Revolutionary War. Buell served in the militia until 1805, retiring with the rank of a major. The Sackett military tradition continued through the Civil War, where George's father, farmer Nathan C. Sackett, enlisted at age eighteen to serve in the 97th Regiment Indiana Volunteer Infantry. See: Buell Sackett, CMSR, 5th Connecticut Regiment (Revolutionary War) and RG 15, E 23, Pension; Buell Sackett, biography in (Southern New York); Nathan C. Sackett, CMSR, 97th Indiana Infantry, and RG 15, E 23, Pension. Captain John R. M. Taylor translated captured Philippine insurgent documents that referenced Sackett's desertion and sent them to the War Department for action on February 21, 1905. RG 94, E 25, 981378.

133. Adopting an alias: Green was the son of a flamboyant pioneer of the West, Donald R. "Cannonball" Green, who operated a stagecoach line across southwestern Kansas. Running service from Kingman to Wichita, "Cannonball" Green was known for his speed; hence the nickname. His coaches were pulled by teams of six or eight horses, and changed every eight to ten miles, ensuring lightning speed. Advertising for the Cannonball Stage Line claimed even "Father Time" couldn't keep up with the "Cannonball." Green's lucrative stagecoach business flourished in the 1870s and 1880s, until the extension of the railroads destroyed his business. In 1889, Green was elected the county's first representative to the Kansas legislature.

Records of the Daughters of the American Revolution show that William Duff Green's great-grandfather, William Green, born in 1762, was a volunteer drummer recruited by his second cousin, General George Washington, and was with Washington at Valley Forge at the age of fifteen. In 1781, William Green served with General Morgan at the Battle of Cowpens. See also new accounts: "Owned Stage Coaches but Railroads Came," *The Dallas Morning News*, February 5, 1911; and US Army records. Enlistment Record, William Duff Green, 1891, RG 94, E 91b; Medical exam RG 94, E 638 (for William Duff Green); William Duff Green's apprehension for desertion, 1896: RG 94, E 25, 26666; GCM, 1896: Headquarters Department of the Missouri, SO No. 14, GCM of William Duff Green, Chicago, Illinois, January 23, 1896. RG 153, E 15, 2883; RG 15, Pension, Census Records: 1850–1930. Enlistment papers under alias Frank McDonald on February 5, 1899; Medical Exam (as Frank McDonald) RG 94, E 638.

133. The sentence was harsh: Captain C. H. Bonesteel, 21st Infantry, commanding, to Assistant Adjutant General, 3rd Brigade, 1st Division, 8th Army Corps, Manila, P.I., August 5, 1899. RG 395, E 18, Box 2. For the second general court-martial in the Philippines, including Frank McDonald's confession, August 25, 1899, see: RG 153, E 15, 13151.

133–34. The cheerful Langford: Along with three soldiers on a three-day leave, Langford had missed the last train to Manila the previous evening. The group set out to reach the sea by river on the chance they might find a sailboat heading to the capital. Two soldiers rowed the boat down the moonlit river, while Langford sat at the stern with his trusty double-action revolver—it was, he claimed, a weapon that had gotten him through Texas and Arizona with nary a scratch. Private Dunlap, 3rd Artillery, sat at the bow with his rifle. The ambush came hard and fast at three in the morning. A head shot instantly killed Dunlap, who splashed headlong into the water. The two other soldiers, Corporal Otto

Sheu and Private Charles Wilander, both with the 3rd Infantry, dove into the water with Langford and swam for the opposite shore. The *insurrectos* hunted them down, one by one. Robbed, stripped, and bound together, they were marched to Tarlac, where their fortunes changed. After meeting with Aguinaldo, they were clothed and issued a daily per diem. Over time, a number of American soldiers, including Sheu and Wilander, were brought south and traded with the US Army for their own comrades as part of prisoner exchanges. Langford, a civilian of limited value, had been held behind.

For an account of the attack, see "He Speaks Well of Aguinaldo," *New York Journal,* October 24, 1899. One of Corporal Otto Sheu's captors, Mariano Sandel, who *"threatened to kill him, spat on him, and struck him,"* was convicted of the abduction and sentenced to pay a fine of $500 Mexican and confined in prison for one year at hard labor. Report of the Judge at the Provost Court, Malabon, P.I., February 18, 1900. RG 395, E 18.

For background on Langford: "With Gillmore Party, Story of an American Volunteer who Painted Signs on Cliffs," *Dallas Morning News,* December 5, 1902; Edwards, 52; Huber, 90.

134. In fact, Baker had gone: Records relating to Charles Baker's death, RG, E 25, 305567; Enlistment, RG 94, E 25, 203692; CMSR, Company A, 14th Pennsylvania Infantry; Medical Exam, RG 94, E 638.

134. The column's load lightened: In a report by Captain E. M. Lewis, Adjutant, 20th Infantry, information and corroboration of the death of Private Charles Baker by bayonet were provided by fellow prisoners Langford and McDonald during their debriefings, as well as by unnamed Spanish prisoners. Langford directly implicated General Tinio in the murder, adding "the General himself rode back and killed Baker." Other informants provided details into the soldier's abduction and captivity. To add weight to the argument that Baker did not voluntarily desert his regiment, fellow captives added that when offered a captaincy in the Army of Liberation by his captors, Baker reportedly replied that "he would not fight for a nigger." Baker's body was never recovered. Memorandum in the Case of Charles Baker, Private of Battery L, 3rd US Artillery, RG 94, E 25, 305567.

CHAPTER 12: THE CENTER OF GRAVITY

135. "Rebel Brutes": *Los Angeles Times,* May 24, 1899.

135. On August 16, 1899, the *New York Times* broke: "In Filipino Prisons," *New York Times,* August 16, 1899.

136. During this rain-swept lull: The declaration of war against Spain, and the patriotic fervor sweeping the United States following the sinking of the USS *Maine* at Havana, led to the rapid creation of some 212 infantry, artillery, and battery units, drawn from 45 states, the District of Columbia, and the territories, the latter covering Arizona, Oklahoma, Indian Territory, and New Mexico. Only a fraction of the volunteer forces—a third of the units created—departed from US soil, and the majority went to Cuba and Puerto Rico. Only 16 of the 212 units were deployed in the Philippines, given the brevity of the conflict: the 1st California and California Artillery; 1st Colorado; 1st Idaho; 51st Iowa; 20th Kansas; 13th Minnesota; 1st Montana; 1st Nebraska; 1st Troop, Nevada Cavalry; 10th Pennsylvania, 1st South Dakota; Utah Artillery; 1st Washington; and the 1st Wyoming and Wyoming Light battery. Of the 183,687 men mustered into service for the Spanish-American War, only 208 were killed in action; with 169 killed in other ways, the average volunteer had about an even (and remote) chance of being killed on the battlefield as dying from drowning, an accident, suicide, or being murdered. By far, the greatest risk was death due to disease, which killed 3,948, twenty times the number killed in the fighting. Another 3,069 deserted, representing 1.7 percent of the American forces. Synthesis of material found in "Statistical Exhibit of Strength of Volunteer Forces Called into Service during the War with Spain," Adjutant General's Office, Government Printing Office, 1899. Calculations are based on the author's own math.

136. With a decisive victory: For a full discussion, see Stuart Creighton Miller, *Benevolent Assimilation: American Conquest of the Philippines* (New Haven, CT: Yale University Press, 1982); Linn, 3–25; Nugent, 265–73.

137. MacArthur's men would then advance: Sexton, 174; Linn, 139–59.

137. They had covered: Linn, 114; Sexton, 176–80.

137. Enlisting as a sergeant: In that fight, Wheaton sprang through an embrasure against strong fire of artillery and musketry and was the first to enter the enemy's works.

138. At the outbreak of war: Linn, 93; Sexton, 105–6.

138. As a young lieutenant: The incident at Colfax was, in fact, a pitched battle between blacks and whites following a disputed electoral contest for governor, leading to the mass killing of black prisoners.

138. In 1876, Hare survived: Hare, a scout in Major Marcus Reno's Battalion, was engaged in violent fighting during the subsequent retreat and was commended for his bravery.

138. In that engagement, with Reno's battalion: Interview with Frederick Benteen, *Atlantic Journal*, May 24, 1897; Charles K. Mills, *Harvest of Barren Regrets: The Army Career of Frederick William Benteen, 1834–1898* (Glendale, CA: Arthur H. Clark, 1985), 261; Nathaniel Philbrick, *The Last Stand*, (New York: Viking, 2010), 197.

138. A year later, Hare joined: At the Battle of Canyon Creek, the 7th Cavalry attempted but failed to subdue bands led by Chiefs Looking Glass and Joseph, who had earlier abducted and killed several tourists at Yellowstone National Park.

138. Over the years, Hare: Luther Rector Hare: CMSR, 1st Texas Cavalry; CMSR, 33rd US Volunteer Infantry; RG 94, E 297, 3587acp1875; RG 92, E 273; RG 94, E 25, 257793 and 129532; RG 15, E 23, Pension.

139. By the time the first landing: Sexton, 188–89.

139. Found within them: Ibid, 180.

140. Young's proposal was unconventional: Ibid, 181.

140. At the end of the Civil War: Samuel Baldwin Marks Young: Sexton, 176–77; United States Army biography (www.history.army.mil/books/cg&csa/Young-SBM.htm).

140. Infantry on foot: Sexton, 183–84.

142. Above all, they were hungry: Ibid, 185.

142. On November 11, eleven companies: Ibid, 189.

142. One battalion, led by Major Marcus D. Cronin: Harper's, 306–7; Sexton, 189; "The Battle at San Jacinto," *New York Times*, December 28, 1899.

143. Awarded the Congressional Medal of Honor: Unschooled until age fourteen, John Logan rose to become a successful lawyer and friend of young Abraham Lincoln. He entered politics as a Jacksonian Democrat and was elected to Congress twice. At the outbreak of the Civil War, Lincoln authorized Logan to raise his own regiment of Union troops, the 31st Regiment Illinois Volunteers, which fought in eight campaigns. A well-regarded Republican in later years with an adoring public following, Logan narrowly lost a vice presidential bid.

143. Credited with establishing Decoration Day: So beloved was General John A. Logan that upon his death, Congress authorized a lifetime pension for his wife, Mary, in the amount of $2,000 annually. Since then, General John A. Logan's achievements as a patriot and hero have been honored with equestrian statues in Chicago's Grant Park and Washington, D.C.'s, Logan Circle, and his name has been bestowed on several streets, boulevards, and neighborhoods, schools and a college, one county in Kansas, a National Guard Base and rifle range, and a US Navy transport ship. Primary sources: CMSR, John A. Logan, 31st Illinois Infantry (Civil War), including casualty sheet for wounds incurred during Siege of Fort Donelson; CMSR, John A. Logan, Company H, 1st Illinois Infantry (Mexican War); RG 15, E 23, Pension. See also a detailed biography posted at the John A. Logan Museum's website at www.loganmuseum.org.

143. On November 10, 1884, faced with dismissal: Court-martial of John A. Logan Jr. at West Point, August 12, 1884. RG 153, rr473. The story of Logan's first court-martial was also covered in the media: "General Logan's Son Acquitted," *New York Times*, August 22, 1884. Court-martial of John A. Logan at West Point, November 5, 1884 (recommendation for dismissal and subsequent resignation). RG 153, E 15, RR-605.

143. Three years later, Logan married: Wealthy Republicans in Ohio pushed to have Chauncey H. Andrews, "worth not less than $2.5 million," run for the state's highest office: "The Ohio

Governorship," *New York Times*, April 1, 1883. His will listed $3 million in assets: "Chauncey Andrews Will Probated," *New York Times*, January 4, 1894.

143. At the age of twenty-three: See the biographical sketch of John A. Logan Jr. in Edwin C. Hill, *The Historical Register: Biographical Record of Men of Our Time who Have Contributed to the Making of America* (New York: Edwin C. Hill, 1919).

143. The shadow of his father's legacy: Logan raised his own unit in the state militia, called the "Logan Rifles," and paraded about in a red-jacketed outfit described as a "jazzier uniform than even the United States Marines." See: History of Youngstown College, Youngstown State University Oral History program, Harriet Wick Schaff to Randall Dicks, February 28, 1974.

When his son John A. Logan III was born, Logan Jr. had the child commissioned in the unit as a first lieutenant at the age of six weeks, perhaps the only infant ever to serve his country in a military capacity. See: *Poughkeepsie Daily Eagle*, March 24, 1890.

144. On August 17, 1899, the War Department: Ibid.

144. "a certain class of men: Letter from 1st Sergeant R. Stanley Clarke, Company L, 33rd Infantry, to his family, June 7, 1900. John A. Logan Museum.

144. "Go for them, men: Account of the Battle at San Jacinto, entitled "The Gillmore Expedition," written by Sergeant Major Albert E. Gebert, 33rd Infantry. Charles F. Manahan Papers, UCSB.

144. "Look in the trees: Gebert, 4.

145. "instantly killed by a missile: John A. Logan Jr.: CMSR, RG 15, E 23, Pension.

145. The surgeon called: Born in Berlin, Germany, Oscar H. Mercier had married his sweetheart Otillie at age twenty and immigrated to Louisiana with his bride. She gave him four children—Clara, Mamie, and Gus, and a fourth child whose name is not in the records, whose birth cost Otillie her life. In 1883, at twenty-seven, like many women of her time, the mother succumbed to puerperal septicemia, a deadly genital tract infection caused by a lack of hygiene while giving birth. Mercier remarried four years later, to Martha Sego of Mammoth Cave, Kentucky, and a year later, Oscar Jr. was born. Sadly, their second child didn't survive, and the failed birth triggered another case of puerperal fever, which took the young mother's life. With five children ranging in ages from four to twenty, Mercier tried one final union, marrying Gertrude Walker in January 1895, and added a sixth child, Harold, to their brood. Unable to support his large family on his meager earnings as a real estate agent, Mercier seized the opportunity to enlist and was shipped to the Philippines. Oscar Mercier: CMSR, 33rd Volunteer US Infantry; RG 15, E 23, Pension.

145. "knocking them out of: "The Fight near San Jacinto," *New York Times*, December 28, 1899.

145. "water-soaked rice fields: Ibid.

145. A thirty-year-old sergeant: Lovel E. Casteel: CMSR, Company H, 33rd UVI.

145. Another private was luckier: Lazaro Castillo: CMSR, Company E, 33rd USVI.

146. Losses included Major Logan: Return of Casualties, 33rd Infantry, at San Jacinto, P.I., November 11, 1899; Linn, 151.

146. Throughout the night, Aguinaldo: Sexton, 186; Wolf, 288; Robert D. Ramsey III, "Savage Wars of Peace: Case Studies of Pacification of the Philippines, 1900–1902." Long War Series Occasional Paper No. 24 (Fort Leavenworth, Kansas: Combat Studies Institute Press, 2007), 23–25.

147. "The only reason that the guide: Sexton, 187.

147. "Oh yes, he was there: Ibid.

148. A company of soldiers: Balete Pass was the site of fierce fighting between Japanese and American forces, being one of the remaining strongholds in Luzon of the Japanese Imperial Army during the liberation period in 1945. The pass was renamed Dalton Pass, in honor of Brigadier General James Dalton II, who was killed by a sniper's bullet on May 16, 1945, while leading thousands of Filipino and American soldiers in pursuit of Japanese forces retreating toward northeast Luzon. The fall of Balete Pass further weakened the Japanese forces, paving the way for the surrender of General Tomoyuki Yamashita, commander of the Japanese Imperial Army, in Kiangan, Ifugao, and the eventual liberation of the Philippines from Japanese occupation in 1945.

148. At some point, the mission failed: On January 28, 1899, Aram K. D. Minassian enlisted as a hospital corpsman and arrived in the Philippines on the USS *Relief* that following March. Gifted as a linguist and conversant in nine languages, the dark-haired private had been pulled out of the Hospital Corps by General MacArthur, first serving as an interpreter, and then, pressed into the US Army's "Secret Service" as an American spy. Private Aram K. D. Minassian to Adjutant General, US Army, San Fernando, P.I., August 29, 1899. RG 395, E 13. Minassian's enlistment record, January 28, 1899: RG 94, E 91b. Minassian's physical examination: January 27, 1899. RG 94, E 638.

148. Canon, the son of a watchmaker: For a biography of Fernando Canon, see: Carlos Quirino, *Who's Who in Philippine History* (Manila: Tahanan Books, 1995).

149. On November 28, Munro: Statement on Private Aram K. D. Minassian by 2nd Lieutenant James N. Munro, 4th Cavalry, February 27, 1900. RG 94, E 25, 82117.

149. The successful ruse: Letter certifying Aram K. D. Minassian's exploits at Bayombong, issued by Don Antonio Sastre y Rameres, Spanish Army Major and former Spanish Governor of Nueva Vizcaya, November 30, 1899. RG 94, E 25, 82117.

149. two *Yorktown* sailors: Woodbury recalled his fellow prisoners at Bayombong: *"With us were at the last 12 or 14 other Americans of various ranks—privates, civilians, teamsters and a kid mascot from one of the Western States Regiments—I think it was Kansas."* Woodbury to Manahan, April 21, 1940, 10; Woodbury to Manahan, June 26, 1940, 5.

149. "the natives of this province: Woodbury to Manahan, 8. April 21, 1940. Charles F. Manahan Papers, UCSB.

149. "That old pirate Rynders: Ibid, 7–8.

149. On December 2, 1899: Ibid, 8.

149. A rail-thin Woodbury tipped: Ibid, 9.

150. "feeding up & drinking bottled beer: Ibid, 9.

Chapter 13: Pursuit

151. Having advanced almost 150 miles: The events that follow draw upon, in part, original entries made in the record of events of the 33rd and 34th Infantries. These include (i) Captions, Records of Events, and Casualties for the 33rd USVI, including a comprehensive report from Colonel Hare to Adjutant General, District of Northwestern Luzon, Vigan, P.I., dated March 1900, which covers regimental events from November 16, 1899, to January 5, 1900; and individual records for Companies E, F, G, H; and (ii) Captions, Records of Events, and Casualties for the 34th USVI, including a report filed by Colonel Kennon on March 29, 1900; and individual records for Companies A, B, C, D, E, F, G, H, I, L, and M. See also: Sexton, 201; Linn, 154.

151. "to prevent the uniting: Sexton, 201.

151. "was too small to allow: Ibid, 203.

151. "I need forces but: Ibid, 203.

152. One of Young's officers: Ibid.

152. In a joint assault: Ibid.

152. The column arrived: The town of Namacpacan, La Union, has since been renamed Luna.

152. "My forces are much depleted: Sexton, 204.

153. Without General Otis's approval: Ibid. James Parker: CMSR, Staff, 45th USVI.

153. Once the smoke cleared: Sonnichsen, 353–57.

153. The Astor Battery: Astor, worth an estimated $100 million to $200 million at the time, was the wealthiest victim of the *Titanic* disaster on April 15, 1912. As legend has it, after the ship hit the iceberg, Astor quipped, "I asked for ice, but this is ridiculous." "Noted Men Lost on Titanic," *New York Times*, April 16, 1912.

153. The unit attracted: Astor Battery, RG 159, E 9; Casualty Reports, RG 94, E 662.

154. Although forty of his men had dropped: Sexton, 296.

154. For this effort, Howze: The twenty other Medals of Honor, awarded to Colonel Forsyth and his men for their actions at Wounded Knee two days earlier, remain a point of debate and subject to a recall movement by Native Americans. For Robert L. Howze: CMSR, 34th US Volunteer Infantry; RG 94, E297, 3965acp1888; Biography at Committee on Veterans Affairs, United States

Senate, Medal of Honor Recipients, 1863–1973 (Washington: GPO, 1973); Veterans Administration Records, WNRC Request.

154. "President wires me: Telegram from Oyster Bay, New York, dated July 6, 1899, from Theodore Roosevelt to Captain Robert L. Howze. RG 94, E 297, 3965acp1888.

154–55. Separately, it was reported, Tinio's Brigade: The account at Tangadan Pass draws on Julius A. Penn's *A Narrative of the Campaign in Northern Luzon, P.I.* (Privately printed, 1933); and Juan Villamor's unpublished account, "Guerra Americano-Filipino" (Manila, 1924).

156. Young, with Howze's battalion: Sexton, 206.

156. For three hours, the flanking force: Major Peyton March's account of the Battle at Tirad Pass, Headquarters 2nd Battalion, 33rd Infantry, December 8, 1899. RG 94, E 25, 99769. See also: Sexton, 207; Linn, 156; Villamor, 37–43, 53–57.

157. From this vantage point, Tompkins: Lieutenant Frank Dean Tompkins; CMSR, RG 94, E 25, 99769. In one recommendation for his military appointment, a family friend employed with the IRS wrote, "He is a fine specimen of physical manhood and a most intelligent man of high moral character. ... He is a fine businessman and has had large interests entrusted to him in a business way." That reputation would be in tatters by 1903, when, as treasurer and internal revenue collector for the province of La Union, Tompkins faced nine criminal cases for forgery and theft of public monies, and faced a term of seventeen years in prison. See: *Manila Times*, September 11 and September 25, 1903.

157. Despite a five-to-one advantage: The two American soldiers killed at the battle of Tirad Pass were Privates Henry F. Hill and John W. Joyner, Company G, 33rd US Volunteer Infantry. RG 94, E 527, 33rd USVI Summary Cards.

157. Yet, March's men spilled over: American soldiers wounded at Tirad Pass included Elmo Crawford, with gunshot wounds to the head and right shoulder, and Chester L. Kilpatrick, with a bullet wound in the abdomen. Six others were wounded less seriously, including two sergeants, Marvin P. Hughes and Henry J. Smith, each with wounds to their left feet, and Corporal Harry D. Brown, with a gunshot to the groin. RG 94, E 527, 33rd USVI Summary Cards.

158. "resting the men and sifting: Major Peyton March's account of the Battle at Tirad Pass, Headquarters 2nd Battalion, 33rd Infantry, December 8, 1899. RG 94, E 25, 99769.

158. The precious day's delay: Ibid.

158. With his forces out of steam: Ibid.

159. Unknown to Young at the time: Penn, 8–12.

159. At that pace, they aimed: Colonel Hare's eight staff officers were Lieutenant Colonel John J. Brereton, a quiet and unassuming officer who had led the 24th Infantry, a regiment of African Americans, at posts across the West just as the Indian Wars on the south plains were coming to a close; Major Marcus Daniel Cronin, a tall, lanky native of Worcester, Massachusetts, who, as a former instructor of Spanish and French at the Academy, was more of a lecturer than a warrior; a newly minted major, Edgar Alexander Sirmyer, of Bay City, Michigan, who had just jumped a grade with Logan's untimely passing; Major (and Surgeon) Albert Lieberman, a slight, 137-pound physician from Kansas City, Missouri, and the only Jewish officer of the regiment; Captain (and Surgeon) Frederick Hadra, a Berlin-born, bearded and bespectacled physician from San Antonio, Texas; Captain James Burroughs, a practicing attorney from Houston; and two lieutenants, Tilman Campbell, a former assistant cashier at the Bank of Augusta, Arkansas; and Hugh Williams, former bookkeeper from Louisiana.

John J. Brereton: CMSR, 33rd USVI; RG 94, E 297, 2078acp1880; RG 15, E 23, Pension.

Marcus D. Cronin: CMSR, 33rd USVI, RG 92, E 256.

Edgar A. Sirmyer: CMSR, 33rd USVI; RG 92, E 256, rp696713.

B. Albert Lieberman: CMSR, 33rd USVI; CMSR, 3rd Missouri Infantry (Spanish War); RG 94, E 501, 658188.

Frederick Hadra: CMSR, 33rd USVI; CMSR, 1st Texas Cavalry (Spanish War); Texas AGO 8495; RG 94, E 561, rp656450.

James M. Burroughs: CMSR, 33rd USVI; CMSR, 1st Texas Cavalry (Spanish War); Texas AGO 2961; RG 92, E 256; RG 94, E 25, 171494.

Tilman Campbell: CMSR, 33rd USVI; CMSR, 2nd Arkansas Infantry (Spanish War); RG 92, E 256; RG 94, E 25, 168616 and 1297997; RG 94, E 501, 674431 and 73606.

Hugh Williams: CMSR, 33rd USVI; CMSR, 2nd Louisiana Infantry (Spanish War); Summary Card.

159. The *New York Times* ran: "Was Logan Killed by His Men?," *New York Times*, December 14, 1899.

159. Widowed twice and left: In 1886, at the age of twenty-seven, John J. Brereton married Nettie Bullis. Their first child, Alice Eleanor, was born at Fort Supply, Indian Territory, a year later. At their next post outside Silver City, New Mexico, tragedy struck: Nettie lost their second child at birth. The event affected her deeply—a year and a half later, she too was dead, recorded at the time as "nervous prostration following miscarriage." The loss left Brereton on his own, to raise two-year-old Alice. To cope with the new responsibility, he asked to be reassigned closer to home, to New Jersey, where he settled with his daughter and served as a professor of military science and tactics at Rutgers College. Ten months later, Brereton married a divorcee with two sons, Minnie Denslow, and adopted her two teenage sons, Edwin and fifteen-year-old Tallmadge, who was studying at the New York Military Academy at Cornwall-on-Hudson. The semblance of normality, however, was short-lived. Minnie died of Bright's disease—kidney failure—fifteen months later, in July 1893.

Edwin Porter Denslow and Tallmadge Hepburn Denslow both petitioned the court to change their names to Brereton on May 31, 1892, just one month after their mother's marriage to John James Brereton. See: Laws of the State of New York (116th Legislature), Volume 2 (Albany, NY: James B. Lyon Printers, 1893), 1886.

160. The pain, headaches, and severe discomfort: The bouts of optic neuritis never ceased for the pain-wracked Brereton. Seemingly triggered by severe stress or physical exertion—essential factors related to his work—they required lengthy sick leaves, anywhere from two to six months. These occurred in 1877 after graduation, in 1881 while campaigning in Indian Territory, in 1891 after his first wife's death, and in 1898, following his wounding at Santiago. Despite this medical constraint, and perhaps due to his well-educated and serious demeanor, Brereton moved up through the ranks. He was appointed lieutenant colonel in July 1899 and reported to Fort Sam Houston, Texas, before sailing to the Philippines. John J. Brereton: CMSR, 33rd USVI; RG 15, E 23, Pension; RG 94, E 297, 2078acp1880; RG 94, E 502, 630534.

160. "beyond a doubt: Major B. Albert Lieberman, Surgeon, 33rd Infantry to President, Board of Officers, February 4, 1900, Vigan Luzon. RG 15, E 23, Pension, Lieutenant Colonel John. J. Brereton, 33rd Infantry, RG 94, E 297, 2078acp1880.

160. They found Brereton: Ibid.

161. "raised Cain: Handwritten letter from Major B. Albert Lieberman to Colonel Luther Hare, December 2, 1899, while at San Tomas. RG 395, E 20.

161. At 5:50 a.m., as the tropical sun began: RG 15, E 23 Pension, John J. Brereton.

Chapter 14: Buying Time

162. More beguiling to Young, the report: Captions and Records of Events, Companies E, F, G, H, 33rd USVI; Record of Events, 34th USVI, Report filed March 29, 1900, by Colonel Kennon, Commanding, Regimental Papers; Gebert, 5; Sexton, 206.

162. The interconnected labyrinth: This description of the Tangadan Pass defenses was provided in a report written by Lieutenant Colonel Robert L. Howze to Adjutant, 34th Infantry, Vigan, P.I., January 7, 1900. Charles F. Manahan Papers, Huntington Library.

162. In any event, if the approaching Americans: Ochosa, 81–83; Sexton, 210.

163. In his late twenties, Villamor: Juan Villamor, *Unpublished Chronicle of the Filipino American War* (Manila, Philippines, 1924), Part I, 42. This detailed account of the battles in northern Luzon was written by Blas Villamor's older cousin, Juan Villamor, who was serving, ostensibly, as the director to the Abra Red Cross at the time. Just as educated as his cousin, Juan Villamor had attended the San Juan de Letran College in Manila, where he earned his law degree, and had worked in the courts in Ilocos Sur and Abra until he was banished to Bangued by the Spanish governor-general Weyler in

1890. Forced to join the Spanish Army during the Revolution of 1896, Juan Villamor was captured by the *insurrectos* at Bataan. Later, in order to be useful to the revolution, he was ordered by Apolinario Mabini, the intellect behind Aguinaldo's movement, to join the editorial staff of *El Heraldo de la Revolucion*, a newspaper being published in Malolos. Following the fall of Tarlac to the Americans on November 12, 1899, Juan Villamor escaped north toward his home province and joined forces with Tinio. See also: Orlino A. Ochosa, *The Tinio Brigade*, 60.

163. They were to attack the Americans: Villamor, 43–53; Ochosa, 85–88; Sexton, 209.

163. In sum, the American force at Vigan: The events at the Battle of Vigan are drawn from (i) official report by Lieutenant Marcus Cronin, 33rd Infantry to Lieutenant Colonel James Parker, 45th Infantry, January 29, 1900 (in Villamor); (ii) the firsthand account in the memoir: James Parker, *The Old Army* (Philadelphia: Dorrance & Company, 1929), 274–95; (iii) Case of Webb C. Hayes, Application for Congressional Medal of Honor, RG 94, E 25, 79214. See also: Sexton, 209; Harper's History, 321.

164. On the periphery of the plaza: Arthur Wright, a twenty-four-year-old engineer from Iowa, was killed. Arthur Wright: Summary Card, RG 94, E 527.

164. He was killed instantly: Norman M. Fry: CMSR, Company L, 33rd Infantry; CMSR, Company C, 160th Indiana Infantry (Spanish War); RG 94, E 501, 694925.

164. Hearing that Epps required reinforcements: A Board of Officers convened at Manila in 1901, comprised among others of Major Generals Bates and Wheaton, and Brigadier General Funston, which recommended that Epps only be given a certificate of merit for distinguished gallantry at Vigan; this was overridden by Washington, and Epps was awarded the Medal of Honor in 1902. Joseph L. Epps: Summary Card, Company B, 33rd USVI; RG 94, E 25, 345788.

The soldier assisting Epps was Private William O. Trafton. William O. Trafton: Summary Card, Company B, 33rd USVI.

165. "to hold that position: Lieutenant Colonel Parker, 5th Endorsement, Recommendation of Certificate of Merit for Private John A. Weimer, Nueva Caceres, P.I., March 20, 1900. RG 94, E 25, 441268.

165. With his blazing rifle: At any time, Weimer could have retreated to a more-defensive position, especially as half of his sixteen or so comrades engaged in the firefight at the hospital were killed, but then he would have given up his advantageous point of fire. For Weimer's "conspicuous bravery," he was recommended by both his regimental commander, Colonel Hare, and the commanding officer at Vigan during the firefight, Lieutenant Colonel James Parker, for a Medal of Honor, but the recommendation was downgraded to a Certificate of Merit by an Army review board that convened in Manila on November 15, 1900. While issued in Washington, the certificate never reached the soldier, as his home address was not on file. When Weimer wrote to request the certificate in December 1902, the army bureaucracy noted the downgraded recommendation lacked a "legal basis," as it did not derive from the commanding officer, and requested a further review by the War Department. On February 2, 1903, George Davis, the judge advocate general, determined that the Certificate of Merit had been incorrectly issued and that Weimer should instead be given a Medal of Honor, as "there seems to be no question that the act of gallantry was performed." The Medal of Honor and Certificate of Merit Board in Washington reviewed the issue further, and on March 19, 1904, disapproved both the already-awarded Certificate of Merit, and the properly recommended Medal of Honor application, determining "the conduct of this soldier was not distinguished in the sense contemplated by the regulations as justifying the granting of a certificate of merit or medal of honor. He was simply doing his duty." In the end, Weimer was given nothing. John A. Weimer: CMSR, Company B, 33rd USVI; Summary Card; CMSR, Company F, 21st Kansas Infantry (Spanish War); RG 15, E 23, Pension; Case of John A. Weimer, Subject: Propriety of the issue of the certificate of merit award to this soldier for distinguished bravery in action at Vigan, Philippine Islands, December 4, 1899, RG 94, E 501, 703560, dated December 18, 1902.

165. "fought for hours, lying: Medal of Honor citation, Medal of Honor Recipients: Philippine-American War, James McConnell Center for Military History, United States Army. James McConnell: CMSR, Company B, 33rd USVI, Summary Card, RG 94, E 527.

165. Finally, the Americans decided: The other American soldiers killed at Vigan on December 4, 1899, included Sergeant Frederick J. Bell, a thirty-two-year-old soldier from San Antonio, Texas, who left behind his wife of one year, Teresa Lopez; Sergeant Lawrence L. Spencer, a farmer from Alabama;

Corporal Alfred P. Wachs, a German-born butcher; Private James A. Bennett, a railroad man from Arkansas; Private William Brandon, a farmer from Oklahoma Territory; and Private Dale Puckett, a bridge builder from Texas. Most had served just four months, and nearly all were in their twenties.

Frederick J. Bell: Summary Card, RG 15, E 23, Pension.

Lawrence L. Spencer: Summary Card, RG 95, E 527.

Alfred P. Wachs: Summary Card, RG 95, E 527.

James Bennett: Summary Card, RG, E 527.

William N. Brandon: Summary Card, RG, E 527.

Dale Puckett: Summary Card, RG, E 527.

165. **Another three American soldiers:** The three wounded privates included William H. Bostwick, an electrician from Michigan; John Patterson, a farmer from Kentucky; and Fred W. Loyeaa, a farmer from Michigan. The unmarried, twenty-eight-year-old Loyeaa seemed to have the worst of it. At Vigan, he received two severe gunshot wounds to his left leg, one bullet entering through the calf, severing the plantaris tendon, and another entering through the middle of the inner thigh, exiting four inches higher on the outside. Recommended for special mention for gallantry, Loyeaa arrived aboard the USS *Relief* hospital, which anchored off Vigan, on December 7, 1899, with both wounds infected. These were cleaned and slowly healed. The battle, however, left the young private severely traumatized, and his mental state failed. Diagnosed with "acute dementia," Loyeaa was shipped home to the United States in October 1900, to be admitted into the Government Hospital for the Insane at Washington, D.C. Subject to "epileptic fits" and "incoherent statements with periods of emotional disturbance," Loyeaa spent most of his time in a "sluggish mental state, [with] no interest in his surroundings." Discharged on January 16, 1901, with a certificate of disability, Fred Loyeaa apparently never recovered from the mental trauma and post-traumatic stress from the Battle of Vigan. He died of tuberculosis on January 8, 1908, while at the soldiers' home in Marion, Grant County, Indiana, at the age of thirty-three.

Fred W. Loyeaa: Summary Card, RG 94, E 527; CMSR, Company E, 33rd USVI.

William H. Bostwick: Summary Card, RG 94, E 527.

John Patterson: Summary Card, RG, E 527.

165. **Over the course of the bloody morning:** For their distinguished gallantry at Vigan, Parker and two privates—McConnell and Epps—received the Congressional Medal of Honor. Quartermaster Sergeant Norman M. Fry, the ailing ammo runner killed at the balustrade, was also recommended for a Congressional Medal of Honor by his superiors. Still wearing his bloodied uniform and wrapped in his blanket, Fry was buried in grave #6, plot #1, at the newly established soldiers' cemetery in Vigan. The contents of his pockets—a purse containing $2 Mexican and a few copper coins and a string of beads—were forwarded up the chain of command and then sent to his wife, Delia, in Syracuse. However, without sponsors to argue his case, as well as a prohibition at the time on the awarding of medals posthumously, Fry's heroism at Vigan was never formally recognized.

A fourth hero of sorts stumbled onto the scene, eleven hours after the battle. At age forty-three, the tenacious Lieutenant Colonel Webb C. Hayes, 31st Infantry, Cornell dropout and presidential son, was now serving as a "freelance" staff officer. Hearing the city was under attack, Hayes had rushed to Vigan, and was in the palace by 9:00 p.m., typing an urgent letter to the commander of the ship that had delivered him, asking for reinforcements. For undertaking what the commander of the *Princeton* described as "the coolest and nerviest bits of work we saw, hazardous but not foolhardy," and by Young as "the chivalrous and daring action . . . in pushing through the enemy lines alone . . . from the beach to our crippled force in Vigan, to ascertain their conditions and needs," Hayes—who arrived half a day too late to the party—was awarded the Congressional Medal of Honor.

See: Personal letter from Henry Knox, Commanding Officer, USS *Princeton*, in Shanghai, China, to Brigadier General Young, October 29, 1900, at Vigan; Brigadier General Young's Report on Hayes to AGO, November 15, 1900. RG 94, E 25, 355740. Medal of Honor Recipients: Philippine-American War, James McConnell, Center for Military History (CMH), United States Army.

166. **Despite his rich experience, Penn:** Julius A. Penn: CMSR, 33rd USVI; RG 94, E 297, 3762acp1886; Summary Card, RG 94, E 527; biography: "In Memoriam, 1934," Charles F. Manahan Papers, Huntington Library.

The balance of Howze's company commanders and junior officers were a cast of characters drawn from civilian life. Captain Frank G. Russell, Company F commander, a thirty-six-year-old carpenter from Concord, New Hampshire, had worked as a clerk in a railroad office, as a businessman and a civil engineer, and finally, as a building contractor, which took him west to Arizona and then into the army. Under Russell were two lieutenants: Wilson G. Heaton, a thirty-one-year-old traveling salesman from Glasgow, Iowa; and Denny Verdi, a twenty-four-year-old from Washington, D.C. Captain Christopher J. Rollis, commanding Company G, a Norwegian immigrant, had previously enjoyed an uneventful eight-month tour with the 4th Wisconsin Volunteer Infantry Regiment.

Supporting Rollis was Lieutenant Stewart M. Decker, a lawyer from Pennsylvania whose claim to fame was his work sixteen years earlier as one of the first professional baseball umpires for the National League. Decker officiated at over a hundred games through three seasons, but by his third season, the job had turned sour, with an unforgiving sports press brutally excoriating his bad judgment and alleging that he threw games. In one contest in Providence, Decker required a police escort to leave the field. In his final game, he was booed by the crowd and, in the ninth inning, he was pelted with seat cushions launched from the bleachers.

Finally, there was Captain Frank L. French, the commander of Company H, a merchant from Sparta, Wisconsin.

Frank G. Russell: CMSR, 34th USVI; CMSR, 1st Territorial USVI (Spanish War); Summary Card, RG 94, E 527.

Wilson G. Heaton: CMSR, 34th USVI; rp668465; RG 94, E 501, 204043; RG 92, E 256; Summary Card, RG 94, E 527.

Denny Verdi: Summary Card, RG 94, E 527.

Christopher J. Rollis: CMSR, 34th USVI; CMSR, 4th Wisconsin Infantry (Spanish War); RG 92, E 256 and E 257; Summary Card, RG 94, E 527.

National League Umpires, Rick Stattler, 2002.

Frank L. French: CMSR, Company H, 34th USVI; CMSR, 3rd Wisconsin Infantry (Spanish War); RG 92, E 256 and E 257; Summary Card, RG 94, E 527; The Laws of Wisconsin, Joint Resolutions and Memorial Passed at the Biennial Session of the Legislature, et al; Madison, Wisconsin, 1901, 711.

167. Under heavy duress: Penn, 9.

168. The men labored with bolos: Penn, 12.

168. Down below, as if on cue: Colonel Hare's senior officers included Captain James Butler, commanding Company A, a tall, strapping farmer from Yazoo City, Mississippi; Captain Charles W. Van Way, commanding Company B, a married mechanic from Winfield, Kansas; tall, dark, and ruddy Captain Edmund G. Shields, commanding Company C, a married civil engineer from Hannibal, Missouri; Captain John Augustus Hulen, commanding Company D, an energetic insurance and real estate agent who had dabbled in the "Gainesville Rifles" for eleven years; and finally, Captain Richard T. Ellis, a corporate secretary and treasurer from Ohio, commanding Company I.

169. The unlucky private would live: The blue-eyed Whalen and his seven siblings had been raised in the slums of London by Catherine, their widowed mother. To break his family's grinding cycle of poverty, Whalen escaped to America, where he labored as a stone paver. Like everyone he knew, he rushed to enlist with the 1st Texas Infantry in May 1898, when the Spanish-American War offered the opportunity. He even saw a bit of service in Cuba. Now on the other end of the world, the thirty-one-year-old Whalen pulled his hat over his eyes and began to doze. For James Whalen's illiterate and aging mother back on Old Kent Road in England, it took almost three years of letter writing and pleading with the War Department's pension office—until June 3, 1902—for her to receive her overdue mother's dependent pension of $12 per month. She enjoyed the financial support for a short nine months, until her death on March 23, 1903, at age sixty-five. See: James A. Whalen: Summary Card, RG 94, E 527; RG 15, E 23 Pension.

169. In plain view, hundreds: Penn, 12.

170. For the Americans: Penn, 13; Villamor, 56–57.

170. "Cease firing!: Etienne Bujac in his application for a Medal of Honor, August 9, 1905, in a report submitted by AG to SecWar, April 24, 1912, RG 94, E 25, 1904511.

170. Bujac sprang over the parapet: Bujac's superior officers in the 33rd Infantry, Captain Hulen and Colonel Hare, both noted Bujac's *"conspicuous gallantry"* in being the first man over the parapet at Tangadan Pass, and recommended the Medal of Honor be awarded. Notably, Lieutenant Colonel Howze, 34th Infantry, declined to support the recommendation, noting that being over the parapet first was *"a point of small importance, and impossible to determine, as it was very dark."* Howze suggested instead that Bujac be urgently brevetted captain. Case of Etienne Bujac, Application for Medal of Honor, Report submitted by AG to SecWar, April 24, 1912, RG 94, E 25, 1904511.

170. The impregnable Tangadan Pass: The American victory came at a cost. During the charges toward the trenches, Private Oscar E. Dollen, Company G, 34th Infantry, a twenty-two-year-old farmer from Iowa, was severely wounded by a Remington round that entered his back, just above the base of his spinal column, and fractured his pelvis. The oldest of seven siblings—including his twin brother Otto, who followed by twenty minutes—Private Oscar E. Dollen was a reluctant recruit into the army. Driven to enlist in order to escape a troubled family life in the fertile rural town of Avoca, Dollen was the last of the large brood to leave home; his twin had run away at age fifteen. Why Dollen stayed for as long as he did, we do not know—perhaps out of duty as the eldest child, or because of his heavy responsibilities, farming rented land to supplement his mother Carolina's meager income earned from milk and butter sales from a single cow, and eggs from a handful of chickens. His father, John Von Dollen, was a financial and personal disaster with a lifelong streak of bad luck. The hard-drinking, abusive German opened a saloon and liquor store, only to have the county go dry on him. He then converted the closed hall into a "moving picture show," which subsequently burned down, leaving him with nothing more than a bare lot. With one arm crippled and suffering from a hernia that would later kill him, the elder Dollen cruelly beat his wife with ugly regularity. It was a fact well known by their neighbors, despite Carolina's efforts at concealment, and they despised him for it. Young Oscar Dollen finally had no choice but to leave, likely with a heavy heart as he abandoned his mother to the fate of his father's gnarled, angry hands.

Following the battle, Private Dollen was transported on a stretcher down to Vigan for urgent medical care. There, he awaited transfer to the hospital ship *Relief,* anchored offshore. The delay, however, was deadly. The gunshot had ruptured his bowels and abdomen, allowing dangerous bacteria to invade his system. Within hours, peritonitis took hold, presenting a surgical emergency. Death arrived three days later. Dollen was buried at Vigan in the soldiers' cemetery, leaving behind no personal effects. His commanding officer, Captain Rollis, later wrote to his parents, noting that their son "was given every possible attention, and all that the best medical skill could accomplish was done, but the wound proved too serious and recovery impossible." Rollis added, "The position my company occupied in the fight was a dangerous one, at point-blank range within 150 yards of the enemy's trenches and subject to cross-fire, resulting in a large percentage of injured, but Private Dollen never failed me. His was the death of a hero."

While Oscar Dollen would not know it, his death ultimately brought some relief to his struggling mother. Once her husband passed on from a strangulating hernia in 1915, Carolina Dollen summoned up the courage to apply for a long-overdue dependent mother's military pension, bringing her a $20 monthly income—totaling some $9,000 over the course of more than two decades—which she received until her death, at age seventy-nine, in 1937. See: Oscar E. Dollen: RG 15, E 23, Pension; Captain C. J. Rollis, 34th USVI, Commanding Company G, from Laoag, to Ed Leach, Avoca, Iowa, January 23, 1900.

170. Total American losses: Nine privates from the 33rd and 34th Infantries were wounded in the assault on Tangadan Pass, mostly slight gunshot wounds to the flesh from Mauser rifles (three were shot in their arms, two their elbows, two their thighs, and another in the right soft buttocks). Private Gilbert Baron, Company C, 33rd Infantry, was shot through the left shoulder, the bullet fracturing his left clavicle and then penetrating the soldier's esophagus and left lung. Like Dollen, Baron was mortally wounded and would live for only another five days. The 3rd Cavalry also had their losses: one trooper killed and two wounded.

The casualties reported as wounded of December 5, 1899, included (i) 34th Infantry: Sergeant John Murphy; Private James Smith; Private Oscar E. Dollen; Private Samuel Faust; and Private Frederick Carr, all Company G; (ii) 3rd Cavalry: Private Frank Kaiser and Private Hubert Muggy, both Troop K; and (iii) 33rd Infantry: Corporal George Marin; Corporal Simon Borison; and Private Gilbert Baron, all Company C. A report from Headquarters, Cavalry Brigade, 1st Division 8th Army Corps (in the field) to Chief Surgeon, 8th Army Corps, Manila, Vigan, P.I., December 5, 1899. Also: Consolidated Report, Wounded in the Battle with Insurrectos at Tagnadin [*sic*] near San Quintin, December 4, 1899, 34th USVI, submitted by Captain F. W. Foxworthy to Chief Surgeon's Office, Manila, P.I., February 2, 1900.

170. Found amid the bloody carnage: Juan Villamor, in his unpublished chronicle, provides an incomplete and inaccurate account of the battle, but his detailed insights are telling. He attributed the loss of Tangadan Pass first and foremost to the taking of "indispensible forces defending Tangadan for the fight at Vigan," which reduced "the efficacy of the patrolling forces intended to guard the flanks." As a result, Major Penn's flanking maneuver was possible, and came as a total surprise to Tinio's men entrenched in the pass. A second factor, according to Villamor, was the return of dispirited and exhausted soldiers from the battle at Vigan earlier that morning, which sent a ripple of fear and failure through the ranks. Finally, Villamor obliquely places blame at the feet of his cousin Blas, who he states retreated due to his two gunshot wounds and thereby left his forces without a senior officer in command in the trenches to rally them to victory. Instead, they abandoned their positions. General Tinio, for his part, was several miles behind the fortifications, at San Quintin. Villamor covers up the disaster by noting that his forces were focused on the guerrilla war to come, and that Tangadan Pass was given up "without waste of lives and blood as expected." By every other account, that seems grossly inaccurate. See: Villamor, 53–56.

170. Filipino losses were estimated: Report on the Battle at Tangadan Pass by Robert L. Howze to Adjutant, 34th Infantry, Vigan, P.I., January 7, 1900. Charles F. Manahan Papers, Huntington Library.

CHAPTER 15: THE EXPEDITION

171. Following orders from General Young: Penn, 16.

171. After a ten-mile hike: Ibid.

172. To ensure this did not happen: *The Gillmore Expedition,* unattributed account in Charles F. Manahan Papers, NHF.

172. The forward advance: The following account of the Gillmore party rescue expedition that follows here is assembled from a number of sources, including Penn, *A Narrative of the Campaign in Northern Luzon;* Gebert, "The Gilmore [*sic*] Expedition" in the Manahan Papers at NHF; a detailed though unattributed account of the expedition by a 33rd Infantry soldier, entitled "The Gilmore [*sic*] Rescue Expedition," found in the Manahan Papers at UCSB; Edwards's memoir, *Prisoner in the Philippines.*

172. "I will find Gillmore: Penn, 10.

172. No one knew: Penn, 16.

173. Hopefully, one of them would pick: Ibid.

173. "Never did a circus: Penn, 17.

173. All told, roughly one thousand impoverished: Ibid.

174. A few houses: Penn, 18.

174. "dispose of them where: *The Gillmore Expedition,* unattributed account in Charles F. Manahan Papers, NHF.

174. The senior officer on duty: Penn, 19.

175. escape had been discussed: Edwards, 48.

175. All agreed that this setup: Edwards, 49.

175. When they passed: Ibid.

176. There they lay in silent agony: Ibid.

176. Thankfully, their novelty: Ibid.

176. Carried along on the current: Edwards, 50.

177. "We landed almost a mile: Ibid.

177. "It was some time before we: Ibid.

177. If American forces: Ibid.

178. "Hunger got the best of: Ibid.

178. "Let's take a shot: Edwards, 51.

178. *"Quien esta?:* Ibid.

178. With two bolos: Ibid.

178. "You must be hungry: Ibid.

179. Now, they would need: Edwards, 52.

179. "What of it; that would*:* Ibid.

179. The soldiers demanded: Ibid.

182. "The Bureau has no further: Chief of Bureau, US Navy to Senator Joseph Simon, July 6, 1899. LS, 169700. Venville, OMPF.

182. The starved prisoners: Ibid.

183. The retreat of Tinio's forces: Penn, 20.

183. Taking advantage of the tragic outcome: Edwards, 53.

183. When the Americans regrouped: Penn, 21.

184. "would have delighted: Penn, 21.

184. Their best guess: Gebert, 6.

184. Into that abyss: Penn, 22.

185. Scrawled on a boulder: Gebert, 9.

186. Without the time: Edwards, 53.

186. "It was a slaughter: Edwards, 54.

186. Now near Banna: Penn, 23.

187. Hare ordered each company commander: Gebert, 9.

187–88. Challenged to catch his counterpart: *The Gillmore Expedition,* unattributed account in Charles F. Manahan Papers, NHF.

188. All told, the private had completed: Grose's exploits on the trail near Banna earned him a Silver Star in 1926. He would later settle in Arkansas, and live to the age of eighty-one, passing away on January 7, 1950. Squire Grose: CMSR, Company A, 33rd USVA. The tale is also retold in Penn, 23–24; and *The Gillmore Expedition,* unattributed account in Charles F. Manahan Papers, NHF. See also: "Hero," *Pharos-Tribune* (Logansport, Indiana), June 17, 1926; obituary, *Northwest Arkansas Times,* January 9, 1950.

189. Held for more than eighteen months: Penn, 24.

189. After these outrages: On December 15, 1899, Chinese merchants Lim Leco, Cu Chinco, and Sy Siatio, and thirteen other similarly aggrieved Chinese shop owners filed a complaint against two of Tinio's officers, Major Joaquin Natividad and Lieutenant Yuson with the US Army's commanding officer at Laoag. The merchants alleged the two Army of Liberation officers were in charge of the looting, and listed the value of merchandise and provisions taken at $117,640. In addition, 2,356 bales of tobacco were signed over as forced "donations" to the war effort, with a value of $15,000, and $2,200 worth of opium was stolen. In closing, the liberated Chinese appealed for justice, noting that they suffered "ill treatment, insult, annoyance, hunger, misery and iniquity of all kinds until, thanks to the happy and triumphal arrival of Your Excellency with your bellicose and valiant troops, we were saved from the infernal claws of those evil insurgents." Résumé of Statements by Lim Leco et al., December 16, 1899, "Report of the Condition of Affairs in Northwestern Luzon," December 17, 1899, Brigadier General S. B. M. Young, US Army, Commanding, Enclosure 3. RG 94, E 25, 315552.

189. It was later learned that Tinio: Martin I. Tinio Jr., *Manuel Tinio y Bundoc.*

190. Cornered into what the tattered map: Penn, 24.

190. Over the past six days: Ibid, 25.

190. A count revealed just twelve: Ibid, 24.

191. The surgeon quickly made the cut: Ibid, 27.

191. The troika was assigned: One more soldier was attached to Company G, a Filipino-American scout named Eugenio Espino. The short, thick, thirty-four-year-old had been born at Candaba,

Pampanga, but now held American citizenship. Espino was invaluable to Howze, serving as the eyes and ears to the often-uninformed if not blundering American advance. Conversant in English, Tagalog, Kapampangan, and Ilocano, Espino kept the Americans up-to-date on the latest intelligence and provided important cultural cues. He came well-trained, having served with a unit called Lowe's Scouts, an odd fighting unit composed of soldiers and contracted civilians that edged into the territory of mercenaries for hire.

The idea of tapping the indigenous population as native scouts was not a new one and had been tried and tested with the Pawnee during the Indian Wars in the American West fought against the Cheyenne and Sioux tribes. In the Philippines, the context was vastly different, as most Filipinos were not native trackers or able to read their natural environment beyond the limited domain of their hometowns any better than anyone else. They did, however, bring other valuable attributes. Tapping into a group of Filipinos from Macabebe and Pampanga who had served in the Spanish military, and exploiting their deep-seated animosity against their neighboring Tagalogs, the US Army organized several companies of Macabebe scouts as guides and scouts. Once mobilized, drilled, and equipped with Krag carbines—but notably not given uniforms or rations—the scouts quickly demonstrated their worth in battle and in suppressing guerrilla attacks. After several months of arduous advances through northern Luzon, the remnants of the Macabebe scouts assisting Young, like many of the American units pushing north, finally collapsed in exhaustion around December 6, and were sent back to Manila for rest, recuperation, and their long-overdue salaries. This experience served as the prelude to the establishment of the Philippine Constabulary, which would help the Americans garrison the archipelago over time and evolve into the country's local police force. Following from the success of the experiment with the Macabebe scouts, General Lawton ordered the organization of a company of division scouts, tasking Captain Percival G. Lowe Jr., 25th Infantry, and Lieutenant Joseph C. Castner, 4th Infantry, with the job. Lawton envisaged a lean, mean, and highly mobile unit that could leap ahead of any US Army column bogged down in the Luzon mud, and achieve quick gains against the nimble and vaporous rebels. Lawton chose the right men for the job: Lowe and Castner had successfully created a unit of Seminole scouts, were accomplished Indian fighters, and as navigators, were credited with creating the first map of Alaska's Yukon River. The thirty-five-year-old Lowe, trained as an engineer at the Pennsylvania Military Academy, pulled together a core group of forty-four enlisted men, each "chosen for their especial adaptability for the work in hand," who were excused from all other duties from wherever they were drawn: the 4th US Cavalry, 1st North Dakota Infantry, 2nd Oregon Infantry, 22nd US Infantry, 4th US Infantry, and 13th US Infantry.

Augmenting these scouts were fifty-three Filipinos, including Espino, and thirteen civilians, the latter being a colorful cast of adventurers kicking around the Philippines. Among them, Captain Hector McAllester, a former sea captain and African ivory hunter; Felio, a former sergeant in the French *cuirassiers* (cavalry); McKay, formerly of the British Army's Gordon Highlanders; Paddy Walsh, a failed Catholic priest who had served in two armies; Manners, a former Methodist minister from the American South; a Frenchman named Bargereau; and Denny Mason, an old army veteran and professional gambler. One of the more notable was Luther S. "Yellowstone" Kelly, a Shakespeare-quoting hunter and trapper who had earned his nickname scouting the Yellowstone River Valley on government expeditions in the 1870s and '80s. Kelly had served as chief of scouts for Nelson Miles, and had fought in the battle against the Lakota and northern Cheyenne in the foothills of the Wolf Mountains in Montana. He also helped to chase down the Nez Perce at Cow Island and in the Bear Paw Mountains.

The challenge of managing the scouts in the Philippines took a heavy toll on Lowe, whose chronic drinking and bouts of sunstroke cascaded into a series of increasingly serious medical diagnoses, from "chronic dementia" to "mental derangement" to "circular insanity." By 1903, at age forty, Captain Lowe was retired from military service and committed to the Government Hospital for the Insane at Washington, D.C. For Lowe's Scouts, see the colorful account by Major Edward S. O'Reilly, *Roving and Fighting* (London: T. Werner Laurie, 1918). See also: "Lowe's Scouts," *American Oldtimer*. For the tribulations of Percival G. Lowe Jr.: RG 94, E 297, 1332acp1889. See also: Linn,

154; Sexton, 176; and the master's thesis, Allan D. Marple, Major, US Army, *The Philippine Scouts: A Case Study in the Use of Indigenous Soldiers, Northern Luzon, The Philippine Islands, 1899* (Kansas: Staff College, Fort Leavenworth, 1983).

192. The five companies: Penn, 27.

192. Two of his men, too lame to keep up: Gebert, 9.

192. Now the phrases took on a touch of biting sarcasm: Gebert, 9; Penn, 30–31; Gillmore, *McClure's*, 404; *The Gillmore Expedition,* unattributed account in Charles F. Manahan Papers, NHF.

CHAPTER 16: CORDILLERAS

193. "All about us were: Gillmore, 404.

194. The column pushed: Walton, 438.

194. The march needed to continue: Erroneously lumped together under the term Igorots, the mountain-dwelling and rice-terracing tribal peoples of the Cordilleras fall into unique and diverse ethnic classifications, numbering seven ethno-linguistic groups—the Bontoc, Ibaloi, Ifugao, Isneg (or Apayao), Kalinga, Tinggian, and Kankanaey. Historically, each was a self-contained unit, carving out sustenance from the mountains as best it could, with terracing or slash-and-burn *kiangin* farms, and each potentially hostile to another, some with blood feuds dating back to time immemorial.

194. The bags of currency: Huber, 93;

195. An infuriated Tinio arrived: Walton, 439.

195. "One of the Spanish officers with: Walton, 438.

195. "If it was prime: Huber, 94.

196. Gillmore and his party elbowed: Huber, 95.

196. In the absolute dead of night: Ibid, 96.

197. For nearly three hundred years, the Isneg: Isneg, broken down to *Is,* "to withdraw," and *uneg,* "interior," suggests the probable history of these mountain dwellers, proto-Austronesians who arrived along the northern Luzon coast from South China thousands of years ago. Over the centuries, they were pushed up into the rain forest following subsequent waves of arrivals. The Spaniards established religious missions by 1610, but 150 years of effort to Christianize the animist Isneg failed miserably, and they were abandoned by 1760. In 1888, a Spanish military expedition accepted an invitation to a feast in the mountain town of Kabugao, but it ended badly. In a case of exceptionally poor cross-cultural miscommunication, seventeen unarmed Isneg were massacred, including the host. The furious Isneg retaliated, killing a party of Ilocano traders and attacking lowland towns. In 1891, the Spaniards tried one last time to bring the Isneg around, when Father Julian Malumbres was sent to resurrect the abandoned mission. Almost upon arrival, he was accused of working in concert with the Spanish military, which was chasing down, killing, and imprisoning Isneg leaders. The padre's two servants were killed and the failed missionary left Apayao, never to return. In 1895, the Isneg added insult to injury, delivering a decisive defeat to the Spaniards, driving them out once and for all. See: William Henry Scott, *History of the Cordilleras: Collected Writings on Mountain Province History* (Baguio City, Philippines: Baguio Printing and Publishing Co., 1975).

197. That afternoon brought a change in circumstances: Statement of Joaquin Natividad, December 15, 1899. "Report of the Condition of Affairs in Northwestern Luzon," December 17, 1899, Brigadier General S. B. M. Young, US Army, Commanding, Enclosure 3. RG 94, E 25, 315552.

198. "Don't be discouraged: Statement of Joaquin Natividad, December 15, 1899. "Report of the Condition of Affairs in Northwestern Luzon," December 17, 1899, Brigadier General S. B. M. Young, US Army, Commanding, Enclosure 3. RG 94, E 25, 315552.

198. Separated from the massive column: The identity of the Filipino lieutenant, not provided in any known account, is confirmed through Major Joaquin Natividad's statement to the US Army on December 15, 1899, and is reflected again in the statement by Chinese merchant Lim Leco. Both references can be found in Young's "Report of the Condition of Affairs in Northwestern Luzon," RG 94, E 25, 315552. A careful analysis of the original handwritten statements in Spanish and their English translations note that the Americans incorrectly identified Yuson as "Tuson" and "Toson."

198. The strong current tugged: Huber, 96–97.

198. Again, they camped: Ibid, 97.

198. They cut up and bundled the flesh: Ibid, 97.

198. "The penalty of a single misstep: Gillmore, *McClure's*, 404.

198. "a veritable devil's causeway: Ibid.

198. "more dead than alive: Huber, 97.

199. "I was so far gone: Leland S. Smith, "Diary Account of the Period L. S. Smith Was a Prisoner of the Filipinos," 1899–1900. USMHI.

199. At this point, another prisoner: Huber, 98.

199. "We looked so desperate: Ibid.

199. "We also got some tobacco: Ibid.

199. A downcast Huber: Ibid.

200. Seizing the opportunity: Statement of Joaquin Natividad, December 15, 1899. "Report of the Condition of Affairs in Northwestern Luzon," December 17, 1899, Brigadier General S. B. M. Young, US Army, Commanding, Enclosure 3. RG 94, E 25, 315552.

200. "to kill them one by one: Ibid.

200. "When I heard this barbarous: Ibid.

201. "present himself with all his: Statement of Joaquin Natividad, December 15, 1899. "Report of the Condition of Affairs in Northwestern Luzon," December 17, 1899, Brigadier General S. B. M. Young, US Army, Commanding, Enclosure 3. RG 94, E 25, 315552.

201. The united column: Penn, 28.

202. The trail then dropped down: Ibid.

202. The Americans assumed these soldiers: Ibid, 29.

202. Just as the Filipino raised his rifle: Edwards, 55.

202. "Don't shoot: Ibid. See also: Penn, 29.

202. It was sailor Norman Godkin von Galen: Penn, 29.

203. Once they heard shouting in English: Ibid.

203. Langford's colorful graffiti: "With Gillmore Party, Story of an American Volunteer who Painted Signs on Cliffs," *Dallas Morning News*, December 5, 1900.

204. In that case, a navy boat: The message sent by Colonel Hare through two runners to General Young was transmitted in part by General Otis as an update to the War Department in Washington, D.C. Otis to AG, December 23, 1899: *"General Young reports twenty-first instant from Vigan still in pursuit through mountains of insurgent column, having our prisoners of whom four captured; Captain Gilmore [sic] remaining prisoners one day in advance; pursuit continued; these pursuing troops have encountered great hardships but will probably strike Aparri . . ."* RG 94, E 25, 292248.

204. "Here we are, God knows: Penn, 31.

204. At that point, the group of twenty: Gillmore, *McClure's*, 406.

205. "General Tinio gave me: Huber, 101.

205. "It was terrible: Ibid.

205. "But I do not want: Ibid.

205. "My soldiers have left: Ibid, 102.

205. "Adios: Ibid.

206. "formidable weapons in: Ibid.

206. Gillmore, coughing, pale, and dazed: Huber, 102.

206. Panicked, Gillmore and his men: Ibid, 103.

206. They would need at least six rafts: Ibid.

207. Behind him, another Isneg: Ibid, 104.

207. Soon, the five muscular Isneg: Ibid.

207. The same guard arrangements: Ibid.

207. One razor-sharp stake: Ibid.

207. Startled, the men instinctively: Ibid, 105.

CHAPTER 17: SALVATION

208. They concluded that the prisoners' captors: Penn, 31.

208. "Get down, get down!: Smith, 17.

209. "Are you all here?: Huber, 105.

209. Hare and Howze: Realizing the importance of the moment, both Colonel Hare and Lieutenant Colonel Howze prepared handwritten reports listing the names of the officers and men present at the rescue. Their foresight would allow their men to receive Silver Stars for this accomplishment decades later, and for the event to be reconstructed with some precision for this narrative. These documents are: (i) "List of Officers and Men of the 33rd Infantry USV Present at the Capture of American Prisoners from Insurgents, in Mountains, Monday, Dec. 18, 1899," found in Regimental Papers, 33rd USVI; and (ii) "In the Mountains near Cabaugaoan, Monday, Dec. 18, 1899, 8:30 a.m.," memorandum prepared by Major Julius Penn for Lieutenant Colonel Robert L. Howze, found in Regimental Papers, 34th USVI.

209. They had not the slightest idea: Gebert, 12; Penn, 33.

209. Although he missed, the former deserter: Penn, 32.

210. He carefully placed the expended cartridge: Edwards, 58; Huber, 105.

212. With luck, the rescue expedition: Penn, 33.

212. Two more soldiers: Gebert, 12.

212. Grossly insufficient: Ibid; Huber, 107.

213. By nightfall, the column had thirty-five well-made rafts: Gebert, 13.

213. Arising from the jumble of rafts: Gillmore, *McClure's*, 409.

213. The command raft, with Gillmore: Lieutenant Gillmore to Admiral Dewey, January 1900.

213. When a Chinese *cargador* was thrown: Gillmore, *McClure's*, 410.

213. At one point, one of the liberated prisoners: Ibid.

213. "The scenery was so grand: Gillmore, *McClure's*, 411.

213. "We were well satisfied: Gebert, 13.

214. Turns were taken: Ibid, 14.

214. More homes were felled: Private Lawrence Benton, 33rd USVI, provides a strikingly honest account of the Gillmore rescue expedition, providing rich details that do not appear in other accounts. On the raft construction: *"By tearing down all the huts we could find we secured bamboo poles for our rafts. We bound two bamboo poles together, then with cross pieces, bound a pole about two feet out on each side to act as "stabilizers." It required several barrios to furnish enough bamboo to float the entire column."* In contrast, Major Penn writes in his account, without mentioning the source of the bamboo for the rafts, *"In all our travel down the river the strictest orders were given not to molest or take or destroy private property."* Lawrence Benton, "Memories of the 33rd US Vol. Infantry," *American Oldtimer*, 1934; Penn, 38.

214. A few of the men shared: Penn, 38.

215. A fight broke out: For Private Burke, of Homestead, Pennsylvania, the incident would add a string of six summary court-martial convictions that would lead to a general court-martial seven months later, on July 22, 1900, and his dishonorable discharge from service and confinement for six months at hard labor at his post in Vigan. Patrick Burke: CMSR, Company I, 33rd USVI; SO 89, para. 30, AAG, Headquarters Department of Northern Luzon, Manila, P.I., July 22, 1900; Summary Card; RG 94, E 25, 1135770.

215. The twenty-six-year-old teamster: Gebert, 14.

215. It was a four-day journey: Ibid.

216. Some of the Filipinos: Ibid, 15.

217. Two hours into New Year's Day: Ibid, 16; Huber, 110; Penn, 39.

217. His filthy trousers: Edwards, 61.

217. On Tuesday, January 2, 1900: Late that afternoon, the command attended to the burial of Private Day at the town of Abulug. His remains were laid to rest in the local churchyard with military honors. A Filipino Catholic priest led the service, and Hare made some remarks. Huber, 110; Penn, 40.

218. "God bless you, Hare: Gillmore, 410; Gebert, 16.

218. Little did they know at the time: Offloaded with the men of the 33rd Infantry was another corpse. Overnight, one of the anonymous Chinese *cargadores* in the party succumbed to exhaustion and disease, his name not recorded. Buried in the cemetery in Vigan, he was another casualty of the Gillmore rescue expedition. Gebert, 16.

On January 5, 1900, Young's telegram from Vigan read: *"Schwan Manila: Hare and Howze have just arrived with all our prisoners; their work unparalleled. I urge Hare and Howze be appointed Brigadier General, Volunteers and all officers and men, who will be mentioned by name, for medals of honor. Young, Brigadier General."* AGO 440429.

218. He also had problems: Report on William Walton, medical journal for the period January 23–August 25, 1900, USS *Solace*, entry dated January 25, 1900, 14. RG 24, Medical Journal of USS *Solace*, 2 vols.

218. Edwards had deep ulcers: Edwards, 62.

220. Apprentice Albert Peterson's heart: Albert Peterson, RG 15, E 19, Pension.

220. Vaudoit and Woodbury: Report on Paul Vaudoit, medical journal from January 15, 1899, USS *Solace*, entry dated January 21, 1900, 451. RG 24, Medical Journal of USS *Solace*, 2 vols. Report on Orrison W. Woodbury, medical journal for the period January 23–August 25, 1900, USS *Solace*, entry dated January 25, 1900, 14. RG 24, Medical Journal of USS *Solace*, 2 vols.

220. Lieutenant Gillmore was nothing more: Report on James C. Gillmore Jr., medical journal for the period January 23–August 25, 1900, USS *Solace*, entry dated February 11, 1900, 61. RG 24, Medical Journal of USS *Solace*, 2 vols.

220. "Well, you fellows have: Brad Prowse, "American Prisoner of War in the Philippines," 1899, *Military History Magazine*, February 1999.

220. Before returning anywhere: At Fort Santiago, the army adjutant and his staff again interviewed the liberated captives, going over the details of their captivity and arrangements to return to their units. Most were ordered to report to the Army's 1st Reserve Hospital, as all were suffering from one ailment or another. Most of the liberated prisoners spent weeks (or months) in the sprawling, 1,540-bed facility, enjoying the care of its 14 surgeons, 9 stewards, 180 privates, and 56 American nurses. Life on the wards provided much-needed rest, medication, and an abundance of meals, three times a day, consisting of eggs, corn mush, oatmeal with hot milk, hot tomato and macaroni soups, and heavy dinners of escalloped oysters, stewed and roasted mutton, and fried chicken. Inspection Report, 1st Reserve Hospital, January 29, 1900. RG 159, E 9, Box 17.

220. A number were crippled: They added to the hospital's roster of those suffering from disease—on average since June 1899, comprising 75 percent of the hospital patient population, with the balance being split by those wounded or injured—13 percent—and those suffering from venereal disease—12 percent. Inspection Report, 1st Reserve Hospital, January 29, 1900. RG 159, E 9, Box 17.

221. Sackett was running a high malarial fever: George T. Sackett, RG 15, E 23, Pension.

221. In subsequent court-martial trials: James Curran: RG 94, E 25, 425189.

221. Ironically, the troublesome private: Frank McDonald: RG, E 25, 196685.

221. LIEUTENANT GILLMORE'S PARTY ARRIVES SAFELY IN MANILA: *Manila Times*, January 7, 1900.

222. To further manage the media: An interesting anecdote suggests that Gillmore knew what was on the line. When they first arrived in Manila, while on the tender ride to Cavite, Gillmore and Walton stood in a huddle near the ship's quartermaster. One of the tender's deck hands approached Apprentice Peterson, who was animatedly recounting the story of their captivity. Suddenly, Gillmore spotted them and angrily ordered Walton to intervene. The boy was dressed down and ordered not to talk to anyone—in short, to keep his mouth shut. William D. Caley, in a letter to Charles Manahan, August 14, 1938. Charles F. Manahan Papers, NHF.

222. LEFT AMONG SAVAGES: *Washington Post*, January 8, 1900.

223. The easy-go-lucky Lyman Edwards: Following his liberation, the young Edwards clearly had had enough of the navy, and was now pushing for an early discharge. While he had asked Lieutenant Gillmore to assist him with the request, likely unknown to him, over the following months an appeal was initiated by his parents, L. B. and Margaret Edwards, from their home in Mexico, Indiana.

Both of his parents were worried that their son would become caught up in a new conflict, the Boxer Rebellion in China. Their letters triggered appeals from both Indiana congressman George W. Steele and Missouri congressman James Cooney to Navy Secretary Long, requesting that the landsman be allowed to terminate his three-year navy enlistment early. See: LR, Bureau of Navy, 211673 and 215049.

223. On Friday, March 9, 1900: Most of the men transferred directly to the Naval Hospital at Mare Island. Vaudoit was released, though sadly found himself back aboard the USS *Solace* just seven days later in urgent need of medical attention. On his first liberty ashore, he apparently headed straight to the port's raucous bars, ended up in a tussle, and was assaulted. The assailants—their names and number unknown—knocked out his front teeth, crushed his cheekbone, and left him unconscious with contusions about the face and head. Tragically, the French-born sailmaker's mate had survived a deadly insurgent ambush and eight months of deprivation as a prisoner of war, only to be beaten senseless, less than a week after his arrival home, by his own countrymen. Report on Paul Vaudoit, medical journal for the period January 23–August 25, 1900, USS *Solace*, entry dated March 13, 1900, 142. RG 24, Medical Journal of USS *Solace,* 2 vols.

223. Maybe something could be salvaged: Leland S. Smith, "China Relief Expedition 1900–1901, "Boxer Rebellion, 1899–1900." MHI, 1.

223. Only one image was any good: Ibid.

223. "I am in great distress: Emily Mash to Navy Secretary Long, May 30, 1900. Bureau of Navigation, RG 24, E 88, 220092. RG 15, E 19, Pension, Denzell G. A. Venville.

224. "The loss of my son: Ibid.

BOOK III

CHAPTER 18: GARRISON

228. And then, on December 19, 1899: General Henry W. Lawton had ventured outside Manila on the evening of December 18, in the middle of an unseasonal monsoon rain—and on the very day the Gillmore party prisoners were rescued—to lead a "scout-in-force" against insurgent forces at San Mateo. Planned quietly to effect surprise, the expedition consisted of one battalion each of 27th and 29th Infantries and two squadrons of 11th Cavalry, one being mounted. They marched all night through mud and rain, arriving at the Marikina River, on the edge of the town, at daylight. The following morning, with some of his forces delayed by rain, and others unable to ford the swollen river, Lawton's engagement quickly went awry. His command, concentrated on a bluff, began to take heavy, albeit inaccurate, enemy fire from trenches across the river. Lawton, true to his custom, stood exposed, presenting a strikingly rich target in a yellow slicker and pith helmet.

Lawton was walking the firing line, issuing orders for his men to spread out, when his aide, Lieutenant Breckenridge, hit by a bullet, called out, "I've got it," and sank to the ground. The general and three men rushed the officer to a sheltered position to have his wounds dressed. When asked if the gunshot wound was serious, the general replied that it wasn't; Breckenridge lacked the peculiar ashen face of a mortally wounded man. General Lawton advised that he needed to return to the lines, and again moved out into the open. One later rumor suggested that the general, suffering from tuberculosis, was actually seeking his early demise on the field of battle. In any event, without warning, it came. Lawton raised his arm in a strange manner, exclaiming, "Jesus!" Captain King asked, "What's the matter, General?" to which he replied, "I'm shot." "Where?" King asked. "Through the lungs," Lawton responded, gritting his teeth as he lay down. The general turned his head to one side and blood gushed from his mouth. A lieutenant propped the dying general's head on his knee, but nothing could be done. In minutes, the fifty-six-year-old general was dead—the first American Army general killed outside the United States, coincidentally, by a sharpshooter under the command of General Licerio Geronimo, a namesake for the Apache leader whose capture had gained Lawton his fame. It was 9:30 a.m. San Mateo was later taken without event, and the general's body was brought over in a *banca,* wrapped in native mats, and brought to Manila the following day.

Report on the death of General Henry W. Lawton, Major William D. Beach, Inspector General, US Volunteers to Inspector General USA, Washington DC, June 7, 1900, Manila, P.I., RG 159, E 9, Box 10. Inspection Report, 1st Division, Major William D. Beach, Inspector General, US Volunteers to Inspector General USA, Washington, D.C., February 2, 1900, Manila, P.I., RG 159, E 9, Box 10.

228. While half of the country's seventy-three provinces: Linn, 185.

229. By now, though, Aguinaldo: Ibid.

229. The prospect of a William Jennings Bryan: Linn, 186.

229. Over the course of the year: Gates, 166.

229. Through 1902, American forces: "Making Riflemen from Mud: Restoring the Army's Culture of Irregular Warfare," James D. Campbell, October 2007, Strategic Studies Institute, US Army War College; Sexton, 283.

229. Northern Luzon remained: With the disintegration of the formal Army of Liberation, General Otis divided northern Luzon—a chunk of territory thirty thousand square miles in size, and home to two million inhabitants—into three districts: north, north-west, and central. Some twenty-five thousand troops, half of the total American military strength in the islands, were dedicated to its pacification. In March 1900, the three districts were reorganized into six smaller districts. See: Robert D. Ramsey III, *Savage Wars of Peace: Case Studies of Pacification in the Philippines, 1900–1902* (Fort Leavenworth, KS: Combat Studies Institute Press, 2007), 44; Sexton, 242.

229. The frontal assaults: The impetus behind the heightened brazenness of the assaults was attributed to the fiery Ilocano lawyer turned Catholic priest and revolutionary, Gregorio Aglipay, whose anti-American rhetoric had worked the insurrectionists into a state of religious zealotry. Linn, 261–263.

229. "Much of the fighting: Linn, 49.

230. After a brief pause: Ramsey, 49.

230. Brigadier General Frederick Funston: Thomas W. Crouch, *A Leader of Volunteers: Frederick Funston and the 20th Kansas in the Philippines, 1898–1899* (Lawrence, KS: Coronado Press, 1984), 32–33.

233. Finding insufficient excitement: Not having encountered any insurgent resistance, Funston also ordered his scouts and one company of soldiers, the 34th Infantry's Company D, back over the mountains to headquarters in San Isidro.

233. Captain Clark Magwire Carr: Eugene Asa Carr, West Point graduate, Class of 1850, was a hardened Indian fighter in America's Southwest whose star rose at the outbreak of the Civil War. Brevetted a lieutenant colonel for his actions in the Battle of Wilson's Creek in 1861, Carr rocketed to colonel a week later. He was wounded three times at the Battle of Pea Ridge, Arkansas, March 7–8, 1862, where his efforts in an eleven-hour battle fought off a flanking maneuver by Confederate troops. His division led the assault on Vicksburg three months later, and was the first to reach the Confederate breastworks after four days of fighting. By the close of the war, Carr was brevetted twice more, to major general, and was known nationally as "the black-bearded Cossack." Back on the Southwest frontier, Carr won new accolades for his campaigns against hostile Sioux and Cheyenne in succeeding decades, employing as civilian scouts both James Butler (Wild Bill) Hickok and William F. (Buffalo Bill) Cody, both of whom became lifelong friends. For his gallantry at Pea Ridge, Carr was awarded the Medal of Honor in 1894.

233. Among the remaining men were: Acting Assistant Surgeon Andy Hall's father, Colonel H. W. Hall, served in the Mexican War under General Taylor's command, had seen action at Fort Donelson, Shiloh, Corinth, Vicksburg, Jackson, Mississippi, Missionary Ridge (where he was shot through the arm), and Kennesaw Mountain, around Atlanta, and after the fall of that stronghold, Sherman's march to the sea. One of nine children, Andy entered the medical department at Chicago's Northwestern University and opened a successful practice in Mt. Vernon, Illinois. Establishing himself as a leading citizen in his community, he was a local leader of the Republican Party, and elected mayor of the city in 1897. When the Spanish-American War broke out, he was compelled to relinquish the post, leave his young wife and two toddler children, and sign up as a surgeon for duty in Cuba. Andy went back to his practice in Mt. Vernon, but after five boring weeks, reenlisted to serve again in the

Philippines. Andy Hall's son, Wilford Hall, was also a physician and distinguished US Air Force officer, rising to the rank of major general. His groundbreaking work on medical air transport led to Wilford Hall Medical Center at Lackland Air Force Base, Texas, being named in his honor. Source: Wall's History of Jefferson County, 1909, 518–523; Fact Sheet: The Man behind the Name. Wilford Medical Hall Center, Office of Public Affairs.

Major Shunk's lieutenants included Harry W. Newton, from West Superior, Wisconsin; John Tipton Dunn, from Santa Monica, California; Ode C. Nichols, from Illinois; Harry G. Peterson, from Piqua, Ohio; and Samuel McAlister, from Nashville, Tennessee. Lieutenant Dunn's military lineage was particularly noteworthy: He was the grandson of Brigadier General John Shields Tipton, a prominent Indian fighter who served in General Harrison's "Yellow Jackets" at the Battle of Tippecanoe in 1811, part of the war against Shawnee leader Tecumseh's Indian confederacy, and subsequently was elected as a senator from Indiana. Dunn was also the nephew of a former brigadier general for the US Volunteers in the Civil War, William McKee Dunn, who served as a delegate to the Indiana Constitutional Convention in 1850, was an elected US congressman, and a judge advocate general to the US Army. Lieutenant Dunn, wounded at El Caney and succumbing to disease after his stint in the Philippines, died on July 23, 1902, in Hot Springs, Arkansas, at the age of thirty-seven. RG 94, E 501, 698546.

234. The prisoner finally admitted: John E. Priest to Manahan, July 16, 1935. Charles F. Manahan Papers, NHF.

234. "I, Teodorico Novicio: Novicio oath, Baler Post records, RG 395, E 3038.

236. Once inside his house, Rubio: Dr. Andy Hall account.

236. According to reports: Lucio Quezon was the father of future Philippine president Manuel Quezon, and the murdered son, Pedro, was his brother. In his memoir, *The Good Fight* (1946), President Quezon writes sparingly of his childhood in Baler, of going to Manila for his studies at the University of Santo Tomas in 1894, and about never seeing his father again. Once his studies were disrupted by the occupation of Manila by the Americans in late 1898, Quezon returned to Baler. "I had not been in communication with my father or anyone from Baler since the siege of Manila and was naturally very anxious about the fate of my family," Quezon wrote. "When I arrived in Baler, I learned that my father, with my younger brother who had gone to the provinces before the siege of Manila, had been murdered by bandits on their way home." Quezon adds that as a young lawyer, he was involved in a subsequent criminal legal case against some of Novicio's men who had been involved in the attack. As a Supreme Court ruling in 1906 shows, given that their crimes were committed under the military orders of a superior, Captain Novicio, and at a time of revolution, the defendants would be entitled to benefits of the amnesty declared on July 4, 1902. As a result, the charges were dropped and the defendants were set free. See: Quezon, *The Good Fight*, 38; Supreme Court, Manila, En banc decision, *United States v. Manuel Querijero, et al.,* July 13, 1906. G.R. No. L-2626.

236. Most importantly, sources gave up the name: The actual name of the Filipino lieutenant was left unrecorded in US Army records.

238. "Doctor, these men: Dr. Andy Hall Account. Charles F. Manahan papers, UCSB.

238. They dragged the man: Minaya refers directly to a near hanging of Simaco Angara: *"He was condemned to be hanged from a tree in order to frighten him into revealing our whereabouts,"* Minaya, 96. Dr. Andy Hall, in his thirteen-page account of the rescue, states more obliquely, *"I and some soldiers took Sim out under a tree and interviewed him concerning the prisoners."* See: Andy Hall, "Rescue of Juan Lopez and Felix Minaya, Imprisoned Franciscan Priests, by 34th USV. Inft. Baler, P.I.," Charles F. Manahan papers, UCSB.

239. A furious Carr: Ibid.

239. "two half-naked priests: Lieutenant Ode C. Nichols to Manahan, March 24, 1935. Charles F. Manahan Papers, NHF.

240. But he had nothing: Dr. Andy Hall account. Charles F. Manahan Papers, UCSB.

240. As Novicio seethed: Ibid.

CHAPTER 19: VENVILLE

241. When the besieged Spaniards finally: According to the priests' deposition, Novicio's total armed force comprised an officer, Manuel Querijero, Sergeant Tomas Carillo, 2nd Sergeant Valenzuelo Alijo, Corporal Marguerito, known as "Guerito," and about twenty-eight soldiers.

241. The prisoners were moved: The first house where the prisoners were held was owned by one of Novicio's aides, Cipriano Valenzuela, in the barrio of Suklayin. In September 1899, under Novicio's orders, Venville and the priests were moved to a house within the town proper of Baler.

241. Finally, on February 16, 1900: Report of Captain Charles H. Howland, 21st Infantry, Interview of Spanish Priests Juan Lopez and Felix Minaya, November 11, 1901. RG 395, E 2140.

242. On February 19: The guard was led by Mariano Espinosa, Corporal Placido of Pantabangan, and a soldier known as "Barro." Ibid.

242. Warned that the arrival of American forces: Joining the *presidente* was his wife, Brigada, and their seven children, four boys and three girls; the *presidente's* brother Luis and his wife, Asenield, the sister of Brigada, and their two children, a son and daughter; Benigno Bitong, who had married the sister of the *presidente,* with five children; a brother-in-law of the *presidente,* his wife, and another four children; and Pedro, the Ilocano house servant. Also joining were two of the *presidente's* adult sons, his eldest, Apolinario Gutierrez, and Protacio Gutierrez, who was about twenty-four years old. Report of Captain Charles H. Howland, 21st Infantry, Interview of Spanish Priests Juan Lopez and Felix Minaya, November 11, 1901. RG 395, E 2140.

242. It was a regular ritual: Among those in the group were Luis Gutierrez, brother of the *presidente;* Protacio, the *presidente's* son; Victor, a prospective brother-in-law who was intimately involved with the *presidente's* daughter; and Pedro Campos, the Ilocano servant.

243. "Where is Venville: The dialogue that follows comes from Minaya's diary.

243. "Oh! He is all right: Ibid.

243. *"Na dispacha na:* Ibid.

243. "Why?: Ibid.

243. "He is a bad man: Ibid.

243. "Was it wrong for my: Ibid.

243. Around 1:00 p.m., two members: Those returning from the fishing party included Louis Gutierrez Victor, the suitor of the *presidente's* daughter Liriaco, and Pedro, the Gutierrez clan's house servant. Report of Captain Charles H. Howland, 21st Infantry, Interview of Spanish Priests Juan Lopez and Felix Minaya, November 11, 1901. RG 395, E 2140.

243. "Have you really done that: Minaya.

244. "Novicio orders that I separate: Report of Captain Charles H. Howland, 21st Infantry, Interview of Spanish Priests Juan Lopez and Felix Minaya, November 11, 1901. RG 395, E 2140, 2.

244. "asserted that [Venville] had been: Ode. C. Nichols to Manahan, March 24, 1935. Charles F. Manahan Papers, NHF. Lieutenant Nichols suggests a scenario that is at odds with other accounts—that it appeared Venville and the two priests elected to stay behind at Baler after the Spaniards left, and fled themselves to the jungle when the American forces approached the town in February 1900. He adds that he was tasked to search Novicio's house, but found nothing incriminating.

244. "had been the personal slave: John William Ganzhorn, one of Funston's scouts at Baler, to Manahan, November 8, 1931. Charles F. Manahan Papers. See also: Jack Ganzhorn, *I've Killed Men* (London: Robert Hale Limited, 1910). In this colorful tale, loaded with half-truths and inaccuracies, Ganzhorn recounts a previous encounter with the *Yorktown* crew while aboard the USS *Mohican* himself, and adds his own spin to the tale of the apprentice's ambush, captivity, and death: *"Venville, hardly more than a boy, made a heroic fight before his capture by Filipinos and was wounded three times. He was then kept as a body slave to his captors and later, when about to be rescued by American troops, was buried alive."* Ganzhorn, 123.

244. Embracing another opportunity: Just a week after Novicio's arrest and Lopez and Minaya's liberation, the garrison hatched a plan to rescue Father Gil. Lieutenant Harry Newton, along with four privates and Rubio, the translator, outfitted the garrison's small boat—an eighteen-foot cutter—with ten days' rations, 2,200 rounds of ammunition, tools, and other supplies. After three days of rowing up the turbulent coast, Lieutenant Newton and his men landed at Casiguran in the dead of night, stormed the *presidente*'s home, and, like the previous goose chase for Minaya and Lopez, were taken to multiple locations by various guides. At the house of the *vice presidente*, a stunned local executive finally explained that the priest was perhaps at some distant location. As time was of the essence—the raiders needed to exit the town by sunrise—diplomacy gave way to coercion. The local leader was backed up against the rough stone wall and a revolver held to his chest. One of the soldiers began to count backward from thirty. After ten counts, the frantic *vice presidente* sputtered that he would take them to the priest. At a final location, Lieutenant Newton climbed into the hut and found the emaciated priest curled up in a heap of corn husks. Newton handed the terrified Father Gil a letter from the other priests, which explained who they were and why they had come, and held up the candle to illuminate the darkened room. The priest, his hands shaking uncontrollably with palsy, began to read. As soon as Father Gil comprehended the contents of the letter, his eyes widened, he grabbed Newton's hand, kissed it, and then went completely to pieces. Newton had the disabled priest carried back to the landing site. He demanded that the *vice presidente* provide a second boat—fully provisioned with a crew—by daybreak. If the *vice presidente* failed, Newton warned, American warships standing in the bay would shell the town.

At daybreak on June 13, the *vice presidente* arrived as instructed with a *banca* and a ten-man sailing crew. As the sun rose and broke over the bay, he anxiously stood up and looked around, curious to see the warships that he understood were poised to attack. Lieutenant Newton explained that the cutter was their gunboat, and the men they saw were the totality of their force. "I thought he was going to have a stroke," recalled Newton. After a tortuous return trip in which the two boats were separated in rough weather and Newton was left stranded for a time, the red-faced, sunbaked crew pulled into Baler with the liberated priest and his chest of books, papers, and personal possessions.

245. "value not to exceed $5.00: Order No. 29 issued by Captain Newbill, July 13, 1900, Baler. RG 395, E 2269.

245. And yet, despite this success: The navy initiated its own investigation of the *Yorktown* incident at Baler, augmenting that of the 34th Infantry at the garrison. The USS *Quiros* dropped anchor at Baler Bay on June 30, 1900, to allow the ship's commander, Lieutenant P. J. Werlich, to delve into the case. He called on Major Shunk, retraced Gillmore's route up the river, and visited the site of the ambush. The lieutenant examined witnesses over a two-day period. Among his findings, he determined that while Lieutenant Colonel Simon Tecson, a former druggist from the Escolta, was the senior military officer in charge during the ambush, it was *Kapitan* Novicio who had overseen the burial of the four sailors on the muddy banks of the Sabali River. Werlich questioned Novicio for five hours, reporting that the prisoner "*. . . contradicted himself several times and denied all connection with the burial; admitting however, that it was a common report, that the men were buried alive. He could not bring a single witness to testify to his whereabouts at the time of the burial, claimed that he was in the battery at the mouth of the river manned by his own company. He told me three distinct stories of his movements on that day, each differing from the other, and then told me that he lied, but that his last statement was correct.*"

The naval officer also struggled to shake the truth out of the many rumors regarding Venville's fate. "*Novicio told me a number of contradictory stories about the matter, claiming that the* presidente *was alone responsible for the prisoners and that the man fled when the Americans took San Jose, and had not been heard of since. Novicio now stands charged with burying alive an enlisted man of the Navy and while responsible for the safety of another enlisted man, taken a prisoner, had him taken to the Illongotas [sic] country with the intention of having him murdered by those savage mountain tribes.*"

Werlich visited the grave of his fellow navy men. With the post's surgeon present, he had the grave opened to confirm the presence of the bodies. As the "bodies were not in the condition for removal," Werlich had the grave closed. Finally, he inquired whether he could offer the three freed priests passage to Manila. The post commander, Major Shunk, politely declined; the three priests were still providing very useful intelligence to the army at Baler; hence, their leaving would be premature. Report by Lieutenant P. J. Werlich, Commanding USS *Quiros,* to Commander in Chief, US Naval Force on Asiatic Station, Cavite, P.I., Operations Report: June 23–July 12, 1900, Cavite, P.I., July 12, 1900. RG 395, E 2140.

246. "Oh dear Sir, think of my: Mrs. Emily Mash to General MacArthur, May 24, 1900. RG 395, E 2140.

246. "Elongots (mountain Savages): Wheaton to Mash, Venville, OMPF.

246. "Novicio is now in confinement: Ibid.

247. "I received notice from: Mash letter to Navy Secretary, Ibid.

247. "The money earned by an: Lieutenant Commander [illegible] to Emily Mash, August 10, 1900, Ibid.

248. "to be by him made: Major William A. Shunk, 34th Infantry, Commanding Port of Baler, July 21, 1900. RG 395, E 2269.

248. "if the soldiers got near: Ibid.

248. "Captain Novicio is a prisoner: Ibid.

249. RAISING A RANSOM: *Portland Oregonian*, August 18, 1900.

249. "If this brave boy still: Ibid.

249. With great sadness: "Ransom for One of Gillmore's Men," *Washington Post*, August 21, 1900.

249. The marble shaft was inscribed: Lambert Florin, *Boot Hill: Historic Graves of the Old West* (New York: Bonanza Books, 1966).

Chapter 20: Trial

250. Order No. 202: Emilio Aguinaldo, Order No. 202, Tierra Virgen, Cagayan, June 27, 1900.

250. "Aside from this: Ibid.

251. Officers from other regiments: SO 123, August 29, 1900; SO 140, September 15, 1900; Special Orders 142, September 17, 1900; Benjamin Alvord, AAG.

251. President of the commission: John H. Beacom went on to become military attaché to the American Embassy in London from 1903–1907, and continued to rise through the ranks until his sudden death (at age fifty-eight) as a colonel in the 6th Infantry, while on an expedition in Mexico that marched on San Antonio, on September 17, 1916. Oberlin College Archives RG 30/82.

253. The insurgent *kapitan* pleaded: Courts Martial transcript, Trial of Teodorico Novicio, RG 153, E 15, 23994.

253. "They were lying on the ground: Ibid.

255. The post surgeon, David Hogan: Ibid. Exhibit A, Trial Transcript, Certification by Acting Assistant Surgeon David D. Hogan, September 27, 1900.

256. "Because I was afraid: Ibid.

257. "the defense does not see fit: Ibid.

257. "could not be proved: Ibid.

257. "And the Commission does: Ibid.

258. FOUND GUILTY OF BURYING ALIVE AN AMERICAN SEAMAN: *New York Tribune*, October 28, 1900, page 8.

258. "The rebel Captain Novicio: Ibid.

259. "the tribesmen bound Venville: Ibid.

259. SENTENCED TO DEATH FOR BURYING A MAN ALIVE: *San Francisco Call*, October 28, 1900.

259. FILIPINO SENTENCED TO DEATH: *Richmond Dispatch*, October 28, 1900.

259. BURIED AN AMERICAN ALIVE: *Nebraska State Journal*, October 28, 1900.

259. MUST DIE FOR BLOOD SUCKING: *Salt Lake Herald*, October 28, 1900.

260. *Dear Sir:* Venville, CMSR.

260. After a careful legal review: Headquarters Division of the Philippines, Case of Teodorico Novicio, December 26, 1900, Major General Arthur MacArthur.

262. "Charge: Murder, in violation: Ibid.

Chapter 21: Bones

264. Rhodes had sailed: Two years earlier, just after the Battle of San Juan Hill, Rhodes had organized the Quartermaster Burial Corps to bring home America's war dead from the foreign shores of

Cuba. Through the first half of 1899, Rhodes's team disinterred and returned to the United States 1,222 casketed remains. Notably, with improved recordkeeping and better field practices in marking bodies and graves, only 13.63 percent of those bodies recovered remained unidentified, a significant improvement over the 42.5 percent figure from the Civil War. See: Edward Steere, "National Cemeteries and Memorials in Global Conflict," *Quartermaster Review,* December 1953. See also: "Burial Corps for Manila," *New York Times,* October 11, 1899.

264. By December, Rhodes: Conditions at Cavite, home to the navy and marine dead, deeply irked the fastidious and detail-oriented Rhodes. The naval commandant in charge of the post, Lieutenant Commander John C. Fremont, was unaware of who was buried where, and cared even less. Rhodes found twice as many graves than on the official lists, a number of graves incorrectly marked, and some remains simply missing from their gravesites altogether. An exasperated Rhodes confronted Fremont, who deflected any blame. "I know nothing about graves, or marines," the captain retorted, "nor do I want to know about them." Rhodes could not restrain himself in his report. "[I]t will be observed that nothing short of gross carelessness or rank stupidity has had full sway with respect to the manner of the graves of the dead at this Naval Cemetery, during the past two years. Common respect and decency, both for the dead and their relatives and friends, demands better treatment, to say nothing of the unnecessary, extra labor devolved upon the burial corps," lamented Rhodes. "The present system and management of affairs pertaining to the dead at Cavite, is a disgrace to all concerned." *'I know nothing about graves:* David H. Rhodes in his Report on American Soldiers, Sailors and Civilians Disinterred by the United States Burial Corps in Honolulu, Guam, Philippines, September 30, 1901, 5. RG 92, E 677.

265. Another team hiked: Three privates had died while on garrison duty at Baler: William R. Davis, who succumbed to pyemia, a bacterial infection of the blood, on July 20, 1900; William D. Harper, a hospital corpsman who was shot and killed by insurgents ten days later; and David Crozier, due to a liver abscess, two days after Christmas, 1900. During the Burial Corps's expedition, Rhodes collected some fifteen bodies with the same cause of death, almost surely brought on by the invasion of a parasitic amoeba—the tissue-destroying *E. histolytica*—from contaminated food and water. The amoeba then bored through the men's intestinal walls, reached their bloodstream, and attacked their livers. The men likely first suffered from lengthy bouts of bloody diarrhea, weight loss, fatigue, and stomach pain, before the invasion of tissues led to the fatal abscesses in their livers. Reference on Rhodes's party and the disinterment: Captain George Detchemendy's monthly report on Baler post operations to Adjutant, 22nd Infantry, April 1, 1901. RG 391, E 1706.

266. Burial in this instance: A. Galloway, "The Process of Decomposition: A Model from the Arizona-Sonoran Desert," in W. D. Haglund and M. H. Sorg, eds., *Forensic Taphonomy: The Postmortem Fate of Human Remains* (Boca Raton, FL: CRC Press, 1997), 139–50.

266. Had the bones been left: Arpad A. Vass, "Beyond the Grave—Understanding Human Decomposition," *Microbiology Today,* Vol. 28, November 2001.

266. "After many months: Shunk to AA General, Department of Northern Luzon, Manila, P.I., November 30, 1900.

266. "As the relatives of: Ibid.

268. "Novicio and his family say: Ibid.

268. Soon after his arrival at Baler: Detchemendy was copied on Emily Mash's letter to Rear Admiral Kempff, on September 25, 1900, and another to Army Headquarters, on February 9, 1901.

270. "exceedingly sad affair: Capt. Detchemendy to Adjutant General, Report on Venville, September 6, 1901. RG 395, E 2269.

270. "From the start: Ibid.

270. Furthermore, informants would: Ibid.

270. "and seemed to be: Ibid.

270. The captain "allowed her: Ibid.

270. "There being absolutely: Ibid.

271. Finally, on September 6, 1900: See David Bain, *Sitting in Darkness* (Boston: Houghton Mifflin Company, 1984) for a compelling account of the capture of Aguinaldo at Palanan.

271. In an engagement: Report to the Committee on Military Affairs. House of Representatives, by Captain George A. Detchemendy (retired), April 15, 1902.

271. On the evening of March 14, 1901: The eleventh navy gunboat to roll off the line after the USS *Yorktown*, and thus named PG-11, the USS *Vicksburg* was similarly named after a siege in 1863, at the fortified city of Vicksburg, Mississippi, where Confederate forces held out for more than forty days before capitulating to Union forces in a campaign that claimed nearly twenty thousand casualties.

271. With the Americans posing: Captain Edward Buttevant Barry would rise to the rank of rear admiral and serve forty-five years in the navy, until 1911, when a scandal involving a liaison between the sixty-two-year-old officer and a cabin boy aboard the USS *West Virginia* broke in the *San Francisco Chronicle*. The allegations forced the admiral to resign in disgrace. Although he denied the charges, he was ostracized by his fellow officers nonetheless. Barry waited for the sun to set on January 16 before taking a launch to shore under the cover of darkness and quietly ending his career. Taking over the helm of his ship was none other than Chauncey Thomas Jr., the former executive officer aboard the *Yorktown* during Gillmore's debacle at Baler. See: "Rear Admiral Forced from Navy," *San Francisco Chronicle*, January 16, 1911.

272. AGUINALDO TAKEN: *Washington Post*, March 28, 1901.

273. Along with the letter, the former rebel general: This incredible letter from Emilio Aguinaldo to Emily Mash, along with the photo of her son, was crafted within weeks of his imprisonment on the palace grounds of Malacañang in Manila. While we do not have the original letter Emily Mash wrote to the rebel general on March 31, 1901, we can imagine the excitement she felt as news broke of Aguinaldo's capture; finally, here was someone who might know, firsthand, what had happened to her son. On the bottom of the typed English translation is written: "For this translation Prof. Bach, Pacific University, F.G., is responsible." Letter, Emilio Aguinaldo to Emily Mash, June 9, 1901, Oregon Historical Society.

275. "I questioned probably a thousand: Captain George Detchemendy's monthly report on Baler post operations to Adjutant, 22nd Infantry, August 1, 1901. RG 395, E 2140; RG 391, E 1706.

275. They belonged to the band: Ibid.

275. " 'Augustin,' a well-known full-blood: Ibid.

275. "[I]t is considered that a war: Ibid.

276. The final straw: Ibid.

276. "Every effort will be made: Ibid.

276. An American detachment: Captain George Detchemendy's monthly report on Baler post operations to Adjutant, 22nd Infantry, September 1, 1901. RG 391, E 1706.

277. This time the soldiers: Report of 2nd Lieutenant Parker Hitt, 22nd Infantry, USA, in regard to the discovery of the remains of D. G. A. Venville near San Jose de Casignan, September 4, 1901, Baler.

277. "denied even that he knew: Ibid.

277. The soldiers fell: Bitong trial transcript.

277. "The size of the tree: Report of 2nd Lieutenant Parker Hitt, September 4, 1901.

278. He supposed the remains: Ibid.

280. "All of the schoolchildren: Florin Lambert, *Boot Hill: Historic Graves of the Old West* (New York: Bonanza Books, 1966).

280. The thirteen bone fragments: Ibid.

282. On December 24, 1901, John David Long: "Binds Navy to the Army: Secretary Long Expresses Appreciation of Soldiers' Conduct," *Washington Post*, December 29, 1901.

284. It was believed "the trying service: Report of the Medical Members, Examining Board, in the case of George A. Detchemendy, late Captain, 22nd Infantry, March 18, 1903. RG 94, E 25, E 297, 4452acp1887.

284. A third conspirator: Telegrams: AG Macomb to Commanding Officer, Baler, P.I., April 12, 1902; AG Macomb to Commanding Officer, Baler, P.I., April 22, 1902; Taylor to AG, 2nd Brigade, Baler, P.I., May 2, 1902. RG 395, E 3038.

284. But on November 21: Telegram, AAG Furlong to Commanding Officer, Baler, November 21, 1902. RG 395, E 3038.

284. The outcome of the civil cases: An extensive effort has been undertaken to hunt down the details of the Gutierrez cases, but no documents have yet been located. A letter to the editor of *American Old-timer* (a veterans' magazine published in Manila) from former Sergeant Harry R. Andreas, Company K, 28th Infantry—who reports he was stationed in Baler with the Mindoro Lumber Company in 1901—provides an intriguing insight. The former newspaperman from Lehigh, Pennsylvania, wrote, *"The Gutierrez brothers were captured at Baler and hanged while I was there . . ."* Unfortunately, Andreas provides no further details. Letter to the editor dated April 21, 1940, *American Oldtimer*, May 1940, 47.

285. From June 1901 through June 1902: The US Army's Annual Report on June 30, 1902, outlined the great progress that had been made in pacifying the Philippines. The peace and order situation had stabilized, and "lawless acts have been clearly those of marauding *ladrones*, rather than as having any connection with insurrection against the United States." Filipino prisoners held under military control were released as part of a general amnesty. Native scouts were being recruited and deployed, and *"their conduct has been good and their worth, efficiency and general appearance in proportion to the quality of their company commanders, some better than others."* Supply lines—using railroads, wagon roads, and trails by land and steamships and *cascoes* by water—had been established across the island, ensuring the timely delivery of provisions. Some 625 miles of telegraphic lines were up and running, managed by the Signal Corps. All in all, the American Army had achieved what it had set out to do—pacify the country and create conditions for peaceful civilian control.

285. Once all the views were on the table: Baler's Town Proclamation presented to Captain Kilburn, April 10, 1902. RG 94, E 25, 451692.

CHAPTER 22: DEAD MAN'S ISLAND

287. On April 3, 1901, Corporal Frank Hanson: Corporal Frank Hanson, 22nd Infantry. RG 94, E 91b; Also in Captain George Detchemendy's monthly report on Baler post operations to Adjutant, 22nd Infantry, April 1, 1901. RG 391, E 1706.

287. The trip completed without event: Completed by the Spaniards in 1866 at a cost of $800,000, Bilibid Prison, known then as the *Carcel y Presidio Correccional*, was laid out as a great square enclosed by a high stone wall and overseen by defensible sentry boxes. The prison consisted of one-story buildings arranged in elliptical fashion, fifteen buildings arranged radially like the spokes of a wheel. Nearly four decades later, the decrepit cells mixed men with boys and hardened criminals with first-time offenders. The prison had two sides, the city side and presidio side, each holding around 550 inmates, an eclectic mix of criminal, military, and political prisoners. At the same time, Bilibid also held some fifty American soldiers and sailors, most sentenced by court-martial and awaiting transfer to either Alcatraz or Fort Leavenworth prisons in the United States. Those prisoners, along with any women, were housed separately.

287. In harsh and unsanitary conditions: In 1900, both the prison, and wider Manila, battled the threat of bubonic plague. Thought to have been passed by rat fleas, over a thirty-two-month period, plague was killing twenty-four of the city's residents per month. The figure was estimated to be fourfold higher among Chinese who failed to seek medical attention. With a mortality rate of 81 percent among Filipinos, the disease was spread through a deadly mix of "poverty, poor food and dwellings, and ignorance." A major campaign of trapping and killing the city's disease-carrying rat population—some five thousand to ten thousand rats were killed per month—beat down the scourge to manageable proportions, only to be replaced in March 1902 by a new deadly visitor—cholera. Caused by poor sanitation, bad habits and customs, filthy water, and contaminated food, cholera ravaged Manila and the countryside. By April 1904, when the epidemic was declared over, 166,252 cases had been reported, resulting in 109,461 deaths, with perhaps a third more never reported. The death toll from cholera was five times more deadly than the war itself. See William J. Calvert, "Plague in the Orient," *Bulletin of the Johns Hopkins Hospital*, 14 (1903): 60–63. War Department, *Annual Report of the Secretary of War*, 1904, 12 (part 32): 86, 114, 132; Mary C. Gillet, *The Army Medical Department 1865–1917* (Washington, D.C.: Center of Military History, US Army, 1995), specifically Chapter 11: *Public Health in the Philippines*, 304.

287. For seventy-seven: War Department, Annual Report of the Surgeon General, 1903, 69.

288. Ten prisoners: War Department, Annual Report of the Surgeon General, 1903, 96–97.

288. "By acknowledging and accepting: Proclamation of Formal Surrender, General Emilio Aguinaldo, April 19, 1901.

288. Recalcitrant "incorrigibles": Among the deportees: Aguinaldo's political strategist Apolinario Mabini; General Artemio Ricarte, a determined fighter nicknamed "the Viper"; and Lieutenant Colonel Simon Tecson, the level-headed officer who had spared the lives of Gillmore and his sailors at Baler.

288. Declared a "hotbed of: Worse, the cost of feeding and managing the prisoners fell on the new civilian Insular Government, even though most were, in a sense, "federal" prisoners of the War Department and not under their jurisdiction. In 1903, the Insular Government filed a reimbursement claim with the US government for $32,368.67, which was rejected out of hand by the War Department's comptroller; the funds simply weren't available. The issue was elevated and given to the War Department bureaucracy to sort through, and the decision was ultimately reversed. The US Congress, on February 18, 1904, approved an appropriation of $46,667.87 to reimburse the Insular Government for costs incurred for feeding and housing a group of prisoners reclassified as either US soldiers that had been sentenced by court-martial; civilian employees and camp followers sentenced by military commissions; prisoners of war; or, as in the case of Novicio, prisoners sentenced by courts-martial or military commissions for violation of the laws of war. See Judge Advocate General to Chief of Staff, War Department, November 25, 1903. See also: "Prison Road Building to Escape Disease," *Washington Times,* April 5, 1905.

288. Those prisoners with sentences: Judge Advocate General to Secretary of War, February 2, 1905.

288. Convicts looking at imprisonment: Around 500 prisoners were sent to the province of Albay to build roads, with another 150 sent to an island off Palawan. Hundreds more were shipped to Iligan, Mindanao, to help build a new railroad line. "Prison Road Building to Escape Disease," *Washington Times,* April 5, 1905.

289. Seven watchtowers: Elsewhere on the small island, facilities had been built to support the four companies of 20th Infantry assigned to oversee the prison—quarters for officers, staff, and civilian employees; mess hall, hospital, storehouses, and laundry; stables for the thirty draft mules and fourteen draft horses; a condensing plant for electricity, a bakery, and a blacksmith. See: Inspection Report, Malahi Island Military Prison and Post, Laguna de Bay, P.I., June 20, 1905. Office of the Inspector General. RG 159, E 7.

289. Amid this waterborne bounty: General Vicente Lukban, the insurgent commander of Samar Island, was brought to Malahi on April 10, 1902, following his surrender, prior to his deportation to Guam. Assigned to special quarters, Lukban settled into prison life at Malahi, and was later sentenced to five years' imprisonment along with his brother Cayetano, the former secretary of the revolutionary junta at Hong Kong. See "Gen. Lukban in Malahi Island Prison," *New York Times,* April 11, 1902; "Filipino Plotters Sentenced," *New York Times,* April 21, 1904.

Lukban was an Ateneo scholar and lawyer trained at Santo Tomas and Colegio de San Juan de Letran, some of the best schools that Manila had to offer, and served on Aguinaldo's staff while in exile with the revolutionary junta in Hong Kong. Returning to the Philippines, Lukban proclaimed himself governor of Samar under the First Philippine Republic, and led an organized resistance that frustrated American attempts to pacify the island. His successful resistance led, in part, to the brutal slaughter at Balangiga, where Filipino bolo men decimated a garrison post on September 28, 1901. A severe American military response resulted in the capture of Lukban on November 17, 1901, but not until after a spirited fight that left thirty insurgents gunned down in a barrage of machine-gun fire and a deadly assault on Lukban's near-impregnable fort along Samar's Caducan River.

290. The shift from the mind-numbing idleness: Among the soldiers who passed through to help manage the hard-core prison population was a young greenhorn second lieutenant with 30th Infantry, twenty-three-year-old George C. Marshall, who remembered the one-month duty in September 1903 at Malahi as particularly offensive and distasteful. "The prisoners," Marshall recalled, "were the dregs of the Army of the Philippine Insurrection; they were the toughest crowd of men I have ever seen. You had to count them twice every night. To go through the barracks where they were lying stark naked on those gold metal cots was a very depressing sight."

The filth, squalor, and malevolence swirling around Malahi shocked the young lieutenant, who recalled his company's state of mind when relieved a month later, in October 1903, by elements of the 7th Infantry. "The depression when they saw the place was very great," the future five-star general recollected. "Our elation when we left was even greater." See Forrest C. Pogue, *The Education of a General, 1880–1939: George C. Marshall* (New York: Viking, 1963), 83. Marshall, of course, would later become chief of staff of the US Army and would manage and help win World War II. (Winston Churchill once called Marshall the "organizer of victory.") He would later launch the Marshall Plan to rebuild war-torn Europe and modernize its economy along American lines. George C. Marshall was named *Time* magazine's "Man of the Year" in 1944, and again in 1948. In 1953, for his work on the Marshall Plan, he was awarded the Nobel Peace Prize, the only US Army general ever to receive the honor.

290. "The Republican Party stands for: "Judge Parker Talks on Philippine Issue," *New York Times*, October 16, 1904.

291. "Shall we forbid the Filipinos: Ibid.

291. ". . . [O]ur work should be to: Ibid.

292. At midnight, the president: "The President Starts for the St. Louis Fair," *New York Times*, November 25, 1904.

292. "golden milestone in: Ex-Secretary of the Interior and President of the Louisiana Purchase Exposition D. R. Francis. "American Society Dinner in London," *New York Times*, February 24, 1903.

293. Bright electrical lights: Visitors could also enjoy seventy-five miles of roads and paths; seven churches, each a replica of a well-known house of worship; a 2,257-room hotel; and a slew of eateries, including one massive affair that could seat 4,800 patrons at a time. For those less educationally inclined, the fair offered more base entertainment. One could gawk at African pygmies, ride Ferris's 265-foot-high Observation Wheel, and line up for autographs from the captured Apache chief, Geronimo. A twenty-five-cent ticket bought a seat to reenactments of the battles of the Anglo-Boer War, conducted by six hundred actual veterans from both sides of the conflict, and the Battle of Santiago Harbor, played out by a miniature flotilla of electric-powered battleships, cruisers, torpedo boats, and a submarine.

For the more amusement-minded, there was the Pike: a mile-long, lowbrow carnival strip offering an array of rides, games, circus oddities, contortionists, and even a team of nurses tending to a room of premature babies—collected from the local orphanage and poor families—who struggled to survive in special incubators. The shocks and surprises found at each turn on this attraction gave rise to the term "coming down the pike." One could also sample new taste sensations—waffle ice-cream cones, Dr. Pepper, and puffed-wheat cereal—along with a number of other treats that would later become cemented into America's popular food culture by the some twenty million visitors who sampled them over the course of the temporary Exposition run: hot dogs, hamburgers, peanut butter, cotton candy, and iced tea.

293. On this day, they were ordered: The Americans named the islet "Mule Island" after a mysterious skeleton of a mule was found on the small spit of land. Today, it is officially known as Bunga Islet.

294. The majority of the inmates: Among the inmates was Venancio Cueto, who had been sentenced to death (later commuted to life in prison) for the murder in 1900 of the *presidente* of his hometown of Bay, Laguna. Cueto had been tagged an *Americanista* for supporting the invaders. In 1897, he is also attributed with helping Josephine Bracken, the widow of executed revolutionary Jose Rizal, to flee from the Spaniards through Laguna after the fall of the insurgent stronghold of San Francisco de Malabon, on April 6, 1897. Cueto assisted the barefoot Bracken sneak back into Manila, where she was able to sail for Hong Kong, to safety. Gabino de la Cruz had earned a death sentence after murdering an intoxicated American soldier he had found lying in the street, but his sentence had been commuted to thirty years. Roque Escarios, convicted for the murder of two American soldiers he had hacked to death with a bolo, had also escaped execution and was serving a term of life in prison. Mariano Zales was serving twenty years for killing four fellow Filipinos, for collaborating with the American pacification effort. Evaristo Lacuesta and his brother Prudencio were both in for twenty years for dousing an old woman in oil and burning her to death.

Then there was Regino Cervantes, serving fifteen years for his involvement in the stabbing death of Jose Buencamino, brother of one of Aguinaldo's cabinet ministers, the wealthy and educated Don Felipe Buencamino. Jose had been abducted along with five American soldier escorts on October 30, 1900, after his election as the new *presidente* of San Miguel de Mayuno, Bulacan. Jose Buencamino was killed with a dagger; the five American privates who were accompanying him were marched into the Candaba swamp with their hands tied behind their backs, stabbed to death, and left unburied. See: Augusto V. de Viana, "A Glimpse into the Life of Josephine Bracken," National Historical Institute website (www.nhi.gov.ph); "Convicts Appear to Elude Arrest," *Manila Times*, November 29, 1904; Frederick Funston, *Memories of Two Wars*, 438.

294. In their hands, the prisoners: The *Denver*'s civilian crew comprised Gregorio Seijo, captain; Juan de Lara, engineer; Pelapio Ingaran, his assistant; several wives of the crew; Francisco Garcia, the wheelsman; Bernadino Tigas, the stoker and fireman; and several deckhands.

294. Moments after shoving off: The assault on the launch *Denver* and escape by Malahi prisoners is detailed in the Record of Court-Martial, Case No. 1, SO No. 265, Headquarters Department of Luzon, December 6, 1904. RG 153, E 15, 42495. Malahi Prison post pommander, Major Edward E. Hardin, was tried for neglect of duty and acquitted.

294. "What are you doing?: Record of Court-Martial, Case No. 1, SO No. 265, Headquarters Department of Luzon, December 6, 1904. RG 153, E 15, 42495.

294. The stock of the swinging rifle: "Convicts Corralled and Cordon Remains Intact," *Manila Times*, November 30, 1904.

294. The prisoners relieved Tummet: A letter of condolence sent to John Tummet's father, George, a cooper in Menasha, Wisconsin, by the soldier's commanding officer, 1st Lieutenant Charles F. Leonard, explained, *"My company then opened fire on the fiends and avenged to a certain extent their loss."* Noting a rosary under Private Tummet's pillow, Leonard added, *"[H]e did not forget his religion, and He will not forget your boy."* Letter from Lieutenant Charles F. Leonard, Company E, 7th US Infantry, Commanding, to George Tummet, November 29, 1904.

294. "Hold the engineer!: Record of Court-Martial, Case No. 1, SO No. 265, Headquarters Department of Luzon, December 6, 1904. RG 153, E 15, 42495.

295. They double-timed: Among the soldiers was a sharpshooter and recent departmental gold medal winner for marksmanship, thirty-two-year-old Captain Alexander Thompson Ovenshine. Ovenshine, drawn from strong military stock, would later rise to the rank of brigadier general, matching the level attained by his father, Brigadier General Samuel Ovenshine, a Civil War and Indian Wars veteran who had commanded troops at the Battle of Zapote Bridge, considered the most ferocious fighting to occur in the Philippines during the war. Captain Ovenshine's son, Richard Powell Ovenshine, followed in their footsteps, serving in the Korean War and retiring as a brigadier general in 1954. See Arlington National Cemetery website.

295. Four other companies: Report of the Philippine Commission, Malahi Island.

295. Prisoner Hipolito Bautista: Inmate Hipolito Bautista had been a member of a criminal gang led by Norberto Pre. Malahi Prisoner Card, Hipolito Bautista: RG 94, E 530.

296. One prisoner, thinking: Record of Court-Martial, Case No. 1, Special Orders No. 265, Headquarters Department of Luzon, December 6, 1904. RG 153, E 15, 42495.

296. Reports later suggested: Novicio's (and his fellow prisoners') escape from Malahi was considered "the most daring ever accomplished in these islands," and triggered a massive manhunt that would see nearly all of the prisoners either killed or recaptured. The plan also encouraged a similar uprising and attempted escape at Manila's Bilibid Prison just twelve days later, when seven hundred inmates overran the blacksmith's shop, armed themselves with steel bars, and charged the gates. The American guards, however, were in no mood for any more of this sort of behavior. They opened up with a Gatling gun from the prison's central tower, killing sixteen inmates on the spot, mortally wounding six others, and leaving thirty-four wounded. The attempted jailbreak was thwarted. See: "Killed Their Soldier

Guards," *Manila Times*, November 26, 1904; "Outbreak at Bilibid," *Manila Times*, December 7, 1904; "Bloody was Price Paid for Folly," *Manila Times*, December 8, 1904.

297. "probably gunshot wound: Medical Card, Todorico Novisio [*sic*], Military Prisoner, Malahi Island Military Prison, November 25, 1904. RG 94, E 530.

297. "Body was not inspected: Ibid.

297. Novicio's corpse: Official Record of Interments, Post Cemetery, Malahi Island, Philippines. RG 395, E 4294.

298. the collection of tribal villages: At the Igorot Village, composed of a mix of Bontocs, Benguet Suyocs, and Tinggians, a tribal chief presented a photo album to the president while a classroom of tribal schoolchildren serenaded him with the song "America." At the Negrito village, a collection of forty tribal representatives demonstrated their music, dancing, and archery. The Lanao Moro Village gifted President Roosevelt with a hammered silver dish and a set of silver bottles, while those at Samal Moro Village presented him with a *pira*, a large bladed weapon. Speaking through an interpreter, Chief Facundo explained, "I give you my *pira*, which has been my own individual weapon, and with which I have killed three enemies. There will be no more fighting in my country, and I will have no more use for my *pira*. I will give it to nobody but you." Roosevelt expressed his thankfulness that war was at an end, and noted that the disposal of weapons was emblematic of peace. At the Visayan pavilion, the president was serenaded again and given a carved cane; at the Bagobo Village, more gifts and banter.

298. The scouts were the talk: The 1st Battalion Philippine Scouts comprised the 4th, 24th, 30th, and 47th Companies, Philippine Scouts. The 4th Company was formerly Company D, Batson's Macabebe Scouts, which had been formed on September 24, 1899; this company joined General Henry Lawton's command and was assigned to Brigadier General Young's expedition into northern Luzon. Reformed as Troop D Squadron Philippine Cavalry, the unit saw more action, most notably in a fierce engagement against one of Aguinaldo's last holdouts, Luciano San Miguel, at "Corral na Bato" in Rizal province on March 27, 1903. Led by 1st Lieutenant Boss Reese, the scouts stormed an entrenched stronghold in a near-suicidal assault, killing the rebel leader San Miguel and seventy-five of his men. Considered nothing more than a band of renegades, or *ladrones,* San Miguel's men called themselves the "New Katipuneros." In the battle, Reese was wounded, with a gunshot wound in the thigh; three scouts were killed, and another six wounded. See "The History of the 4th Company Philippine Scouts," in a report issued at the Louisiana Purchase Exposition by 1st Lieutenant Boss Reese, commanding, January 14, 1905. RG 94, E 25 972992. See also: James Richard Woolard, "The Philippine Scouts: The Development of America's Colonial Army," master's thesis, Ohio State University, 1974, 103–105.

299. And today they: On orders of the War Department, they had assembled in Caloocan on August 1, 1903, intensively drilled for more than six months, and then set sail for San Francisco on the USAT *Thomas*, the famed transport that had delivered "Thomasite" teachers to the Philippines. After their arrival at the fair by rail, the scouts had served as the escort to over thirteen state governors, the secretary of war, and a prince from the German empire. The scouts had been called to drill in front of senior military officers of the US Army, including Major General Samuel S. Sumner, Brigadier General J. Franklin Bell, Major General John C. Bates, Lieutenant General Samuel B. M. Young, and, surprisingly enough, Lieutenant Gillmore's brother-in-law, Colonel Butler D. Price.

299. "the little brown soldiers: Ibid.

299. The president was beside himself: Later that evening, President Roosevelt remarked on the Exposition. "It is beyond description," he noted, "and exceeds my fondest expectations. I have had the best time I ever had in my life." "President at Fair Spends Busy Day," *New York Times*, November 27, 1904.

299. "the greatest fighting tune: Ibid.

300. President Roosevelt clapped: President Roosevelt's inaugural was held in Washington, D.C., on Saturday, March 4, 1905. Following his swearing-in on the portico of the US Capitol, a massive military and civil parade followed. Led by a corps of army cadets, twenty-three separate groups of battalions, brigades, squadrons, companies, and troops marched in formation, including a battalion

of Philippine scouts wedged in between the Puerto Rico Provisional Regiment and a battalion of the US Marines. See: Souvenir Programme of the Inaugural of Theodore Roosevelt, March 1, 1905.
300. "Hip hip hooray: "President at Fair Spends Busy Day," *New York Times*, November 27, 1904.
300. Pacification was complete: Eleven months later, the desolate garrison on Malahi Island, with its dank wooden prison, ceased to exist. On September 26, 1905, the most violent typhoon of the year ravaged the island of Luzon in the dead of night, killing scores, toppling telegraph lines, sinking the gunboat *Leyte* in Manila Bay, and wiping the Malahi military post off the map. Damage estimates in Manila alone exceeded $750,000. On Malahi, the large wooden prison, barracks, and all other structures were ripped apart in violent winds and thrashing rain, scattering the 90 prisoners, 14 officers, and 267 enlisted men of the 16th Infantry to the elements. The prison was never rebuilt, and the island was abandoned, its malevolent history forgotten. See "Typhoon Destroys Post at Malahi," *New York Times*, September 27, 1905.

CHAPTER 23: EMPIRE'S END
302. "maldistribution of political power: Friend, *Between Two Empires*, 151.

EPILOGUE: THE COST OF CONQUEST
305. From January 1900: Author's calculations.
305. of the total 16,000 Filipino fighters: Author's calculations.
306. He died less than three years: Walton: OMPF.
306. Found dead in his bunk: Vaudoit: OMPF.
306. "I do not think: After Peterson's pension was granted in 1925, a follow-up medical exam just a year later determined that his condition had improved slightly, which led to a reduction of his pension. Three years later, another examining physician disputed the findings, noting serious stomach trouble, dyspepsia, and alternate constipation and diarrhea with loss of weight and weakness. The doctor linked all of these ailments to the severe dysentery the sailor had contracted while in captivity as a prisoner of war. Peterson: OMPF; RG 15, E 19, Pension
306. After a series of fainting spells: Peterson: OMPF, RG 15, E 19, Pension.
306. He drew a small navy pension: Brisolese: OMPF, RG 15, E 19, Pension.
306. The hard-drinking, foul-mouthed Coxswain Ellsworth Pinkham: Following a funeral in Kittery, Maine, that included a naval band, a company of marines, and six petty chief officers as bearers, Pinkham was buried in the family plot in Orchard Grove Cemetery: "Was Prisoner of Aguinaldo," April 28, 1924, *Portsmouth Herald*; "Ellsworth E. Pinkham," April 30, 1924, *Portsmouth Herald*.
307. He died in Solano, California: William Rynders's wife pursued a posthumous Purple Heart for her husband in 1953, which she noted had been bestowed on the similarly wounded sailor Woodbury. Her petition was denied. Rynders: OMPF, RG 15, E 19, Pension.
307. After an extended petition process: A January 15, 1900, report on Woodbury's medical condition stated: "Diagnosis: General debility. In line of duty; result of exposure and fever during seven and a half months' captivity with the insurgents. Was wounded in lower portion of right chest at the time of capture with Lieut. Gilmore [*sic*], USN, at Baler, P.I." Without this one notation, the award would not have been possible. OMPF.
307. In his later years, Edwards: The seventy-seven-page memoir by Edwards, *Prisoner in the Philippines*, includes sixty-three photographs and a copy of a letter, dated March 3, 1901, from Gabino Castro, the doctor at Vigan whom Edwards credits for saving his life. In the letter, translated from Spanish, the former lieutenant thanks Edwards for the gift of a watch chain sent the previous Christmas. He noted that Abra, Ilocos Sur, and Ilocos Norte were still not pacified, adding, "We are working to bring about peace; as I belong to the federal party, we'll see whether we can influence all those who are armed in the mountains to deliver themselves."

A devoted family man, Edwards left a living will for his grandchildren. In it, he wrote, "Set your sights high, and don't just dream about being great, do something about it. Remember always that the easy things to do can and are done by the ne'er-do-wells, and the hard things ... are the ones that bring success and the everlasting feeling of a task well done." Edwards, excerpts from his living will, provided by his granddaughter, Virginia Edwards, to the author.

307. Tragically, the attending army physician: Dr. Zauner, Medical Report on William Bruce. CMSR.

307. Keen to stay in the Philippines: He was buried in the native cemetery in Bangued, grave #4, leaving his impoverished mother Bertha in Kentucky with a monthly widow's pension of $12. Bruce, CMSR; RG 15, E 23, Pension.

308. He died on February 15, 1903: Private Sackett's early death precluded an investigation into a document seized from Aguinaldo's command that raised eyebrows in the US Army bureaucracy. Bylined Tarlac, September 10, 1899, notes taken during his interrogation by his Filipino captors explained that Sackett had deserted his 3rd Infantry regiment on the night of July 25, 1899, without arms, and had surrendered to the Filipino line at San Miguel, Bulacan. The soldier stated that he had deserted "because he is tired of fighting and he sympathizes with every man who is fighting for his liberty," and "if his services can be useful to our government he offers them thereto; if not, he will remain in the country at the termination of the war and go into business; for the present he does not wish to return to America." The report, written by General Aguinaldo himself, concluded with the notation that Sackett was given $5 by the Army of Liberation and a daily per diem of twenty cents. It seemed that revolutionary blood still coursed through the young Sackett's veins, four generations removed. This document was located by Captain John R. M. Taylor, 14th Infantry, noted US Army archivist of insurgent records, in 1905. Taylor transmitted the document to the adjutant general for follow-up action on Sackett. The report had been prepared for the "Archives of the Military Chamber" of the Filipinos, and was written by General Emilio Aguinaldo. See: Philippine Insurgent Records, M 254; RG 94, E 25, 981378.

308. British civilian John O'Brien: O'Brien traveled to Japan and China to buy cheap cast-iron cookstoves, calico, pins, needles, thread, and beads—items difficult to find in Manila—to trade for raw sugar, sisal, hemp, and tobacco in the Philippines. John O'Brien's trading company was formed with Captain Frank L. French, one of his rescuers from the 34th Infantry, and the officer's $2,000 investment. See: Edwards, 67.

308. Left unclaimed in the city morgue: Responding policemen found a suicide note and various letters scattered, including those from fellow prisoner George Langford, which cautioned O'Brien to avoid marriage, as "such entanglement would bring grief and sorrow to dear ones when time came to fulfill pledges, unless fortune soon smiled on them."

308. To raise money for his care: Thirty-five signatories pleaded with the former prisoner of war in the local newspaper to deliver a lecture in order to raise funds for his care. On August 10, 1900, McKissick's Opera House opened its doors to 380 people who paid a fifty-cent admission each to hear the soldier's colorful tale of captivity. The event netted $187.65, after $3.50 was deducted for the janitor.

308. A massive outpouring: Honnyman: CMSR, RG 15, E 23, Pension.

308. Fireman 1st Class John James Farley: Farley: OMPF.

308. He died at the age of forty-four: Curran: CMSR.

308. Army Private Frank Stone: Ellsworth: OMPF.

309. Both men descended on Langford: Memorandum on Murder of George Langford at Atong-Atong, Basilan; Lieutenant Manuel Cadiz, Philippine Constabulary, Zamboanga to Department Adjutant, October 3, 1917.

309. Dead at forty-five, Langford: Among the effects of his personal estate: farming instruments, tools, household furniture, forty-five novels, several hundred magazines, a French-English dictionary, a phonograph, and nineteen musical records. Death Report for George Langford, Provincial Commander, Philippine Constabulary, Zamboanga, P.I., October 5, 1917.

309. Sonnichsen's father approached: Father's letter, November 9, 1900.

309. "As to the conduct: Ibid.

309. "not able to say anything: Ibid.

309. Whether the letter helped: The deal offered a royalty of 10 percent on the retail price of all copies sold, together with an advance of $100 on the day of publication.

310. "Some of the hardships: Sonnichsen, 387.

310. *Ten Months a Captive:* Albert Sonnichsen wrote four books: *Ten Months a Captive among Filipinos* (New York: Charles Scribner's Sons, 1901); *Deep Sea Vagabonds* (New York: McClure, Phillips, 1903); *Confessions of a Macedonian Bandit* (New York: Duffield, 1909); and *Consumers' Cooperation* (New York: Macmillan, 1919). Sonnichsen's writing morphed from a personal diary of his captivity, to seafaring fiction, to battlefield journalism, to social advocacy. His final book was a paean to the radical, anti-capitalist Cooperative Movement, which sought social justice and equality for the masses through the abolition of private profit and the transformation of all members of society into workers who would toil in all-inclusive collectives for the greater good.

310. Edward Burke: Infractions ranged from drunk on board, destroying government property, leaving the ship without permission, late from leave, willful disobedience, and being disrespectful to senior officers. The final violent blowup on December 21, 1905, at the Cavite Navy Yard in the Philippines resulted in charges for drunkenness, resisting arrest, using obscene and abusive language, and assaulting a fellow navy man. The incident landed Burke in the navy base's prison for an eighteen-month term, with his transfer to captivity ironically signed by the Cavite port commander at the time, Commander James C. Gillmore Jr. But Burke's bad behavior did not stop behind bars. While in prison, he was caught with a knife on his person, and again, found intoxicated; both infractions earned the prisoner bread-and-water rations and the loss of good behavior service. Burke served his time and sailed home to Mare Island, California, where he was dishonorably discharged on July 6, 1907. See: Edward Burke, Service Number 1852481: OMPF.

310. Settling in Seattle: Burke: OMPF.

310. "I believe you know: William Duff Green / Frank McDonald to Gillmore. Green: RG 94, E 25, 320381.

310. "As far as I know: Gillmore to William Duff Green / Frank McDonald, Ibid.

311. On May 15, 1900: Incredibly, Green attempted to reenlist again in Kansas City in 1905, despite his dishonorable discharge. His argument: "My record up till my mistake was as clear and good as any man on earth . . . my crime is for taking some Mexican money from Phillipinos [*sic*] going through our lines and not turning it in. I was a corporal at the time. When I was asked about it, I never denied it but told the truth . . ." He pleaded, "Of course I did rong [*sic*], I was punished for it. I don't drink or gamble, can prove it all. All I want is a chance to re-enlist. I will make a model soldier. I give you my word on it. Give me a show pleas [*sic*]." The enlistment request was denied. RG 94, E 25, 1058305.

311. "complete outrage: William Duff Green to Pension Appeals. Pension, RG 15, E 22.

311. Herbert succumbed: A first-class pilot holding a commercial license as a Master of Oceans, Herbert married his wife, Irene, and settled in Baltimore. He joined the US Naval Reserve in 1928 as a lieutenant commander. In 1941, six days after Pearl Harbor, the sixty-five-year-old sailor pressed for active service in World War II, only to be put on the reserve list due to his age and relegated to running transports between New York and forward army bases in Greenland. A physical exam in 1942 sealed his fate; he would not be able to return to active service. Herbert: RG 15, E 19, Pension, OMPF.

311. Hospital Corpsman Harry Huber: "Held Prisoner for a Year by the Filipinos," *San Francisco Call*, April 22, 1900. Among the images and illustrations, the article provides a photograph of Harry Huber, in civilian clothes, standing beside a Filipino in military uniform, his arms crossed, identified as "the insurgent lieutenant" who led and then abandoned the Gillmore party in the mountains of Apayao.

311. In a collegial competition: A copy of Huber's 111-page account can be found at the American Historical Collection, Rizal Library, Ateneo de Manila University, Quezon City, Philippines.

311. Following his liberation: In China, Smith witnessed the multinational assault—undertaken by American, British, French, German, Japanese, and Russian forces—on Chinese Imperial Army positions in the ancient walled city of Tientsin. At Beijing, in the Forbidden City's dimly lit Temple of Heaven, the adventurous Smith set up a photographic darkroom, using chemicals scavenged from a local camera shop that had been heavily shelled. Smith left a two-chapter memoir of his experiences in the Philippines and China, 1898–1902, which can be found at MHI.

312. Other prisoners in the Gillmore party: Landsman Norman Godkin von Galen, tagged a straggler after his abduction and captivity while in search of chicken and eggs at San Fabian, Pangasinan, surrendered to his ship, the USS *Baltimore*, on January 7, 1900. The sailor wasn't aboard for long. At a port call at Kobe, Japan, on May 2, the young man jumped ship while on shore liberty and ran, deserting his service. Von Galen next turned up in the dead of night in the bedroom of Oceana Fackler, the fifty-four-year-old wife of the chief of police in Tacoma, Washington, as a self-professed palmist who insisted on reading her palm. He was promptly arrested. In later years, von Galen managed to apply for military service medals and a pension, his confusing dual service in both the army and the navy obscuring his desertion at Japan. Von Galen relocated to the comfort of British Columbia, appearing in photographs proudly bedecked with medals for his service in the Spanish-American War and Philippine Insurrection. See: "Brief News of the State," *Morning Olympian*, November 21, 1900.

Private Albert O. Bishop, Battery H, 3rd Artillery, originally from Polk County, Iowa, battled acute dysentery on his return to Manila. Bishop was discharged on February 12, 1900, and later married. He applied for a Philippine Congressional Medal in 1919, at the age of forty-six. See: Albert O. Bishop: Enlistment Papers, RG 94, E 91b.

312. "Preacher Brown had better change: *Macon Telegraph*, January 6, 1900.

312. It appears that Brown: Brown, as referenced in *American Oldtimer*, May 1940.

312. The soldier from Bonner Springs: Private Deming left behind seven stepsiblings, a stepmother, and father, a Civil War veteran, in Bonner Springs, Kansas. Deming's own mother died in 1876, when he was two, after the birth of her fourth child (two of her children died in infancy). His father, Jason T. Deming, served as a private in Company I, 13th Ohio Volunteer Infantry and the Signal Corps in the Civil War, and outlived Elmer by twenty-three years, dying in 1923 at the age of eighty-five. Elmer L. Deming: Summary Card, RG 94, E 627, CMSR, Company G, 34th USVI; Jason T. Deming, RG 15, E 23, Pension and Census Records.

312. His effects were burned: Private Brogan was hospitalized for five days in Bangued before his death. Upon receipt of the news back home at Fort Smith, Arkansas, the "Relatives Union of American Soldiers of the Philippines" convened on March 11, 1900, in the law office of T. C. Humphrey to issue a resolution in honor of the fallen soldier, noting "his last service being the memorable march which resulted in the release of Lieut. Gilmore [*sic*] . . ." Neal Brogan: Summary Card, RG 94, E 627, CMSR, Company C, 33rd USVI.

312. Less than a month later: Bert W. Hayden: Summary Card, RG 94, E 627, Company H, 33rd USVI.

312. Three other soldiers: Frank D. Hawes was a twenty-three-year-old cook from Massachusetts; William A. Holt, an eighteen-year-old boilermaker from Texas; and William Sisk: Summary Cards, RG 94, E 627, Company A, 33rd USVI; William A. Holt: Summary Card, RG 94, E 627,

312. One of the soldiers wounded: William H. Bostwick: Summary Card, RG 94, E 627, Company A, 33rd USVI.

312. Death for the men: Those not succumbing to disease were redirected to protect the garrisons at Vigan and Bangued, which continued to suffer from attacks by General Tinio and his zealous followers. Bangued came under violent night attacks throughout 1900—three times in June, twice in September, and three times in October—from regrouped elements of Tinio's Brigade. Ambushes outside of the fortified garrisons were common.

On a five-raft expedition to bring hard-drinking Lieutenant Bujac down from Bangued to Vigan for a trial to ascertain his sanity on the afternoon of October 25, 1900—he was acting increasingly irrational beyond his normal boisterous behavior, and was drifting into the realm of apparent madness—a nineteen-man contingent led by Surgeon Frederick Hadra was jumped by insurgents. The attack left the former gardener from Edmund, Oklahoma, Sergeant Vincent Burgstaller, and Private Joseph Marek, both in their early twenties, dead along the riverbanks of San Quintin.

While station at Bangued for most of 1900, Lieutenant Bujac's heavy drinking and long family history of insanity—he repeatedly shared that his father, grandmother, and uncle had all died in insane asylums after battling mental health problems for years—finally caught up with him. With his fits triggered by "whiskey, 'vino', fear, remorse, hallucinations of persecution or whatnot," Bujac became "a maniac of the most violent and ungovernable type," wrote Surgeon Frederick Hadra, and was only controlled through the use of heavy sedatives.

Known among his fellow officers for being unusually articulate, intelligent, and brave in battle, Bujac was "of an intensely emotional and excitable temperament" that "would often fluctuate between hilarity and depression: at times he was reverential, at another blasphemous; from threatening to pleading to crying." By the time Hadra was taking Bujac to Vigan to assess his sanity, the mentally unstable lieutenant was facing a raft of charges: appearing drunk on duty; trying to shoot and then beating and jailing the town's priest after the man refused to help the lieutenant hunt for more "vino" in the middle of a late-night debauch; demanding the town's president provide him with "a woman of easy virtue," and when the man claimed he did not know any, offering money to procure "certain respectable ladies of Bangued for immoral purposes"; intimidating his commanding officers with an unholstered revolver on his hip, stating he would hold them all personally accountable after the war; and, while in an enraged and drunken state among a group of enlisted men, spewing such a torrent of invective against his commanding officers and becoming "so violent and mutinous" that his comrades were forced to have him gagged and bound.

Rumors circulated that he was responsible for burning a number of local residents' homes in Bangued. At times boasting about—or being haunted by—the some nineteen Filipino insurgents he claimed to have killed, Bujac often slipped into a state of paranoia, believing he was being hunted. In the last episode of madness before heading to Vigan, Bujac threw up his hands, proclaiming, "My arms are red with the blood of the people I have murdered!" After being held at Vigan Military Hospital for three weeks of observation, a panel of US Army surgeons determined Bujac's mental condition was "normal." See: Captain and Assistant Surgeon Frederick Hadra to Lieutenant Colonel Peyton March, Bangued, Abra, November 16, 1900. RG 94, E 501, 657184.

An insight into the tempo of attacks in northern Luzon throughout 1900 can be seen in Lieutenant Arthur Thayer's "Report of Operations of Troop A, Third Cavalry, in the Province of Ilocos Norte, Luzon, P.I., December 20, 1899 to May 4, 1900," in which he details his troop's six engagements over a period of eight days in April 1899. Confronting at one point a force of three hundred insurgents, the cavalrymen faced broad frontal assaults, hidden snipers, and insurgents who then evaporated into the local communities or the mountains beyond. See: RG 94, E 25, 336503. Captions, Record of Events, and Casualties reports, 34th USVI, Regimental Papers.

313. "assault with intent to kill: Walter B. Rose, Company D, 33rd USVI: CMSR. See also: Summary Card, RG 153, E 7.

313. Private George Strauss: Lieutenant Decker's letter of recommendation for a certificate of merit for Private Strauss noted that while on the rescue, the private displayed *"great strength and untiring energy"* while blazing trails on point, approaching the enemy under fire, and dislodging sharpshooters. Serving as an *"inspiration by example,"* Strauss was *"energetic and aggressive"* until the point when, *"in climbing one of the dangerous trails, he unfortunately fell a distance of twenty feet, and although he complained little at the time, it . . . almost wholly incapacitated him from further duty."* Despite being endorsed up the chain by seven levels of superiors—Captain Rollis, Major Penn, Lieutenant Colonel Howze, Colonel Kennon, Brigadier General Funston, Major General Wheaton, and Major General MacArthur—the War Department rejected Decker's recommendation more than two years later, on June 20, 1902, and exactly three months after Strauss had died. See original recommendation: Lieutenant Decker to Adjutant, 34th USVI, Laoag, Ilocos Norte, May 21, 1900. RG 94, E 501, 693149; and final decision that it was not sustained: RG 94, E 501, 993149, and RG 94, E 25, 348795. See also: George Strauss, G, 34th USVI: RG 15, E 23, Pension.

313. Another private, Carl Burrage: Carl Burrage, Company C, 33rd USVI: Summary Card, RG 15, E 23, Pension.

313. The army belatedly rejected: John Thomas, Company F, 34th USVI: CMSR, RG 15, E 22, Pension.

313. He died of pulmonary tuberculosis: Norman L. Knibbs, Company F, 34th USVI: CMSR, RG 15, E 23, Pension.

314. "no evidence he is now: Peter R. Lavick, Company F, 34th USVI: RG 15, E 23, Pension.

314. Lavick enjoyed the long-denied benefit: The records of many other pension claims make for depressing reading indeed. The majority of the enlisted men, poorly educated and not in the habit of keeping written records, were often at the mercy of outright belligerent and offensive pension examiners. Private John J. O'Neil, Company G, 34th, a carpenter from Ogden, Utah, is a case in point. Following his wife's death during childbirth in Ireland, John had immigrated to America with his infant daughter Kate in 1885. At the battle at Tangadan Pass, he was wounded by flying gravel and left with a badly cut face. Later, on the rescue, he was one of the unfortunate soldiers to have a bamboo stake driven through his right foot, between the big toe and the second toe, while hunting for food at one of the Isneg villages deep in the Cordilleras. He mustered out with the regiment in April 1901 and attempted to reenlist a month later at Fort Douglas. He was rejected, however, due to disease of the eyes and ears, rheumatism, and deafness. O'Neil entered civilian life as a railroad man, during which his health failed. In 1906 he applied for a disability pension but was denied. By 1913, O'Neil was still trying to prove his case, busy collecting affidavits from the officers in his regiment to document his injuries for the army's insatiable bureaucracy. On August 25, 1913, Special Examiner F. W. Tuckerman reported on his visit to O'Neil at his bunkhouse to take a deposition. The railroad man could only vaguely recount dates and events:

"The first trouble I had is what I call a ricochet. A rifle ball from the enemy hit the gravel and threw it with great force, hitting me on the left side of the face near the left ear. I believe it was the cause of my deafness in the left ear, but I did not notice the deafness until I went to re-enlist. I was in northern Luzon when it happened, and I do not know the place. I think it happened in December 1899. We were making a charge. I had no treatment. We had no hospital or doctor."

He went on: *"My right foot was wounded while foraging at Laoag, P.I. I cannot say when it was. I was on a detail under Corporal Deming, who was also wounded in a similar manner. He died at Laoag. The natives fixed sharp bamboo stakes in the ground in a path. The stakes were poisoned. I wore low shoes, which we got on the* Princeton. *A stake struck through my shoe sole and entered my foot between the first and second toes, and came out of the top of my foot. I pulled it out. It was not at Laoag when I got hurt, but up in the hills, I do not know the place. They brought me down the river to Laoag and put me in the hospital."*

Examiner Tuckerman responded with caustic sarcasm in his report. The "claimant lacks education and his mind seems to work sluggishly," he wrote, and "[O'Neil] contradicts himself about once a minute"; "he has not accurate memory of dates and places," his "countenance is puffed and waxy in appearance and his hands and legs swollen," and "his breath would make one sick." Tuckerman concluded, "Claimant has filed no evidence at all. He seems to have no conception of the necessity of filing testimony; he is a good deal a simpleton. He said he would give me $100 if I would secure a pension for him. What with his stupidity, and half a dozen drunken men in the room, it was a hard job securing his statement. He could furnish but meager data." On November 26, 1913, O'Neil's claim was rejected for the last and final time. See: John J. O'Neil, Company G, 34th USVI: RG 15, E 22, Pension.

314. Scores of other enlisted men: Corporal Theodore Roddy, Company I, 33rd Infantry, served through 1905, when he was discharged, and returned to civilian life as a laborer. He entered a soldiers' home five years later, at age thirty-two, with a fractured and deformed right ankle, a history of chronic dysentery and rheumatism, and impaired hearing. Roddy languished for fifteen years from dementia praecox, later reframed as schizophrenia, a chronic, deteriorating psychiatric disorder characterized by rapid cognitive disintegration. He died at age forty-seven in Wister, Oklahoma. Theodore J. Roddy: CMSR, 33rd USVI; CMSR, Company H, 4th Texas Infantry (Spanish War); Texas AGO; RG 15, E 23, Pension; Application for Headstone.

314. The officers: Calculated by the author.

314. Lieutenant Colonel Robert L. Howze: Lieutenant Colonel Robert L. Howze, 34th Infantry, rose to be appointed Commandant of Cadets at West Point. He returned to active duty in 1916 as a major in General John J. Pershing's punitive expedition into Mexico to help chase down Pancho Villa. Howze served in World War I, and, in 1925, presided over the court-martial of General Billy Mitchell, the crusader for airpower who was found guilty of insubordination. The son of a wealthy Wisconsin senator, William Lendrum "Billy" Mitchell was deputy director of the Air Service and a staunch advocate for increased investment in American airpower, which he saw as a "dominating factor in the world's development." He strenuously argued that armored battleships, considered unsinkable at the time, were in fact vulnerable to aerial bombing. In 1925, after two air disasters,

Mitchell issued a public statement that accused the army and navy senior hierarchy of "incompetency, criminal negligence, and almost treasonable administration of the national defense." He promptly faced a court-martial and was found guilty, but elected to resign from service, advocating his view until his death in 1936. Ultimately, Mitchell would be vindicated, posthumously promoted to the rank of major general, and settle into history as the "father of the Air Force." In the 1955 film, *The Court-Martial of Billy Mitchell*, Gary Cooper starred in the title role, and Howze's character was downgraded to an anonymous "court judge." For a thorough account of the trial, see: Alfred F. Hurley, *Billy Mitchell: Crusader for Air Power* (Bloomington: Indiana University Press, 1975).

Named in Howze's honor were Camp Howze in South Korea, which closed in 2004, and the USS *General R. L. Howze*, a 523-foot, 9,950-ton World War II transport ship that carried troops, supplies, and Japanese prisoners of war in combat areas throughout the Pacific. Robert Howze's son, Hamilton Howze, began his military career in the horse cavalry, served in the tank corps during World War II, and rose to the rank of general. Helping to develop helicopter-warfare tactics that were used in Vietnam, Hamilton Howze was credited as the intellectual force behind the concept of air mobility and the current Army Aviation doctrine.

314. The majority of other officers: Major Julius Penn completed three more tours of duty in the Philippines, served as an instructor at the Army War College, and sailed to France in 1918 to join World War I. He retired as a brigadier general in 1919 at age fifty-four. In 1933, at the prodding of his fellow veterans, an ailing Penn belatedly completed "A Narrative of the Campaign in Northern Luzon, P.I.," which serves as an important account of the Gillmore rescue expedition. He died eleven months later, at age sixty-nine. Julius A. Penn attempted to write his account many years earlier, and in October 1913, wrote General Manuel Tinio in Manila to request his version of events. It does not appear Penn received an answer. See: Major Penn, 1st US Infantry at Hawaii to General Manuel Tinio, Manila, P.I., October 9, 1913. Charles F. Manahan Papers, Huntington Library. Penn died of cardiovascular disease at Batavia, Ohio, on May 13, 1934, State of Ohio, Division of Vital Statistics, Certificate of Death, File No. 54, May 13, 1934.

314. "I renew my recommendation: RG 94, E 26, 440429.

315. General Otis's refusal: Lieutenant Frank Dean Tompkins in a letter marked "Confidential" to General Entrekin, Collector of Internal Revenue in Chillicothe, Ohio, February 21, 1900. RG 94, E 25, 99769.

315. "I call special attention: Hare report and recommendations for special medals.

315. On June 26, 1902: A summary of the various requests for medals from Young, Howze, and Hare can be found in a letter from the Adjutant General to Oklahoma senator Robert L. Owen more than a decade after the event. Howze's recommendation for a special medal was rejected by the War Department on August 1, 1902, with the conclusion that *"there was no authority of law for presentation of such a medal."* Howze requested the War Department to present the request to Congress, an approach that was rejected again by the Secretary of War on September 13, 1902. See: RG 94, E 26, 440429. For details on Howze's unsuccessful efforts, see: Robert L. Howze, rp69413; RG 94, E 26, 440429.

316. It was not until 1924: Serial list of campaign badges issued, Silver Stars, 1924.

316. George Hindman of Terrell: Unattributed five-page account entitled "The Gilmore [*sic*] Rescue Expedition," in Charles F. Manahan Papers, NHF; See also: George Hindman: CMSR, Company A, 33rd USVI; Texas State Bureau of Health, Certificate of Death, November 11, 1929; Application for Headstone, Spanish-American War Veteran.

316. "The story of his boat-battle: Gillmore, *McClure's*, August 1900.

316. "I was with Aguinaldo's family: "Lieut. Gillmore Delighted," *New York Times*, March 29, 1901.

317. The cataclysm had obliterated: The molten flows ignited huge bonfires, exploding thousands of barrels of stored rum, and left only two survivors in its wake: a severely burnt shoemaker, and a convicted felon who had been saved by the thick walls of the town's prison. US Consul Thomas T. Prentis was killed, along with his wife and two daughters. His body was found in his home, "but almost too charred to be recognizable"; the identification of his wife and daughters was in doubt. US Vice Consul Amedee Testart was also killed. See: William A. Garesche, *Complete Story of the Martinique and St.*

Vincent Horrors (Chicago: L. G. Stahl, 1902), 150, 219; See also: "The Horrors of St. Pierre," *New York Times*, May 13, 1902; "Graphic Story of Survivor," *New York Times*, May 11, 1902; "Exploring Martinique," *New York Times*, May 18, 1902, which references Gillmore by name.

317. Again, a disingenuous Gillmore: For the second infraction, Gillmore *"solemnly"* stated that while he had gone ashore at Shanghai the evening prior with some friends, he *"had nothing to drink from three in the morning until ten, when the Captain put me under suspension, except for one glass of beer, a pint, with a guest."* In answer to unfavorable report #7 in fitness file, James C. Gillmore Jr., to Commander Osterhaus, Commanding USS *Cincinnati*, at Cavite, P.I., December 6, 1904; Examining Board Proceedings, April 29, 1905. James C. Gillmore Jr., Dead File, NPRC.

317. On June 28, 1905: Patient Files, Government Hospital for the Insane, Washington, D.C., Case Number 154233, Mary S. Gillmore, June 28, 1905.

317. In a flurry of activity: Ibid.

317–18. In any event, the boy recovered: "Wounded While Hunting, Philip Edelin, of Washington, Victim of Strange Shooting," *Washington Post*, September 26, 1906.

318. She was awarded: Letter from Secretary of Navy (Division of Operations) to Captain Gillmore, Commanding USS *Maryland*, January 12, 1911. James C. Gillmore Jr., Dead File, NPRC.

318. On July 1, 1911: Over the course of his career, Gillmore had served on twenty-four warships and commanded five. The full record can be found in Abstracts of Service Records of Naval Officers, R 5, Vols. 8–9, M 1328, NARA.

318. But for Gillmore, it was a star: The ship that had so defined Gillmore's career, the USS *Yorktown*, continued in service in the Asiatic Squadron, serving in pacification operations off China. She later operated off the coasts of Mexico, Honduras, and Nicaragua, and by 1907, was assigned to seal patrols in Alaskan waters. By 1912, she was again decommissioned, being twenty-four years old and obsolete in every way. Overhauled once more, she again served off Mexico, where she experienced one final rescue adventure. On July 18, 1917, she arrived off Clipperton Island, a barren, ring-shaped coral atoll located some 945 kilometers off the Mexican coast. The low-lying island, named after an English pirate and privateer who, while fighting the Spanish during the early eighteenth century, made it his base, was now the site of a British camp that had been established to mine guano—bat feces—from its caves, under an agreement with the Mexican government. By 1914, one hundred men, women, and children had settled there, relying on a shipment of supplies from Acapulco for survival. Once the Mexican Revolution was under way, the atoll was no longer reachable by ship, and the inhabitants were left to their own devices. By 1915, most had died from an outbreak of scurvy. Survivors were offered evacuation on a US Navy warship, the USS *Lexington*, but the Mexican military governor, Ramon Arnaud, keen to fulfill his duty, declared that such a drastic step was not necessary. Within two years, all the island's male inhabitants had died, save the lighthouse keeper, Victoriano Alvarez, who promptly declared himself king. He began a rampage of rape and murder before being killed by one of the women, the widow of the garrison commander. At long last, the *Yorktown* came to the rescue on July 18, 1917, and unlike at Baler, this time succeeded. The ship's crew collected the handful of starving, sorry survivors: three women and eight children. See: RG 45, E 520, box 520, Folder 1.

The far-flung atoll, home to a successive number of shipwrecks and currently uninhabited save for a large population of brown and masked boobies, was first discovered by the French in 1711, though by the mid-nineteenth century its ownership was in dispute by the United States, Mexico, and France. Through a process of international arbitration concluded in 1931, ownership of the island finally shifted from Mexico to France, with its name reverting to the original Île de la Passion.

For the rich history of this startlingly busy atoll in the middle of nowhere, see: Jimmy M. Skaggs, *Clipperton: A History of the Island the World Forgot* (New York: Walker, 1989). See also: "Marooned Two Years on Isle," *New York Times*, August 13, 1917; "Little Clipperton Island Long Disputed Territory," *New York Times*, July 9, 1933.

The rescue at Clipperton was to be the last major mission for the *Yorktown*. She cruised Central and South America through 1918, transited the Panama Canal, and then returned to New York to escort a coastal convoy to Halifax, Nova Scotia. She then headed back to California on January 2, 1919, her last voyage before final decommissioning. In September 1921, stripped of her guns and armor, she was sold at the lowest bid, through the involvement of California congressman John Arthur Elston, to an Oakland scrap and salvage business, to be "dismantled for junk." In circumstances that remain unclear, the former warship avoided the scrap heap and was instead resold to the Union Hide Company in Oakland, California, serving as an anonymous cargo ship with the ignominious task of hauling tanned cattle hides to markets abroad. In a quirky and surely unrelated twist of fate on December 15, 1921, less than three months later, the forty-seven-year-old Elston, who had helped to broker the original *Yorktown* sale, found himself "in a chain of circumstances that spell[ed] ruin," and leapt to his death from a Washington, D.C., bridge into the Potomac River. The shocking suicide was attributed to the legislator's failure to secure a naval base for his constituents in Alameda, California.

See: "Yorktown for Junk Heap," *New York Times*, October 24, 1921; Consolidated Index Card, Purchase of USS *Yorktown*, Inquiry by Hon. J. A. Elston on "lowest cash price," August 12, 1920. Consolidated Index Card (6363-1281-F).

See: "Worry of Alameda Navy Base Believed Reason for Suicide of Congressman J. Arthur Elston," *Oakland Tribune*, December 17, 1921. See also: "Representative Elston of California, Facing 'Ruin,' Takes Life in Potomac," *New York Times*, December 16, 1921. Elston's suicide note, left at the Long Bridge with his hat, coat, and bottle of medicine prescribed earlier in the day, said, *"I am in a chain of circumstances that spell ruin, although my offense was innocently made in the beginning. I hope all the facts come out. My stay means embarrassment to my district and to a worthy people, clean and generous."* Before electing to jump off the bridge, Elston had taken a taxi to Great Falls, Virginia, presumably to end his life there, but due to impassable roads, returned to Washington. The roiling water of Great Falls would take Gillmore's son Stuart two decades later (see subsequent endnote).

The *Yorktown* would suffer one final indignity before being sold for scrap. The commandant at Mare Island, having suggested to Washington that the ship's bell might be preserved for the sake of posterity, received a reply on July 20, 1921, directly from the Secretary of the Navy: "In view of the enforced economy in Naval appropriations, the ship's bell of the *Yorktown* is not considered of sufficient historical value to warrant the cost of shipment to the US Naval Academy." RG 19, E 105, box 349 1-g1.

318. Keenly aware that many: Charles S. Sperry, his commander on the *Yorktown*, rose to serve as senior officer of the Southern Squadron on the Asiatic Station, president of the Naval War College, and with the rank of rear admiral, served on the United States delegation for the Geneva Convention and the Second Hague Conference. Prior to his retirement, Sperry led the US Navy's Great White Fleet on its historic, two-year cruise around the world, beginning in 1907. Its four squadrons, comprising sixteen battleships, their escorts, and a crew of fourteen thousand sailors, was a material demonstration of America's growing military power and blue-water naval capability. Sperry retired in 1909 and died two years later at the age of sixty-three. Named in his honor, the USS *Charles S. Sperry* (DD-697), an Allen M. Sumner–class destroyer, was laid down in October 1943, and saw action at Iwo Jima, Tokyo, Okinawa, and the Korean War. See: Charles Stillman Sperry Papers, MDLC.

In May 1915, Gillmore's former crewmate, Ensign William Harrison Standley, at age forty-two, became commander of the *Yorktown*, surpassing Gillmore in terms of equivalent career achievement, and at an age eleven years younger than Sperry. The bright and intellectually adept Standley was just beginning what would become a storied naval career. The former *Yorktown* ensign who climbed the hill at Baler to sketch the town from the limb of a tree would later rise to the rank of vice admiral and serve as the American ambassador to the Soviet Union. He retired in San Diego and died in 1963, at the age of ninety. Standley was honored with a guided missile frigate, the USS *William H. Standley* (DLG-32), and a California state park that memorialized his name. See: William Harrison Standley Papers, MDLC.

Two other ensigns from the *Yorktown* also rose to greatness. Harry E. Yarnell enjoyed a fifty-one-year naval career, sailing the world with the Great White Fleet, serving in the Navy War College, and rising to commander in chief of the Asiatic Fleet in 1936. Yarnell pioneered carrier tactics and demonstrated Hawaii's vulnerability to naval airpower, notably ten years before Pearl Harbor and under conditions that nearly mirrored the Japanese attack. He served as special advisor to the

Chinese Military Mission in 1941, and retired to Newport, Rhode Island, where he lived to the age of eighty-four. The USS *Harry E. Yarnell* (DLG-17) was named in his honor. See: Harry Ervin Yarnell Papers, MDLC.

Ensign Dudley Wright Knox rose to become a leading figure on naval operational doctrine, commanded Guantanamo Naval Bay Station, and served as naval editor of the *Army and Navy Journal*. He penned *The Eclipse of American Sea Power* (1922); *The Naval Genius of George Washington* (1932); and *A History of the United States Navy* (1936), among other publications. Knox advanced to the rank of commodore in November 1945, after it was temporarily reinstituted, and died in June 1960 at the age of eighty-two. The navy honored him with a prototype of a new class of destroyer escorts, the USS *Knox* (FF-1052), in 1964. See: Dudley Wright Knox papers, MDLC.

318. It was a moniker: The rank of commodore reappeared in the US Navy briefly in April 1943, as a means to recognize the many officers present in the expanded naval service during World War II. It was then phased out, only to reappear again in 1982 with the title of commodore admiral, referring to a one-star rank below rear admiral. In 1983, the rank was again dropped, replaced by rear admiral (lower half), and the term "commodore" was used only to refer to captains in command of more than one unit.

319. Just five weeks before Gillmore's arrival: Al Welsh achieved fame as the first American-Jewish aviator, an immigrant and former bookkeeper who worked with the Wright brothers to test the limits of their "heavier-than-air" machines. During 1910–1911, Welsh established records for speed and altitude at various exhibitions, at one point winning a $3,000 prize for the first flight of over two hours in duration, with a passenger. See: Jewish Historical Society of Greater Washington, www .jhsgw.org.

319. Loaded with 125 pounds of gunshot: "Army Fliers Killed in a 30-Foot Drop," *New York Times*, June 12, 1912.

319. The aeroplane crashed: Ibid.

319. Hazelhurst had been the fourth: In that instance, Lieutenant Thomas Selfridge was killed as a passenger in a biplane piloted by Orville Wright at Fort Meyer, Virginia. At 150 feet in the air, the machine's wing flexed, the propeller blade snapped off, and the contraption simply dropped from the sky. A helmet-less Selfridge died of trauma to his head; Wright survived with serious injuries. "Fatal Fall of Wright Airship," *New York Times*, September 18, 1908.

319. That first fatality was followed: "Aviation Victims Now Number 100," *New York Times*, October 15, 1911.

319. In fact, since the delivery of the first: By 1912, with airplane flight ever more prevalent, the death toll would quickly climb to fifteen deaths a month, and a near tripling of the death toll, to 462 aviators and passengers, by early 1914. See: "Air Deaths Heavy Toll," *New York Times*, April 7, 1914.

320. Trained by the Wright brothers: Milling had already won accolades for his biplane race victory at Boston, where he edged out far more experienced fliers over the 175-mile nighttime route, illuminated with bonfires to guide the way across a darkened sky. See: Thomas DeWitt Milling Document Collection, Accession No. XXXX-0133, Biographical Note, Smithsonian National Air and Space Museum Archives. "Intercity Flight Won by Ovington; Milling, Biplane Victor," *New York Times*, September 5, 1911.

320. "Good-bye, Commodore; have you: "Navy Officer in Air," *Washington Post*, July 24, 1912.

322. "It is a pleasant sensation: Ibid.

322. Gillmore continued: Ibid.

322. The following day, the *Washington Post*: Ibid.

323. Settling into retirement: By 1921, he was fully estranged from his wayward son Stuart, who was serving in Europe with the army, and refused to honor unauthorized checks being illicitly drawn by Stuart on his bank account. "Scriven Heads Carabao," *Washington Post*, September 26, 1915. James C. Gillmore Jr., Letter to Bureau of Navigation, April 1, 1921. N-5/R/H 4644-38, James C. Gillmore Jr., Dead File, NPRC.

323. It was the same facility: Report of Medical Survey, US Naval Hospital, Washington, D.C., April 13, 1926. James C. Gillmore Jr., Dead File, NPRC.

323. A burial was held: Gillmore's progeny were fated to meet further tragedy. His son, Stuart H. Gillmore, served in World War I and was commended for his gallantry, but later in life, working odd sales jobs, muddled through four marriages. On August 31, 1941, at age forty-nine, Stuart slipped on some rocks along the Potomac River at Great Falls while fishing, a misstep while carrying his ten-year-old son, Stuart Jr., on his back. Stuart kept the boy above water until his wife, Mary, could save the child. Stuart was swept away and drowned, his body recovered the next day, downstream. Stuart left behind four children, including a daughter, diagnosed as a helpless schizophrenic at age six, and a sixteen-month-old son, James C. H. Gillmore. See RG 15, E 23, Pension, Stuart Hagner Gillmore; "Bethesdan's Body Removed from Potomac," *Washington Post,* September 2, 1941.

323. "We regret and deplore: Navy Secretary Theodore Robinson to Stuart Gillmore, June 15, 1927. Nav-327-ADD, James C. Gillmore Jr., Dead File, NPRC.

323. "Commodore Gillmore Dies: "Commodore Gillmore Dies; Renowned Fighter," *Washington Post,* June 14, 1927.

324. The story recalled: Ibid.

324. Two weeks later, *Time* magazine: *Time* magazine, June 27, 1927.

Appendix C

332–333. List of Disinterments made by US Burial Corps under D. H. Rhodes from October 10, 1900, to June 30, 1901. RG 92, US Burial Corps Report, Quartermaster General's Office, War Department, July 10, 1901. RG 92, E 677.

Selected Bibliography

US Government Records Groups, National Archives, Washington, D.C.
RG 15. Records of the Department of Veterans Affairs.
RG 19. Records of the Bureau of Ships.
RG 21. Records of the District Courts of the United States.
RG 24. Records of the Bureau of Naval Personnel.
RG 45. Naval Records Collection of the Office of Naval Records and Library.
RG 80. General Records of the Department of the Navy, 1789–1947.
RG 92. Records of the Office of the Quartermaster General.
RG 94. Records of the Adjutant General's Office, 1780–1917.
RG 107. Records of the Office of the Secretary of War.
RG 108. Records of the Headquarters of the Army.
RG 111. Records of the Office of the Chief Signal Officer.
RG 112. Records of the Office of the Surgeon General (Army).
RG 125. Records of the Office of the Judge Advocate General (Navy).
RG 127. Records of the United States Marine Corps.
RG 153. Records of the Judge Advocate General's Office.
RG 159. Records of the Office of the Inspector General (Army).
RG 165. Records of the War Department General and Special Staffs.
RG 233. Records of the United States House of Representatives.
RG 287. Publications of the US Government.
RG 350. Records of the Bureau of Insular Affairs.
RG 391. Records of the United States Regular Army Mobile units, 1821–1942.
RG 395. Records of the United States Army Overseas Operations and Commands, 1898–1942.
RG 407. Records of the Adjutant General's Office 1917–[AGO]
Microcopy 254. Philippine Insurgent Records, 1896–1901, with Associated Records of the US War Department, 1900–1906.

Archival Collections and Manuscripts
Philippines
American Historical Collection, Rizal Library, Ateneo de Manila University, Quezon City
Personal Diary of Harry Huber, An Account of Captivity by the Filipinos from January 27, 1899, to December 16, 1899. Unpublished manuscript.
Lopez Museum and Library, Pasig City
National Archives of the Philippines, Manila

Spain
Archivo Franciscano Ibero-Oriental, Madrid
Felix Minaya, *Defensa de Baler*. Unpublished manuscript in three parts.

United States

Archives and Library, Sharlot Hall Museum, Prescott, Arizona
 Bowers Papers
Hitt, Parker. Day Book for 1901–1905. Unpublished. Part of a collection of privately held Parker Hitt papers, used courtesy of Dave and Eric Moreman and Jennifer Mustain.
Huntington Library, San Marino, California
 Emilio Aguinaldo y Famy Papers
 Charles F. Manahan Papers
 John H. Hobart Peshine Papers
Special Collections, Davidson Library, University of California, Santa Barbara, California
 Charles F. Manahan Papers
Joyner Library, East Carolina University, Greenville, North Carolina
 Nelson M. Ferebee Papers
John A. Logan Museum, Murphysboro, Illinois
 John A. Logan Papers
Manuscripts Division, Library of Congress, Washington, D.C.
 Charles S. Sperry Papers
 William H. Standley Papers
Special Collections, Navy Department Library, Naval Historical Center, Washington Navy Yard, Washington, D.C.
 Charles F. Manahan Papers
Rare Books and Manuscripts Divisions, New York Public Library, New York, New York
 Albert Sonnichsen Papers
Research Library, Oregon Historical Society, Portland, Oregon
 Emily Mash Papers (mother of Denzell G. A. Venville)
 George H. Himes Papers
Manuscript Collections, University of Oregon, Eugene, Oregon
 Harry L. McAlister Papers
 Herbert C. Thompson Papers
 Arthur R. Wilson Papers
US Army Military History Institute, Carlisle Barracks, Pennsylvania
 W. C. Brown Collection
 Luther R. Hare Collection
 Hamilton H. Howze Collection
 Lyman W. V. Kennon Collection
 Julius A. Penn Collection
 Leland S. Smith Collection
 Spanish-American War Survey
Naval Historical Foundation, Washington, D.C.
 Charles F. Manahan Papers
Virginia Lee Edwards
 Lyman Paul Edwards, *Prisoner in the Philippines*. Privately published manuscript provided to the author.
Gloria C. Morrisette
 An account of Norman Godkin von Galen's life. Unpublished manuscript provided to the author.

GOVERNMENT PUBLICATIONS AND DOCUMENTS

Ahern, George P. *Important Philippine Woods*. Manila: Forestry Bureau, 1901.
Annual Reports of the Navy Department, 1899–1902.
Annual Reports of the War Department, 1899–1902.

Filth Flies: Significance, Surveillance and Control in Contingency Operations. Technical Information Memorandum No. 30, Armed Forces Pest Management Board, Washington, D.C., January 2001.

Gillmore, J. C., Jr., arranged and compiled. *California, Bay of San Francisco, Magnetic Ranges.* Special Publication No. 1. Washington: Government Printing Office, 1898.

Lewis, George G. and John Mewha. History of Prisoner of War Utilization by the United States Army, 1776–1945. Department of the Army Pamphlet No. 20-213, Department of the Army, June 1955.

Report of the Philippine Exposition Board to the Louisiana Purchase Exhibition, World's Fair, St. Louis, Missouri, 1904.

Newspapers

Philippines

Aparri Times
Manila Freedom
Manila Times
The American

Spain

El Imparcial (Madrid)
La Epoca (Barcelona)

United States

Army and Navy Register
Baltimore Sun
Bangor Daily Whig and Courier
Bismarck Daily Tribune
Boston Daily Globe
Brooklyn Eagle
Chicago Tribune
Dallas Morning News
Los Angeles Times
Nebraska State Journal
Newark Daily Advocate
New York Herald
New York Sun
New York Times
New York World
Portland Oregonian
Richmond Dispatch
Salt Lake Herald
San Francisco Call
San Francisco Examiner
Steubenville Herald–Star
Trenton Times
Washington Post

Books

Alger, R. A. *The Spanish-American War.* New York: Harper & Brothers, 1901.

Angara, Eduardo J. *Baler, Aurora.* Quezon City: Rural Empowerment and Assistance Foundation, 2007.

Armstrong, LeRoy. *Pictorial Atlas Illustrating the Spanish-American War.* Chicago: Robert Grainger, 1899.

Bain, David H. *Sitting in Darkness: Americans in the Philippines.* Boston: Houghton Mifflin, 1984.

Bellairs, Edgar G. *As It Is in the Philippines.* New York: Lewis, Scribner & Co., 1902.

Beyer, W. F., and O. F. Keydel. *Deeds of Valor.* 2 vols. Detroit: Perrien-Keydel Co., 1906.

Blount, James H. *The American Occupation of the Philippines, 1898–1912.* New York: G. P. Putnam's Sons, 1912.

Boot, Max. *The Savage Wars of Peace: Small Wars and the Rise of American Power.* New York: Basic Books, 2002.

Bradford, James C., ed. *Crucible of Empire: The Spanish-American War and Its Aftermath.* Annapolis, MD: Naval Institute Press, 1993.

Brown, Charles H. *The Correspondents' War: Journalists in the Spanish-American War.* New York: Charles Scribner's Sons, 1967.

Brown, John C. *Diary of a Soldier in the Philippines.* Privately printed (author's copy No. 22 of 50 copies printed, all numbered). Portland, ME: Philip G. Brown, 1901.

Cerezo, Saturnino Martin. *El Sitio de Baler,* 5th edition. Madrid: Ministerio de Defensa, 2000.

———. *El Sitio de Baler.* 4th edition, with prologue by Azorin. Madrid: Masia Alonso, 1946.

———. *El Sitio de Baler.* 3rd edition. Madrid: Cleto Vallinas, 1934.

———. *El Sitio de Baler.* 2nd edition. Madrid: Antonio G. Izquierdo, 1911.

———. *El Sitio de Baler.* Guadalajara: Taller tipografico el Colegio de Huerfanos, 1904.

———. *Under the Red and Gold: The Siege of Baler.* Translated and edited by F. L. Dodds, Major, US Army. Kansas City, MO: Franklin Hudson, 1909.

Chaligne, Paul, ed. *Le siege de Baler.* France: Dole, 1906.

Chamberlain, Frederick. *The Philippine Problem.* Boston: Little, Brown and Company, 1913.

Chicago Record's War Stories by Staff Correspondents in the Field. Chicago: Chicago Record, 1898.

Cirillo, Vincent J. *Bullets and Bacilli: The Spanish American War and Military Medicine.* New Brunswick, NJ: Rutgers University Press, 2004.

Coffman, Edward M. *The Hilt of the Sword: The Career of Peyton C. March.* Madison: University of Wisconsin Press, 1966.

Cole, Fay-Cooper. *The Tinguian: Social, Religious and Economic Life of a Philippine Tribe.* Chicago: Field Museum of Natural History, 1922.

Commercial Directory of Manila. Manila: 1901.

Crouch, Thomas W. *A Leader of Volunteers: Frederick Funston and the 20th Kansas in the Philippines, 1898–1899.* Lawrence, KS: Coronado Press, 1984.

Davis, Richard Harding. *Notes of a War Correspondent.* New York: Charles Scribner's Sons, 1910.

De Bevoise, Ken. *Agents of Apocalypse: Epidemic Disease in the Colonial Philippines.* Princeton, NJ: Princeton University Press, 1995.

Dooley, Daniel A., ed. *Official History of the Operations of the Tenth Pennsylvania Infantry US Volunteers in the Campaign in the Philippine Islands.* Privately printed. Ligonier, PA: 10th Pennsylvania Volunteer Infantry Last Man Association, 1963.

Everett, Marshall, ed. *Startling Experiences in the Three Wars.* Chicago: The Educational Company, c. 1901.

Eyot, Canning, ed. *The Story of the Lopez Family: A Page from the History of the War in the Philippines.* Boston: James H. West, 1904.

Faust, Karl Irving. *Campaigning in the Philippines.* San Francisco: Hicks-Judd Company, 1899.
    Alternate editions with regimental histories:
    1st California USVI; 1st Colorado USVI;
    1st Montana USVI; 1st South Dakota;
    1st Washington USVI; 1st Wyoming USVI;
    2nd Oregon USVI; 10th Pennsylvania USVI;
    13th Minnesota USVI; 20th Kansas USVI;
    51st Iowa USVI.

Feuer, A. B., ed. *American at War: The Philippines, 1898–1913.* Westport, CT: Praeger, 2002.

Florin, Lambert. *Boot Hill: Historic Graves of the Old West.* New York: Bonanza Books, 1966.

Fry, Howard T. *A History of the Mountain Province.* Revised edition. Quezon City: New Day, 2006.

Funston, Frederick. *Memories of Two Wars.* London: Constable and Co., 1912.

Gantenbein, C. U. *The Official Records of the Oregon Volunteers in the Spanish War and Philippine Insurrection.* Salem, OR: J. R. Whitney, 1903.

Gates, John M. *Schoolbooks and Krags: The United States Army in the Philippines, 1899–1902.* Westport, CT: Greenwood Press, 1973.

Gatewood, Willard B., Jr. *Black Americans and the White Man's Burden, 1898–1903.* Urbana: University of Illinois Press, 1975.

———. *Smoked Yankees and the Struggle for Empire: Letters from Negro Soldiers, 1898–1902.* Urbana: University of Illinois Press, 1971.

Gleek, Lewis E., Jr. *The American Half-Century.* Revised edition. Quezon City: New Day, 1998.

———. *The Manila Americans, 1901–1964.* Manila: Carmelo and Bauermann, 1977.

Halstead, Murat. *The Story of the Philippines: The Eldorado of the Orient.* Chicago: Our Possessions Publishing, 1898.

Harper's Pictorial History of the War with Spain. 2 vols. New York: Harper & Brothers, 1899.

Interesting Manila: Historical Narratives Concerning the Pearl of the Orient. Manila: B. C. McCullough, 1919.

Kamen, Henry. *Empire: How Spain Became a World Power, 1492–1763.* New York: HarperCollins, 2003.

Karnow, Stanley. *In Our Image: America's Empire in the Philippines.* New York: Random House, 1989.

Keesing, Felix M., and Marie Keesing. *Taming Philippine Headhunters.* Stanford: Stanford University Press, 1934.

King, W. Nephew. *The Story of the Spanish-American War and the Revolt in the Philippines.* New York: Peter Fenelon Collier & Son, 1901.

Langellier, John P. *Uncle Sam's Little Wars.* London: Greenhill Books, 1999.

LeRoy, James A. *The Americans in the Philippines.* 2 vols. Boston: Houghton Mifflin, 1914.

Leslie's Official History of the Spanish-American War. Washington, DC: War Records Office, 1899.

Linn, Brian M. *The Philippine War, 1898–1902.* Lawrence: University Press of Kansas, 2000.

———. *The US Army and Counterinsurgency in the Philippine War, 1899–1902.* Chapel Hill: University of North Carolina Press, 1989.

Mabey, Charles R. *The Utah Batteries: A History.* Salt Lake City: Daily Reporter Co., 1900.

May, Glenn A. *Battle for Batangas: A Philippine Province at War.* New Haven: Yale University Press, 1991.

McCallus, Joseph P. *Gentleman Soldier: John Clifford Brown & the Philippine-American War.* College Station: Texas A & M University Press, 2004.

Military Order of the Carabao. *The Military Order of the Carabao, 1900–1913: Historical Sketch, Constitution and Register.* Washington, DC: W. F. Roberts Co., 1914.

Miller, Stuart C. *"Benevolent Assimilation": The American Conquest of the Philippines, 1899–1903.* New Haven: Yale University Press, 1982.

Mills, Charles K. *Harvest of Barren Regrets: The Army Career of Frederick William Benteen, 1834–1898.* Glendale, CA: Arthur H. Clark Co., 1985.

Navy Guide to Cavite and Manila for the Battleship Fleet. Manila: 1908.

Nugent, Walter. *Habits of Empire: A History of American Expansion.* New York: Alfred A. Knopf, 2008.

Ochosa, Orlino A. *The Tinio Brigade: Anti-American Resistance in the Ilocos Provinces, 1899–1901.* Quezon City: New Day Publishers, 1989.

O'Reilly, Edward S. *Roving and Fighting: Adventures under Four Flags.* New York: The Century Co., 1918.

O'Toole, G. J. A. *The Spanish War: An American Epic—1898.* New York: W. W. Norton, 1984.

Palmer, Frederick. *With My Own Eyes.* Indianapolis: Bobbs-Merrill, 1933.

Parker, James. *The Old Army: Memories, 1872–1918.* Philadelphia: Dorrance & Co., 1929.

Penn, Julius A. *A Narrative of the Campaign in Northern Luzon, P.I., of the Second Battalion, 34th US Inf. Volunteers in November and December, 1899 and January,* 1900. Batavia, OH: Privately published, 1933.

Phelan, John L. *The Hispanization of the Philippines: Spanish Aims and Filipino Responses, 1565–1700.* Madison: University of Wisconsin Press, 1959.

Prentiss, A., ed. *The History of the Utah Volunteers in the Spanish-American War and in the Philippine Islands.* Salt Lake City: Tribune Job Printing Company, 1900.

Quezon, Manuel L. *The Good Fight.* New York: Appleton-Century Company, 1946.

Rosaldo, Michelle Z. *Knowledge and Passion: Ilongot Notions of Self and Social Life.* Cambridge, UK: Cambridge University Press, 1980.

Rosaldo, Renato. *Ilongot Headhunting, 1883–1974: A Study in Society and History.* Stanford: Stanford University Press, 1980.

Roth, Russell. *Muddy Glory: America's "Indian Wars" in the Philippines.* West Hanover, MA: Christopher Publishing House, 1981.

Sawyer, Frederick. *Sons of Gunboats.* Annapolis, MD: Naval Institute Press, 1946.

Schneller, Robert J. *Breaking the Color Barrier: The US Naval Academy's First Black Midshipmen.* New York: New York University Press, 2005.

Schott, Joseph. *Ordeal on Samar.* Indianapolis: Bobbs-Merrill, 1964.

Scott, William H. *Ilocano Responses to American Aggression, 1900–1901.* Quezon City: New Day Publishers, 1986.

Sexton, William T. *Soldiers in the Sun: An Adventure in Imperialism.* Harrisburg, PA: Military Service Publishing Co., 1939.

Silbey, David J. *A War of Frontier and Empire: The Philippine-American War, 1899–1902.* New York: Hill and Wang, 2007.

Smallman-Raynor, Matthew, and Andrew D. Cliff. *War Epidemics: An Historical Geography of Infectious Diseases in Military Conflict and Civil Strife, 1850–2000.* Oxford: Oxford University Press, 2004.

Sonderman, Joe, and Mike Truax. *Images of America: St. Louis, The 1904 World's Fair.* Charleston, SC: Arcadia, 2008.

Sonnichsen, Albert. *Ten Months a Captive Among Filipinos.* New York: Charles Scribner's Sons, 1901.

Stickney, Joseph L. *Admiral Dewey at Manila and the Complete Story of the Philippines.* Philadelphia: J. H. Moore, 1899.

Storey, Moorfield, and Marcial P. Lichauco. *The Conquest of the Philippines by the United States, 1898–1925.* New York: G. P. Putnam's Sons, 1926.

Taylor, John R. M. *The Philippine Insurrection against the United States, 1898–1903: A Compilation of Documents and Introduction.* 5 vols. 1906. Reprint, Pasay City, Philippines: Eugenio Lopez Foundation, 1971.

Top, Gerhard van den. *The Social Dynamics of Deforestation in the Philippines.* Copenhagen: Nordic Institute of Asian Studies Press, 2003.

Trask, David F. *War with Spain in 1898.* New York: Macmillan, 1981.

Tucker, Richard P. *Insatiable Appetite.* Berkeley: University of California Press, 2000.

Victor, Maurice, Raymond D. Adams, and George H. Collins. *The Wernicke-Korsakoff Syndrome and Related Neurologic Disorders Due to Alcoholism and Malnutrition,* 2nd edition. Philadelphia: F. A. Davis Company, 1989.

Villamor, Juan. *Inedita Cronica de la Guerra Americano-Filipina en el Norte de Luzon, 1899–1901.* Manila: Juan Fajardo, 1924.

Watterson, Henry. *History of the Spanish-American War.* New York: Werner Company, 1898.

White, John R. *Bullets and Bolos.* New York: The Century Company, 1928.

Wilcox, Marion, ed. *Harper's History of the War in the Philippines.* New York: Harper Brothers, 1900.

Wilson, Laurence L. *Ilongot Life and Legends.* Manila: Bookman, 1967.

Wolff, Leon. *Little Brown Brother: How the United States Purchased and Pacified the Philippine Islands at the Century's Turn.* Garden City, NY: Doubleday, 1961.

Worcester, Dean C. *The Philippines Past and Present.* New York: Macmillan, 1930.
Wright, Marcus F. *Story of American Expansion.* 2 vols. Washington, DC: War Records Office, 1904.
———. *Wright's Official History of the Spanish-American War.* Washington, DC: War Records Office, 1900.

ARTICLES AND PAPERS

Alonso, Rogelio Vigil de Quinones. "Espana en Filipinas, La Muy Heroica Defense de Baler," *Revista de Historia de Militar,* Servicio Historico Militar y Museo del Ejercito, No. 56 (1984): 159–185.
Andreas, H. R. "A Saga of Baler," in two parts, *American Oldtimer* (July, August 1934).
Armengol, Pedro Ortiz. "La Defensa de la Posicion de Baler, Junio de 1898–Junio de 1899, Una Approximacion a la Guerra en Filipinas," *Revista de Historia Militar,* Servicio Historico Militar y Museo del Ejercito, No. 68 (1990): 83–178.
Benton, Lawrence, "Memories of the 33rd US Vol. Infantry," in four parts, *American Oldtimer* (December, 1933; February, March, April, 1934).
Burgess, Harry L. "Malahi Military Prison and Post," *American Oldtimer* (March, 1937).
Camagay, Maria Luisa T. "Prostitution in Nineteenth-Century Manila," *Philippine Studies,* Ateneo de Manila University, Vol. 36, No. 2 (1988): 241–255.
Campbell, James D. "Making Riflemen from Mud: Restoring the Army's Culture of Irregular Warfare." Carlisle, PA: Strategic Studies Institute, Army War College, 2007.
"The Capture and Rescue of Lieutenant Gillmore and Party," *American Oldtimer* (April, 1940): 13–14.
"Cronica (Biography of Father Juan Lopez)," *Archivo Ibero-Americano,* No. 58 (July–August, 1923): 394–404.
Deady, Timothy K. "Lessons from a Successful Counterinsurgency: The Philippines, 1899–1902," *Parameters* (Spring, 2005), 53–68.
Dery, Luis C. "Prostitution in Colonial Manila," *Philippine Studies,* Ateneo de Manila University, Vol. 39, No. 4 (1991): 475–489.
DeWardener, H. E., and B. Lennox, "Cerebral Beriberi (Wernicke's Encephalopathy): Review of 52 Cases in a Singapore Prisoner-of-War Hospital," *Lancet* 1 (1947): 11–17.
Echevarria, Antulio J., II, "Reining in the Center of Gravity Concept," *Air & Space Power Journal* (Summer 2003).
Gates, John M. "War-Related Deaths in the Philippines, 1898–1902," *Pacific Historical Review,* Vol. 53 (August, 1984): 367–378.
Gillmore, James C., Jr., "A Prisoner among Filipinos," *McClure's,* Vol. 15, No. 4, Part 1 (August, 1900): 290–302.
———. "A Prisoner among Filipinos," *McClure's,* Vol. 15, No. 5, Part 2 (September, 1900): 399–410.
"Guerra de Filipinas: El Destacamento de Baler," *La Ilustracion Artistica,* No. 924 (September 11, 1899), 588–591.
Hanks, Carlos C. "The Affair at Baler," *United States Naval Institute Proceedings,* Vol. 63, No. 3, Whole No. 409 (March, 1937): 335–340.
Howe, Hamilton H. "The Rescue of Lieutenant Gillmore," *Army,* Vol. 11 (June, 1961): 59–69.
Laurie, Clayton D. "An Oddity of Empire: The Philippine Scouts and the 1904 World's Fair," *Gateway Heritage, Quarterly Magazine of the Missouri Historical Society,* Vol. 15, No. 3 (Winter 1994–95): 44–55.
Lewis, Charles F., Merle M. Musselman, A. D. Thompson, and E. J. Marshall. "The Natural History and Pathophysiology of Wernicke's Encephalopathy and Korsakoff's Psychosis," *Alcohol and Alcoholism* 41(2). (2006): 151–158.
May, Glenn A. "Filipino Resistance to American Occupation: Batangas, 1899–1902," *Pacific Historical Review,* Vol. 48 (November 1979): 531–556.
Miller, Gary L. "Historical Natural History: Insects and the Civil War," *American Entomologist,* No. 43 (1997) 227–245.

Motoe, Terami-Wada. "Karayuki-san of Manila: 1890–1920," *Philippine Studies*, Ateneo de Manila University, Vol. 34, No. 3 (1986): 287–316.

"The Northern Advance," *American Oldtimer* (May, 1940) 5–6, 32–35.

Parezo, Nancy J. "The Exposition within the Exposition: The Philippine Reservation," *Gateway Heritage, Quarterly Magazine of the Missouri Historical Society*, Vol. 24, No. 4 (Spring 2004): 30–39.

Perez, Lorenzo. "Los Ultimos de Filipinas: Tres Heroes Franciscanos," *Archivo Ibero-Americano*, No. 63 (July–September, 1956): 1–89.

Prowse, Brad. "American Prisoner of War: 1899," *Military History* (February, 1999).

Ramsey, Robert D., III. "A Masterpiece of Counterguerilla Warfare: BG J. Franklin Bell in the Philippines, 1901–1902," *The Long War Series Occasional Paper 25*. Fort Leavenworth, KS: Combat Studies Institute Press, 2007.

———. "Savage Wars of Peace: Case Studies in Pacification in the Philippines, 1900–1902," *The Long War Series Occasional Paper 24*. Fort Leavenworth, KS: Combat Studies Institute Press, 2007.

Ratcliffe, Brett C. "A Matter of Taste or the Natural History of Carrion Beetles," *University of Nebraska Lincoln News*, Vol. 59, No. 31 (April 24, 1980).

Reeve, Horace M. "The Defense of Baler Church," *The Century Illustrated Magazine*, Vol. 70, No. 2 (June, 1905).

Ruiz, Rosa. "Odisea en Baler," *Revista Espanola de Defensa*, No. 213 (November 2005): 30–37.

Staunton, S. A. "A Battle-Ship in Action," *Harper's New Monthly Magazine*, No. 527 (April, 1894): 653–663.

Tracy, Benjamin F. "Our New War-Ships," *North American Review*, No. 415 (June, 1891): 641–655.

Vass, Arpad A. "Beyond the Grave: Understanding Human Decomposition," *Microbiology Today*, Vol. 28 (November 2001): 190–192.

Viguera, Enrique de la Vega. "Vigil de Quinones, Medico Militar, Heroe en Baler," *Boletin de la Real Academia de Buenas Letras*, Vol. 2. Sevilla: Graficas Mirte, 1987.

Walton, William. "Lieutenant Gillmore's Captivity," *Frank Leslie's Popular Monthly*, Vol. 1, No. 5 (September, 1900): 419–443.

Welch, Richard E., Jr. "American Atrocities in the Philippines: The Indictment and the Response," *Pacific Historical Review*, Vol. 43 (May, 1974), 233–253.

"Wheaton's Expedition to Pangasinan," *American Oldtimer* (May, 1940), 7–14.

Worcester, Dean C. "Head-Hunters of Northern Luzon," *National Geographic*, Vol. 23, No. 9 (September, 1912).

MASTER'S THESES AND DOCTORAL DISSERTATIONS

Andrews, Frank L. "The Philippine Insurrection (1899–1902): Development of the US Army's Counterinsurgency Policy." Master's thesis, Louisiana State University, 2002.

Craig, James R. "A Federal Volunteer Regiment in the Philippine Insurrection: The History of the 32nd Infantry (United States Volunteers), 1899 to 1901." Master's thesis, US Army Command and General Staff College, Fort Leavenworth, 2006.

Guerrero, Milagros C. "Luzon at War: Contradictions in Philippine Society, 1898–1902." PhD dissertation, University of Michigan, 1977.

Marple, Allan D. "The Philippine Scouts: A Case Study in the Use of Indigenous Soldiers, Northern Luzon, The Philippine Islands, 1899." Master's thesis, US Army Command and General Staff College, Fort Leavenworth, 1983.

Mulrooney, Virginia F. "No Victor, No Vanquished: The United States Military Government in the Philippine Islands, 1898–1901." PhD dissertation, University of California at Los Angeles, 1975.

Woolard, James R. "The Philippine Scouts: The Development of America's Colonial Army." PhD dissertation, Ohio State University, 1975.

INDEX

ABOUT THE AUTHOR

Matthew Westfall is a writer, urbanist, and award-winning documentary filmmaker who has devoted much of his professional career to tackling poverty in the developing world. Based in Asia for nearly three decades, his work as a development banker addresses some of the most intractable issues in our increasingly urban world: megacities, slums, and managing the urban environment. For his documentary *On Borrowed Land,* executive produced by Oliver Stone and funded by the John D. and Catherine T. MacArthur Foundation, Matthew received the prestigious Paul Davidoff National Award for Advocacy Planning from the American Planning Association. Born in New York City and raised in Brookline, Massachusetts, Matthew currently resides in the Philippines with his wife, three daughters, and their ever-loyal French bulldog, Magnum. He spends his free time reading, writing, and collecting as a means to explore the fascinating history of his adopted country. *The Devil's Causeway* is his first work of narrative nonfiction. Visit matthewwestfall.com